career (cross) roads

Gerry Crispin & Mark Mehler

MMC Group
Kendall Park, NJ
mmc@careerxroads.com

CAREERXROADS

©1999 by **Gerry Crispin & Mark Mehler**
Published by MMC Group

Fourth Edition

0 9 8 7 6 5 4 3 2 1

ISSN 1088-4629

ISBN 0-9652239-3-0

TRADEMARKS
A number of words in which we have reason to believe trademark, servicemark, or other proprietary rights may exist have been designated as such by use of initial capitalization. However, no attempt has been made to designate as trademarks or service marks all personal computer words or terms in which proprietary rights might exist. The inclusion, exclusion, or definition of a word or term is not intended to affect, or to express any judgement on the validity or legal status of any proprietary right which may be claimed in that word or term.

Every effort has been made to obtain up-to-date and reliable information.

We assume no responsibility, however, for errors or omissions and reserve the right to include or eliminate listings as well as edit and comment on the sites reviewed based on our judgement as to what is useful for job-seekers and recruiters. We will post corrections as part of our updates.

With the Internet's World Wide Web growing at a rate unlike any phenomenon known before, we have offered the purchasers of CAREERXROADS an option of registering with our site and receiving updates via e-mail.

We offer new job-related sites the opportunity to be included in these updates at no cost based on our determination of their value to our audience. A form for new site reviews is available at http://www.careerxroads.com. Please send new information, comments, corrections or any other correspondence to: mmc@careerxroads.com.

MMC Group
P.O. Box 253
Kendall Park, NJ 08824
732-821-6652
mmc@careerxroads.com
http://www.careerxroads.com

Register for
CAREERXROADS® Updates

Send us your e-mail address (and any new sites, changes, or comments when you can). We promise to e-mail you **FREE** updates (for at least three months) to keep your copy of *CAREERXROADS®* fresh. Tell your colleagues. Help your friends. To register, go to **http://www.careerxroads.com** or e-mail us at: **mmc@careerxroads.com**. Type "Register" in the body of the e-mail message.

We agree to *ONLY* send you our updates. We will not share, sell or otherwise abuse your e-mail address.

Thank you for purchasing *CAREERXROADS®*.

Gerry Crispin & Mark Mehler

More praise from recruiters & job seekers for **CAREERXROADS:**

"I am a career consultant in New York City, specializing in online/internet job searching and career information. Love your book. May adopt it for my New York University class in using the Internet for career counseling. Look forward to your updates."
Tuvia Mozorosky

"I found your book extremely useful and have received over 15 telephone calls from companies who found my resume online or posted to some of the sites you suggested."
Keith Gormezano

"Great Book! I've made my selections, now I have to get on board."
Andrew J. Della Gatta

What a great book! Very timely and it will help me in so many ways!
I will recommend your book to all I meet. It is terrific!"
Mike Ruskin

"I just found your site and am excited by the information and research you have compiled."
Allison

"I think *(CareerXroads)* is a terrific tool which I will use many times over and you can be sure I will be leading the cheering squad."
Christine J. Paul

"I love your book! I have been meaning to compile and manage a living list of career/resume websites for a long time, and now it's done for me!"
George LaRocque

"I have been attempting to find my way through to good international web sites for recruiters. I found your book this weekend, and I'm thrilled."
Sezen Yilmaz

"Your Internet site has provided a way for me to realize the potential of how many employers are actually out there and need working individuals."
Aven Norfleet

Where Talent and Opportunity Connect on the Internet

"I have read all of the great research from your newest book, and will be quoting applicable sentences at our first conference."
Rachel Bell, JobDirect

"Thanks for keeping me on the cutting edge of Internet job seeking!"
Barry Rubenstein

"I'd also like to pass on my compliments to *CareerXroads* for putting out such an excellent recruiting resource. I use your book all the time to evaluate new partnerships and links on the web."
Heidi Stipsits
Positionwatch Limited

"Purchased your book and it's great. I have been recruiting on the Internet for a year (no other source) and I have been able to keep up with or surpass my colleagues."
Sue Cascella

"If you two don't know, it's not out there!"
Suzanne Wrenn

"Your book is only 12 inches away from my terminal because I use it so often."
Monica Reed

"I don't have time to waste and I find it a wonderful resource. I have been recommending it to friends, colleagues—and even new acquaintances."
Joy C. Omelanuk

"If you want excellent job-related links for your new site, you must check out *CareerXRoads*. We just got the book into our office and I am excited about all of the great links I can recommend right away!"
Grace Gravestock
Career Counselor, Andrews University

"It is the only publication that addresses my interest in international employment."
K.J Kadziauskas

Acknowledgements

For our fourth edition, there are many individuals who helped us along the way:

Our spouses, Diane and Beth, who wonder sometimes whether we've taken leave of our senses. Without them we would not have had any reason to do this or anything else for the last twenty odd years.

Our children Jaime Beth, Gerry, Dara, and Lauren. It's amazing what they've put up with.

Mark's daughter, Lauren, who worked two jobs this Summer and after viewing over 1,000 links has become our "researcher par excellence."

David Mehler, Mark's nephew who we coralled when we needed more links to be viewed.

Janet Gallo, the graphic designer who gave us our "new look" and proofread what we could only humbly try to do.

Sal Madalone and his assistant Judy of Premier Graphics who have helped our fledgling business become a reality over all these years.

The members of the Princeton Human Resource Network Group both new and old, who share a commitment to one another's success.

And to Dick Stone, the groups founder, a true professional who bought a laptop this year.

Mike Goodman, Cornell University's NYSSILR NY Campus Director who sponsors our workshop in the HR community.

Our HR cybersupporters and cyberfriends. We literally spoke with hundreds of web designers, web owners and web heads about what they are doing or trying to do. We thank them all for sharing. We are particularly indebted to the insights of the authors who participated in this edition: Rachel Bell, Suzanne Cohen, Ed Gagen, Nancy Heimbaugh, Lori Kameda, Bob Levinstein, Anna Mooney, Lynn Nemser, Ed Struzik, John Sullivan, Camille Trapp and Peter Weddle.

We look forward to your comments about *CAREERXROADS: Where Talent and Opportunity Connect on the Internet.*

Gerry Crispin & Mark Mehler

mmc@careerxroads.com
http://www.careerxroads.com
732-821-6652

About the Authors

Gerry Crispin and Mark Mehler have each been involved in the employment field for their entire careers. Nationally recognized experts, they have pooled their knowledge of the hiring process and emerging technology to chart the developing strategies & tactics of job seekers and company recruiters.

The authors share their knowledge with human resource professionals about how to best integrate recruiting technology into daily practice through Cornell University's School of Industrial and Labor Relations, Extension Division. They are frequently quoted in publications such as *Fortune, Inc., BusinessWeek, Newsweek, NY Post, LA Times, Chicago Tribune* and *Wall Street Journal*.

CAREERXROADS is partly the result of Gerry's and Mark's volunteer involvement as contributors to a networking group of human resource professionals seeking new employment. The group meets every third Saturday morning (at 7 a.m.) and shares job leads. As the speed and accuracy of technology improved a job seeker's access to these leads through the Internet, Mark and Gerry joined forces to share what they've learned about the World Wide Web.

Gerry Crispin has been active in the human resource profession for more than 25 years and counts his certification as a Senior Professional in Human Resources (SPHR) among his most satisfying accomplishments. An engineering graduate from Stevens Institute of Technology, he began his career in human resources with Johnson & Johnson's largest consumer products company after completing a graduate degree in Organizational Behavior. Today, as vice president of Shaker Advertising Agency, Inc., one of the nation's largest independent advertising firms specializing in recruitment advertising, he creates and places help-wanted advertisements and consults with clients on their staffing strategies. Gerry chairs the Society for Human Resource Management's national committee on employment and speaks frequently on emerging technology topics.

Mark Mehler is a highly-successful consultant to major corporations on high-volume recruiting strategies and systems. With over 20 years of human resource experience, Mark founded the MMC Group in 1992 and focuses his company's efforts on staffing process improvements by applying emerging technology solutions to set new standards for performance and cost savings. His work with clients such as Johnson & Johnson, Martin Marietta and G.E., has given him experience with the "best of the best" in this field.

Table of Contents

Making Sense of the Cyberspace Sizzle:
How Talent & Opportunity Connect on the Internet

by Gerry Crispin and Mark Mehler

Reprinted with permission from Employment Management Today, October, 1998
A publication of EMA and the Society for Human Resource Management (SHRM)

The pace of change, punctuated by the rapid growth of the Internet and its emerging technology spin-offs, seems to add an exclamation point to everything we do. Too often the hype exceeds the reality, and this contributes to the confusion and stress about what to do and how to do it. The changes we've seen in the employment arena during the last two years are no exception. Human resource practitioners who can keep from being distracted, and instead focus their attention on the fundamentals of how people interact and how they respond to technology, will be less likely to succumb to the pressures to adopt the newest solutions to problems they often didn't even know they had. The fictitious scenario that follows is just one opinion, one story about how emerging technology, and the people that use it, could come together. Hopefully it will stimulate HR professionals to spend a little time creating their own personal scenario as they evaluate, choose and integrate emerging technology into their hiring strategies and tactics.

It was Tuesday, and Jaime was having a bad day at Black Rock, Inc. , her high tech employer located in Grass Valley, a growing, "almost suburban" community nestled in California's historic gold mining country. Her mom had called earlier from just outside Charlotte, NC where she had moved after her dad's retirement nearly a decade ago. Now it seemed certain that her mom's "minor" infirmities were getting worse...and that spelled trouble with a capital "T." Future financial support of her one remaining parent notwithstanding, Jaime's drive to build a successful career developing engineering applications for the health care industry was increasingly in conflict with an equally strong desire to be near her mom, and that had her second guessing her decision to relocate across the continent two years earlier. She wanted to make a difference in all aspects of her life, and it seemed something had to give.

On top of all that Jaime's spouse Jim was struggling as an administrator in a nonprofit agency that was resistant to his progressive ideas. He was usually patient, but lately he had become increasingly frustrated. Sally, their daughter, the bright light in their life, was showing exceptional academic potential, but the school system seemed so limited in offering her the challenge she needed that both Jim and Jaime were becoming concerned.

A call to Black Rock's Human Resources Department confirmed that the company had limited elder care support although Jason, the HR Manager whom she had gotten to know through their joint participation in company projects, was quick to point out that Black Rock was flexible and creative enough to work with her to try and solve her issues. He said he wanted to check something out and get back to her.

Still rattled at lunch, Jaime decided to do a little research on her options outside Black Rock.

Using the techniques she had learned in the required Career Management course she had taken as an Engineering senior just six years ago, she went to the Career Center at her alma mater and checked out an "Alumni in Transition" area to find the newest recommended starting points for a job search. She immediately created a file in her browser's "bookmark" section.

The Internet will provide colleges and universities with tremendous continuous, remote learning opportunities. Tulane University's Career Planning efforts, as one example, received an award at this year's NACE (National association of College's and Employers) conference for it's web based services to students and alumni.

Number one on her list of places to go was her technical professional association. A member of a national technical society since her student days, Jaime first updated her skills profile and formal resume that she kept in the association's "Registry". These two documents had been on an "inactive" status since joining Black Rock, which meant that no one had access but her. Now with a simple click she changed the status to "active". She also added a note that the States surrounding the Research Triangle area were preferred. When active, the Registry feature allowed anyone with the URLs to view them or, should a recruiter use the registry's search engine, her profile minus contact information could be accessed. A quick search of current jobs posted at the site returned nothing of interest but, in the resources section, there was a great article recently written by a member of the association about a job transition as well as several links to technical and scientific sites.

The internet will breathe new life into literally thousands of professional associations who can now provide new services with a sense of urgency to their members without increasing staff. In the case of staffing, this will also mean a significant dollar increase.

Jaime downloaded the former and saved the latter to her growing bookmark "next job" file, she clicked on another link which led her to a newspaper association search engine and, moments later, links to the help-wanted classified sections of all 8 daily newspapers in North Carolina. A convenient tool at this association site allowed her to search all of last Sunday's ads from all of the papers simultaneously. While doing that, an intrusive window opened up advertising that the largest paper in North Carolina had a special feature allowing her to search the jobs pages of more than 100 area company web sites and she immediately opted to "click -through" after saving several more links for herself and Jim. Jaime soon found and highlighted two positions that fit her interests which weren't going to appear in print until next Sunday's classifieds, but had already been posted to the newspaper's site.

903 Daily newspapers in the US are attempting to compete for the classified dollars they once took for granted

Returning to her bookmark file and a link to a related association for Health Care Technology turned up several more possibilities that led to a unique site, RT Careers, a consortium of 50 companies in the Research Triangle area that had gotten together with the local Chamber of Commerce to attract more candidates from outside the area (instead of competing for the folks already in the state). This was a gold mine. In addition to finding more job possibilities, there were local spousal assistance services, links to all the local school systems and a online real estate service that provided video stream reviews of houses on the market- all supported by the consortium. Book mark that one. Taking a moment to use the site's "benefits" search engine she noted five companies offering elder care benefits packages and saved the company links to those companies to research later.

Collaboration and cooperation over competition is a trend that will explode in communities throughout the country and internationally during the next year.

With time running out Jamie next: found a major search engine allied with 20 large independent 'Career Hubs' listing hundreds of thousands of openings from everywhere and the means to search all of them simultaneously. More possibilities.

Finally, she sent a message to two technical e-mail discussion groups (listservs) she subscribed to and asked colleagues living or working in the Research Triangle area to contact her off line as she had a couple questions about relocation.

Communication between colleagues, especially the best and the brightest is already established in tens of thousands of growing online "communities."

Enough for now. Happy there were options she could review in more depth at her leisure, Jaime sent several new files to her home e-mail address and returned to work to move her projects forward.

Jason hung up from his conversation with Jaime with a nagging sense that her concerns had a sense of urgency attached to them. A quick check of her performance included a note that Jaime was considered a "key" employee to the success of the company's business plan and was also listed as a high potential candidate for any one of three team leader positions expected to come open during the next year. Ironically, on Jason's list of goals to finish this week was a plan for staffing up Black Rock's workforce to twice its current size in the next 12-18 months. Ignoring a key retention problem was only going to complicate meeting his goal.

In the back of his mind, Jason knew that his boss had been lobbying the company Board of Directors to develop project teams using a new virtual project and conferencing technology.

One of the issues was how to quantify the expected benefits of these alternative work issues with the investment required and Jason was thinking that Jaime might be the perfect candidate in more ways than one. He made a mental note to discuss the possibility with his boss before she left at the end of the day.

How "plugged-in" are professional staff to corporate plans? What are the costs of losing a key employee?

In the meantime, Jason decided to test how well his sourcing systems were shaping up, and rolled up his sleeves to see if, in a worst case scenario, how hard it would be to come up with a replacement for Jaime's projects. While it wasn't yet time to be advertising on the Internet or in one of the newspapers or technical journals, Jason first checked on how well his previous print and online ads and banners had been in driving a stream of potential candidates to his web site

From a browser control panel built into the staffing area of Black Rock's Intranet, Jason checked his e-mail "Interest" database. This was the result of visitors to Black Rock's web site who were invited to leave a "non-work" e-mail address for positions that weren't yet open. Black Rock promised that when these positions became available, they (the visitors) would be the first to receive announcements via e-mail along with an invitation to either respond (if qualified) or, to connect to a special web page, an online screening tool, and answer a series of questions. Jason found fewer than 50 e-mails matched his search parameters, and, curious about their source, he ran a report which showed, as expected that most e-mails were visitors driven to the site through ads in newspapers, journals and banners on association and third party sites. Several e-mails were obviously agencies Jason occasionally worked with who wanted to monitor the company's newest openings, and a few, surprisingly, came from local library and college resource centers. One was from a community service agency specializing in helping the physically challenged that Jason had been reaching out to.

The centerpiece of most staffing strategies will be an interactive web site that provides the employment professional real time monitoring capability

Next, Jason searched his company resume database nearing 5000 resumes. He kept it at that level through traditional advertising and online posting, and, in addition, subscribed to an automated "robot" service that sought out fresh resumes every night, and then merged them into his database where the resumes were "read" and "ranked" and eventually available for detailed search. The current database wasn't as helpful as he expected, and Jason made one note to change the specs on what the resume robot searched for, and another note to strip out the e-mails from some of the older resumes, and invite these unhired applicants to update their profiles. Jason also had recently downloaded a neat application that he could customize to a dozen public resume databases that he wanted to track. He could use it to search them all- simultaneously and in real time. Maybe later.

The future of the Internet will be more about communication than content.

Finally, checking the web site of the media consulting/advertising agency that Black Rock partnered with, Jason noticed that their resource list included a new job fair in Philadelphia with a focus on just the candidates he sought. Normally Jason wouldn't have considered a job fair so far away, but this one was offering a virtual component which would allow him to interview attendees from a PC in his office in Grass Valley. He sent a message to the account representative handling Black Rock to have him check into it and supply details.

Remote interviewing capability will be technically feasible, low cost and widely available in 1999.

Before getting back to the more mundane issues at hand, Jason was curious about an article he had just read describing corporate direct sourcing techniques. Following the text example, he surfed to a specialized search engine that "drilled" into tens of millions of archived e-mails from hundreds of e-mail discussion group. With a little effort, and some creative phrasing, Jason uncovered dozens of online conversations related to the areas of expertise that his company had designated as "critical" skills. He would have to think more carefully about this when the staffing plans began heating up, and he brought on contract recruiting help.

Corporate direct sourcing strategies will raise issues that impact policy, case law and professional standards as the technology enables anyone to reach anyone else...directly.

Returning to his planned tasks for the day, Jason left an voice mail message for his boss outlining his interest in discussing her virtual teams project, and then e-mailed Jaime to see if she might be available to meet on Thursday hoping he might be able to run a couple ideas by her by then.

Home an hour earlier than expected Jaime saw Jim's message that he and Sally were out at soccer practice, and thought she might as well follow up on her lunch time efforts. Still thinking back to Jason's intriguing e-mail which she received just before leaving work, Jaime also hoped there might be a solution at Black Rock, but she was also going to what else she could develop, and quickly logged onto the net, downloaded her files, and stripped out the duplicates from all the links she had collected earlier.

Next, Jaime researched the web sites of more than a dozen companies high on her list using a business search engine. Five were of immediate interest based on what she could see from the content available on the site. One company had a great section on "Getting to know us" with video and audio streams from employees describing the challenges and opportunities that had convinced them to join it. Most companies had a "resume builder" form or offered an opportunity to receive more info, but all of them indicated they would accept a resume e-mailed directly. This she did by returning to her association's registry and pasting in all the e-mail addresses. A special "Send one at a time" button allowed her to deliver the resumes all at once, but make it appear that each was sent separately.

To be effective, company web sites must share more than job content. They must provide a glimpse of their company culture, values and vision, engage the visitor and give him or her the means to self-select (realistic previews, match values and interests, etc.) before taking an action

Jamie was glad that she had gotten into the habit of saving most of the e-mail addresses of headhunters she had spoken with over the years. In five minutes she composed an e-mail broadcast letter, and attached the abbreviated skills profile from the registry (with limited contact data and a separate return e-mail address) Jamie had learned the hard way the last time she searched for a job that control of who had her full resume was a important consideration.

Checking e-mails, Jaime saw two from colleagues on her listservs and replied with a series of questions about the Research Triangle area. Coincidentally, one message was from a member who was working at a company she had just applied to minutes before and she asked if she might give him a call if things progressed.

As Jaime worked, e-mail responses to her earlier messages were coming back acknowledging her interest, and promising to keep in touch if her qualifications matched their openings. One message even described how to use the company web-site to track the progress of her application, and, at the same time invited her to answer a few optional questions on gender, race and age which would be analyzed separately to help the company better understand how to reach a diverse audience. She replied.

Companies must decide at what point a person becomes an applicant, and why. The debate will continue, but companies that have better data will also make better plans.

A sudden flashing icon appeared at the bottom right of her screen indicating that someone was online and inviting her into a chatroom for a quick discussion. Someone was working late. Clicking on the icon, Jaime found herself at a message board reserved for use by a national placement agency with John, a recruiter located in Chicago who was in receipt of her earlier profile. He was working on two related assignments in North Carolina, and, after a bit of back and forth, Jaime agreed to forward her full resume for review. He also asked if she would be available for a quick PC-PC video interview, but Jaime replied that she hadn't invested in the program and equipment he was using and anyway, her home lines weren't fast enough to really support it. "No problem," he said and suggested that if one of a national chain of hotels was nearby, he would arrange for an interview before work the next morning in the hotel's business center. Jaime agreed to a 7 a.m. meeting after emphasizing that she was just beginning to explore her options, and not ready to make a commitment.

Logging off, Jaime couldn't help thinking that it was a busy day at Black Rock, and there was a lot to discuss with Jim.

An unrealistic scenario? Perhaps. Your company size, human resource capabilities, location(s), staffing needs, budget, scarce skills, business plans, investment processes, or relationships with colleges, industries, communities, vendors, professional associations, etc. may be very different . The technology described above however, is very real. All of the products and services implied in this story...and more exist today or are about to be announced. While few companies can claim they have seamlessly integrated their hiring process, technology is no longer the problem.

The real challenge, developing a staffing vision for your company won't be easy, but here are a few thoughts about researching the tools and toys in this rapidly growing industry.

1. Follow the Job Seeker. Conduct focus groups with new employees as part of the orientation process. How they were found or found you will go a long way to arming your HR department with data about your company's "readiness" for emerging technology. Survey the employees who have left you. Not only for the typical traditional reasons, but increasingly, you'll find that the techniques they used once they decided to look...or not, have a bearing on your policies and choices about the tools and techniques you might use. After all, retention has a direct impact on the employment function.

2. Network. Get involved in regional and national meetings of professional associations like EMA where the best practices, issues and ideas are discussed in a setting that maximizes professional learning. Join online discussion groups and message boards where recruiting discussions take place, and where practitioners share tactics and strategies.

3. Measure everything. Reread Gary Cluff's excellent article from the August issue of Employment Management Today entitled "Metrics for the Recruitment and Staffing Function." There is no substitute for results that can be measured in relation to your company's business plans. Look for research related articles and surveys where hard data minimizes the hype, and instead focuses on the facts so you can compare products that claim to meet your needs in terms of "apples and apples."

4. Imagine the possibilities. Think about what could be. The first step to getting there is knowing where you want to go.

RESOURCES FOR
RECRUITERS AND JOB SEEKERS

Here are some starting points for getting content, getting connected and getting integrated:

BOOKS

Recruiters and jobseekers will benefit from the reading material listed below: All of the books below can be found at Amazon.com or where indicated, at the Author's website

Resumes for Dummies
by Joyce Lain Kennedy
IDG Books Worldwide. Approximately 300 pages.
Finally, an intelligent resource for the job seeker on how to handle resumes on the net. Joyce Lain Kennedy obsoletes every other resume "how to" with a 70 page comprehensive section on "Going Digital with your Kickbutt Resume". She makes the case for how to best address issues of optical scanning, formatting and distribution while giving great tips on everything from confidentiality to resume builders. This is required reading for job seekers and a must for the library in every outplacement firm and "career coach" office. ($13)

The Guide to Internet Job Searching
by Margaret Riley Dickel, Frances Roehm and Steve Oserman
VGM Career Horizons (co-published by the Public Library Association)
This handbook for the novice job seeker was put together by research librarians with a long term interest in jobs on the net and the skills to help. This is more than an update of their 1996 book and it has solid organization, hundreds of recommended sites and good advice. Margaret (The Riley Guide: http://www.dbm.com/jobguide) is our pick for "queen of the links" if they ever honor pioneers in the online recruitment field.

Job Searching Online for Dummies
by Pam Dixon, Ray Marcy
IDG Books Worldwide. Approximately 300 pages
We didn't have our copy in time for comment but we think very highly of Pam's earlier work and we fully expect you'll find this version a quality effort as well.

The Internet Recruiting Edge

by Barbara Ling

http://www.virtual-coach.com

Approximately 250 pages. This is a wealth of information for the proactive recruiter with a strong understanding of "Direct Sourcing" protocols. A must for headhunters looking to track down candidates for the toughest assignments.

The Employer's Guide to Recruiting on the Internet

by Ray Schreyer & John McCarter

Impact Publications – approx. 250 pages ($24.95)

703-361-7300   http://www.impactpublications.com

Excellent starting point for novice recruiters looking to get their feet wet and develop a plan or cybersavvy staffing pros trying to get their hands around the net's business models. We even enjoyed "Billybob's Secret Sauce" recipe listed at the end. Nice touch. Great taste.

A Human Resources Guide to Global Sourcing

by George Zambos, Recruitment Technologies

Simon & Schuster ($49.95) – Recruitment Technologies

http://www.netcruiting.com/book   153 Shelley Avenue, Campbell, CA 95008

Ph: 408-278-7837   E-mail: info@netcruiting.com

George Zambos also conducts Internet training for HR professionals

E-MAIL (FREE)

Many job sites are linking to some of the resources that offer free e-mail.

Free Stamp	http://www.freestamp.com
Geocities	http://www.geocities.com
Hot Mail	http://www.hotmail.com
Juno	http://www.juno.com
RocketMail	http://www.rocketmail.com
Yahoo	http://www.yahoo.com
Switchboard	http://www.switchboard.com
Tripod	http://www.tripod.com

HIRING SYSTEMS

"Web-based," "Web-enabled" and other network-based staffing systems have exploded onto the marketplace in recent years. Features and capabilities differ from vendor to vendor and range from data warehousing and sophisticated applicant tracking reports to multiple posting options, optical scanning and Intranet/Internet site templates . Those listed below are just a few of the quality vendors out on the market. Many HRIS sytems also offer staffing modules and vendors announce new products nearly every day. As the core component around which a company strategy is built it is important to understand the capital and ongoing cost, labor, technical support and compatibility of these systems with your hiring processes. A directory to many of these products can be ordered from Advanced Personnel Systems at http://www.hrcensus.com

Alexus	http://www.alexus.com
Best Internet Recruiter	http://www.bestrecruit.com
CareerBuilder	http://www.careerbuilder.com
Greentree Systems Homepage	http://www.greentreesystems.com
Hot Jobs (SoftShoe)	http://www.hotjobs.com or
	http://www.softshoe.com
HR Sites	http://www.hrsites
I Search	http://www.isearch.com
Intelligent Search Tools	http://www.intell-search.com
Personic	http://www.personic.com
Restrac	http://www.restrac.com
Resumail Network	http://www.resumail.com
Resumix	http://www.resumix.com
Web Recruiter	http://com.sortium.com
World Hire	http://www.world.hire.com

DISCUSSION GROUPS: LISTSERVS & FORUMS

If you would like to exchange ideas with recruiters on-line to keep up on the goings on all over the world, here are a couple discussion groups you might want to join. Check out other discussion groups through the ListServ Directory at http://www.lsoft.com/lists/listref.html or LISZT at http://www.liszt.com

Electronic Recruiting Exchange
http://www.erexchange.com/
David Manaster has built one of the most active listservs for corporate and third part recruiters on the net to exchange ideas

EMA (Employment Management Association) Bulletin Board
http://www.shrm.org/hrtalk (must be a SHRM member)

RECNET – Recruiter's Network
Internet Recruiting, Best Practices for Recruiting, HR Software, etc.
Hosted by: http://www.recruitersnetwork.com

MULTIPLE-SITE JOB POSTING SERVICES

Best Internet Recruiter	http://www.bestrecruit.com
CareerBuilder	http://www.careerbuilder.com
HR Sites International	http://www.hrsites.com
Recruit-Net	http://www.recruit-net.com
Smart POST Network	http://www.smartpost.com

ONLINE NEWSLETTERS

Lots of advice for free and for a fee on how to recruit on the net. Job seekers should check out the Career Management index in the back of *CareerXroads* or search:

Online Newsletters
http://www.lemaze.com/Business_News/newsletters/newsletter to find more.

CAREERXROADS Updates (6x a year)
http://www.careerxroads.com

Curry Business Systems (Newsletter)
http://www.curryinc.com

Electronic Recruiting Daily
Subscribe by going to:
http://www.erexchange.com/

Intelligent Search
"RealTools" and "BenchMark" (free)
http://www.intell-search.com/realtools/index.html
http://www.intell-search.com/benchmark/index.html
Internet Business Network (Research/Seminars/Newsletter)
http://www.interbiznet.com

IT Recruiter (Monthly–Fee)
a publication by Pinnacle Publishing

Recruiter's Network (Monthly)
http://www.recruitersnetwork.com

WEDDLE'S Wildly Useful, Up-to-the-Minute Newsletter
about INTERNET RESOURCES for Successful Recruiting
http://www.recruiternetwork.com
http://www.pinpub.com

Wet Feet Press (Monthly)
http://www.wetfeet.com

PC-PC VIDEO/AUDIO INTERVIEWING

SearchLinc (See CXR Listing for CareerMagazine)
http://www.careermag.com

RESUME SWAPPING

RRI Resume Swap   http://members.tripod.com
                              ~RecruiterResources/index-3.html

ROBOTS AND SPIDERS

ITTA- ProRecruiter   http://www.it-ta.com
Personic Resume Agent/RoboSurfer   http://www.personic.com

SEARCH ENGINES

The two sites listed below include excelllent advice on how to refine your
search skills. Everything you ever wanted to know about them is there.
Search Engine Watch   http://www.searchenginewatch.com
Spider's Apprentice   http://www.monash.com/spidap.html

Hundreds of new products will help test and screen. Here are a few with a track record.

Apview	http://www.aspentree.com
Aspen Tree	http://www.aspentree.com
ijob	http://www.ijob.com
Qwiz	http://www.qwiz.com

RESOURCE DIRECTORY

Advanced Personnel Systems (Directory)
Dick Frantzreb

http://www.hrcensus.com   E-mail: frantz@hrcensus.com   Ph: 916-781-2900

1873 Hiddenview, Roseville, CA 95678

Site states it monitors 2300 HR software products from 1300 vendors and 3500 courseware products from 300 suppliers. Everything from affirmation action programs to training management modules are reviewed. You can look at their evaluation of up to 20 systems for $30. The 64 applicant tracking systems listed will be of interest to most employers. If you need a starting point to see what is available this site will be of help. If you are looking for a detailed evaluation of each system you may be asking for too much.

Alexus (System)
Paul Rowson

http://www.alexus.com   E-mail: sales@alexus.com   Ph: 888-253-9878

Alexus, 555 Quince Orchard Road, Suite 480, Gaithersburg, MD 20878-1437

Instead of purchasing software, hardware and scanning equipment, recruiters use the Alexus site as a web-based, applicant resume database. Some reporting and tracking capability adds

Apview (Screening and Testing)
http://www.aspentree.com   E-mail: marketing@aspentree.com   Ph: 800-899-7451

SHL Aspen Tree Sofware, Inc., 700 Grand Avenue, P.O. Box 1347, Laramie, WY 82070

A telephone interview screening service (interactive voice recognition system) that has gone to the net. Apview features detailed pre-screening programs where employers can set the questions to keep in or screen out candidates that do not meet job criteria. While this is not a low cost solution, Apview is geared for larger organizations that are trying to organize high-volume recruiting, the use of automated screening software can reduce the labor...and cost involved in processing large numbers of applications. Company has recently merged with SHL so we will see what the future holds for changes.

Best Internet Recruiter (Multiple Job Posting/Hiring Systems)
http://www.bestrecruit.com   Ph: 813-579-1111

Best Software, 888 Executive Center Drive W., Suite 300, St. Petersburg, FL 33702

Best Internet Recruiter claims employers can quickly and conveniently place job listings on some of the Internet's "better known" employment sites (OCC, CareerWeb, Classifieds 2000, 4Work, JobBank USA and JobOptions), and then select and analyze resumes submitted for those jobs. Employers enter job listings once and the site will place the listings on the desired recruiting boards. Applicants e-mail their resumes to the Best Internet Recruiter, where they are stored and organized. We like the fact that users pay only the actual advertising feeds to the job listing sites. The Internet Recruiter handles all of the billing for the job list sites, providing the customer with a simple statement of charges.

Brave New Work World (Research)

Gary Johnson

http://www.newwork.com   E-mail: gjohnson@pclink.com

New York News

Brave New Work World collects articles from major publications all over the world on work related issues. The information is updated on a daily basis with a synopsis of each article and a link to the document. Some very challenging ideas and concepts are addressed- from "discrimination in the workforce" to where have all the "hi-tech workers gone". A career management site with a difference.

Career Builder (Hiring Systems)

Jennifer Giles

http://www.careerbuilder.com   E-mail: info@netstartinc.con   Ph: 703-709-1001

CareerBuilder, Inc., 11495 Sunset Hills Road, Reston, VA 20190

Employers using CareerBuilder's system have access to a set of web-enabled recruiting tools that begins with company Intranet and Internet Templates. *(See CXR Listing)*

Greentree Systems Homepage (R:/Resume Database System)

Andrea Collins

http://www.greentreesystems.com   E-mail: info@GreentreeSystems.com   Ph: 408-879-1410

3131 S. Bascom Ave 200, Campbell, CA 95008

Greentree Systems provides applicant tracking and resume scanning software for recruiters who need to get the paperwork off their desks. This windows based system tracks job applicants, produces reports and makes it easy for recruiters to find resumes in a flash. Priced for the mid market client(under 500 to over 10,000 employees they continue to improve and, when you are looking to put in an optical scanning system this is one that should be considered. A new web based hiring manager module is due out and we will provide an update review when it is released.

Hot Jobs/SOFTSHOE (Systems)

Kelly Michaelian

http://www.hotjobs.com   E-mail: kelly@hotjobs.com   Ph: 212-302-0060

Otec Inc., 24 West 40th Street,11th floor, New York, NY 10128

Hot Jobs is a site that connects job seekers to employers who use the site's web-enabled product SoftShoe. *(See CXR Listing)*

HRSites International (Systems/Multiple Posting)

Art Koff

http://www.hrsites   E-mail: artkoff@enteract.com   Ph: 888-921-9400

HR Sites International, 820 North Orleans,Suite 218, Chicago, IL 60610

HRSites has raised the bar when it comes to posting jobs to the Internet. *(See CXR Listing)*

I Search (Private Resume Database)
John Reese

http://www.isearch.com   E-mail: info@isearch.com   Ph: 800-459-4747

Interactive Search, 5959 West Century Blvd. #1122, Los Angeles, CA 90045

For recruiters inundated with resumes and looking to take some of the paper pushing out of staffing, I-Search might be the answer. A private online database, resumes are sent (via fax, e-mail, snail mail) directly to I-Search and quickly scanned into their system so each company's recruiters can access their "private reserve" from anywhere.

ijob (Resume Database/Screening)
Judy Ward

http://WWW.ijob.com   E-mail: jward@ijob.com   Ph: 405-936-2600

13800 Benson Road, Edmond, OK 73034

ijob provides recruiters with an online staffing system. *(See CXR listing)*

Intelligent Search Tools (Research/Seminars)
http://www.intell-search.com   E-mail: info@intell-search.com   Ph: 888-999-8844

35 S. Main Street, Hanover, NH 03755

Intelligent Search Tools is becoming well known for its seminars among the "recruiting search community". This site is a great starting point to understanding the changes the WWW is making among the staffing industry. A free newsletter for staffing professionals.

Internet Business Network (Research/Seminars/Newsletter)
John Sumser

http://www.interbiznet.com   E-mail: info@interbiznet.com   Ph: 415-380-8244

346 Starling Road, Mill Valley, CA 94914

The Internet Business Network (Interbiznet) provides hundreds of links, training and newsletters. *(See CXR listing)*

ITTA – ProRecruiter (Resume Robot)
Tom Murray

http://www.it-ta.com   E-mail: tmurray@it-ta.com   Ph: 602-953-4870

ITTA LLC, 5759 E. Acoma Drive, Scottsdale, AZ 85253

ITTA's resume robot provides employers up to four queries per night. *(See CXR Listing)*.

ListServ Directory (Search Engine)
http://www.lsoft.com/lists/listref.html   E-mail: sales@lsoft.com   Ph: 800-399-5449

L-Soft international, Inc., 8401 Corporate Drive, Suite 510, Landover, MD 20785

CataList is a complete list of nearly 20,000+ LISTSERV addresses. Here you can browse links and subscribe to those topics that interest you.

Online Newsletters (Research/Search Newsletters)
Len Canning
http://www.lemaze.com/Business_News/newsletters/newsletter
E-mail: candocdx@lemaze.com   Ph: 403-249-1100
LeMaze Studio, 207 Coachway Road SW, Calgary, Alberta, Canada T3H 1B2
Online Newsletters provides hundreds of resource links to newsletters, mailinglists and discussion lists. These are nicely indexed and show the frequency of publication as well as whether there is a related web site available. What is particularly convenient is that the links are 100% live meaning you can click on what you like from the description and subscribe to the publication on the spot.

Personic (Hiring Systems)
Mike Silvester
http://www.personic.com   E-mail: info@personic.com   Ph: 650-829-6800
1000 Marina Blvd, Brisbane, CA 94005
Personic (formerly EZ Access) provide Human Resource professionals with a sophisticated set of hiring tools. Applicants can fax or e-mail resumes in directly as well as through optical scanning devices. Recent acquisition of Robosurfer adds software that automatically locates resumes by searching newsgroups, individual resume pages and major Internet search engines. Personic has become a major player.

Postmaster Direct (E-mail collection software)
http://www.PostMasterDirect.com   E-mail: sales@postmasterdirect.com
PostMaster Direct is for those who are into a particular type of direct. Some recruiters enjoy flying the "Jolly Roger" and e-mailing (read spamming) the world. Site will cut, dice and slice thousands of e-mails anyway you want it. Prices seem to start at $.15 per address. This seriously intrusive approach has some downside potential and should be thought through carefully. Lots of competitors in this category.

Qwiz (Testing/Screening)
Lisa
http://www.qwiz.com   E-mail: quiz@quiz.com   Ph: 800-281-9713
8601 Dunwoody Place, Suite 420, Atlanta, GA 30350
Quiz provides PC-based testing and training for software applications, technical, secretarial and business skills. Systems automatically score and time applicant performance. Site provides additional information.

Recruitment Extra (Research)
Madeline Krazit
http://www.recruitmentextra.com   E-mail: jkraz@aol.com   Ph: 201-750-0521
Recruitment Extra provides industry information for the savvy recruiter. Layoffs and jobfair calendars are only a small part of the information here.
(See CXR Listing)

Recruit-Net (Automated Job Posting/Seminars)
Tracy Claybrook
http://www.recruit-net.com   E-mail: request@recruit-net.com   Ph: 813-282-3005
1100 S. Hoover Blvd., Suite 203, Tampa, FL 33609
For recruiters who are tired of posting to multiple sites manually Recruit-Net has developed technology to post at the click of a button. At press time they had over 175 different groups you could place your openings with and this will grow rapidly. Cost for this service runs $300-$400 per month for 50 job postings depending on the number of accounts you require. Owner also conducts seminars.

Restrac (Hiring Systems)
Anna Mooney
http://www.restrac.com   E-mail: annam@restrac.com   Ph: 781-869-5000
Restrac, Inc., 91 Hartwell Avenue, Lexington, MA 02173-3125
Restrac answers the question "what do I do with all of these resumes?" Their optical scanning intelligent software and their new web internet product WebHire is one of the important elements driving the changes in the hiring process and eliminating the need for paper. Restrac' systems accept resumes via e-mail, fax and, if contracted, they will do the hard copy scanning for you. Company has made alliances with several websites so that all replies go seamlessly into their database. Infinite reports. Along with Resumix, these systems are the Cadillacs of the industry.

Resumail Network (HiringSystems)
Steve Rofey
http://www.resumail.com   E-mail: srofey@resumail.com   Ph: 800-916-7638
Opportunity Network, Inc., 6309 North O'Connor Road, Suite 216, Irving, TX 75039-3510
Visitors to Resumail Network can download Resumail(TM) software for free to develop and send resumes to employers.*(See CXR Listing)*

Resumix (Resume Database System)
http://www.resumix.com   E-mail: info@resumix.com   Ph: 408-744-3800
Resumix Inc., 890 Ross Drive, Sunnyvale, CA 94089
Resumix resume database systems take care of the problem of too many resumes on a recruiter's desk as well as many other hiring functions. Among the early leaders in the industry, Resumix , Restrac and Personic are likely candidates for high volume multi site systems that need to do it all.

Search Engine Watch (Research)
Danny Sullivan
http://www.searchenginewatch.com   E-mail: susanl@internet.com
Mecklermedia
Search Engine Watch is a wealth of information about search engines. Interesting tips, all types of explanations on how they work and how to use them. A shareware model, the owners ask that if you like what you see, subscribe and, for $29, become a paying member. Hundreds of links to different engines with simple explanations of each. A great tutorial on the subject.

Skill Set- Desktop Recruiter (Hiring Systems)
Dan White

http://www.skillset.com   E-mail: sales@skillset.com   Ph: 925-468-7420

Skill Set Software, Inc., 3875 Hopyard Road, Suite 250, Pleasanton, CA 94588

Skill Set is based on Lotus Notes and includes all the tools for a paperless hiring process with the added benefit of integrating the hiring manager into the process.

Smart POST Network (Multiple Job Posting)
Stephanie Ralston

http://www.smartpost.com   E-mail: eralston@the webdesk.com   Ph: 254-539-6178

The WebDesk, LLC
5813 Wrightsville Avenue, Suite 121, Wilmington, NC 28403

SmartPost is a job posting tool that takes the drudgery of sending job copy to multiple websites The product has some very interesting reports and technical features. As their agreements with job posting sites grow so will this product.

Spider's Apprentice (Research)
http://www.monash.com/spidap.html   Ph: 781-861-8700

Monash Information Services, 430 Marrett Road, Lexington, MA 02173

Spider's Apprentice is a research tool on how to use search engines. One of the best tutorials on the web. Check out "How to Use Web Search Engines" to learn what goes on behind the scenes. Some very interesting information and the owners ratings of the different aspects of each engine should be taken seriously.

Ultimate White Pages
Scott Martin

http://www.theultimates.com   E-mail: scott@scottmartin.net

The Ultimate White Pages provides links to research sites for finding those corporations, telephone numbers, names of individuals, or anything else that your heart desires. Yahoo, WhoWhere, Switchboard, Four11, Infospace and Worldpages and others are all listed here.

US Resume/M2C (Resume Robot)
http://www.usresume.com   E-mail: info@m2c.com   Ph: 914-627-2600

Market 2000 Corp. (M2C), One Blue Hill Plaza, 11th Floor Box 1536, Pearl River, NY 10965

The US Resume/M2C agent search engine looks for resumes on all websites EXCEPT tradtional (read "paid") resumes databases. Agent picks up folks that have posted their resumes on personal web pages, company directories, etc. Job seekers can post their e-mail address for their resume for free. Recruiters have a choice of packages that run from $1,475 per month for 150 resumes to $3,995 for 1,000 resumes per month.

Web Recruiter (System)
http://com.sortium.com   E-mail: info@comsortium.com   Ph: 212-557-7000

535 Fifth Avenue, Suite 911, New York, NY 10017

WebRecruiter is COM.sortiums intranet based recruiting module. Product will accept resumes via fax, email or from websites and then place them into an automated intranet system. Matching of candidates skills against job specs and then delivering resumes to managers is what this and other systems are all about.

World Hire (Hiring Systems)

Hank Stringer

http://www.world.hire.com   E-mail: hank@world.hire.com   Ph: 800-953-4473

World Hire, 6101 Balcones Drive, Suite 201, Austin, TX 78731

World.hire's system has most of the bell's and whistles from applicant tracking applicant applicant screening to job posting and resume collection. Clients use it as a template for their Intranet and Internet web sites.

Tips and Advice
from Experts in the Field

What Is The Future Of Recruiting?

by Dr. John Sullivan
Head and Professor of Human Resource Management
College of Business, San Francisco State University

johns@sfsu.edu

The process of recruiting has changed dramatically in the last few years. Web pages, electronic resume scanning, E-mail, and other innovations have forever changed the way we look for candidates. The employment process will continue to change and rely more and more on technology due to:

The growth of "easy to use" technology, cheap at home PCs and the increasing willingness of candidates and recruiters to use them.

The globalization of firms and world wide worker shortages means recruiters must now search the globe for candidates

The growth of "remote" and at home work will make looking for jobs less and less tied to firms located within a commuting distance from home

The continuing shift away from physical labor toward knowledge workers who are more willing to search for a job on the web

The decline in newspaper subscriptions (and their want ads as recruiting tools)

Additional contributing factors to the change in the recruitment paradigm is the low unemployment rate, vacant jobs are everywhere and the expectation of long term employment with a single firm is becoming the exception. As a result, there will be a dramatic increase in the number of times in our lifetime that we will be in the job search mode. For recruiters it means more work and for individuals it means that great job search skills will become a life long skill rather than something we will just occasionally need!

Some breakthrough firms like Cisco, Intel, Silicon Graphics and Microsoft have dramatically changed the way they recruit as a result of new technology and the Web. Some of the tools and strategies they pioneered are included below. But the wave of change has just begun in recruiting. If you want to get ahead of the wave, read on.

NEW RECRUITING TOOLS

The recruiting tools outlined below are already being tried at some of the more progressive companies. As a recruiter or a job seeker you need to be prepared for these new approaches if you are to have a competitive advantage in the search process.

Relationship Recruiting: Most "old style" recruiting is done on a hit or miss basis. I call it "they are looking just when I have an opening" approach. The approach assumes that the best candidate is LOOKING for a job AT EXACTLY THE SAME TIME A COMPANY HAS AN OPENING!

If you want to get the best people it is a mistake to rely on this "blind coincidence." If you are looking for the perfect recruit (or job) you can no longer rely on these lucky coincidences.

A better approach is what I call "Relationship Recruiting." The basic premise is that recruiting stops being a one-time reaction to an "open requisition." Instead recruiters are continually looking for "names" and are continuously building "relationships" with the best potential hires in a given field through a "Personal Courting" approach.

Recruiters use relationship building tools such as occasional calls, e-mails, lunches and "Push" E-Newsletters (periodic E-Mail newsletters sent by the company) to build a relationship BEFORE an opening occurs. This allows most (or all) of the "prequalifying" and assessment of candidates to be done in advance. Executive recruiters and hi-tech recruiters already use this approach and you can use it to stand out from the rest of the "I need to find a candidate right away" crowd! Because the candidates know you in advance offer acceptance rates are as much as 25% higher than under the traditional approach.

As an applicant you can become a "Relationship Hire" by preselecting companies and jobs you want and building relationships with their recruiters before you "need" a job. There is reduced pressure "because you don't need a job tomorrow" which allows you more time to provide examples of your skills and work than in a normal Look/Opening recruiting situation.

Change Your Recruiting Targets: Stop recruiting unemployed/unhappy people! If you are targeting the very best in a field to recruit expect them NOT to be active job seekers. They are by definition good at their jobs and do not "read want ads" or post their resume on the Web. In fact they might not even have a current resume. You need to have a different strategy to attract people who are not looking for a job. You should also assume you are going to have to build a long term relationship with them in order to get them to work for you.

Remote Hiring (PC Hiring): Traditionally, all hiring was done on a face-to-face basis. Candidates came to the office and interviewed in front of the hiring manager. This can slow the hiring process considerably (trying to coordinate availability of meeting times), increase costs (flying the candidate in) and is often an unrealistic expectation in a global corporation. One company (Hewlett Packard) has already begun introducing relatively simple technology to allow for real time "video-conference" interviews. They have set up a network of video equipped computers on college campuses to allow for remote interviewing. Other companies can take advantage of this new technology through their own video conferencing set-ups and/or those at chain copy centers that also have video setups.

Remote Work's Impact Upon Recruiting (Hire From Anywhere): New technology (fast modems and video equipped PCs) and changing corporate policies now allow many people (especially knowledge workers) to do their work from home, or on the road. This will expand your geographic recruiting area because applicants will no longer have to live in the same city as the company. This will allow "all recruiting to become global." Recruiters can now ignore the lack of "local" talent and search the web for candidates anywhere in the world. These "remote jobs" might only require you to visit the company headquarters once a year.

"Push Cast" Technology To Automatically Notify Candidates of Job Openings: In the future the process of searching for jobs will shift from the current approach where you must actively look in a multitude of sources (want ads and web pages) for jobs to a new "automatic" approach. This automatic "push" technology starts when a candidate "pre-registers" (or when recruiters pre-selects you as a viable candidate) for certain types of jobs. Once registered, job openings are automatically sent (or pushed) to you by a vendor or software package via confidential e-mail. This "reduced effort" approach will make job searching significantly easier because the targeted openings will come automatically to you.

Resume Robots/Job Opening "Mining": There are two basic elements in recruiting: finding the candidate and assessing them. The first (finding candidates) which used to be a relatively difficult task for recruiters is becoming increasingly easy as a result of large modern databases, online "yellow" pages and Job Posting Web pages. Firms use data mining techniques that will supply complete lists (directories) of qualified candidates to companies. By sorting professional organization membership data, journal mailing lists, online "yellow pages and WEB "registration hits" agents are able to provide candidate profiles instantaneously to subscriber firms, worldwide. Resume "robots" (sometimes called spiders or snakes) are automated tools that scan every corner of the Web to find resumes and candidate names for recruiters (examples include ResumeRobot, "Resputin")

Finding people tools: Electronic "phone book" search engines like "411" and "Who Where') are new tools that let us rapidly track down people no matter where they work or live. These systems make "capturing names" a much more valuable asset because you can now find their address(s) so easily and then use e-mail to communicate with them.

A "Futureview" Interview: In a world of rapid and constant change companies must learn to focus on the future (and in some cases learn to forget the past). Most selection tools unfortunately focus on what candidates have done in the past. Fortunately, most progressive companies are starting to ask different questions like "What WILL you do for me in the FUTURE" and "What tools will you use to solve my problems?." I call that type of interview a "Futureview." Companies need to know if candidates can solve their problems and use new tools and methods that didn't exist the last time "you" solved the problem. Actually, even if the candidate has never done the task before it is to your advantage to ask them to show you how they WOULD do it!

Virtual Reality Job Simulations: Advanced technology will also allow companies to better assess the capabilities of its recruits. Computerized simulations (like flight simulators for pilots) allow corporations to put employees in "what If" situations to see how they can perform BEFORE they are actually hired. This will help applicants who perform poorly in interviews but who do well in the actual job.

Web-Based Simulations to Assess Candidates: Web-based "video games" that both excite the candidate and enable us to assess their skills remotely. Technical skills assessment can now also be done on the Web using interactive testing tools (like tech chek) that allows a firm to assess the skill level of programmers and other technical hires.

Sharing Job Openings Among Strategic Partners: Many major firms, especially in high-tech, have developed "strategic business partnerships" with other firms in their industries (a strategic partnership is where firms cooperate on the development of new products without having to merge). The next step is a joint internal job posting system where the partners share "selected" job openings. This "cross pollination" between each other's teams further builds the relationship between the two firms. These placements may be temporary assignments, job rotations or even permanent placements, in some cases.

Listservers and Chatrooms to Find and Assess Candidates: The Net has become a tool for learning and exchanging ideas. Automated e-mail lists (listservers) and chatrooms are used by professionals to learn rapidly. Recruiters can use these venues to learn about the hot issues professionals are talking about but they can also use them to "remotely" find and assess the skills of the people that comment on the list. Often these people are thought leaders and the Net allows us to assess their ideas over time, as opposed to a one time, quick resume assessment.

Virtual Job Fairs/Open Houses: Firms can now attract people through virtual job fairs, where they would not normally participate. They are cheaper and are more likely to "WOW" a candidate than the boring traditional kind. Cisco's "friends" program on their web site is an excellent example of this type of virtual relationship building

Profiler (You Don't Need a Resume): Top recruiters know that many of the best performers are "too busy" to update their resumes. Normally they won't pursue a new job until they get around to finishing their resume. You can get them without a resume using Web site "resume builders" that help candidates write a resume or, in some cases profilers allow candidates to avoid needing a resume at all by just responding to interactive questions posed to them on the web site.

Extranet: Shared databases between external recruiters/placement agencies and firms now allow companies to electronically search for candidates 24 hours a day from a recruiting/temp firms shared database of candidates.

Tips for the Recruiter's Toolkit

by Dr. John Sullivan
Head and Professor of Human Resource Management
College of Business, San Francisco State University

johns@sfsu.edu

This is a list of employment practices a recruiter might consider as you attempt to move into 21st Century HR.

Do a survey of all hires and ask them why they accepted the job (and what were their concerns).

Do a survey of all rejected offers and find out what were the deciding factors in their decision.

Every employee is a recruiter! Use large referral programs to turn every employee into a name finder and candidate sourcer. Don't assume they know how, develop a list of your companies "WOW's and show them how/where to find referrals. Give larger bonuses for finding top performers and people for key positions

Involve your sales force in the process. They have mega contacts in the industry and also know how to sell your firm.

Consider your "retail" customers as a recruiting source. Who else respects our firm and might be inclined to want to work for us. You might also involve large corporate customers in the selection process so that you improve the likelihood that new hires meet your customers needs. It might also build customer loyalty, as they feel some "ownership" of those selected.

Give your managers and teams "ownership" of recruiting. Make them aware of the impact of good hiring on team performance. Employment consults and teaches but does not DO hiring.

Sign on to a HR Listserver to exchange recruiting ideas and ask questions (i.e. HRNET, E-RECRUIT).

Develop an E-Newsletter (a periodic e-mail newsletter) to keep potential candidates interested in your company.

Begin tracking recruiters/recruitment tools/and sources used in the hiring process. See which produces high performers, long tenure employees, and bad hires.

Identify and prioritize key jobs and key managers. Stop treating all jobs as having equal importance.

Stop looking at the cost of hire and filling "reqs" and begin focusing on the Quality of the hire and/or any potential business gains from a great hire.

Start with a "blank sheet" HR. Prove that everything you do results in a higher quality hire. Stop assuming old practices still work and "good people trying hard" always produce a quality hire. Drop all employment practices that don't make a significant difference.

Consider "weekend" hires, consultant to hire, temp to perm. and job simulations to improve the accuracy of the selection process by putting the candidate "in the job."

Develop "prequalifying" systems (tell them in advance that they are qualified for an internal transfer) to increase the number of internal transfers and also to increase retention rates.

Develop "Personal Courting" and relationship building programs with potential recruits so that candidate assessment occurs over time and are not just one time "flash" assessments.

Realize one of the primary functions of recruitment and hiring is to build and reinforce the corporate image and culture as well as to increase corporate capabilities and productivity. Remember recruiting is marketing and all potential recruits are also potential customers.

Start forecasting the future (unemployment rates, the pool of qualified candidates, business cycles, the changing needs of your customers etc.) and stop just "reacting to reqs" when they hit your desk. Realize that openings and trends can often be anticipated.

Do internal customer satisfaction surveys to see what managers and applicants want "more of and less of."

Identify how your employment practices differ from your direct competitors. Develop a plan to make EACH program element superior to your competitors. You can't beat the competitor if you all do the same things the same way.

Drop forever the idea that recruitment and hiring must be done face to face. Develop remote recruitment and hiring practices that are superior to face to face ones.

Begin the process of becoming an Employer of Choice in your industry. Gather information on what is needed and sell it to top management.

Develop JIT hiring systems like "corporate resources" (hiring a superstar even when there is no current opening) to capture superstars who are likely to be on the market for only one week or less.

Develop metrics (in conjunction with the CFO) to identify and prove the business impacts of a great hire and the costs of a bad hire. Make hiring great employees THE corporate competitive advantage over your competition.

Develop forecasting tools which "forecast corporate FAT" (excess employees) before a RIF is necessary and identify future retention issues so that you will have to do less recruiting.

Develop a rotation program where employment specialists spend time each year working in the field and "learning the business."

Get line managers to "sponsor" and "own" changes and revisions in employment systems so employment doesn't have to spend it's time in political battles.

Consider creating "feeder channels" for future University hires. For example sponsor "Learn to be a _____ training classes, student clubs, internships, "Professor summer internships" and short term professor/manager swap programs).

Develop and sponsor internet business chat rooms and listservers to develop relationships with potential applicants.

Capture reference names given by high performers and new hires. Consider them as potential hires.

Track down high-performers that "voluntarily terminated" within the last year and attempt to get them to return.

Track candidates that turned down your offer within the last 2 years and contact them again at periodic intervals to see if they would consider your firm again.

Track candidates that were rejected for "needing more experience" and contact them again after an interval of time that would now "make them qualified"

Develop a "Real Time" speed of hire program. Drop or weaken employment "rules" and approvals to decrease your time to hire. Identify things that slow down the hiring process and that you can't prove make a difference (No you don't need a job description in order to hire someone etc.).

Calculate the average performance rating, bonus pay, awards, promotions and productivity of those hired this year and compare it to last year's hires. Smile if you see an improvement! Change if they aren't.

Get employees when they talk to other professionals (during benchmarking at conferences, through e-mails etc.) to "capture the names" of people that are impressive. Have them keep a log or just write it on their calendar for later transfer to the database.

Ask applicants for their references and capture them as possible candidates. References should also be asked for additional names when they are called

Ask new hires, from "target" companies, on their first day, "Who else is good there?" and capture the names. Also ask them who are good mentors, managers and trainers.

Identify key idea people from listservers and chat rooms/newsgroups. Occasionally post questions to draw out the best ones.

Capture the names of speakers at conferences from junk mail brochures, AMA type catalogs, web sites etc. Also authors of articles, books and technical information pieces are captured.

Consultants we hire are asked for names. Consultants themselves are names to capture if there is a chance they may sometime return to making an "honest" living (joke).

Capture attendance lists at conferences.

Look at award winners and runners-up at professional associations. Board members and officers are noted and they are also asked for names of "up and comers" in their professional organizations.

Add someone with market research experience to your employment staff to help you refine your name capture system.

Put some "cool" people and outside the box thinkers on your recruiting advisory team. Ask them how to attract other similar thinkers.

Ask the best people you meet "who is almost as good as them?" and "who do you learn from?" Capture those names.

Track the top 10% of college recruits (and interns) that we identified but did not hire. Interns and recent grads should be asked for the names of mentors, fellow students or great people they have met in informational interviews, shadow days etc.

Ask our employees that speak at conferences to get the business cards of people that ask good questions.

Individuals with WOW personal web pages on technical topics are added. People they visit our web site technical areas are added to the list with a "cookie."

Give away gifts at conferences and capture the business cards that are put in the hopper.

Hire interns or temps to surf the web for names you might have missed from the web pages of professional association, magazines, listserver archives etc.

Ask the best we hire to search their e-mail address book/daytimer for names.

The Value of Internet Recruiting: Reasons to Recruit on the Web

by Dr. John Sullivan
Head and Professor of Human Resource Management
College of Business, San Francisco State University

johns@sfsu.edu

The Web is *the* recruiting tool for the 21st Century. There are numerous reasons you must have a presence on the Web, including:

Speed: Posting jobs and finding candidates is faster on the web. There is no need to "wait until Sunday" to post a job. It's faster and easier to screen candidates through the use of a computer key word search than it is by reading hard copy resumes.

Cost: It's much cheaper than most newspaper ads and fewer people even read newspapers every year while more and more people are Internet savvy... Most job boards are cheap (and some are free) compared to the high costs of newspaper ads or job fairs. It's usually as much as 1/3 cheaper than paper ads. Some of the "new" types of sites are even free to candidates and employers. It's virtually paperless and that cuts cost and helps the environment.

It's Exciting: A great web site can excite candidates and encourage "passive" people to visit the site. The best candidates are also more likely to be "playing" on the web.

Larger markets: The Internet can reach global masses...newspaper hits small demographic areas. The web allows us to find the best anywhere while newspapers have less than a 50 mile range.

Self Service: Using the web lets the candidates find their own answers and to assess their "fit" with the firm. This also helps limit unsolicited phone calls.

Better Candidates: You can find "better people" on the Web than through hard copy ads. People who post their resumes on the web show they are accepting of change and that they are familiar with technology. This means that they are also more likely to help a business use technology to grow and change.

Gaining A Competitive Advantage: HR professionals that begin by using the web to find candidates usually soon learn to progress to using the web to gather other information and data. This additional learning will help them beat the competition in areas of business other than hiring (purchasing. market research, advertising etc.). Recruiters can also use listservers (e-mail networks) and chatrooms to ask questions, to share problems and solutions for free with other recruiters and consultants.

More Choices: Targeting candidates for a specific job is noticeably easier now that there are an increasing number of "focused" functional job boards that mean that you don't have to surf through the large and complex "monster" job boards.

POTENTIAL PROBLEMS WITH WEB RECRUITING

Recruiters that use the web find it has great value but it also has its share of problems. Some common recruiting problems include:

Old resumes: Many large web sites go for volume and worry little about the currency of their resumes. A site might have thousands of resumes for high demand fields that are weeks old. As a result, business have to "sort out" the candidates that are no longer looking.

Volume: The largest sites have such a large volume of non-targeted resumes that it can become a burden just to sort through them.

A National Scope: Because many businesses only hire locally, having a web site that attracts national candidates that require expensive relocation might be of little value. This is especially true for California where the high cost of living may "eliminate" many candidates that haven't lived in California before.

Overpicked: Some resume databases are overpicked so that all of the good candidates are "gone." The smaller sites get few "hits" and may not be worth the effort.

Limited Access to the Internet: Not everyone has access to the Internet (not everyone gets the paper either). An adverse impact is also possible if less minorities and women have access.

Privacy Issues: Access to resumes needs to be security protected so that they can't be "stolen" by competitors or seen by their applicants current employers.

How To Pick a Web site for Your Recruitment Ad

by Peter D. Weddle

Reprinted with permission from *WEDDLE'S Wildly Useful, Up-to-the-Minute Newsletter about INTERNET RESOURCES for Successful Recruiting*

http://www.recruiternetwork.com
pdweddle@worldnet.att.net

As in print publications, recruitment advertising on the Internet usually has several objectives. Obviously, the first and most important is to locate high caliber candidates for an organization's open positions at the lowest possible cost. Often, a second objective is to build the public image of the organization, both as an attractive employer and as a high quality provider of goods or services. And increasingly, at least in cyberspace, yet another goal is to cut the time and effort involved in identifying prospective candidates so that recruiters can devote more attention to evaluation and selection.

In order to meet these objectives, recruitment web sites must capture eyeballs. In other words, they must generate both initial and sustained traffic by visitors to their site. First, they have to promote their location on the Internet as an attractive destination for the kinds of people an organization is seeking to recruit so that these prospective candidates will *visit the site the first time,* and then they have to provide an experience at the site that is interesting, educational, entertaining and/or worthwhile enough to get those prospective candidates to *return to the site over and over again.*

Market share is one way to measure a site's effectiveness in attracting visitors, but there are other factors which should be considered, as well. Indeed, a strong promotional campaign will often get a person to visit a site one time (which is clearly important), but it is the site itself—its design—that will determine if they ever come back. Barb Ruess, former Director of Marketing at E.Span (now JobOptions), puts it this way: "There were three key tenets to our site's design: functionality, which made it easy for visitors to get to where they wanted to go on the site; graphics, or the look and feel of the site, which made it easy to use and enjoy what they found there; and content, which gave them a reason to pay us another visit."

All of a site's visitors are important (and measured in market share) as they make up the pool of prospective candidates who will read a recruitment ad, but repeat visitors are the engine of successful recruiting. They are the "loyal audience" to which a site can offer employers access—consistently and with confidence—whether an ad is posted this week or next year. So, what determines the number of repeat visitors to a site and the level of their loyalty?

Basically, people come back to a site when it satisfies two criteria: (1) they get what they want and/or expect and (2) they enjoy themselves in the process. And the only way to determine which sites meet those criteria (and hence, represent a good potential return on your investment) is to *walk awhile in the job seeker's shoes* on the "information superhighway."

For both active and passive job seekers, the key to the first criterion is great jobs with great employers. In other words, one of the most effective ways to evaluate whether or not candidates will visit, stay for any length of time at and return to a site—and thereby give your recruitment ad a chance to work—is to determine the company your organization will keep at the site. Ask the sites you are considering for a list of those organizations which have recruited with them in the last 90 days and for the kinds of jobs (i.e., occupational field, skill level, salary) they posted. Then ask yourself, whether those opportunities with those employers would attract the kind of candidate you are seeking. If the answer is yes, move on to the second criterion; if the answer is no, move on to another web site.

The only way to evaluate a recruitment web site against the second criterion is to pay it a visit online. Indeed, I strongly recommend that you never place an ad on a site until you have "test driven" it from a job seeker's perspective. If you don't enjoy the experience, chances are the candidates won't, as well; and when that happens, your ad will either get ignored, or worse, your organization's image will be tarnished by its association with the site. Here are some other issues you should consider when visiting a site:

HOW EASY IS IT TO OPEN THE DOOR? Although seemingly a small point, ease-of-entry can have a huge impact on whether a site is major on-off ramp on the Internet or a back road with much less traffic. As more and more people begin to visit cyberspace for the first time, a site's appeal will be based on such factors as the length and complexity of the site's name (e.g., compare www.disserv3.stu.umn.edu/COL to www.occ.com, and it's easy to figure out which is more "candidate friendly") and how long it takes to download the site's content (i.e., you can forget about it if the site takes more than two sips of coffee to move its images and words from the Internet to your—or a candidate's—computer).

HOW EASY IS IT TO FIGURE OUT WHAT'S THERE? Is the lay-out of the first page of the site (i.e., what you see when you initially arrive) intuitively obvious to the first time visitor? Does it clearly identify the different sections or areas of the site (e.g., for job seekers, employers) and provide easy access to them? Does it provide a Table of Contents or a "site map" (usually an outline of the site's content) for each or all of those areas so that visitors can quickly determine what's available on the site (for first time visitors) and what has recently changed there (for repeat visitors)?

HOW EASY IS IT TO GET WHERE YOU WANT TO GO? Does the site provide good navigability? For example, if you click on a word or image to go to one area of the site, there should be a clearly identified way to return to your original location. A good web site design will make it easy to go "forth and back." It will also provide a way (a) to return to the first or home page of the site, so that you can start all over again if you lose your bearings within the site's content and (b) to move from one major content area (e.g., the database of job openings) to another (e.g., the database of resumes).

Building on the Basics:
How to Write Ads to Promote Opportunities

By Nancy Heimbaugh

JobOptions (formerly E-Span)
http://www.joboptions.com

If you were looking for a job, would that ad get your attention? Even if you could decipher it, would you apply? Probably not. Yet, to save space and money, that's the way many classified ads appear.

Look at employment ads on the Internet. You'll see that old habits die hard. Many employers/recruiters use abbreviated, bland online ads. They're not matching the message with the medium or the audience.

The major online employment sites have information and resources that will help make your online ads more effective. Visit some of the sites for how-to advice on writing online ads. Then pretend you're a job seeker and skim online ads. You'll quickly see why a good, comprehensive ad can get 10 times as many responses as a "just the basics" ad.

Space and connections are advantages unique to the Web. Make the most of them to provide comprehensive information. The more information you give candidates, the more likely you are to attract the right candidates.

While some online recruiting services ask you to limit your ads to one or two pages, you don't have the space restrictions you have with print classifieds. (In print advertising, the more space you use, the more you pay!) Generally, online ads cost the same whether you use 25 words or 250, so don't mince words!

Make the most of the Web's linking capabilities, too. If your company has a Web site, connect candidates to it. Most online employment services can connect viewers of your ads directly to your Web site where they'll get a good overview of your company. Ask online services you're considering if they will provide this connection. If you don't have a site, ask if they will create a mini-site with information about your company and link ads to it.

Use your ads and your links to give candidates a complete picture of your company and your positions.

THE A-B-Cs OF ONLINE AD CONTENT.

Your online ads should tell and sell. Following are points to consider and information to include in your ads.

Audience. Remember, it's the world-wide Web! Your Internet ads will attract candidates from across town and across the country. Many online job seekers may not be familiar with your geographical area or with your company. Think of your ads as dynamic advertisements designed to sell your company and your location to candidates!

Not only do you need to keep in mind who's looking at your ads, but also how they're looking at them. Online job seekers view ads at their convenience. They use keywords to search for ads. It's much more scientific and precise than flipping through a Sunday classified section. Candidates usually have many ads to choose from, and they have a "remote control" in their hand—a mouse. If your ads are not appealing and descriptive, they'll move on. Fast. Your ads are often the first impression a prime candidate has of your company. It pays to create ads that set your company and your positions apart.

Benefits.   Give a complete list of the benefits of working for your company— not just the traditional employment benefits! Different candidates have different hot buttons, so hit them all! Include all that are applicable and appropriate for the position you are posting.

Company.   Even if you're a leading employer in your area and your industry, outsiders may not have heard of your company and its products and services. So tell candidates what your company does and why it's a good place to work. Convince them that your company has a future—and they have a future with it!

Description.   Give a comprehensive description of the position and the qualifications. Most companies now have formal job descriptions. In order to attract the right candidates, every online ad should include a detailed overview of the responsibilities the position entails and the requirements for consideration. But don't stop there! Include any of the following that are applicable and positive such reason for the opening; strategic corporate focus on this area of the business; recent achievements of department; role within the organizational structure.

E-mail address.   The online audience wants to find and respond to openings quickly and conveniently. To the Net's computer-savvy candidates, that usually means via e-mail. In an article on June 16, 1998, USA Today reported that e-mail is used by more than 85% of U.S. homes connected to the Net. Be sure to include an e-mail address in your ads. With most services, candidates can respond online while they're viewing the ad. (Also provide a fax number and address so that you have all the bases covered.)

Fields and Format   Complete all of the fields (blanks for information) when you post your ads. Different online employment services request different information. Fields frequently include the following: job title; reference number; reply e-mail address; Web URL; company name; job location; education level and experience required; job classification; management level and more. Some of this information will not be seen by candidates, but it will be used by the search engine. It's important to complete all the fields to ensure that your ads are selected properly in response to candidate searches.

Submit your ad in the correct format.   Most online employment services request ASCII text for ads posted via e-mail. ASCII is like the "universal" format. When you use the specified format, you avoid strange glitches in your ad or symbols that look like a secret code.

Geography.   What if you were looking for a position and saw an ad for the ideal job, but it was located in Podunk? You probably wouldn't consider it. But what if the ad told you the following:

"Podunk is nestled in the fabulous Finger Lakes region of New York state. The scenic area offers great recreational opportunities, including camping, downhill skiing, golfing, and snowboarding. You'll enjoy the inviting atmosphere of a small, friendly town, yet the excitement of (major city) is just 60 miles away." Even if your company is located in a large, well-known area, don't assume that candidates will think of the good things. Mention San Francisco, and some people will tremble at the thought of earthquakes, while others will thrill at the thought of the Golden Gate Bridge or the Giants. Remember, people frequently have misconceptions about various areas of the country.

Give an overview of the community where the job is actually located. Emphasize all lifestyle institutions and opportunities

Keywords.   O.K. We skipped a few letters in the ABCs of online content. Keywords are the last critical element. Candidates use keywords to search for positions. Most online job sites perform full text searches and give candidates a list of all ads that include their keywords. However, if your position is for an accountant and a candidate uses "CPA" as a keyword, your position won't appear. To ensure that all appropriate candidates see your ad, include all applicable keywords. For example, keywords candidates might use to search for accounting positions include: accountant, accounting, auditor, finance manager, CPA, CFO, director of finance, etc.

So that you don't have to do word gymnastics to include all applicable keywords within the text of your ad, many online services suggest adding a keyword listing at the end of your ad.

You can use these ABCs of online ad content as a checklist to help you create effective ads. They emphasize what to say. But how you say it is important, too.

THE 1-2-3s OF ONLINE AD STYLE.

Your ads should give a feel for your company as well as facts about the position. Convey an image that's appropriate for your company. If yours is a button-down, stuffed shirt environment, don't be overly casual. Conversely, if you're sitting there in your tennis shoes and have a dart board on your wall and a basketball hoop on your door, don't make your ads sound formal, prim and proper.

Whether yours is an established Fortune 500 company or a new business, the following tips will help make your ads more readable and involving.

1. Use a conversational tone. Think of your ads as talking one-on one with individual candidates.
2. Use "you" instead of "the candidate." Talk directly to candidates by using the second person (you) instead of third person (the candidate or applicant).
   Example:
   Third-person: "The candidate will find that this is a very challenging and rewarding position."
   Second-person: "You'll find this job challenging and rewarding!
3. Use active voice and action words. Your ads will be more exciting and compelling.
   Example:
   Passive voice: "Resumes may be sent to jdoe@company.com"
   Active voice: "Rush your resume to jdoe@company.com"

In the second example, notice the sense of urgency the word "Rush" gives as compared to the standard "Send."

TAKE ADVANTAGE OF TECHNOLOGY TO MAKE YOUR JOB EASIER!

Use a standard header and footer to simplify writing and posting your ads.

You don't have to get out your thesaurus and create great prose every time you post an ad. Many online services let you create a standard header and footer that you can use as a "shell" for all your ads. Use the header to entice the reader with detailed information about the geographical area and the company, and the footer for a call to action and information on how to respond. Make sure all the information in the header and footer applies to all of the positions you'll post so you don't have to change them each time.

Once you have an effective header and footer, simply customize the middle, job-specific portion of the ad. Include a complete description of the position and list the qualifications. Then read the whole ad to make sure it tells the whole story!

ONLINE RECRUITING IS MORE THAN ADS!

Effective ads can significantly improve your Net results. But don't stop there! There's a whole arsenal of online weapons you can use to win today's hard-fought recruiting wars.

- *Resume database services you can search to find qualified candidates*
- *Resume e-mail updates that automatically alert you to prime candidates*
- *Display ads that make your company stand out and get noticed*
- *Ancillary employment-related services*
- *Links to great resources and information*

Make the most of your online ads, options and resources. That can boost your career!

Building A College Online Recruiting Presence: Tactics, Tools and Tips

By Rachel Bell and Sara Sutton
founders, JobDirect.com

http://www.jobdirect.com

The diverse crop of college students stepping out into the "real world" has something in common that no past class has shared: many of them are on their way to jobs they found with the help of the Internet. The past two years have brought an explosion of online tools for job-seekers and recruiters—everything from simple electronic classified ads to sophisticated database systems to online storefronts—for traditional headhunting services.

With unemployment down, demand for college grads up, and average cost-per-hire reported by the Employment Management Association reaching $6,359, these new tools couldn't have come at a better time. But the path that brought us to this point has been anything but smooth. Chances are, if you can imagine a type of recruiting tool that might exist on the web, an enterprising company has already invented it, marketed it, and promptly gone out of business.

At last, the dust is settling. The Internet services that have withstood the trials of the last few years are now delivering stable, high-quality, high-value results that make them strong additions to any company's recruiting arsenal.

This column will take a quick look at the latest trends in online recruiting, then examine in detail some of the strengths and weaknesses of the different types of Internet services, and the most successful tactics for incorporating these new tools into the hiring process.

NEW TACTICS, JUST IN TIME

A major stumbling block for all Internet tools has been the chicken-and-egg dilemma of finding acceptance with employers, while still perfecting the process of attracting good candidates. The past six months, however, have largely solved this problem, as online companies have moved rapidly to address the needs and preferences of students and other online job-seekers. Armed with improved products, and bolstered by widespread media coverage, these companies have promoted themselves aggressively to a population of job-seekers that increasingly expects to find the answers to its needs online. CNN reports that in 1998, 92% of college-level students will use online resources as part of their job hunt—a clear sign that online recruiting's day has come.

Corporate America has watched with well-justified caution through the early stages of the Internet's evolution into a practical recruiting tool and is now moving decisively toward full participation. Whereas pioneers in online recruiting sought and found electrical engineers and computer programmers, employers today are taking advantage of the diversity of candidates using the Internet to fill positions of all kinds: sales, administrative, technical—anything goes. In a market with the lowest unemployment rate in a quarter-century, where demand for college grads is expected to increase by almost 20%, no employer can ignore the opportunities afforded by online recruiting. Specifically, the National Association of Colleges and Employers (NACE) projects a nearly tenfold growth—from $48 million in 1998 to $460 million in 2002—in the money spent by employers on online recruiting efforts. The rate of increase in online use by both employers and candidates is likely to accelerate dramatically as the 1998-99 academic year starts up in the fall. Colleges and universities, having had time to assess and evaluate the Internet's offerings, are beginning to make their selections and endorse particular services for their students. It seems probable that most schools' career counseling offices will incorporate some recommendation into their materials for students by the start of the coming school year—a boon for recruiters who take advantage of online tools.

BUILDING YOUR INTERNET PRESENCE

Once an organization has recognized the value of online recruiting tools as a part of its staffing solution, a clear decision must be made to define the role the service—or services—is to play, and then to choose those services can best take on the challenges of that role. The key players in the online recruiting market have each chosen different models for what services they provide. Having a clear organizational vision and set of expectations will make evaluating these services much more manageable.

BASIC TYPES OF ONLINE SERVICES

Job Listing Boards   The pioneers of online recruiting, these services, variously known as "job boards," "bulletin boards," "posting services," or "electronic classifieds," are high-tech versions of their print predecessors, newspaper classified ads. Easier to search through than traditional paper ads, job bulletin boards can be quickly scanned by keyword or geographic location, allowing job-seekers to find your ad and respond. Some services also allow candidates to store ASCII (industry jargon for "plain text, with no fancy formatting") resumes online, which can be emailed to a recruiter with a click of the mouse.

Job listing boards can be an excellent tool for increasing the volume of resumes received for your jobs. Because of the speed with which your staff can post jobs on multiple boards, and because anyone with web access can quickly respond to your posting, these services may generate thousands of resumes in a short period of time. (One established service requires candidates to obtain a secret password from their alma mater before applying.)

This advantage, however, can become a disadvantage if your staff is not prepared to handle the diverse range of ages, locations, skill levels and educational backgrounds of applicants who find your job listing on the Internet.

Because these services make it easy for candidates to apply to many jobs at one sitting, the ratio of qualified candidates to inappropriate submissions may be disappointingly low. (To help solve this problem when recruiting students, some services will target your job to particular schools.)

Resume Databases   The second generation of online recruiting tools has focused on putting more control in the hands of recruiters, by collecting and organizing candidates' resumes for recruiters' review. Services in this category span a wide range of sophistication and flexibility: at the low end, resumes can be searched out by keyword; more advanced systems integrate keyword matching with specification of detailed criteria (e.g., dates of availability, willingness to relocate, etc.) to provide more accurate results.

Resume databases can be highly effective at finding and pre-screening candidates when you have a particular profile in mind, and are particularly effective routes to instant gratification, generally showing results in a matter of a few seconds. They avoid the job-posting services' predicament of delivering unqualified resumes by allowing the recruiter to define the characteristics of an acceptable resume.

This type of service clearly requires a higher degree of participation and activity on the part of the recruiter. The full responsibility for sourcing candidates is yours in this case. No resumes are delivered when you are not actively searching, which makes this type of tool more effective for just-in-time sourcing than for regular, semester or year-long projects. Also, early systems often had large accumulations of out-of-date resumes, though most modern systems have set "expiration dates" on candidates in their database.

Matching Services   The most complete solution presently available, matching services combine the strengths of job listing services and resume databases to continuously deliver prescreened candidates. Services of this kind offer both the option to create job listings and to search for resumes in real time. Job listings range in sophistication from bare-bones classified ads to interactive tools that publicize your position and automatically filter applicants based on criteria you set.

The most effective services of this kind will provide a high level of automation, both for employers and for candidates, providing maximum efficiency for busy people. Typically, job-seekers are notified (via email) of new positions for which they are qualified, while recruiters are notified whenever new applicants matching the requirements of any open postings are entered into the database.

Because they are combinations of the two other types of systems, matching services are able to overcome the problem of handling inappropriate resume submissions and provide detailed search capabilities without requiring constant activity on the part of the recruiter.

The coming year will show a broad trend toward this level of service; indeed, companies who have offered more simplistic products have already begun a flurry of announcements heralding their impending upgrades and enhancements.

Search Engines   Though not recruiting services, per se, Internet search engines deserve a mention, as they can sometimes be useful for finding web-savvy candidates, and they have the advantage of being free to use. Search engines' usefulness, however, is limited by the complexity of the process for job-seekers: creating an online resume in this manner can be a daunting and time-consuming process, and requires a high level of web programming savvy. Search engines allow you to search for resumes by keyword.

OTHER CONSIDERATIONS

Once you've decided which model of service best fits your needs, you'll need to choose a particular product, or combination of products. The range of services and options offered by the different companies is too broad to cover here, but there are certain basic questions which should always be considered:

Customer service The market presently offers everything from turnkey solutions (read: you're on your own) to full-service Internet recruiting experts, in some cases with on-site training and dedicated account support. Taking a quick inventory of your staff's web-savvy will help you determine which level of support is appropriate.

Access to candidates You're expecting the service to supply new candidates— it's important to know what the vendor is doing to attract new candidates and publicize opportunities at your company. This year, companies were advertising online and in traditional media, establishing relationships with schools, and getting involved with student-related events. One company even had a team of students driving souped-up buses from school to school!

Accountability Some services can help you determine how well they're working for you. This can be a very valuable piece of information to help you coordinate your recruiting strategy, particularly if your staff is working from multiple locations.

MAXIMIZING YOUR RETURNS

One of the greatest challenges of adding online recruiting tools to your routine is, well, adding online recruiting tools to your routine. For most people the prospect of changing a time-honored practice is daunting, and can seem like a lot of unnecessary work. And some "early adopters" (industry jargon for "people who buy into a new technology before it's really ready") may feel that it was just that, having learned to work with a product or service that has since disappeared from the market. Fortunately, having read the section above on choosing a service, you've identified a company with a proven track record and a service that matches your company's needs, so you stand to make a major gain by learning to use it effectively in conjunction with your other recruiting tools.

It's important to set expectations for your new acquisition: on what basis will you determine whether or not it is adding value to your efforts? Will you measure by number of resumes? By quality of resume? By number of interviews generated? Number of candidates hired? Once expectations for the tool have been established, they'll need to be communicated to your recruiters—how, and how much, are they expected to use the new service?

A recruiter at a Fortune 500 company related a story about one instance where this communication broke down, and the company's careful planning was undone. After careful analysis, the decision to use a particular set of tools was made by a recruiting manager. There seemed to be a clear benefit to the new system, and it could be integrated with minimal change to the daily routine. But these advantages were not clearly communicated to the recruiters who were supposed to benefit from the new tools. As a result, the tools were underused (where they were used at all), and little of the expected benefit was realized. When asked how well the new service performed, the recruiters answered that it hadn't delivered any results or added value—it must have been a bad investment.

Fortunately, that type of organizational disaster can usually be avoided by following a structured approach to incorporating new online (or offline) tools:

1. Set expectations for each new tool or service, and decide how you will measure its effectiveness.
2. Translate these expectations into specific recommendations for recruiters on how and when to use the tool or service.
3. Communicate the purpose and benefits of the new tool or service to the people who are expected to use it on a day-to-day basis. Remember that they may not have had the benefit of seeing a sales presentation! They may not have had the chance to get excited about the ways in which they can put the company's new tools to work.

WORKING WITH YOUR VENDOR

In the early rush to "get on the Internet," many businesses did not ask hard questions about performance, and now face the difficult task of evaluating their Internet recruiting programs without clear metrics. A good online recruiting service will help you set these goals, define what constitutes "success," and offer you different options for measuring their performance.

In fact, the service you choose may be able to adapt to your business model in ways you wouldn't expect. In your initial "needs analysis" discussion, the company providing the recruiting service may suggest ways in which the service can be specially tailored to your needs. Sometimes this can be as simple as designing an online account structure that mirrors your organization or finding creative ways to distribute your job postings; other times, it may go as far as arranging on-campus promotions for your company, or other forms of exposure to candidates.

What you should know:
How Applicant Tracking and Resume
Retrieval Systems Work

Anna Mooney

Restrac
http://www.restrac.com

The Internet continues to revolutionize the way companies do business, and recruiting is no exception. In fact, job seekers interested in technical and engineering careers realized early on that the Internet provides the means to reach more people faster than traditional recruiting tools. Today, the Internet has become the cornerstone of recruiting strategies for countless companies in a broad range of industries, and Web-based job boards are a candidate's first stop in the job hunt.

International Data Corp. predicts that 98 percent of all companies will perform some or all of their recruiting on the Internet by the year 2000. The popularity of the Internet as a recruiting vehicle is obvious. It's fast, so companies can begin receiving responses to a job posting minutes after an ad goes online. It's convenient, as job seekers can search for jobs 24/7 rather than having to wait for the Sunday paper. The global reach of the Internet enables companies to reach high-quality candidates beyond their local areas. And when combined with a powerful Internet-based recruiting and candidate management system, the Internet can lower recruiting costs by as much as 50 percent, since print advertising and recruiting agency fees are greatly reduced.

Recruiters can use the Internet to harvest online resumes in several ways from posting their available jobs on corporate Web sites or by contracting with Web-based job sites and subscribing to any number of candidate sites that house more than 2.5 million resumes.

THOUSANDS OF RESUMES, NOW WHAT?

Despite an industry-wide shortage of skilled workers, many resumes are available to recruiters. In fact, successful online recruiting strategies can yield thousands of candidate resumes. But this success creates another problem: How to quickly uncover the top 25 resumes out of a sea of thousands?

Who has the time or resources to sift through thousands of resumes by hand? Jobs need to be filled fast and efficiently, and to accomplish this, companies are implementing automated recruiting systems. These systems include Internet-based candidate management services that help employers identify, qualify and process candidates via an easy-to-use browser interface. These systems also give HR professionals desktop access to a broad range of Internet resources to post jobs, search resumes and manage other recruiting activities.

Once resumes have been collected, candidate management systems employ advanced search techniques to hone in on the few applicants with the most relevant skills and experience for your open positions.

CANDIDATE MANAGEMENT SYSTEMS AUTOMATE THE SEARCH AND HIRING PROCESS

1. Regardless of how resumes were received by a company æ from online resume pools, resumes received by a corporate Web site, resumes attached to emails, and paper resumes scanned into the digital formats æ a candidate management system uses real-time indexing to allow new resumes to be immediately available to recruiters. All resume searching and candidate tracking functions are consolidated within a single screen environment.

2. Search technologies can take different forms. Many search applications implement simple keyword program searches, which scan resumes quickly for specified words and phrases. Another search technique known as skills extraction, creates summaries of resumes for faster and easier processing and administration. However, the fairest, most accurate and least biased search approach preferred by most companies is full-text, concept-based searching.

3. Full-text searching enables entire resumes to be searched automatically and quickly for any word or phrase that a recruiter specifies. Search terms are often housed in a "topic library," pre-defined terms numbering in the thousands. Recruiters use these terms to construct sophisticated queries on the fly to match candidates to jobs, or jobs to candidates. With this functionality, recruiters can generate concept-based, context-sensitive searches for skills such as "multimedia," or highly focused expertise, for example, "video capture."

4. Candidates can be matched to jobs in a number of ways. Job posting information can be used to generate queries automatically. These queries can be saved, modified and rerun. More sophisticated candidate management systems include automated help systems to assist with selecting search criteria and building queries. Advanced query tools also enable users to use any combination of search terms and phrases to create a highly flexible and effective search.

5. Other candidate management tools enable recruiters to quickly receive snapshots of how applicants and requisitions relate at any point in the hiring process. Companies can quickly know what positions a candidate is being considered for, when a resume was routed and what the next steps in the process are. Recruiters can also automatically rank selected resumes based on company-specific and job-appropriate skills and requirements.

6. Recruiters can then view activities associated with a specific job. You can quickly determine open jobs, jobs where interviews have been arranged, positions with outstanding offers and jobs that have been filled. Recruiters can also easily find out the details of specific jobs including the job posting, attached documents, recruiting team members, and relevant candidate activity.

7. Once resumes have been matched against job specifications and concept-based searching has produced the top 10-to-20 candidates, the candidate management system can be used in conjunction with a company's email or corporate intranet to share resumes electronically with the hiring team. Team members can provide online comments and additional candidate rankings.

8. Candidate management systems also enable hiring teams and recruiters to schedule in-person interviews and document candidate status online. Recruiting team members can provide their impressions of the candidate and offer opinions on next steps.

9. Once a job is filled, the remaining resumes are returned to a company's candidate database and the system is updated to reflect a new hire and a closed job requisition.

10. Automatically generate and track correspondence to communicate with candidates at any point in the hiring process. Recruiters can produce letters individually or create batch runs. A candidate management system provides templates for acknowledgments, offer letters, competitive offer letters as well as customizes and creates letters to meet your company's unique needs.

Candidate management systems enable recruiters to gain the benefits of online recruiting—speed, cost-effectiveness, broad reach and access to vast candidate pools—while being able to quickly and easily identify the top 25 candidates for specific positions. People will always continue to make a company's hiring decisions. Applying leading search technology to recruiter know-how can help companies to shorten hiring times dramatically, reduce hiring costs and improve their overall competitive position.

Company Considerations When Purchasing a Recruiting Automation System

by Ed Gagen, Corporate Director of Recruiting, First Union National Bank and Ed Struzik, President, BEKS Data Services, Inc.

http://www.launchsite.com/beks
beks@compuserve.com (Struzik)
gagened@aol.com (Gagen)

Many organizations have or will be purchasing a system to help find, track and hire candidates. The explosion of "Internet recruiting tools" has added a layer of complexity to an already challenging decision. There is no single solution yet that offers everything that recruiting organizations want, including: post openings to internal and external systems, accept/process resumes seamlessly from paper and electronic sources, route requisitions for review and approval, route resumes electronically, allow skill searches based on keywords and on years of service, track requisition and candidate activity, generate necessary reports, feed candidate information into an HRMS once a person is hired, a reasonable cost, and a product that fits comfortably into your technical infrastructure.

When an organization is evaluating solutions or analyzing their current system there are several things that need to be considered. Below is a partial list of considerations and areas to focus on to make your employment management system work for you.

MATCH YOUR RECRUITING PROCESSES TO YOUR TECHNOLOGY

This is a critical element to ensure maximum efficiency of the system(s). What steps and data elements are required and who is responsible to do them is a very important aspect to the success of the system. If different processes are permitted and data is recorded inconsistently then you will have data integrity issues that will compromise the usefulness of the system. Reports will be inaccurate, recruiters won't know where candidates are in the process, and sought after efficiencies and economies of scale will not be achieved.

EXPECT TO USE MORE THAN ONE APPLICATION

No single application does everything (well). The complete solution will enable the creation of a job requisition electronically that can be routed for approval, and forwarded seamlessly into your employment management system, and postable internally and externally. Job seekers can express interest through a variety of media (paper, e-mail, fax) which are fed into a database for recruiters/hiring managers to search. Possible qualified candidates are routed electronically for review, interviews take place, a selection decision is made and the person is hired. All the data collected on a new hire is fed into the HRMS system so the person can be paid.

The above could require several different applications, interfaces or technology enablers including: a core employment management system, web and/or IVR functionality, utilization of e-mail and word processing packages, and an interface to the HRMS.

EASE OF USE FOR USERS AND INTERFACES

Most applications today are easy to use for the average user. Basic Windows and/or web browser skills will enable simple navigation through the system. When multiple applications are involved it is important that they are transparent to the end users. Also, the open architecture and/or web based nature of today's systems make the interfaces easier to create and maintain.

Many candidates still use paper resumes so have multiple ways to input job seekers.

As was noted earlier, job seekers need a variety of avenues to express their interest in your organization. Many people still rely on paper resumes to respond to job opportunities, so resume scanning still needs to be incorporated into any solution as well as e-mail and fax-in capability. Additionally, many organizations are moving to electronic personnel files. So, your employment management system needs to have imaging capabilities for applications, I-9 forms, interview evaluations, etc. This type of facility is a great alternative to expensive Workflow and Document Imaging systems.

Most organizations need applicant tracking capability in addition to job posting and resume retrieval capability.

There are a number of sophisticated applications that enable the posting of job opportunities to an Intranet or Internet site, and receive resumes from interested parties. These systems allow for searching the resumes and then kicking off the interview process. It is important that organizations also have applicant tracking functionality for data management and reporting purposes. A cool web site with lots of resume traffic does not, by itself, help get your applicant flow report accurate.

COST

As with most software purchases, you need to balance your needs and requirements against the price. Don't spend a million dollars if you only handle 5,000 resumes and a couple hundred open positions. Make sure the functionality you need is available, either in the core system or easily obtained through additional software.

VENDOR TRACK RECORD

We believe in focusing on vendors with a proven track record of delivering the functionality you require. Check them out. Talk to current customers (not just the references the sales person gives you), and see if they use the system the way you intend. HR-related Internet listservs are a great source for information from your counterparts at other companies.

Find out if the system can do what you want it to? Who else in your industry is using a particular system? What other applications or technology-enablers are being used?

What is the vendor's support like? After the sale is made, what is the vendor's track record in providing reasonable and reliable consulting support for the installation? How good is routine help desk support once you are up and running? Does the vendor offer process consulting services to help you integrate their new technology into your processes?

TECHNICAL PLATFORM

This point speaks to the need to have your Information Management group involved in the selection process. Employment management systems are available on varieties of technical platforms. Your IM people need to work with you to determine if the application is compatible with your technical infrastructure. If you are planning to purchase a system with resume scanning capabilities, you will need to consider the impact resume Images may have on disk storage and network traffic/performance. There are many other technical points to consider. Don't wait until you've signed the contract to ask your IM people if it will work. You may be in for an unpleasant surprise.

REPORTING

We've seen this area overlooked so many times. Quite often shoppers looking for an employment management system are so excited about the prospects of resume scanning, skill searching, and requisition and applicant data tracking, that they forget that they will need to get structured report data out of their new system.

There are systems out there that offer their own report writing facilities. These tend to be very basic toolsets and may not give you some of your more sophisticated reports, like Applicant Flow or Time to Fill. Alternatively, there are systems out there that bundle off-the-shelf reporting tools. These usually offer more power in reporting, but may impose a need to have a technical person to create the reports.

Lastly, consider the data of the system itself. How is it stored? Technically speaking, is the data stored in an open system, ie. in an Oracle or SQL Server data base. Or, is it stored in some proprietary format. If it's the latter, be careful, standard reporting tools you may already have in-house may not work against it natively. Also, how is the data structured? If the system uses a relational data base structure, make sure you are comfortable with how the data is organized, otherwise you'll find yourself struggling to figure out where to go in the data base to get report results you need. Ask your vendor for a data model and have your IM department review it.

INTERNET CONNECTIONS

This arena is exploding with opportunities, but like many new technologies, standards, relative to all the public job sites out there, are next to non-existent. Many companies, realizing that the Internet has quickly become a new Source, are struggling to develop some sort of Internet recruiting strategy. Such a strategy should contain both technical and nontechnical components. Ask yourself these two questions: How well can you get posting data to targeted public job sites? How well can I receive/process resume submissions from these sites into my system? On the surface these seem like simple questions, but experience has shown us that the lack of standards can make your head spin.

HIGH DEMAND FOR STAFFING METRICS

by Lynn S. Nemser, SPHR

lnemser@nb.net

The interest in newer, more effective staffing metrics has taken off in the last few years. Although staffing functions have measured cost-per-hire and time-to-fill for years, the demand for metrics that allow organizations to reliably benchmark with other organizations and evaluate their staffing methodology has been increasing significantly. This trend is likely to continue.

WHY IS THIS TREND GOING TO CONTINUE?

A Difficult Employment Market Never Experienced Before: We are in the midst of an extremely difficult employment market, In fact, we have never experienced these conditions before. Although we have experienced low unemployment in previous decades, a number of factors did not exist at the same time:

The New Employment Contract: The ease with which people move from job to job has increased as loyalties to an employer have disappeared. The old employment contract was based on a paternalistic company philosophy. The new one is based on a philosophy that involves no loyalties by company or employee and a belief that employees are responsible for their own careers.

A Global Economy: Although many organizations believe that if they are not in international business markets, they can still recruit with a domestic mindset. More and more companies are finding that they are competing for employees globally.

Technology: Technology has finally come to the staffing function. The explosion of availability of tools, such as applicant tracking systems, internet recruiting in many forms, and automated selection devices and voice response systems were not available to recruiters the last time unemployment was at these levels. Not much data exists that points to how cost effective this new technology is or how to use it to get the best results.

OLD BEST PRACTICES MAY NOT WORK TODAY

Staffing functions have relied for decades on tried and true best practices gleaned from research as well as benchmarking efforts. Although only time will tell if some of those best practices apply, many organizations are questioning their validity in today's market.

ORGANIZATIONS DEMAND FASTER & MORE FREQUENT CHANGE

Competitive pressure has created a demand for organizations to determine their effectiveness quickly and make necessary changes even faster. Waiting for thorough research studies to determine the effectiveness of new and costly technology is not an option. Smart Human Resource organizations are designing measurements to determine effectiveness of new technology before it is implemented.

In addition, the traditional metrics of cost-per-hire provided measurements based on average of all hires annually. Today's organizations demand more frequent measures that point not only to how effective a staffing organization is, but how it needs to change in order to improve.

OLD METRICS JUST DON'T DO IT

There has been a gradual realization that traditional recruiting measures have inherent weaknesses that make them of limited value in today's market . Cost-per-hire and time-to-fill do not take into account in enough detail factors such as:

Geographic differences: It is clear that some parts of the country and globe are more difficult and costly markets than others.

Functional & Industry Differences: The old concept of supply and demand means that some types of positions and some industries require greater effort, time and money to locate qualified candidates.

Level of position: In the past highly skilled and knowledgeable workers have been harder to find than entry level ones. Today in some industries and functions the entry level positions may be the most difficult to recruit for the first time.

LARGE BUDGET REQUESTS REQUIRE HARD DATA

Budget requests for technology expenditures are not small items any more. Requests for technology upgrades as well as initial expenditures require hard data to support them. As with any technology, there is never a single purchase; there are always upgrades and maintenance costs. Metrics that support repeated budget requests are a necessity.

RECRUITER BEHAVIOR CHANGES

Some organizations have learned that metrics are an effective way to promote recruiter behavior changes. My observation as a consultant is that while some recruiters welcome change and the benefits that new technology brings, many resist new technology and prefer to stick with their old methods of recruiting.

If this pattern surfaces, an organization that, for example, measures how many hires come from a search of the applicant tracking system will be able to encourage recruiters to use the system rather than their old methods of paper screening

In these cases, customized metrics are more useful for focusing internally than for benchmarking with other organizations. It may mean that the measures change from time to time as the behavior changes are needed.

HUMAN RESOURCES PROFESSIONALS AS BUSINESS PROFESSIONALS

Lastly, current interest in more effective metrics will continue to be fueled by the current philosophy that what you don't measure doesn't count. Staffing functions that want to be taken more seriously as business partners with their senior management need to show hard data on the cost effectiveness of the new technology compared to other methodologies. A simple cost number can be misleading. Low recruiting costs can result in poor quality of hires and low retention rates. As a result, smart organizations are starting to take a much broader approach to evaluating their staffing function and methodology by looking at quality of hires and customer satisfaction, not just cost and time.

Welcome to the World of Push

by Bob Levinstein Vice President
NationJob, Inc.

rlevinstein@nationjob.com www.nationjob.com

A stranger with a clipboard approaches you on the street and asks you to describe your ideal job search process.

You've got better things to do than play lab rat for some junior marketing automaton, but you've already committed the cardinal sin of the city: you've made eye contact. So you decide to put him off by giving him too much of what he's asked for: a completely unrealistic vision of the most annoying chore that the IRS isn't in charge of.

"Well," you say, "first off, I don't want to have to do any work." You look to see if the stranger recoils at this, but he just nods impassively and makes a checkmark on his clipboard. So you continue.

"How about this," you say, a hint of a challenge in your voice. "I'll tell you what kind of job I want: what field, where I want to work, how much money I want to make, etc., and you can spend your time to go out and look for a job for me."

This doesn't seem to faze him either, so you get just a little personal. "And I don't want you to call me to tell me how it's going. In fact, I don't want to even hear from you until you find me a job that matches what I've told you to find—and you'd better not share my information with anyone else, either." Even this gets only a nod and two more check marks. so you lay it on a little thicker.

"And even when you find a job that does fit what I'm looking for, I still don't want to talk to you. Just, oh, pop by my house and slip a detailed description of the job under the door, along with some information about the employer, and I'll look at when I feel like it." No reaction. "And if I'm interested, I'll go ahead and contact the employer directly: I don't want you messing up the contact."

He's still impassive, nodding and looking at the clipboard, but you've saved the best for last. "Oh, and by the way, I'm not going to pay you anything for this service. What do you think of that?" you ask triumphantly.

The stranger nods slowly and checks one last box. He looks up, smiles, and says, "Welcome to the world of push."

Yes, it's available now. In fact, it's been out there since the fall of '95. Call it "push", an "agent service", or an "e-mail alert", but it all comes down to the same thing: a better way to look for a job or recruit new employees.

The technology is simple: you visit a web site and enter your e-mail address and then your qualifications and preferences by checking boxes and/or typing in key words. Then, on an on-going basis, new job listings are compared to what you want, and if a match is found, you're notified automatically via e-mail (ie. the information is "pushed" out to you over the web). A job description is provided, hopefully in the e-mail message itself (or at least though a direct link). Better services will make company profile information easily accessible, as well instructions on how to apply for a given position.

The appeal to job seekers is obvious: this type of service is easy to use, non-intrusive, confidential, and generally free of charge. For anyone at all concerned about their career, whether they're actively looking for a job or not, it's a no-brainer.

Job seekers, are only part of the equation. Agent services are extremely effective for employers as well.

A large part of the value of agent services to employers comes from the same things that make Internet recruitment advertising in general so powerful: reach (hundreds of thousands of job seekers); cost effectiveness (about 1/10 the cost of print advertising); no geographic limitations; very detailed information. Agent services do (if run correctly) deliver results faster than posting on web sites, as the jobs go out to the job seekers rather than waiting for the job seekers to come to them. But the key point is that agent services offer something else: quality of audience.

As any H.R. pro will tell you, employers really don't want the people who are out there combing the classifieds, desperate to find a new job. (If they did, these people wouldn't still be looking, would they?). What employers really want are people who are currently employed, but willing to consider a change. Head-hunters understand this too: in fact, they owe their very existence to it. (It's the main reason why they call you at work.)

With an agent service, employers primarily reach people who already have good jobs. They may be content enough that they're not willing to invest their time in an exhaustive job search; but they're still open to new opportunity. And when that e-mail comes in from an agent service, they know it contains only one thing: jobs that matched what they asked for. Wouldn't you take two minutes just to scan through that e-mail and see if that dream job is in there? Most people would, and this is the real power of this type of service.

Despite all of the promise, all agent services are not created equal. Here are a few criteria to use in evaluating them:

Is anybody else using it? If the site doesn't tell you how many subscribers they have, there's probably a reason.

Does the service send me jobs on a consistent basis? One service I signed up for sent me just one e-mail in five months. I just checked the site, and found several jobs posted over the last few months that matched my preferences that they never bothered to send to me. So, while the technology is fairly simple, that doesn't mean everybody's mastered it. *Note to employers: a quick, free way to test any service out for yourself is to sign up as a job seeker and see what you get.*

Can the service send me the jobs I want? In order to get good results as a job seeker, you need to be able to communicate to the service what it is you're looking for. Services that rely entirely on key word searching make this difficult.

(Try typing in "human resources", for example. You'll get all sorts of jobs that ask you to "Apply to our Human Resources Dept." but not jobs without the specific key words, i.e. those for "H.R. Manager" or "Corporate Recruiter.") Services that consistently code all jobs of a certain type into a particular category (ie. you can select "Human Resources" from a menu and get only h.r.-related jobs) and then allow key word searching (to focus your search even further) produce far more accurate results.

How many hoops do I have to jump through to see the actual jobs? Some sites, in an effort to bolster their traffic numbers, force you to return to their site and log into an account to see the matching jobs. For the job seeker, this is more than an annoyance: in the course of a busy day, it's one more reason not to look at a particular job opening. For the recruiter, more hurdles mean fewer people looking at your jobs. These sites that are more concerned with traffic than service miss the point: after all, it's supposed to be easy.

There are many ways to use the Internet to recruit, just as there are many ways to use it to look for a job. As a company who competes in this business, we use a lot of the various metaphors to promote every job we get: our paid general search site; a network of niche sites; cross-postings to free sites; "meta"-sites that allow search of multiple databases, etc. And while we don't do it, there are plenty of sites where you can post a resume and see who happens to call.

But if there is a "killer app" in this business, and I believe that there is, it's push.

Even now, an employer can reach more quality job seekers than the entire circulation of some major newspapers, with much more detailed information, for 1/10 the cost or less than an ad in that same paper. Job seekers already have access to tens of thousands of new jobs, already narrowed down to the ones that best fit their needs, delivered to them conveniently, without compromising their privacy, and with no effort on their part.

A fundamental change in the way people go about looking for jobs and the way employers go about finding people has already happened, and the job search process will never be the same.

Welcome, my friends, to the world of push.

SEARCH ENGINES: Basic Research Tools

by Suzanne Cohen, Reference Librarian
Martin P. Catherwood Library
School of Industrial and Labor Relations, Cornell University

http://www.ilr.cornell.edu
mailto:sac29@cornell.edu

Both the recruiter and the job seeker often need information to supplement a search for that perfect candidate or that perfect job. As a recruiter, have you ever said, "I want information about these companies where the candidate says she worked." "I need access to job descriptions and salary surveys for the position that I am advertising." "I want to contact professional associations in my industry to see if they will make a link to my company web site or post job notices." As a job seeker, have you ever said, "I want to do research on the company that is advertising this job." "I want to find out more about the city that I would be working in and how much it would cost for me to relocate there." "I need some help with my interviewing skills."

Information to fill these needs may be found on the Internet, using search engines, "Starting Points" web sites, and by taking advantage of the many articles, books, discussion groups and workshops that highlight useful Internet sites for targeted audiences (such as recruiters or job seekers).

SEARCH ENGINES

Search Engines allow you to perform keyword searches of the large amounts of information on the Internet. It is helpful to understand how search engines work when trying to choose the best one to use or the best way to formulate your search.

There are three basic types of search engines: active, passive and meta.

Active search engines (for example, http://altavista.digital.com or http://www.hotbot.com) are what most people think of when they hear the term "search engine". Active search engines use computerized retrieval methods that have been called "crawlers," "robots," "wanderers," or "spiders" to find Internet sites (mostly web pages). Once a web site is found, the keywords in the site are indexed and stored in a searchable database. When you enter your search terms into an active search engine, the computer looks for matches to those terms in its database of web sites that have been found by the "spiders" and then organized by keyword. The "spiders" are constantly finding new web sites, but obviously not every single web site that exists has been indexed in any one search engine.

Passive search engines (for example, http://www.yahoo.com) contain web sites that have been submitted by people to the company that made the search engine. The employees at the company then evaluate the site and choose the most appropriate subject category in which to list that site for easy retrieval. Yahoo has created an excellent directory of subject categories from which you may easily be able to find what you are looking for without actually typing in a keyword search. Remember that when you are searching in a passive search engine, such as Yahoo, you are not searching the whole Internet - only those sites that have been entered into the directory of web sites by the people at Yahoo. This limited searching can be advantage when you are looking for something well known. For example, if you are looking for a company's home page or a university's home page, chances are that it is already in Yahoo's directory and you will quickly find what you are looking for. Instead of typing in the search you could also choose the category "Companies" or "Universities" from the home page screen and find the information by clicking through various menus. If you do that same search in an active search engine, you may find thousands of matches, because that company or university is mentioned in news items, personal web pages, regional directories, and more. I often try my search in Yahoo first, and if I don't get the results I am looking for, I move on to an active search engine.

Most search engines basically use the indexes of other search engines to find matches to your search terms. For example, if you do a search in Metacrawler (http://www.metacrawler.com), you may get results from AltaVista, Yahoo or other search engines not mentioned previously such as Excite, Infoseek, Lycos, and WebCrawler. Metacrawler claims that the search engine removes duplicates from the results list if the same site is found in more than one search engine. With meta search engines you will get a wider variety of sources, which for a more obscure search could be very useful. However, you may also get a more confusing display of results and more than you really needed.

My advice is that people choose one of each type of search engine and become very familiar with the way that it works. I always print off the help screens that are found with each search engine. Every search engine works differently - they require different ways of typing in searches and also use different methods to determine the order that your search results are displayed. The help screens will provide search examples and explanations of all other features available when using the search engine. Most search engines also provide "basic" or "advanced" search levels. Becoming familiar with the "advanced" searching features of a search engine can help narrow your search more effectively.

STARTING POINTS

Another strategy for finding the information you need, is to go directly to "Starting Points" designed for a specific subject area.

Yahoo could be considered a starting point for the whole Internet, but a starting point for the specific category of "jobs" can be found at the specific web site http://www.yahoo.com/Business_and_Economy/Employment/ . From here you may choose links for Internet resources on topics such as "jobs," "salary information," "resumes," or "telecommuting." Recruiters might be interested in http://www.yahoo.com/Business_and_Economy/Companies/Employment/ Recruiting_and_Placement/ which has links on topics such as "executive search firms," "people of color," "students and recent grads," or "temporary."

Cornell University's School of Industrial Relations and Human Resource Executive magazine have teamed up to produce Workindex (http:// workindex.com) which is a starting point for any workplace information. Some categories of particular interest might be "career development and occupations," "human resources," "labor force and labor market," "relocation resources," "recruitment," "staffing" and more. For example, after choosing "career development and occupations," and then choosing "job hunting," I found a link to an interviewing skills site at http://safetynet.doleta.gov/intrview.htm .

The Society for Human Resource Management has a good starting point at http://www.shrm.org/hrlinks/ . Some categories of particular interest here might be "compensations and benefits," "flexible work arrangements," "legal issues and resources," "recruitment and career planning," and more. For example, under "compensation and benefits" is a link for "salary surveys" which leads me to internet resources for salary information.

All of the above starting points allow you to do keyword searching of the site instead of clicking through the subject categories. If you have the time, however, browsing through focused subject categories will sometimes result in finding something useful that might not show up from a keyword search.

OTHER SOURCES FOR USEFUL WEB SITES AND INTERNET SEARCHING STRATEGIES

As you read through newspapers, magazines or professional literature you will see more and more articles devoted to discussion of the Internet. Many times these articles will highlight useful web sites. Instead of just writing down the Internet address and never looking at it again, you should connect to the Internet, see if the site is really useful and then "bookmark" it so it is saved for future use. "Bookmarks" in Netscape's web browser or "Favorites" in Microsoft's Internet Explorer store web sites in a list from which they can be easily re-trieved. There are more and more books devoted to searching the Internet. If you have entered the world of Internet shopping you may be familiar with http://amazon.com or http://barnesandnoble.com . Both of these sites allow keyword searching or browsing by subject and both have "Internet" and "World Wide Web" as subjects. They also have "careers and job hunting" or "recruit-ing." You will also see more and more workshops being offered for Internet training. Some colleges, universities, public libraries, and service agencies are offering these for free while there are other fee-based workshops, often aimed toward a specific audience. If you are thinking about participating in a work-shop, look for those which advertise their program as a "hands-on" experience.

A FINAL THOUGHT

Once you have found a web site that looks useful, you must critically evaluate that site before relying on the information. Ask yourself the following questions: What is the purpose of the site—to persuade? inform? outrage? entertain?; What is the authority of the person or group who created or contrib-uted to this site?; Can the authors be contacted for clarification or to be informed of new information?; Who is the intended audience and how is this reflected in the organization and presentation of the site?; Based on your knowledge, is the information factual, opinion, propaganda, etc.?; What is the currency of this site—when was it produced?; When was it last updated?

There is so much valuable information accessible on the Internet. The challenge is learning how to effectively use search engines and other tools to find that information and then critically evaluate the content. With approximately 130 million Internet users worldwide (source, NUA Internet Surveys: http://www.nua.ie) and governments, educational institutions, and businesses making more and more information available online, it is well worth the investment of time to meet this challenge.

Preparing the Ideal Scannable Resume: Tips for Writing and Formatting a Scannable Resume that Computers Can Read.

Printed with permission from *Resumix*

http://www.resumix.com
lkameda@resumix.com

There's a new technology that could be very helpful to you. It could help you find your next job. It's called electronic applicant tracking, and it's being used by leading businesses and organizations.

By using the latest in document imaging technology, your resume can be scanned into a computer system and kept "active" for years. The computer can search for just about anything in your resume. You could be qualified and considered for jobs you never thought of. The computer can make it easier for you to be considered for more jobs, and it keeps your one resume on file so it's quicker to update your information.

Here's how it works. Your resume is scanned into the computer as an image. The OCR (optical character recognition) software looks at the image to distinguish every letter and number (character) and creates a text file (ASCII). Then artificial intelligence "reads" the text and extracts important information about you such as your name, address, phone number, work history, years of experience, education, and skills.

Why is it important for you to know this? When you prepare a resume for the computer to read, you want it to be "scannable". A scannable resume is clean so the scanner can get a clean image. A scannable resume has standard fonts and crisp, dark type such as a laser printer or typewriter with a new ribbon would produce- so the OCR can recognize every letter. And a scannable resume has plenty of facts for the artificial intelligence to extract- the more skills and facts you provide, the more opportunities you'll have for your skills to match available positions.

A scannable resume maximizes the computer's ability to "read" your resume and maximizes your ability to get "hits" (a hit is when one of your skills matches the computer search).

Preparing a scannable resume is easy; like the traditional style resume, you focus on format and content. To maximize the computer's ability to read your resume, provide the cleanest original and use a standard style resume.

The computer can extract skills from many styles of resumes such as chronological (list and describe up to six jobs in order of date), achievement (describe achievements rather than job titles), functional (organize by skills rather than job titles), and combinations of resume types.

The most difficult resume for the computer to read is a poor quality copy that has an unusual format such as a newsletter layout, adjusted spacing, small font sizes, graphics or lines, type that is too light, or paper that is too dark.

TIPS FOR MAXIMIZING SCANNABILITY

- Use white or light-colored 8 1/2 x 11 paper, printed on one side only.
- Provide a laser printer original if possible. A typewritten original or a high quality photocopy is OK. Avoid dot matrix print-outs and low quality copies.
- Do not fold or staple.
- Use standard typefaces such as Helvetica, Futura, Optima, Univers, Times, Palatino, New Century Schoolbook, and Courier.
- Use a font size of 10 to 14 points. (Avoid Times 10 point.)
- Don't condense spacing between letters.
- Use boldface and/or all capital letters for section headings as long as the letters don't touch each other.
- Avoid fancy treatments such as italics, underline, shadows, and reverses (white letters on black background).
- Avoid vertical and horizontal lines, graphics, and boxes.
- Avoid two-column format or resumes that look like newspapers or newsletters.
- Place your name at the top of the page on its own line. (Your name can also be the first text on pages two and three.)
- Use standard address format below your name.
- List each phone number on its own line.

CONTENT

The computer extracts information from your resume. You can use your current resume; however, once you understand what the computer searches for, you may decide to add a few key words to increase your opportunities for matching requirements or getting "hits."

Recruiters and managers access the resume database in many ways, searching for your resume specifically or searching for applicants with specific experience. When searching for specific experience, they'll search for key words, usually nouns such as writer, BA, marketing collateral, Society for Technical Communication, Spanish (language fluency), San Diego, etc. The computer system will extract the words and information from your sentences; you can write your resume as usual.

TIPS FOR MAXIMIZING "HITS"

- Use enough key words to define your skills, experience, education, professional affiliations, etc.
- Describe your experience with concrete words rather than vague descriptions. For example, it's better to use "managed a team of software engineers" than "responsible for managing, training…"

- Be concise and truthful.
- Use more than one page if necessary. The computer can easily handle multiple-page resumes, and it uses all of the information it extracts from your resume to determine if your skills match available positions. It allows you to provide more information than you would for a human reader.
- Use jargon and acronyms specific to your industry (spell out the acronyms for human readers).
- Increase your list of key words by including specifics, for example, list the names of software you use such as Microsoft Word and Lotus 1-2-3.
- Use common headings such as: Objective, Experience, Employment, Work History, Positions Held, Appointments, Skills, Summary, Summary of Qualifications, Accomplishments, Strengths, Education, Affiliations, Professional Affiliations, Publications, Papers, Licenses, Certifications, Examinations, Honors, Personal, Additional, Miscellaneous, References, etc.
- If you have extra space, describe your interpersonal traits and attitude. Key words could include skill in time management, dependable, high energy, leadership, sense of responsibility, good memory, etc.

TIPS

Some people may want to have two versions of their resume:
- One for the computer to read—with a scannable format and detailed information. Send this one.
- One for people to read—possibly with a creative layout, enhanced typography, and summarized information. Carry this one to the interview.
- When faxing, set the fax to "fine mode"; the recipient will get a better quality copy.

Notes on E-mail Resumes

by Camille Trapp

reprinted with permission ASAE

http://www.asae.org/CareerHeadquarters/library/e-mailnotes.html
ctrapp@asaenet.org

You found the perfect job on the Internet-or at least one that will pay the bills and isn't too unpalatable. The employer or recruiter provides an e-mail address and instructs you to paste your resume right into the body of the e-mail.

Your resume, painstakingly prepared—delicately balanced with hanging indents, bold and italics, neatly aligned columns—will probably be immediately bounced if you try to file attach it.

Why? The fact is most e-mail is scanned for keywords, either by a novice human resources assistant or no human at all—a "program." Programs scan the text for keywords stipulated in the job description. On finding resumes with the required percentage of keywords, the program flags those for further review-all based on how many keywords match the job requirements. This is especially so for technical positions.

Another reason for immediate rejection of file-attached rather than pasted in resumes is that not all organizations use your particular word processing program, and some e-mail programs garble the attachment.

Fact: you can e-mail 100 resumes at less cost than printing, mailing, or even faxing. Direct marketing, and you are marketing yourself, has a percent of return based on targeted volume. So it's worth having an ASCII version of your resume. Saturate your targeted market (job openings) with your product message...you, best employee for that job in the universe.

WHAT IS ASCII?

ASCII (pronounced askee) is an acronym which stands for "American Standard Code for Information Interchange." ASCII is plain text with minimal character set-no fancy curly quotes, no font or formatting capabilities past carriage returns. But ASCII can be imported and read by almost all computer platforms and programs.

Forget underline, bold, italics, tabs, indents, size, justify commands like "center," and forget commentary. Your ASCII resume requires rethinking and reworking to fit a primitive but modern method of communication. Ah...you despair!

HOW TO CREATE AN ASCII RESUME

If you are using Windows (all versions), find a utility called "Notepad" in your accessories directory and launch this program. Notepad is an ASCII text editor. Under the Edit drop down menu, make sure the option "Word Wrap" is checked. Also, only use the return (enter key) to indicate the end of a paragraph or hard line return. Let Notepad wrap the paragraphs rather than inserting a return at the end of each line. Use an extra return between items you want clearly separated. And separate plenty! If you don't use Windows, you can save your resume as a text-only document, which should be an option under your "save as" command.

RESUME CONTENT

Since you don't have the opportunity to wow them with your word processing skills, or impress them with your graphical prowess, you'll have to stick with the basics. Start your resume with the job code and job title listed on the job notice you are applying for (repeat this information on the subject line of the e-mail when you send it). This should be followed by a summary of qualifications section, work experience, education, professional affiliations and any other information (e.g., speaking experience, articles) which is requested. Here's an example:

Job #M10001 Assistant Director, XYZ Association
Jane Quince Sample
123 Street, Apt 12
City, State 12345
(202) 300-4000

KNOWLEDGE/SKILLS/SUMMARY OF QUALIFICATIONS

This is your first and last shot at commentary. Use as many "keywords" and phrases enumerated in the job announcement as possible (without lying of course). No more than five short sentences.

Employment history: *Begin with the most recent.*
Dates
Company
Address
Responsibilities and accomplishments: *Make sure you incorporate the "keywords" enumerated in the job announcement.*
Education: *Begin with the most recent.*
   Name of completed degree or certificate
   Institution
Professional Affiliations/Achievements: *Limit these to what would apply to the job.*

SENDING THE RESUME

After you've spell-checked the resume, use the "Save as" command to file your document in the directory of your choice and then launch your e-mail program. When you're ready to send the resume, select (by highlighting) the entire contents of the Notepad file, select the "copy" command in the edit drop down menu of your Notepad file. Place your cursor in the body of the e-mail, and using the e-mail program's edit command "paste" the text at the insertion point.

Reread your resume for errors (this is usually where job seekers hurt themselves by not checking for typos and grammar) and make any last minutes adjustments to fit the company you are applying for. Address the e-mail to the job contact e-mail address, cc: yourself, and remember to insert the job code and job title in the Subject heading. You're ready to send!

Don't stop there, work down the list of job openings that you would consider and e-mail them all with the same resume. Remember to change the To: and Subject: lines and of course try to incorporate those 'keywords"—which may require a bit of editorial rewrite, but it's well worth it if you want to make sure yours is the resume that gets to the top.

If you'd like the ASAE resume expert to take a look at your resume, click here for details.

"Tools And Tricks" For The Advanced Job Seeker

by Dr. John Sullivan
Head and Professor of Human Resource Management
College of Business, San Francisco State University

johns@sfsu.edu

As a job seeker you must think and act differently if you are going to gain a competitive advantage over others. You must find the jobs faster and sell yourself "better" if you are to "beat" other applicants to that great job. You must have a competitive advantage that goes beyond having a good resume and prudently reading the want ads.

Gaining a competitive advantage in a job search begins with thinking and acting differently—we call that "TOX" (Thinking Outside the boX)! Some of the "tools" listed here are simple tools while others, although they might seem unusual on the surface, are advanced "outside the box recruiter tricks" designed to give you the edge! Remember you have to take risks to get a great job!

BASIC JOB SEARCH TOOLS

Using Key Words. You might not realize it but few resumes submitted to large firms are actually read by "people." At most large firms computerized scanners search all resumes looking for preselected "key words." Typical jobs have between 30 and 100 key words (they are generally skills, problems, management tools, and company or university names). If you don't use these key words you WILL NOT be selected for and interview!

The color of the paper, nice prose and neatness won't impress a computer! To find out if a firm scans in resumes just call the Human Resource department and just ask if they use a scanning system (Resumix and Restrac are common brand names). If you want to know for sure how many key word "hit's" you have in your resume and you are incredibly bold ask a "friend" in any HR to "run" your resume through their system. It will rank you, compared to other candidates, and tell you the keywords you hit!

Pre-Test Your Resume. There are a lot of stereotypes about resumes that no longer hold as a result of the use of new technology in employment. For example "one page only" resume "rules" go by the wayside when a computer is scanning your resume. There are several ways to pre-test your resume to make sure it gets you an interview. Here are a couple of ways to find out how good your resume is.

Circle Test. Have several friends circle all the items in the resume that impress them put an x through all items that they don't like (or are negative), and a ? by all items that confuse them or slow them down. In a great resume the circled items should cover the top three problems, the top five skills, the minimum years of experience required in the job. It should also include your top five accomplishments. Keep revising it until all the important items get circled and all "X ed" and "? ed" items are revised,

Name that Job Test. Cover your name on your resume and give it to a friend who is a recruiter or a manager in your field. Give them two minutes to read it and ask them to "close their eyes" and "name the job" that the resume comes closest to qualifying for. Then revise your resume and repeat until you have developed the most convincing resume possible for your target job. .

Ranking Test. Gather together 4 resumes from friends or coworkers who are in/or seeking the same job as you are. Ask 3-5 professionals to review the job description/Ad for your target job. Put the resumes in a stack with the names covered. Have the individuals rank the resumes from most to least qualified. Revise your resume until you consistently come out on top.

A Partnership With The Recruiter. Start your job search with a new "mindset." Stop thinking that you are a bother to the recruiter. The real truth is that YOU are the goal of their search. Recruiters want to find you. So think of it as a partnership—they want to find you as much as you want to be found. Your job in this partnership is to do your homework, find out the recruiter's exact needs. Then tailor the information you put in your resume to their needs. Also present in the targeted information in your interview so that it provides the recruiter with convincing evidence (ammunition) that you meet their needs.

Ammunition. Many recruiters want to hire you but they can't "sell you" to their boss because you didn't provide them with the right ammunition (information).

Don't just say you can do the job—prove it! Be sure to provide recruiters with examples that show that you have a high level of the competencies and skills they need. Also show that you know the actual problems you will face in the job and that you CAN solve each one. Make a list of all of their job requirements and in simple business language show that you have their required skills and you can solve each of their problems.

A Portfolio. If you were an artist, chef or musician you wouldn't try to sell your self solely based on "words." You would include brief scanable summaries or samples of your actual work (a picture, a menu or a tape). Consider providing them with work summaries or examples with your resume, in an e-mail, through your own web page or by bring them to the interview.

Company WOWs. "Knowing the target company" well is essential if you are to impress the recruiter. Unfortunately, reviewing the annual report and visiting the Web page is becoming so easy to do that it does not give you a competitive advantage over others who have also read them. The real competitive advantage is knowing the companies "inside story" and having a list of what I call "Company WOWs!" WOW's are brief "facts" or best practices that generally only an insider or an expert would know about the firm. Put a few of these WOWs in your conversation, cover letter or interview and you will definitely stand out. WOWs are generally gotten from people "who like to talk."

So call salespeople (and competitors' salespeople), the PR department, read their CEO's articles or speeches (call their assistant and ask for copies) or just visit the restaurant across the street at lunch and ask employees about their WOW products, plans or "problems." It's not that hard. If you are a student ask your professor for an assignment to study the company. Then just ask their receptionist "is there anyone who might mentor a "needy student" or just ask a friend or relative who works there to find the WOWs for you.

OTHER POSSIBLE WOWS

Tell them you own their stock and that you follow the firm's progress (buy one share).

Tell them that you bought their "newest" product and you love it

Go to one of their product presentations and tell them how great it was

If you are trying for an out of state job often companies are reluctant to interview "non-local" candidates because of the travel costs. You might be able to overcome that obstacle by suggesting a telephone or e-mail interview.

MORE ADVANCED TOOLS

I Have The Solution To Your Problem! If you are really bold or if realistically don't meet the job requirements you might try the "Consultants" approach. Ask around or read articles about the company and try to find the biggest problems facing the department or function you want to work in. Be bold and work out your solution to one of these problems (pre-test it on experts to make sure it is good). Then send either an outline of your solution or a part of your solution directly to the Department head and/or the hiring manager. Attach a brief cover page saying this is the solution they are looking for and IF THEY SEE IT WOULD WORK: Call you! It must be brief, easily scanable in two minutes and it must make them curious enough to want to call you in to see the rest! You might try this at a less desirable competitor first to see if the "bait" (solution) is good enough to try on your primary target. If you are a student mail them a copy of your solution or idea and ask them to review it for you. as part of a class assignment. You might get an interview if your idea works.

Ask For A "Tryout." Managers are always skeptical about "words"—they want proof. Offer to work several evenings or a weekend for free to show them how you perform in their operation. It is not uncommon for 1/3 of all hires to come from temporary or contract positions. so "ask for a tryout," just like in sports. Another option is to act as a free "off-site" consultant on a problem and help them solve it with the expectation you could be hired at the end of the tryout!

Get Ahead Of The Competition. Try to find out about jobs before everyone else does. Almost all companies post all jobs internally weeks before they get on their web page. Ask any employee from the firm to share the internal posting list or to look for possible jobs for you. The extra warning will give you time to prepare your "Sales Pitch" and have it on the manager's desk the day the competitors see the public want ad. You can generally also buy the Sunday paper on Friday night and get a day-and-a-half jump on preparation time over regular readers (Web postings are generally also before Sunday). If you know a recruiter, they are the first to know about an new opening (when the "req." is filled out), which may be as much as three weeks before the ad appears.

Go Fishing on the Web! It's possible to find out your worth without actually looking for a job by posting an "anonymous resume" on the web to "test the waters." If you get a lot of "hits" you know your particular mix of skills and experience is in demand.

Recruiters are People Too! Most job seekers only contact recruiters when they are into the job search mode. Contact recruiters when you are not looking for a job and seek their career advice. They know a lot of "tricks" but they can't share them ethically when you are an official candidate. Call them in the "off" recruiting season (December and during a hiring freeze) and they will have more time to help you. During breaks at job fairs and during college campus visits works sometimes also.

Don't Go It Alone! Instead of searching alone, form a job search network with four to six friends. Share what you learn, critique each other, and in general, give support. A team is more likely to have a "friend" that is a recruiter who can help you polish and focus your approach. In addition many firms offer referral bonuses to their employees for referring possible candidates. Get your friends and family to help you, because in some firms, referrals are assured of an interview or at least a close look. In addition the friend gets a handsome reward for their help.

Use Technology To Gain A Competitive Advantage. Today there are numerous "Electronic Bulletin Boards/Chat rooms" and Listservers (automatic e-mail discussion groups) that allow you to ask questions about what are the biggest problems and hottest solutions in your specific technical field. They are fast and the best workers in the field usually participate in them. Listservers allow you to get exposure without having to put on a suit. Recruiters also participate/listen in, so the odds are good that you will be noticed if you post a great idea or solution.

Plot Your Growth Rate. If you run into a manager that is technically or "visually oriented" try giving them a "Plot" or graph of your career growth. Plot raises, great performance appraisals, new competencies, awards and promotions. Plot it on a graph and visually show your rapid and continuous career growth compared to your peers. By seeing it in a "visual" format you might get the attention of technical managers who are impressed with graphs and creativity.

Show You Are A "Better" Hire! Not all employees are equal, even though they may have the same technical qualifications. Managers look (but don't always find) "better employees" with skills like these:

Continuous Learners   Employees that develop and learn on their own, without the need for training classes and mentors.

Low Maintenance: Employees that don't need warnings, discipline or that take up management time.

Agile: Workers that can do multi-tasks simultaneously, that add to "bench strength" and that can fill in for other jobs in a pinch.

Bar Raisers: People who continually expect and get more from themselves and those around them

TOX Thinkers: Those who think differently (outside the box) and can get others to do the same

OTHER TRICKS/CAUTIONS

Call or e-mail recruiters/HR and ask them which Web sites they use/visit when they look for candidates.

Make your resume a "skills and accomplishment" list. It's not just what you did in a job that they want to know it's also how well you did it (quantify the results using numbers and dollars) that really impresses them..

Get a mentor at your target firm.

If you are a college student, invite key managers to your class to present or ask them to review one of your projects. Most managers consider it an honor and they will return the favor if you impress them.

Go to your target firm's executive's speeches and send them e-mail comments.

 Seek out their employees for informational interviews at professional meetings.

Don't let published minimum qualifications keep you from applying for a job. It is not uncommon for as many as 30% of the actual hires not to have the skills listed in the ad. They can't say yes, unless you actually apply!

Bosses at your current firm search the web too! Posting your resume could be "career limiting" because the resume might stay posted for a long time or get transferred to many sites without your permission..

Some firms even post jobs on the Web to "catch" their own employees on the look! So be careful when you apply to a "blind" ad.

Last of all remember firms really do want creative people that are risk takers. Unfortunately most selection processes are designed to weed out and "rule breakers." You have to act differently to gain a competitive advantage but don't be surprised if some recruiters get turned off by your boldness. Keep tying and when necessary circumvent the "personnel" types and go right to the hiring manager. They are usually more focused on what you can do than your ability to fill out the form correctly. Go for it!

CAREERXROADS

The 1999 Directory to the 500 Best Job, Resume, and Career Management Sites on the World Wide Web

How to use this Directory

There are no standards that dictate what a WWW job, resume or career management site should look like—what information it should contain, how it should be organized, how the quality of that information might be measured, what means should be used to search it, deliver it, or even what services might be provided.

Our organization of this Directory and our comments throughout *CAREERXROADS* are framed from the job seeker's point of view:

	WEB SITE NAME
CAREERXROADS	
www.careerxroads.com	SITE ADDRESS (URL)
Mark Mehler/Gerry Crispin, MMC Group	
P.O. Box 253, Kendall Park, NJ 08824	CONTACT INFORMATION
Ph: 908-821-6652 Fax: 908-821-1343 E-mail: mmc@careerxroads.com	

Jobs: **No** Cost to post jobs: N/A Cost to see jobs: N/A	**CAREERXROADS** is now in its fourth edition. If you've read this far and haven't registered at our site for updates—*DO IT NOW*. We won't be sending you anything other than our updates— no spamming, no strange e-mail challenges or opportunities, no advertising.
Resumes: **No** Cost to post resumes: N/A Cost to see resumes: N/A	
E-mail Alert (Push): **Both**	
Specialty: N/A	*"Where Talent & Opportunity Connect on the Internet."*
Industry: N/A	
Feature: N/A	
Location: **US/Int'l**	

SITE REVIEW

SITE INFORMATION

How can I reach this site via the WWW (**URL**)? How can I reach the owners (**CONTACT INFORMATION**)?

Is this site committed to providing opportunity (**JOBS**), advice (**CAREER ADVICE**), or the means to communicate my skills and interests (**RESUME**) to others?

How expensive (**COST**) is it to see the openings that are posted here or to submit my resume? Do employers have any restrictions or expenses associated with postings or searching for my resume?

Can I receive information when new jobs are posted that match my skills (**PUSH**) via e-mail or have these openings sent to me? Is my resume or profile compared with an employer's criteria and either sent automatically when there is a match?

Are most of the jobs posted at this site organized with any critical emphasis such as the educational degree or skill requirements (**SPECIALTY**) or geographic emphasis (**LOCATION**)?

Is the site easy to use? Is the information limited, extensive? How much does it cost? What else can job seekers, or employers, do to connect here (**REVIEW**)?

The 1999 Directory is organized into two distinct sections:

An alphabetical listing of all our reviews and,
A cross reference listing to highlight each site's features, services or areas of emphasis.

The cross reference listings include (See Table of Contents for page numbers):

The Best of the Best: The top 50 sites for 1999.

Career Management: 39 sites whose main focus is information about careers, job search and counseling(see index).

College: 32 sites that focus primarily or exclusively on the entry level job seeker. Some sites with multiple level services have strong enough college presence that they have been included as well.

Diversity: 41 sites that contain gender or minority career information.

Jobs: 444 of the sites in this directory contain jobs. We have specifically indexed those that allow you to post your company openings for a fee or for free.

Location: Sites that focus exclusively on providing services for a specific country or region of the US. Among these are 143 sites that have an international component.

Meta-links: 46 lists of links that can help you find all the rest.

Push: 142 sites that send employment related information directly to the job seeker's or employer's desktop.

Resumes: 295 sites where job seekers and employers can post and see resumes for a fee or for free.

Specialty: Sites or specific pages on a site that emphasize a single academic discipline, industry focus or professional emphasis–104 of these emphasize Information Technology.

RATING SYSTEM

We selected what we considered to be the Best of the Best job, resume and/or career management sites for 1999 based on several criteria.

We looked at the ease of access; value of the content, navigation, business model, real world marketing strategy and technology. For 1999 we reviewed over 2,000 sites, included 539 reviews in this directory and designated 50 as the Best of the Best. Every company and each person must judge their own best sites by the results they achieve.

We have designated this icon as our symbol for these sites.

Alphabetical
Listings & Reviews

100 Careers in Cyberspace

www.globalvillager.com/villager/CSC.html

Global Communications Services, Inc.
3130 Rt. 10 West, Denville, NJ 07834
Ph: 201-989-0501   Fax: 201-943-8137   E-mail: yli@globalvillager.com

Jobs: **Yes**	
Cost to post jobs: **Fee**	
Cost to see jobs: **Free**	
Resumes: **Yes**	
Cost to post resumes: **Fee**	
Cost to see resumes: **Free**	
E-mail Alert (Push): N/A	
Specialty: **IT**	
Industry: **All**	
Feature: N/A	
Location: **US/E/Int'l**	

100 Careers in Cyberspace provides direct contact information for positions listed in their database, and also offers employers "blind" listings (you have to go through the site to get to the company). Employer cost to post is $40 per ad for three months ($500 for unlimited ads). Job seekers can post "position wanted" ads for $15. Recruiters can see these for free. The site's search engine works well, but titles of positions are limited.

100 Careers in Wall Street

www.globalvillager.com/village/WSC.html

Global Communications Services, Inc.
3130 Rt. 10 West, Denville, NJ 07834
Ph: 201-989-0501   Fax: 201-328-9216   E-mail: gv@globalvillager.com

Jobs: **Yes**	
Cost to post jobs: **Fee**	
Cost to see jobs: **Free**	
Resumes: **Yes**	
Cost to post resumes: **Fee**	
Cost to see resumes: **Free**	
E-mail Alert (Push): N/A	
Specialty: **Finance/Business**	
Industry: **Finance**	
Feature: N/A	
Location: **US/E/NY/NYC**	

Like its sister site, 100 Careers In Cyberspace, **100 Careers in Wall Street** had several hundred relevant jobs posted on each of our visits. A long list of the site's clients are also displayed along with links to their home page. Nice starting point for candidates seeking this location. The posting price for a job is $40 for two months. The job seeker is charged $15 to post a resume.

4Work

www.4work.com

Stu Franson, Access Influential Inc.
5650 Greenwood Plaza Blvd., Suite 250, Greenwood Village, CO 80111
Ph: 800-789-0145   Fax: 303-741-9702   E-mail: recruit@4work.com

Jobs: **Yes**	
Cost to post jobs: **Fee**	
Cost to see jobs: **Free**	
Resumes: **No**	
Cost to post resumes: **Free**	
Cost to see resumes: **Fee**	
E-mail Alert (Push): **Job Seeker**	
Specialty: **All**	
Industry: **All**	
Feature: N/A	
Location: **US**	

The good sites just keep getting better. **4Work** is easy to use, and offers a basketful of tools for job seekers and recruiters. Included among them is a workable search format where the job seeker enters the location where they wish to work (state) and the skills they want to search on. **4Work** matches the stated interest with incoming positions and "Pushes" information to the potential applicant via e-mail. For employers, the cost is $50 per month to post a job. Volunteer opportunities and internships are posted for free. This site also contains a human resource directory which houses links to numerous sites for additional help. Helpful articles on different aspects of career management and job search techniques are also well-written and well-placed on the site. Recently, they have added a customized job application for employers who choose this tool, and they soon will have a generic one for all customers. **4Work** is a top site with added features that both job seeker/recruiters want to have. Their biggest flaw is limited marketing to their target audiences.

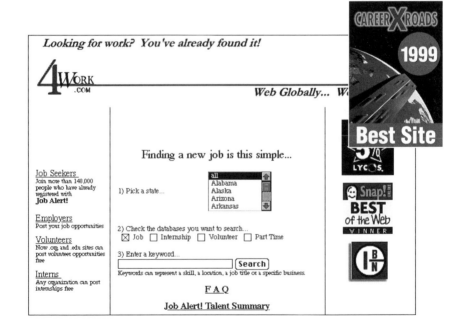

680 careers.com

www.680careers.com

John Foley, Foley & Associates
321 Main St., Suite 512, Sebastopol, CA 95472
Ph: 800-346-5658   E-mail: webmaster@680careers.com

Jobs: **Yes** Cost to post jobs: **Fee** Cost to see jobs: **Free**	
Resumes: **Yes** Cost to post resumes: **Free** Cost to see resumes: N/A	
E-mail Alert (Push): N/A	
Specialty: **All**	
Industry: **All**	
Feature: **Newsletter**	
Location: **US/W/CA/SF**	

680 careers.com is a combined effort by employers and nonprofit organizations along California's East Bay 680 corridor. Site offers links to all employers who are working with this organization. Jobs, career fairs, local lifestyle information, and a newsletter that is Pushed to all who register in a great effort to build a virtual community. Yearly corporate sponsorships range from $1,500 and up. A must see for the relocation minded.

A1A Computer Jobs

www.a1acomputerpros.net/

Ray Osborne, A1A Computer Professionals
816 A1A (So. Atlantic), Daytona Beach, FL 32118
Ph: 904-253-2600   E-mail: rko@a1acomputerpros.net

Jobs: **Yes** Cost to post jobs: **Fee** Cost to see jobs: **Free**	
Resumes: **Yes** Cost to post resumes: **Free** Cost to see resumes: **Fee**	
E-mail Alert (Push): **Job Seeker**	
Specialty: **IT/Human Resources** **Recruiting**	
Industry: **IT**	
Feature: N/A	
Location: **US**	

Ray Osborne, the site's owner, has been slowly building a significant number of e-mail lists for specific IT skill sets including: MS Access, AS/400, Electronic Engineering, Powerbuilder, Informix, Oracle, Windows NT, Java, Unix, Web, Y2K, PeopleSoft, Object, Smalltalk, SAP. For $100, he'll e-mail the employer's opening. The price is right. Human resource professionals and recruiters seeking new career opportunities can also receive job leads by visiting **A1A** or via e-mail to rko@a1acomputerpros.net by including the phrase "Subscribe HRJobs" or "Subscribe RecruitJobs" in the topic heading of the message.

Abag Globe

www.abag.ca.gov/bayarea/commerce/globe/globe.html

Brian Kirking, Assoc. of Bay Area Governments
P.O. Box 2050, Oakland, CA 94604-2050
Ph: 510-464-7900   Fax: 510-464-7970   E-mail: briank@abag.ca.gov

Jobs: **Yes** Cost to post jobs: **Free** Cost to see jobs: **Free**
Resumes: **Yes** Cost to post resumes: **Free** Cost to see resumes: N/A
E-mail Alert (Push): N/A
Specialty: **All**
Industry: **Government**
Feature: N/A
Location: **US/W/CA/San Fran.**

This California Bay Area public employment site offers job seekers direct contact information to its members and salary grades. The site links to other California public sector job sites as well, and has recently added an online application form which, unfortunately, you have to download their software to use.

AboutWork

www.aboutwork.com

Eileen O'Reilly, TMP Worldwide
1633 Broadway, New York, NY 10019
Ph: 212-940-6948   Fax: 212-940-6954   E-mail: eoreilly@tmp.com

Jobs: **No** Cost to post jobs: N/A Cost to see jobs: N/A
Resumes: **No** Cost to post resumes: N/A Cost to see resumes: N/A
E-mail Alert (Push): N/A
Specialty: N/A
Industry: N/A
Feature: N/A
Location: **US**

AboutWork has recently been acquired by TMP advertising, and at press time, was still under construction. We have left it in our work as we feel that if past history is any indication of the future, this will still be a site to watch. We believe that alliances with OCC and the Monster Board may bring job and resume links to this site.

Academe This Week

www.chronicle.com

Mike Snyder, The Chronicle of Higher Education
1255 23rd Street NW, Suite 700, Washington, DC 20037
Ph: 800-728-2803   Fax: 202-466-1055   E-mail: circulation@chronicle.com

Jobs: **Yes** Cost to post jobs: **Fee** Cost to see jobs: **Fee** (Subscribe)	All current positions listed are those published weekly in the *Chronicle of Higher Education*. A broad range of faculty, research, administration and executive positions. 1,000+ openings are searchable by keyword, and can be restricted by region. You must be a subscriber to the Chronicle to see the open positions ($75). Employers must pay for the print and internet combination.
Resumes: **No** Cost to post resumes: N/A Cost to see resumes: N/A	
E-mail Alert (Push): N/A	
Specialty: **Teaching/Admin.**	
Industry: **Education/University**	
Feature: N/A	
Location: **US**	

Academic Employment Network

www.academploy.com

Christopher J. Gaudet,
266 Grey Road, Windham, ME 04062
Ph: 800-890-8283   Fax: 207-892-2614   E-mail: info@academploy.com

Jobs: **Yes** Cost to post jobs: **Fee** Cost to see jobs: **Free**	Educational districts can place an unlimited number of positions on this site for $495 per year or pay $95 per position for a 30-day posting. Newly created search engine will allow the job seeker to go into over 150 school web sites for $19.95 for 30 day access. Job seekers can review posted positions for free (130 openings in 44 states were available on our last visit).
Resumes: **No** Cost to post resumes: N/A Cost to see resumes: N/A	
E-mail Alert (Push): N/A	
Specialty: **Education**	
Industry: **Education**	
Feature: N/A	
Location: **US**	

Academic Physician & Scientist

www.acphysci.com/aps.htm

Martha McGarity, Academic Physician & Scientist
345 Hudson Street, 16th Floor, New York, NY 10014
Ph: 212-886-1350 Fax: 212-627-4801 E-mail: mmcgarit@nyc.lrpub.com

Jobs: **Yes**	
Cost to post jobs: **Fee**	
Cost to see jobs: **Free**	
Resumes: **No**	
Cost to post resumes: N/A	
Cost to see resumes: N/A	
E-mail Alert (Push): N/A	
Specialty: **Health Care/ Physician Research**	
Industry: **Health Care/Education**	
Feature: N/A	
Location: **US**	

The **Academic Physician & Scientist** site includes openings from a bi-monthly print publication that is mailed free to every U.S. faculty physician, scientist, senior resident and fellow at 125 U.S. medical schools, 400 major teaching hospitals and academic and professional societies. Many senior level positions were posted on our visit. The site's search engine is very easy to use.

Accounting.com

www.accounting.com

Ryan Cahill
32 Chauncey Street, Dedham, MA 02026
Ph: 781-329-3660 E-mail: ryan@accounting.com

Jobs: **Yes**	
Cost to post jobs: **Fee**	
Cost to see jobs: **Free**	
Resumes: **Yes**	
Cost to post resumes: **Free**	
Cost to see resumes: **Fee**	
E-mail Alert (Push): N/A	
Specialty: **Finance/Accounting**	
Industry: **All**	
Feature: N/A	
Location: **US**	

Accounting.com is relatively new and open for business. Recruiters pay $45 to post an opening for 30 days. Employers paying for five postings ($175) get access to the resume database. Candidates who fill out a job matching form get to go to " Job Match Land." Job seekers can also search the job bank directly. Several dozen relevant jobs were listed with direct contact information. Site plans a discussion forum in the near future.

AccountingNet

www.accountingnet.com

Jeff Farris, AccountingNet
600 Stewart Street, Suite 1101, Seattle, WA 98101
Ph: 206-441-8285   Fax: 206-441-8385   E-mail: jeff@accountingnet.com

Jobs: **Yes** Cost to post jobs: **Fee** Cost to see jobs: **Free**	
Resumes: **Yes** Cost to post resumes: **Free** Cost to see resumes: **Free**	
E-mail Alert (Push): N/A	
Specialty: **Finance/Accounting**	
Industry: **All**	
Feature: N/A	
Location: **US**	

Partnering with CareerMosaic, **AccountingNet** provides extensive information about the accounting field. Over 2,500 jobs were listed on our visit. 4,500 (short profiles) resumes were available. Recruiters pay $150 to post a job for 30 days. **AccountingNet** owners also have other recruiting sites: http://www.accountingstudents.com and http://www.cpalink.com. We expect the resumes to move to a fee basis.

Acorn Career Counseling

www.acornresume.com

Fred Nagle,
8 Clay Court, Rhinebeck, NY 12572
Ph: 914-876-8617   E-mail: acorn@ulster.net

Jobs: **No** Cost to post jobs: N/A Cost to see jobs: N/A	
Resumes: **No** Cost to post resumes: N/A Cost to see resumes: N/A	
E-mail Alert (Push): N/A	
Specialty: N/A	
Industry: **All**	
Feature: **Resume Service** **Meta-links**	
Location: **US**	

Acorn Career Counseling aka "the Resume Doctor," is a neat place to get advice on how to improve your resume. Site offers a lengthy list of links about where to post your resume. We enjoyed the "doctor's" defective resume designed to help job seekers analyze their own CV's strengths and weaknesses. E-mail your resume to Fred for suggestions and a quote on a price for rewriting it.

ActiJob

www.actijob.com

Claude Gelinas, Logix Communications
1540 Fossambault Blvd N., St-Augustin-de-Desmaures, QC G3A 1WB
Ph: 514-453-3828   Fax: 514-453-9153   E-mail: cgelinas@actijob.com/

Jobs: **Yes** Cost to post jobs: **Fee** Cost to see jobs: **Free**	Canadian employers post jobs for $50 for a one-month listing. **Actijob** is updated each day—most jobs are posted in one hour. Positions can be viewed in French or English. An online job chat room completes a very helpful effort, especially for French Canadians.
Resumes: **Yes** Cost to post resumes: **Free** Cost to see resumes: N/A	
E-mail Alert (Push): N/A	
Specialty: **All**	
Industry: **All**	
Feature: N/A	
Location: **Int'l/Canada (French)**	

Adecco

www.adecco.com

Adecco, Inc.
100 Redwood Shores Parkway, Redwood City, CA 94065
Ph: 415-610-1000   Fax: 415-610-1076

Jobs: **Yes** Cost to post jobs: **Fee** Cost to see jobs: **Free**	This major placement/temporary agency has 3,000 offices in more than 48 countries. Hundreds of positions are posted from their offices and easily searched. All levels/types of jobs are listed. **Adecco** recently acquired Lee Hecht Harrison, a major outplacement firm. Job seekers should keep an eye on a firm like this as they could be a ready source of international leads.
Resumes: **No** Cost to post resumes: N/A Cost to see resumes: N/A	
E-mail Alert (Push): N/A	
Specialty: **All**	
Industry: **All**	
Feature: N/A	
Location: **Int'l (US)**	

Adguide's Employment Web Site

www.adguide.com

Steven Rothberg, Adguide Publications Inc.
3722 W. 50 St., Suite 121, Minneapolis, MN 55410-2016
Ph: 612-915-0076   Fax: 612-915-1102   E-mail: stevenr@adguide.com

Jobs: **Yes** Cost to post jobs: **Fee** Cost to see jobs: **Free**
Resumes: **No** Cost to post resumes: N/A Cost to see resumes: N/A
E-mail Alert (Push): **Job Seeker**
Specialty: **College**
Industry: **All**
Feature: N/A
Location: **US/MW/MN**

Adguide accepts positions for college students, recent graduates and experienced professionals. Corporations have full page advertisements on this site with e-mail capability directly to the recruiter. A new search engine has been added and the cost to post a position is $300 for three months. A career counselor roundtable for advice, and an e-mail newsletter adds to this site's value. The site looks national in scope, but the content is almost all from MN.

AdSearch

www.adsearch.com

Miller Advertising Agency

Ph: 212-691-2929   E-mail: adinfo@adsearch.com

Jobs: **Yes** Cost to post jobs: **Fee** Cost to see jobs: **Free**
Resumes: **No** Cost to post resumes: **Free** Cost to see resumes: N/A
E-mail Alert (Push): N/A
Specialty: **All**
Industry: **All**
Feature: N/A
Location: **US**

This recruitment advertising agency site contains a job database for their clients' openings. Ads are listed for 30 days. Simple site with all levels and titles.

Adweek Online

www.adweek.com

Wright Ferguson, BPI Communications Inc.
1515 Broadway, NY, NY 10036
Ph: 212-536-6527   Fax: 212-536-5353   E-mail: wferguson@adweek.com

Jobs: **Yes** Cost to post jobs: **Fee** Cost to see jobs: **Free**	
Resumes: **No** Cost to post resumes: N/A Cost to see resumes: N/A	
E-mail Alert (Push): N/A	
Specialty: **Advertising**	
Industry: **Advertising**	
Feature: N/A	
Location: **US**	

Online job opportunities are listed from this weekly advertising publication's classified section. A new search engine has been added which shows date of posting, publication date and region of the country. Site allows job posts to seven specific areas with a catch-all "miscellaneous" for the rest.

Africa Online Jobs

www.AfricaOnline.com/AfricaOnline/cgi/showclasscat

Africa Online Inc., Africa
Ph: 161-749-4021   E-mail: webmaster@africaonline.com

Jobs: **Yes** Cost to post jobs: **Free** Cost to see jobs: **Free**	
Resumes: **Yes** Cost to post resumes: **Free** Cost to see resumes: **Free**	
E-mail Alert (Push): N/A	
Specialty: **All**	
Industry: **All**	
Feature: **Diversity**	
Location: **Int'l/Africa**	

Africa Online posts jobs and resumes on a page in no particular order. Dozens of jobs are posted with date of opportunity listed. Descriptions are poorly written and confusing. We have tried to advise the webmaster that this is a difficult way to conduct web commerce.

Afro-Americ@: The Job Vault

www.afroam.org/information/vault/vault.html

Afro-American Newspapers
2519 N. Charles Street, Baltimore, MD 21218
Ph: Fax: 410-554-8213   E-mail: vickyc@afroam.org

Jobs: **Yes** Cost to post jobs: **Fee** Cost to see jobs: **Free**	A very limited number of jobs are listed here from the Afro-American Newspapers. Unrealized potential for reaching a diverse community in the Baltimore area.
Resumes: **No** Cost to post resumes: N/A Cost to see resumes: N/A	
E-mail Alert (Push): N/A	
Specialty: **All**	
Industry: **All**	
Feature: **Diversity**	
Location: **US**	

Airline Employment Ass't. Corps

www.avjobs.com

T. Lahey, AEAC
P.O. Box 462151, Aurora, CO 80046
Ph: 303-683-2322   Fax: 303-471-0226   E-mail: sales@aeac.com

Jobs: **Yes** Cost to post jobs: **Free** Cost to see jobs: **Fee**	If flying the friendly skies is the place you want to be, then this site needs to be one of your destinations. Positions are posted for airline, airport, aerospace or the aviation industry. Job seekers are charged $10 per month to view open positions (which includes the ability to post a resume). This is still trying to get itself off the ground as the resume database is under construction at the time we viewed it. Employers can post openings for 90 days for free. The resume database will also be free to employers. A new feature listing colleges with programs in the aviation industry has also been added.
Resumes: **Yes** Cost to post resumes: **Fee** Cost to see resumes: **Free**	
E-mail Alert (Push): N/A	
Specialty: **All**	
Industry: **Aviation/Aerospace** **Airline**	
Feature: N/A	
Location: **US**	

Airwaves Media Web

www.airwaves.com

William Pfeiffer, Airwaves Media
P.O. Box 100192, Milwaukee, WI 53210
Ph: 888-233-3074   E-mail: wdp@airwaves.com

Jobs: **Yes**	
Cost to post jobs: **Free**	
Cost to see jobs: **Free**	
Resumes: **Yes**	
Cost to post resumes: **Free**	
Cost to see resumes: **Free**	
E-mail Alert (Push): N/A	
Specialty: **Entertainment/ Radio Broadcasting**	
Industry: **Entertainment**	
Feature: N/A	
Location: **US**	

Disc jockeys can share more than their play lists at **Airwaves Media Web**. This site has created an e-mail listserv for individuals to share old radio show tapes and stories. Free job postings and a free resume database make this a site a hit for folks looking to rocket up the charts. Check out "Amazing Anagrams." We give it a 6 for coming to the dance.

Allied Health Opportunities Directory

www.gvpub.com

Kathleen Czermanski, Great Valley Publishing Company
1288 Valley Forge Rd., Valley Forge, PA 19482
Ph: 800-278-4400   Fax: 610-917-9041   E-mail: admin@gvpub.com

Jobs: **Yes**	
Cost to post jobs: **Fee**	
Cost to see jobs: **Free**	
Resumes: **No**	
Cost to post resumes: N/A	
Cost to see resumes: N/A	
E-mail Alert (Push): N/A	
Specialty: **Health Care/ Allied Health**	
Industry: **Health Care**	
Feature: N/A	
Location: **US**	

This allied health care publisher posts positions that are listed in their magazines. Only a dozen positions were listed on our last visit which suggests a model that doesn't fully support their print side. Positions posted ranged from cardio-vascular technologist to pharmacist. Well-written article "The Job Interview: Important Questions" makes this site worth a visit.

AltaVista

www.altavista.digital.com

Jobs: **Yes**
Cost to post jobs: **Free**
Cost to see jobs: **Free**
Resumes: **Yes**
Cost to post resumes: **Free**
Cost to see resumes: N/A
E-mail Alert (Push): N/A
Specialty: **All Search Engine**
Industry: **All**
Feature: N/A
Location: **US/Int'l**

AltaVista is one of the major search engines on the web today. If you click on "careers," both recruiters and job seekers can search for resumes or jobs from major sites that supply their "links" on a weekly basis. A career coach will answer all of your Q&A job seeking challenges

Alumnae Resources

www.ar.org

Bonnie Willdorf
120 Montgomery Street, Suite 600, San Francisco, CA 94104
Ph: 415-274-4710   Fax: 415-274-4715   E-mail: arinfo@ar.org

Jobs: **No**
Cost to post jobs: N/A
Cost to see jobs: N/A
Resumes: **No**
Cost to post resumes: N/A
Cost to see resumes: N/A
E-mail Alert (Push): N/A
Specialty: **All**
Industry: **All**
Feature: N/A
Location: **US/NW/CA/SF**

Alumnae Resources is a nonprofit organization founded in 1977. **AR** provides services to women and men seeking first jobs, job search assistance after layoffs, career advancement and new career direction. Emphasizing career transition and management, **Alumnae Resources** offers workshops, counseling and research facilities. Support comes from individual and corporate fees for services, membership dues and fundraising events. Group supports 8,500 individual members, 100 companies and more than 200,000 client visits, online and offline.

American Assoc. of Fin. & Accounting

www.aafa.com/

American Association of Finance & Accounting

E-mail: aafa-aafa@bii.com

Jobs: **Yes**	
Cost to post jobs: **Fee**	
Cost to see jobs: **Free**	
Resumes: **No**	
Cost to post resumes: N/A	
Cost to see resumes: N/A	
E-mail Alert (Push): N/A	
Specialty: **Finance/Accounting**	
Industry: **All**	
Feature: **Meta-links**	
Location: **US/Int'l**	

This is a network of 250 + search firms that specialize in placing accounting/finance professionals. The site has a search engine that worked well on our visits. Good place to obtain a lengthy list of search firms for this field. Some interesting career articles were also found.

American Astronomical Society

www.aas.org

Dawn-Marie Craig, American Astronomical Society
2000 Florida Ave., Suite 400, Washington, DC 20009
Ph: 202-328-2010   Fax: 202-234-2560   E-mail: dcraig@blackhole.aas.org

Jobs: **Yes**	
Cost to post jobs: **Fee**	
Cost to see jobs: **Free**	
Resumes: **No**	
Cost to post resumes: N/A	
Cost to see resumes: N/A	
E-mail Alert (Push): N/A	
Specialty: **Science/Astronomy**	
Industry: **Education/University**	
Feature: N/A	
Location: **US/Int'l**	

Gives new meaning to the phrase "Ad Aspera per Aspera." The American Astronomical Society has been in existence since 1899, and provides opportunities specifically for Astronomers. Positions listed here are from all over the world. The cost for posting is $100 per opening.

American Banker CareerZone

www.americanbanker.com/

Ernestine Grant, American Banker Publisher
1 State Street, 27th Floor, NY, NY 10004
Ph: 800-221-1910   Fax: 212-843-9636   E-mail: grante@americanbanker.com

Jobs: **Yes**	
Cost to post jobs: **Fee**	
Cost to see jobs: **Free**	
Resumes: **No**	
Cost to post resumes: **Free**	
Cost to see resumes: **N/A**	
E-mail Alert (Push): **Job Seeker**	
Specialty: **All**	
Industry: **Finance/Banking**	
Feature: N/A	
Location: **US**	

American Banker makes it easy for the pinstripe crowd. Job seekers who register here will have jobs "Pushed" to their doorstep that match their skill set. You can also view positions at their site. Recruiters can post a job for $200 for one month. Additional packages are available. The site has a map locator to direct applicants to your exact location. Weekly updated career articles round out this niche site. Well-designed site that does a great job.

AMERICAN BANKER ONLINE

CAREERZONE
Interactive Archive

Mon., Sep. 14, 1998   The Financial Services Daily   163d year

Banker
  Front Page
  Today's Headlines
  Online Exclusives
  Recent Issues
  Daily Digest
  Company Index
  Bank & Thrift Stocks
  Hot Off The Wire
American Banker
Magazines
  Future Banker
  Financial Services
  Marketing
Classified Advertising
  Career Zone
  Resource Directory
How To Subscribe

Quick Jump... [Go]   [Search]

Welcome to American Banker Online's CareerZone. On our CareerZone site you can look for the perfect job as defined by industry, location, salary and job field. You can actively search for available positions meeting your criteria by clicking on the Job Search link, or you can register with our Personal Search Agent® and automatically receive e-mail notification whenever a position is posted that meets your specific criteria. And the service is completely **FREE!**

You can also post available jobs at your company by clicking on the Post A Position link.

▶ **Find A Position**

Access our comprehensive list of professional job opportunities. Find your ideal job (location, industry, salary and field) and apply online. It's free, confidential and easy to use!

▶ **Personal Search Agent®**

Submit your ideal job profile and automatically receive daily e-mail notifications of new postings that match your search criteria. Personal Search Agent® is your own personal career search tool. This service is free and confidential!

▶ **CareerTracks Online**

American Chemical Society Job Bank

www.acs.org

Beth Palubinskas, American Chemical Society
1155 16th Street, NWS, Washington, DC 20036
Ph: 800-227-5558   Fax: 202-872-4615   E-mail: b_palubinskas@acs.org

Jobs: **Yes**	
Cost to post jobs: **Fee**	
Cost to see jobs: **Fee**	
Resumes: **Yes**	
Cost to post resumes: **Fee**	
Cost to see resumes: **Fee**	
E-mail Alert (Push): **Employer**	
Specialty: **Science/Chemistry Chem. Eng.**	
Industry: **All**	
Feature: N/A	
Location: **US**	

Members of the ACS can post free advertisements up to 35 words. All other positions listed are from *Chemical & Engineering News* which has a $460 minimum cost per advertisement. If you are looking for ChemEs, the **ACS Job Bank** has the right formula. Employers should make sure that print ads listed in the C&E News get this internet component. ACS members can join the professional data bank that will match their skills to employers' specific job requirements (if you want this to be confidential and not forwarded to certain employers there is a $40 fee). A new feature allowing members to post their skill sets (brief resume) to the site for employers to view will be out shortly. Costs were being put together as we went to press.

American Compensation Association

www.acaonline.org

Don Griffith
14040 N. Northsight Blvd., Scottsdale, AZ 85260
Ph: 602-922-2005   Fax: 602-922-2005   E-mail: dgriffith@acaonline.org

Jobs: **Yes**	
Cost to post jobs: **Fee**	
Cost to see jobs: **Free**	
Resumes: **Yes**	
Cost to post resumes: **Free**	
Cost to see resumes: **Free**	
E-mail Alert (Push): N/A	
Specialty: **Human Resources/ Compensation**	
Industry: **All**	
Feature: N/A	
Location: **US/Int'l**	

The American Compensation Association (ACA) has recently added job postings to their site. Recruiters pay $150 for a four-week run. Job seekers need to know that "JobLinks" is where posted jobs are located—not links to other sites. Poor choice of title. Resumes posted to the site are dated, as are the jobs. Corporate job postings are kept separate from agency listings. Good start with room for improvement.

American Economic Development Council

www.aedc.org

Nancy Lasselle
9801 W. Higgins Road, Suite 540, Rosemont, IL 60018
Ph: 847-692-9944   Fax: 847-696-2990   E-mail: nlassell@interaccess.com

Jobs: **Yes** Cost to post jobs: **Fee** Cost to see jobs: **Free**
Resumes: **Yes** Cost to post resumes: **Fee** Cost to see resumes: N/A
E-mail Alert (Push): **Job Seeker**
Specialty: **Finance/Economic Development**
Industry: **All/Government**
Feature: N/A
Location: **US**

The American Economic Development Council has over 3,000 members and publishes a monthly newsletter where recruiters can post jobs for $300-$400. This web site is the newsletter's Internet component. Ads run for three consecutive months. For an additional $400-$500, openings will be "Pushed" to registered job seekers within 24 hours. Job seekers pay $50, nonmembers pay $100 to receive the bulletin and get "pushed" listed openings. Several dozen positions are listed by region of the U.S., and all direct contact information can be viewed at the site. Jobs range from township CEOs to city economic development directors.

American Institute of Physics

www.aip.org

American Institute of Physics
Career Services Division, One Physics Ellipse, College Park, MD 20740
Ph: 301-209-3100   Fax: 301-209-0841   E-mail: aipinfo@aip.org

Jobs: **Yes** Cost to post jobs: **Fee** Cost to see jobs: **Free**
Resumes: **No** Cost to post resumes: N/A Cost to see resumes: N/A
E-mail Alert (Push): N/A
Specialty: **Science/Physics**
Industry: **All**
Feature: N/A
Location: **US**

Stripped to the bare essentials, the AIP site allows employers to submit a job for $49 (up to 10 lines for a 4-week posting). Dozens of academic and corporate positions are listed. Date of posting is also listed.

AmericanJobs.com

www.americanjobs.com

Kevin Romney
1625 West Big Beaver Road, Suite A, Troy, MI 48084
Ph: 248-816-8400   Fax: 248-649-3696   E-mail: kromney@ix.netcom.com

Jobs: **Yes** Cost to post jobs: **Fee** Cost to see jobs: **Free**	**AmericanJobs.com** focuses on high tech, computer/IT and engineering openings. Recruiters pay $75 to post a position for a 90-day run. Other packages are available. A resume database is being created as we go to press, and the site has advised us that for the first 3-6 months it will be free. Click on "about us," and you will see a good-faith attempt to provide disclosure about activity at this site.
Resumes: **Yes** Cost to post resumes: **Free** Cost to see resumes: N/A (See Notes)	
E-mail Alert (Push): N/A	
Specialty: **IT/High Tech/Eng**	
Industry: **All**	
Feature: N/A	
Location: **US**	

American Journalism Review Online

www.newslink.org/joblink.html

Rem Reider, American Journalism Review
Univ. of Maryland Foundation, 8701 Adelphi Road, Adelphi, MD 20783
Ph: 301-431-4771   Fax: 301-431-0097   E-mail: feedback@newslink.org

Jobs: **Yes** Cost to post jobs: **Free** Cost to see jobs: **Free**	This site is a joint venture between the **American Journalism Review** and NewsLink Associates, a research, consulting and publishing firm. Job postings remain free for a 5-week trial. There were over 170 jobs posted (for 30 days) on our last visit. The site also lists links to major newspapers and magazines by state. Well-designed, this is a great niche resource.
Resumes: **No** Cost to post resumes: N/A Cost to see resumes: N/A	
E-mail Alert (Push): N/A	
Specialty: **Journalism**	
Industry: **Publishing**	
Feature: N/A	
Location: **US**	

American Medical Association

www.ama-assn.org

Thalia Moss, AMA Classified Advertising
515 N. State Street, 12th Floor, Chicago, IL 60610
Ph:312-464-4169   E-mail:classifieds@ama-asn.org

Jobs:**Yes** Cost to post jobs:**Fee** Cost to see jobs:**Free**	
Resumes:**Yes** Cost to post resumes:**Free** Cost to see resumes:**Fee**	
E-mail Alert (Push):N/A	
Specialty:**Health Care/MD**	
Industry:**Health Care**	
Feature:N/A	
Location:**US**	

The American Medical Association publishes *JAMA*. The recruitment advertisements that are placed there can be seen on this website...in alpha order. Bring your scrolling fingers. Positions wanted (resumes) are at the end (so keep scrolling). Designed with the same efficiency as the doctor's waiting room.

American Physical Therapy Association

apta.edoc.com

American Physical Therapy Association
1111 North Fairfax Street, Alexandria, VA 22314
Ph: 703-684-2782   Fax: 703-684-7343

Jobs: **No** Cost to post jobs: N/A Cost to see jobs: N/A	
Resumes: **No** Cost to post resumes: N/A Cost to see resumes: N/A	
E-mail Alert (Push): N/A	
Specialty: **Health Care/** **Physical Therapy**	
Industry: **Health Care**	
Feature: N/A	
Location: **US**	

A career in physical therapy is the key part of the focus of this association's site. Members number 75,000, and the information here includes how to obtain a license, academic study, areas of specialty, etc. The site has a search engine for finding articles. There are no jobs posted, but when you consider that PT is a critical specialty in high demand, the association will need to offer more concrete help or face "stiffer" competition.

American Society for Quality

www.asq.org

611 East Wisconsin Avenue
Milwaukee, WI 53201
Ph: 800-248-1946   Fax: 414-272-1734   E-mail: cs@asq.org

Jobs: **Yes**	
Cost to post jobs: **Fee**	
Cost to see jobs: **Fee**	
Resumes: **No**	
Cost to post resumes: N/A	
Cost to see resumes: N/A	
E-mail Alert (Push): N/A	
Specialty: **Technical/QA-QC**	
Industry: **All**	
Feature: N/A	
Location: **US**	

The **ASQC** keeps everything related to jobs a secret on their site (must be a test). Only members can access the jobs database in hidden job vault under ASQ Net. Members can post one job for free, and additional postings are $150. Looks like a little over-control problem.

American Society of Mech. Engineers

www.asme.org/jobs

ASME
22 Law Drive, P.O. Box 2900, Fairfield, NJ 07007
Ph: 800-843-2763   Fax: 973-882-1717   E-mail: infocentral@asme.org

Jobs: **Yes**	
Cost to post jobs: **Fee**	
Cost to see jobs: **Free**	
Resumes: **No**	
Cost to post resumes: N/A	
Cost to see resumes: N/A	
E-mail Alert (Push): N/A	
Specialty: **Engineering/ Mechanical**	
Industry: **All**	
Feature: N/A	
Location: **US**	

American Society of Mechanical Engineers posts hundreds of positions to their site. All have direct contact information and date of posting. Recruiters pay $75 per job for a 45-day run. Internships cost $25 to post. Search engine allows job seekers to view positions by title, location, expected responsibilities, job requirements or even company.

American Water Works Jobs

www.awwa.org

Torey Lightcap, American Water Works Association
6666 West Quincy Avenue, Denver, CO 80235
Ph: 303-794-7711   E-mail: tlightca@awwa.org

Jobs: **Yes**	
Cost to post jobs: **Free**	
Cost to see jobs: **Free**	
Resumes: **No**	
Cost to post resumes: N/A	
Cost to see resumes: N/A	
E-mail Alert (Push): N/A	
Specialty: **Environmental**	
Industry: **Water**	
Feature: N/A	
Location: **US**	

Not quite an ocean of possibilities here...more like a "crik." There were over 60 jobs posted in the last 30 days. Many articles for career information are also available. Jobs can be e-mailed to the AWWA site and are posted in 2–3 days for free. This site can be viewed in English and Spanish.

America's Employers

www.americasemployers.com

Rose Emerson, Career Relo Corp. of America
80 Business Park Drive, Suite 303, Armonk, NY 10504
Ph: 914-273-2500   Fax: 914-273-5077   E-mail: profserv@americasemployers.com

Jobs: **Yes**	
Cost to post jobs: **Fee**	
Cost to see jobs: **Free**	
Resumes: **Yes**	
Cost to post resumes: **Free**	
Cost to see resumes: **Fee**	
E-mail Alert (Push): N/A	
Specialty: **All**	
Industry: **All**	
Feature: N/A	
Location: **US**	

The main business of **America's Employers** is as a career counseling service for major corporations. The site claims they get over 1,000 resumes a week and have over 50,000 jobs posted. Employers pay $125 to post on this site for 60 days (although the site made the same claims last year). Unique to AE is a chat room where employers can conduct online interviews with job seekers. An electronic networking discussion group (listserv) actively connects visitors who wish join in and pose questions or just make great contacts. Resumes are coded, and employers have to go back to the site for contact information. $5,000 per year. Interesting career information such as "The 50 Toughest Interview Questions" tops off a site with a lot to offer. Their biggest challenge will be how they can continue to stand out among job seekers in a crowded marketplace.

America's Health Care Source

www.healthcaresource.com

Steve Ludwig, Health Care Source, Inc.
196 Boston Avenue, Suite 3000, Medford, MA 02155
Ph: 888-289-9979   Fax: 781-393-5499   E-mail: info@healthcaresource.com

Jobs: **Yes** Cost to post jobs: **Fee** Cost to see jobs: **Free**	
Resumes: **Yes** Cost to post resumes: **Free** Cost to see resumes: **Fee**	
E-mail Alert (Push): N/A	
Specialty: **Health Care/ Allied Health**	
Industry: **Health Care**	
Feature: N/A	
Location: **US**	

This site targets some of the allied health professions and rehabilitation therapies including: occupational therapy, physical therapy, speech-language-hearing, audiology, hospital pharmacy, and nursing. Site states it has over 2,500 current listings that are updated biweekly, and cover all regions of the country. Links to interesting healthcare related sites, mailing lists and newsgroups. CEUs, seminars, events, colleges and universities, state associations and licensure information is available. Employers pay $95 to post a job for a 2 month run. A resume database has recently been added. Easy-to-use format allows the job seeker to apply online. Note pad allows job seekers to keep track of each opening in which they have an interest.

America's Job Bank

www.ajb.dni.us

US Government

Jobs: **Yes** Cost to post jobs: **Free** Cost to see jobs: **Free**	
Resumes: **Yes** Cost to post resumes: **Free** Cost to see resumes: **Free**	
E-mail Alert (Push): N/A	
Specialty: **All**	
Industry: **All**	
Feature: N/A	
Location: **US**	

Our tax dollars are hard at work at **America's Job Bank.** Supporting the government's 2,000+ employment offices, the site has 665,000 jobs listed. In 1996 The Equal Employment Advisory Council stated: "Three of the Labor Department's offices, the OFCCP, the Office of Veteran's Affairs, and the Employment Training Administration have agreed that using the AJB can satisfy job posting requirements under the particular regulating authority." There are two levels of services for the job seeker: search positions by state, zip code or function directly from the site, and registered users can create cover letters and use the site's electronic resume builder, which posts your CV to America's Talent Bank. The directions for using the services were a little confusing. Maybe Al Gore could lend a hand to simplify.

America's Online Help-Wanted

www2.ohw.com

Karla Ward,
2900 Delk Road, Suite 700-278, Marietta, GA 30067
Ph: 888-850-1115   Fax: 770-850-0671   E-mail: info@ohw.com

Jobs: **Yes** Cost to post jobs: **Fee** Cost to see jobs: **Free**	
Resumes: **Yes** Cost to post resumes: **Free** Cost to see resumes: **Fee**	
E-mail Alert (Push): N/A	
Specialty: **IT**	
Industry: **All**	
Feature: N/A	
Location: **US**	

America's Online Help-wanted specializes in IT recruiting, and is concentrated in 15 major U.S. cities. Job seekers post a listing of their skills for free, and recruiters can view the data and select who they want to contact once they register. Cost to post an unlimited number of jobs runs from $325-$695 depending on the city you choose. Also advised us that they are sending out 150-200 resumes a month. Owners state they filter out the good from the bad resumes for their clients—interesting approach.

America's Talent Bank

www.atb.org

US Department of Labor and State Government

E-mail: mt02633@navix.net

Jobs: **No** Cost to post jobs: N/A Cost to see jobs: N/A	
Resumes: **Yes** Cost to post resumes: **Free** Cost to see resumes: **Free**	
E-mail Alert (Push): N/A	
Specialty: **All**	
Industry: **All**	
Feature: N/A	
Location: **US**	

America's Talent Bank is the government's nationwide resume database that can be searched by employers to find candidates for their openings. 97,000 resumes in their database. Site should be simple, but this is the government. When you enter this site from America's Job Bank, each state's resumes are cordoned off from one another. Employers must register before they can search the database. Every "one stop" State employment center has a contract with the U.S. Department of Labor to implement **America's Talent Bank** as part of their effort to support the labor market. The prototype and development of **ATB** was piloted in 1997 by nine states, and while still growing, it seems to have lost some steam.

America's TV Job Network

www.tvjobnet.com

Bruce Billow, 7250 Westfield Avenue
Pennsauken, NJ 08110
Ph: 800-220-4545   Fax: 609-665-0055   E-mail: info@tvjobnet.com

Jobs: **Yes** Cost to post jobs: **Fee** Cost to see jobs: **Free**	
Resumes: **Yes** Cost to post resumes: **Fee** Cost to see resumes: **Free**	
E-mail Alert (Push): **No**	
Specialty: **All**	
Industry: **All**	
Feature: N/A	
Location: **US**	

This Delaware Valley (Pennsylvania/New Jersey) television show lists job opportunities and gives career guidance. The show appears on Philadelphia public television on Sundays at noon on KYW3. For recruiters, the resume database on their web site is free, while applicants pay $19.95 for having their resume listed for six months. Employers pay $25 per month to post positions, and there are packages to get your job shown on the television show. Job seekers have the capability to search all jobs posted on the site by title and location. If you saw a position on the TV show you can search by the job code as well.

Antenna's Internet Broadcast Jobs

www.theAntenna.com

Dan Naden
7711 Computer Ave., Edina, MN 55435
Ph: 513-241-1440   Fax: 513-241-2440   E-mail: dann@theAntenna.com

Jobs: **Yes** Cost to post jobs: **Free** Cost to see jobs: **Free**	
Resumes: **No** Cost to post resumes: N/A Cost to see resumes: N/A	
E-mail Alert (Push): N/A	
Specialty: **Entertainment/** **Broadcasting**	
Industry: **Entertainment**	
Feature: N/A	
Location: **US**	

The Antenna allows recruiters to post positions in TV/cable and radio for free. There were openings at all levels and in different areas of broadcasting on our last visit. If you want to join the "really big show," this site may get you there.

Arizona Careers Online

www.diversecity.com/jobs.html

Rich Watson, Diverse Data
287-2 North Meyer Ave., Tucson, AZ 85701
Ph: 520-884-1320   Fax: 520-791-0955   E-mail: aztu@azstarnet.com

Jobs: **Yes**	
Cost to post jobs: **Fee**	
Cost to see jobs: **Free**	
Resumes: **Yes**	
Cost to post resumes: **Fee**	
Cost to see resumes: **Free**	
E-mail Alert (Push): **N/A**	
Specialty: **All**	
Industry: **All**	
Feature: **Diversity**	
Location: **US/SW/AR**	

Arizona Careers Online maintains extensive information about the southwest including links to colleges, job hotlines and local real estate. Links to diversity resources are especially rich and useful. Part of the Help-wanted-USA Network, (see Help-wanted-USA), employers can post jobs for $75/2 weeks while also searching their resume database for free. Cost to post a resume for several months is a hefty $89.95, but includes a service to send it to over 700 locations. If you decide to check into this ask "Where exactly is my resume going?"

ASAE Career Headquarters

www.asaenet.org/careerheadquarters

Tammy Cussimanio, American Society of Association Executives
1575 I Street, NW, Washington, DC 20005
Ph: 202-626-2758   Fax: 202-408-9652   E-mail: TCUSSIMANI@asaenet.org

Jobs: **Yes**	
Cost to post jobs: **Fee**	
Cost to see jobs: **Free**	
Resumes: **No**	
Cost to post resumes: **N/A**	
Cost to see resumes: **N/A**	
E-mail Alert (Push): **N/A**	
Specialty: **Non-Profit/ Executive/PR**	
Industry: **All**	
Feature: N/A	
Location: **US**	

ASAE Career Headquarters is devoted to career issues in the association community. Search the job listings by location, job and level. Use the salary calculator to compare cost of living or explore the "Gateway to Associations" to find the perfect job. Visitors who subscribe to "CEO Update" receive a biweekly listing of nationwide nonprofit job openings in the $50,000+ range. Subscribers to "Career Opps'—$30,000 to $50,000 range. There are also bulletins for public relations and hospitality jobs. ASAE members (24,000) can post positions for $200 (first 100 words). Nonmembers pay $250 for 100 words. Each additional word costs $1. Positions may also be advertised in *Association Management* magazine at no additional charge. Great articles, easy-to-use site that gets its message across.

Asia Online

asiadragons.com/employment/home.shtml

Asiadragons.com
E-mail: webmaster@asiadragons.com

Jobs: **Yes** Cost to post jobs: **Free** Cost to see jobs: **Free**
Resumes: **Yes** Cost to post resumes: **Free** Cost to see resumes: **Free**
E-mail Alert (Push): N/A
Specialty: **All**
Industry: **All**
Feature: N/A
Location: **Int'l/Asia**

Asia@Online is a search engine that provides classified directories in many different categories. In their employment section, there is a resume database and job bank where everything to see or post is free. Unfortunately, you can only scroll what's here. No search.

Asia-Net

www.asia-net.com

Dale Bowen-President, TapestryNet
111 Mission Street, Santa Cruz, CA 95060
Ph: 408-469-0781   Fax: 408-469-0782   E-mail: sales@asia-net.com

Jobs: **Yes**	
Cost to post jobs: **Fee**	
Cost to see jobs: **Free**	
Resumes: **No**	
Cost to post resumes: N/A	
Cost to see resumes: N/A	
E-mail Alert (Push): **Job Seeker**	
Specialty: **All**	
Industry: **All**	
Feature: **Diversity**	
Location: **US/Int'l/Asia**	

We have always liked sites that press the edge. **Asia-Net** continues to impress us with their understanding of "community" and the power of e-mail. They continue to change, update their work and look for the next level. If you speak English *and* either Japanese, Chinese or Korean, and are seeking employment throughout the world, **Asia-Net** keeps its commitments. Claiming 20,000+ addresses of bilingual professionals, they promise to e-mail an employer's job specification charging the employer a flat fee ($795 for a domestic position and $995 for an international opening). They have opened an office in Japan, added a newslink to keep their clients up-to-date, while also asking their members to rovide salary data for all to see. A sister site, http://www.developers.net, has been created for software developers.

Association for Women in Computing

www.awc-hq.org

Sojn Hudson, Association for Women in Computing
41 Sutter Street, Suite 1006, San Francisco, CA 94104
Ph: 415-905-4663   E-mail: awc@awc-hq.org

Jobs: **No**	
Cost to post jobs: N/A	
Cost to see jobs: N/A	
Resumes: **No**	
Cost to post resumes: N/A	
Cost to see resumes: N/A	
E-mail Alert (Push): N/A	
Specialty: **IT**	
Industry: **All**	
Feature: **Diversity**	
Location: **US**	

This gender-based, not-for profit national association includes a U.S. map linking to local chapters (once there, you'll find that the job posting policies and content vary). From a recruiter's standpoint, the chapters may be a good resource for potential job postings and candidates. An additional feature is a list of links for professional women to help with career and general issues.

Association of Online Professionals

www.aop.org

Susan Merkel, Association of Online Professionals
6096 Franconia Road, Suite D, Alexandria, VA 22310
Ph: 703-924-5800   Fax: 703-924-5801   E-mail: meraop@aol.com

Jobs: **Yes**	
Cost to post jobs: **Free**	
Cost to see jobs: **Free**	
Resumes: **No**	
Cost to post resumes: N/A	
Cost to see resumes: N/A	
E-mail Alert (Push): **Job Seeker**	
Specialty: **IT/WWW/ Communications**	
Industry: **Computer/Commun.**	
Feature: N/A	
Location: **US**	

AOP does things a little differently, and will e-mail employer openings to their members. Jobs that are Pushed out include: webmasters, systems operators, etc. All recruiters need to do is e-mail a description of the opening with the contact information, and **AOP** will post it in their weekly electronic newsletter. Jobs are not posted on their site. Free service for AOP members.

Assoc. for Computing Machinery (ACM)

www.acm.org/cacm/careeropps/

ACM
Ad Dept., 1515 Broadway, NY, NY 10036
Ph: 212-869-7440   Fax: 212-869-0481   E-mail: acm-advertising@acm.org

Jobs: **Yes**	
Cost to post jobs: **Fee**	
Cost to see jobs: **Free**	
Resumes: **No**	
Cost to post resumes: N/A	
Cost to see resumes: N/A	
E-mail Alert (Push): N/A	
Specialty: **IT**	
Industry: **IT**	
Feature: N/A	
Location: **US**	

Listings in the **Association for Computing Machinery's** (ACM) publications are posted to their web site. Employer are charged $125 for six lines, and jobs are posted for one month. Dozens of positions for C++, Java etc.—typically teaching openings at the university level.

ATI-Net

www.atinet.org/html/jobs.html

Saeed Awan, California Agricultural Technology Institute
2910 E. Barstow Avenue, M/S 115, Fresno, CA 93740
Ph: 209-278-2361   Fax: 209-278-4849   E-mail: webmaster@atinet.org

Jobs: **Yes**	
Cost to post jobs: **Free**	
Cost to see jobs: **Free**	
Resumes: **No**	
Cost to post resumes: N/A	
Cost to see resumes: N/A	
E-mail Alert (Push): N/A	
Specialty: **Science/Agriculture**	
Industry: **Agriculture**	
Feature: N/A	
Location: **US**	

Advanced Technology Information Network is a unit of the California Agricultural Technology Institute at California State University, Fresno. In addition to agricultural information, the site posts dozens of jobs for professionals in education, management, research, sales and marketing. Positions cover part-time/seasonal and temporary.

Au Pair in Europe

www.princeent.com/aupair/

John/Corine Prince
P.O. Box 68056, Blakeley Postal Outlet, Hamilton, Ontario, Canada L8M 3M7
Ph: 905-545-6305   Fax: 905-544-4121   E-mail: aupair@princeent.com

Jobs: **Yes** Cost to post jobs: **Fee** Cost to see jobs: N/A	Ever thought about taking 9–12 months and going to Europe as an au pair? The charge for registering is $425 for this agency's matching service. Some interesting statistics are presented on the site regarding the different requirements and salaries between the countries in Europe. You can select from 16 different countries who may have possible assignments.
Resumes: **Yes** Cost to post resumes: **Fee** Cost to see resumes: N/A	
E-mail Alert (Push): N/A	
Specialty: **Domestic**	
Industry: N/A	
Feature: N/A	
Location: **Int'l**	

AutoCAD

www.acjn.com

Josh Rothman, P.O. Box 1983
Tustin, CA 92781
Ph: 714-648-2261   Fax: 714-242-1406   E-mail: acjn@acjn.com

Jobs: **Yes** Cost to post jobs: **Fee** Cost to see jobs: **Free**	**AutoCad** has been around for two years and still needs a marketing plan. On our visit, we searched the U.S. for open positions and found fewer than a dozen listed. A useful regional map of the U.S. allows a quick search by location. International jobs were supposedly being added, but none were found on our visit. Cost to post a job is $100 for 30 days
Resumes: **Yes** Cost to post resumes: **Free** Cost to see resumes: **Fee**	
E-mail Alert (Push): N/A	
Specialty: **IT/CAD**	
Industry: **IT**	
Feature: N/A	
Location: **US**	

Aviation Employee Placement Service

www.aeps.com

Jim Dent, Sysops, Inc.
P.O. Box 550010, Ft. Lauderdale, FL 33355
Ph: 954-472-6684   Fax: 954-472-8524   E-mail: aeps@aeps.com

Jobs: **Yes** Cost to post jobs: **Free** Cost to see jobs: **Fee**	
Resumes: **Yes** Cost to post resumes: **Fee** Cost to see resumes: **Free**	
E-mail Alert (Push): **Job Seeker**	
Specialty: **Aerospace/Pilot**	
Industry: **Aviation**	
Feature: **Meta-Links**	
Location: **US**	

Here's a low-cost fare still looking to get off the ground. The cost to post a resume is free (for the first 10 days and then the charge is $12.00 per month). Corporations can post their jobs for free. Recently added "Job Alerts" promise to "Push" job information to possible candidates. Most aviation ground and pilot positions are included. Interesting graphics and text "flash" as you navigate the site. We can't decide whether they serve to engage you or simply distract you.

BAJobs (SF Bay Area Jobs)

www.bajobs.com

Andrew Gardiner
652 Bair Island Rd., Suite 301, Redwood City, CA 94063
Ph: 650-261-1149   Fax: 650-261-1061   E-mail: gardiner@bajobs.com

Jobs: **Yes** Cost to post jobs: **Fee** Cost to see jobs: **Free**	
Resumes: **No** Cost to post resumes: **N/A** Cost to see resumes: **N/A**	
E-mail Alert (Push): **N/A**	
Specialty: **All**	
Industry: **All**	
Feature: N/A	
Location: **US/CA/SF**	

BAJobs is the "San Francisco Bay Area and Silicon Valley Employment/Job Search" site which allows employers to post positions for $90 for a 45-day run. Job seekers can either use the search engine or scroll down the jobs or check out an index of companies to find their next employer. Links to local area information are also available. Simple and easy-to- navigate site.

Bakery-Net

www.bakery-net.com

Steve Percifield, Profit.Net, Inc.
1716 Coach Drive, Naperville, IL 60565
Ph: 630-778-6092   Fax: 630-778-6086   E-mail: steve@bakery-net.com

Jobs: **Yes** Cost to post jobs: **Free** Cost to see jobs: **Free**	
Resumes: **Yes** Cost to post resumes: **Free** Cost to see resumes: **Free**	
E-mail Alert (Push): **Yes**	
Specialty: **Food/Bakery**	
Industry: **Consumer Products**	
Feature: N/A	
Location: **US**	

To get a rise out of **Bakery-Net**, employers who are members of their association can post jobs for free. Be prepared to be asked many questions regarding your affiliation with the industry if you register. A chatroom has recently been added to this site.

Be the Boss

www.betheboss.com

TMP Worldwide

E-mail: btbfeedback@betheboss.com

Jobs: **Yes** Cost to post jobs: **Fee** Cost to see jobs: **Free**	
Resumes: **No** Cost to post resumes: N/A Cost to see resumes: N/A	
E-mail Alert (Push): N/A	
Specialty: **All**	
Industry: **All**	
Feature: **Franchise**	
Location: **US**	

Entrepreneurs will certainly find **Be the Boss** a helpful source of information about owning your own business. Browse among 80 franchise types of businesses. For those who are tired of the corporate rat race and are wondering what all that money you have from your "early out" will buy, check out **Be the Boss.** Outplacement firms will all bookmark this spot.

Benefit News Online

www.benefitnews.com/career.html

Pery Serwitz, 1483 Chain Bridge Road
Suite 202, Mclean, VA 22101
Ph: 703-448-0336   Fax: 703-448-0270   E-mail: info@benefitnews.com

Jobs: **Yes**	
Cost to post jobs: **Fee**	
Cost to see jobs: **Free**	
Resumes: **Yes**	
Cost to post resumes: **Free**	
Cost to see resumes: **Free**	
E-mail Alert (Push): N/A	
Specialty: **Human Resources Benefits**	
Industry: **All**	
Feature: **Jobs Wanted**	
Location: **US**	

This specialty magazine in the Thompson publishing stable has a simple and elegant list of openings from its publication as well as a unique "jobs wanted" section that is well-thought-out. If you are looking for a benefits position or to add a person to your staff you have everything to gain, little to lose.

BenefitsLink

www.benefitslink.com/

David Rhett Parker,
1014 East Robinson Street, Orlando, FL 32801
Ph: 407-841-3717   Fax: 407-841-3054   E-mail: erisa@benefitslink.com

Jobs: **Yes** Cost to post jobs: **Fee** Cost to see jobs: **Free**
Resumes: **Yes** Cost to post resumes: **Free** Cost to see resumes: **Free**
E-mail Alert (Push): **Job Seeker**
Specialty: **Human Resources** **Benefits**
Industry: **All**
Feature: N/A
Location: **US**

Benefits positions are now listed at this well-know resource for the benefits profession. The cost for recruiters to post an opening is $150 for a 60-day listing. With their "Agent," **BenefitsLink** will Push job content out to over 999 job seekers who had registered at the time of our visit. Their FAQ message board, where questions can be posted—and answers found—regarding the latest benefit regulations, is one of the best on the net. **BenefitsLink** also offers helpful articles and a resume database. By providing quality tools to attract professionals, this site has become one of the best in its class.

Welcome to the free nationwide (USA) Internet link to information and services for employers sponsoring employee benefit plans, companies providing products and services for plans, and participating employees.

Best Internet Recruiter

www.bestrecruit.com

Best Software
888 Executive Center Dr. W., Suite 300, St. Petersburg, FL 33702
Ph: 813-579-1111

Jobs: **No** Cost to post jobs: N/A Cost to see jobs: N/A	
Resumes: **No** Cost to post resumes: N/A Cost to see resumes: N/A	
E-mail Alert (Push): N/A	
Specialty: **All**	
Industry: **All**	
Feature: **Multiple Job Posting**	
Location: **US/Int'l**	

Internet Recruiter claims employers can quickly and conveniently place job listings on some of the Internet's "better known" employment sites (OCC, CareerWeb, Classifieds 2000, 4Work, JobBank USA and JobOptions), and then select and analyze resumes submitted for those jobs. Employers enter job listings once, and the site will place the listings on the desired recruiting boards. Applicants e-mail their resumes to the Best Internet Recruiter, where they are stored and organized. We like the fact that users pay only the actual advertising fees to the job listing sites. The **Internet Recruiter** handles all of the billing for the job list sites, providing the customer with a simple statement of charges.

Best Jobs USA

www.bestjobsusa.com

Susan Bell, Recourse Communications, Inc.
1655 Palm Beach Lakes Blvd., West Palm Beach, FL 33401
Ph: 561-686-6800   Fax: 561-686-7632   E-mail: rci@bestjobsusa.com

Jobs: **Yes** Cost to post jobs: **Fee** Cost to see jobs: **Free**	
Resumes: **Yes** Cost to post resumes: **Free** Cost to see resumes: **Fee**	
E-mail Alert (Push): **Yes**	
Specialty: **All**	
Industry: **All**	
Feature: N/A	
Location: **US/Int'l/India/Germany**	

Positions that are published in *USA Today*, several IT, sales and other publications allied with this owner under the banner of "Employment Review," are listed on this web site. Cost for recruiters to post is $150 per position, and the job can stay up until you fill it. Viewing resumes is $250 per month. An extensive listing of newsgroups by function/state, where job seekers can post their resumes, is an added feature. Interesting links to best places to live in the U.S. are also available.

Bilingual-Jobs

www.bilingual-jobs.com

Wilson Lee, ICG Consulting Partners
P.O. Box 34069, Department 185, Seattle, WA 98124
Ph: 888-221-5375   Fax: 212-504-8099   E-mail: manager@bilingual-jobs.com

Jobs: **Yes**	
Cost to post jobs: **Fee**	
Cost to see jobs: **Free**	
Resumes: **Yes**	
Cost to post resumes: **Free**	
Cost to see resumes: **Fee**	
E-mail Alert (Push): **Job Seeker**	
Specialty: **All**	
Industry: **All**	
Feature: N/A	
Location: **Int'l/Canada/Japan (US)**	

This site's focus on bilingual careers in the technology and finance/banking related industries is a niche that could benefit from more marketing. Their "Push" methodology delivers bilingual career openings directly to job seekers via e-mail. Resumes are forwarded by interested job seekers to the site's database for employers to view. Recruiters pay $500 if they only want one posting or $200 per position (min. two postings for six months), which includes the ability to search their resume database. Individuals must be fluent in English and a second language. A program which pays $150 for referring applicants who are hired is available, but we have concerns about these practices generally. Communication, not content, is what is important at **Bilingual-Jobs**.

Bio Online

www.bio.com

John D. Turkel, Vitadata Corporation
2855 Telegraph Ave., Suite 210, Berkeley, CA 94705
Ph: 510-548-1171   Fax: 510-548-1173   E-mail: john@bio.com

Jobs: **Yes**	
Cost to post jobs: **Fee**	
Cost to see jobs: **Free**	
Resumes: **Yes**	
Cost to post resumes: **Free**	
Cost to see resumes: **Fee**	
E-mail Alert (Push): N/A	
Specialty: **Science/Bio**	
Industry: **Biotechnology** **Pharmaceuticals**	
Feature: N/A	
Location: **US**	

Supported by over a dozen major players including Wyeth-Ayerst and Baxter, **Bio Online** has carved a visible niche for itself in the bio-tech industry. Extensive industry content is available, searchable and constantly updated. Individual job postings are $145 for a month. A career forum has been created to share life sciences information. **Bio Online's** online application form makes it easy for the job seeker, and has excellent controls for confidentiality and distribution.

BIOCareer Employment Center

www.biocareer.com

Biotechnology Industry Organization
SciWeb, P.O. Box 7119, Menlo Park, CA 94026
Ph: 650-854-6272   Fax: 650-854-6287   E-mail: sales@biocareer.co

Jobs: **Yes**	
Cost to post jobs: **Fee**	
Cost to see jobs: **Free**	
Resumes: **No**	
Cost to post resumes: N/A	
Cost to see resumes: N/A	
E-mail Alert (Push): N/A	
Specialty: **Science**	
Industry: **Pharm-Bio**	
Feature: N/A	
Location: **US**	

The Biotechnology Industry Organization and SciWeb have created this growing site for job seekers in the biotechnology industry. Search engine based on keywords lacked some of the features of better sites and had a few problems narrowing the search to specific companies and locations. Salary survey and online discussion boards are worth a visit. Good attempt, and we expect rapid improvement and plans for a resume database to be implemented.

Bioscience and Medicine

linkage.rockefeller.edu/hum-molgen/index.html

Kai Garlipp, The Netherlands Opthalmic Res. Inst.
P.O. Box 12141, 1100 AL, Amsterdam, The Netherlands
E-mail: see notes

Jobs: **Yes**	
Cost to post jobs: **Free**	
Cost to see jobs: **Free**	
Resumes: **Yes**	
Cost to post resumes: **Free**	
Cost to see resumes: **Free**	
E-mail Alert (Push): N/A	
Specialty: **Ed/Science/ Bioscience**	
Industry: **Higher Education**	
Feature: N/A	
Location: **Int'l/US**	

With over 4,000 professionals in the human molecular genetics field on a subscriber mailing list, employers may want to e-mail for more information about this option by sending a request to: garlipp@informatik.uni-rostock.de (there is also a mail form at the site). Positions have been listed here for universities and corporations all over the world.

BioSpace Career Center

www.biospace.com/sd/career

Timothy Fredel, Synergistic Designs, Inc.
Attn: BioSpace Career Center, 594 Howard Street, Suite 400, San Francisco, CA 94105
Ph: 415-977-1600   Fax: 415-977-1606   E-mail: missioncontrol@biospace.com

Jobs: **Yes**	
Cost to post jobs: **Fee**	
Cost to see jobs: **Free**	
Resumes: **No**	
Cost to post resumes: N/A	
Cost to see resumes: N/A	
E-mail Alert (Push): N/A	
Specialty: **Science/Bio**	
Industry: **Pharm-Bio**	
Feature: N/A	
Location: **Int'l/US**	

Over 40 corporations have signed on to post their open positions in bio sciences fields. Job postings can be viewed through the site's search engine by region and by job category. Direct contact information is available (they emphasize that job seekers should refer to the posting's "ad code" when they reply). Employer cost is $120 per posting for four weeks. Visitors can post the stock symbol for their favorite companies, and the stock information will appear. An attractive touch for an industry in constant change.

BIS Careers/Employment

bisinc.com/pronet/ccc

Buck Information Systems
22 Orchard Hill, Hamilton, Ontario, Canada L8P 2V8
Ph: 800-355-2066   Fax: 905-777-0383   E-mail: careers@bisinc.com

Jobs: **Yes**	
Cost to post jobs: **Fee**	
Cost to see jobs: **Free**	
Resumes: **Yes**	
Cost to post resumes: **Free**	
Cost to see resumes: **Fee**	
E-mail Alert (Push): **Both**	
Specialty: **All**	
Industry: **All**	
Feature: N/A	
Location: **Int'l/Canada/US**	

BIS Careers/Employment has taken over Pro Net Search, and this site now posts all types of positions throughout the world. Employers can get a $29 trial posting (regular price is $85). Site charges an additional $25 if you want your post to be blind. Other packages are available. Job seekers click on the job function of their choice (only highlighted functions have jobs), and then connect to the country and or state of the site's posted positions. Jobs can be viewed by U.S., Canada or International locations. Site will also pre-screen resumes and e-mail them to employers for a fee. Job seekers can register and "Career Alert" will e-mail new opportunities to them each week.

The Black Collegian Online

www.blackcollegian.com

Penny Francis, Black Collegiate Service, Inc.
140 Carondelet Street, New Orleans, LA 70130
Ph: 504-523-0154   Fax: 504-523-0271   E-mail: penny@black-collegiate.com

Jobs: **Yes** Cost to post jobs: **Fee** Cost to see jobs: **Free**	This is the electronic version of the *Black Collegian*, a national career opportunities publication. Employers post jobs for $150 or obtain an annual membership for unlimited postings. The resume database allows students and professionals to post their backgrounds (in confidence if they wish). Interesting career articles for the recent college graduate are well-written and on-target. Site also offers statistics/predictions of expected new hires by corporation. (See its sister site- Minorities Job Bank.)
Resumes: **Yes** Cost to post resumes: **Free** Cost to see resumes: **Fee**	
E-mail Alert (Push): N/A	
Specialty: **All**	
Industry: **All**	
Feature: **Diversity**	
Location: **US**	

Black Data Processing Assoc. Online

www.bdpa.org

Rudy Duke, Black Data Processing Association
1111 14th Street NW, Suite 700, Washington, DC 20005
Ph: 800-727-2372   Fax: 202-789-1592   E-mail: rudy_duke@hunter-group.com

Jobs: Cost to post jobs: N/A Cost to see jobs: N/A	A new home page design brings the **Black Data Processing Association** into the future for their members. Link from this national site to the local chapters to find (or post) job listings. Employers should certainly investigate web advertising opportunities here. Career fairs and information about the BDPA national conference are available.
Resumes: Cost to post resumes: N/A Cost to see resumes: N/A	
E-mail Alert (Push): N/A	
Specialty: **IT**	
Industry: **All**	
Feature: **Diversity**	
Location: **US**	

Black E.O.E Journal

www.blackeoejournal.com/jobsearch.html

Tom Layton, Olive Tree Publishing
22845 Savi Ranch Parkway, Suite H, Yorba Linda, CA 92687
Ph: 800-487-5099   Fax: 714-974-3978   E-mail: publisher@blackeoejournal.com

Jobs: **Yes**
Cost to post jobs: **Fee**
Cost to see jobs: **Free**
Resumes: **Yes**
Cost to post resumes: **Free**
Cost to see resumes: **Fee**
E-mail Alert (Push): **N/A**
Specialty: **N/A**
Industry: **All**
Feature: **Diversity**
Location: **US**

This is an employment magazine which focuses on college and experienced minority professionals. E.O.E. collects resumes from many different sources, and passes on the ones that match to their clients and advertisers. You must place a help-wanted ad in the publication to get the service. The cost for the resume match service is free, and they make sure that everyone who places an ad in their journals receives resumes that match their requirements. A solid search engine allows job seekers to view posted positions.

Black Voices

www.blackvoices.com

Cathy Taylor

Ph: 800-347-6868   Fax: 407-418-5950   E-mail: careers@blackvoices.com

Jobs: **Yes**
Cost to post jobs: **Fee**
Cost to see jobs: **Free**
Resumes: **Yes**
Cost to post resumes: **Free**
Cost to see resumes: **Fee**
E-mail Alert (Push): **N/A**
Specialty: **All**
Industry: **All**
Feature: **Diversity**
Location: **US/FL**

Utilizing a technology that essentially mirrors the jobs posted at an employer's site, visitors to **Black Voices** can search nine major corporations. A chatroom and related business information related to the African American community rounds out this site. Hopefully they will change their pricing policy as sponsorship packages start at significant dollars. Meanwhile, you can post positions individually at $12 each.

Bloomberg Online

www.bloomberg.com/fun/jobs.html

Bloomberg Financial Markets
100 Business Park Drive, P.O. Box 888, Princeton, NJ 08542
Ph: 800-448-5678   E-mail: feedback@bloomberg.com

Jobs: **Yes** Cost to post jobs: **Free** Cost to see jobs: **Free**	With salaries approaching the stratosphere, **Bloomberg Online** is a great place for posting high-level finance positions. Resumes are free. We find it amazing that recruiters can post positions for free—for one week. Jobs are categorized by type of position, although they are listed as "over 5 years" or "under 5 years." This site is impossible to navigate, so bookmark the URL to go direct (someone should tell them about site maps).
Resumes: **Yes** Cost to post resumes: **Free** Cost to see resumes: **Free**	
E-mail Alert (Push): N/A	
Specialty: **Finance/Executive**	
Industry: **Finance**	
Feature: N/A	
Location: **Int'l/US**	

The Blue Line

www.theblueline.com

Checkpoint Press
872 S. Milwaukee Ave., Suite 270, Libertyville, IL 60048
Ph: 800-475-6183   E-mail: kevin@theblueline.com

Jobs: **Yes** Cost to post jobs: **Free** Cost to see jobs: **Free** (See Notes)	**The Blue Line** is a monthly publication for the men and women in uniform—police, fire, EMS, dispatch, corrections and administrative positions. Jobs are free to see, but job seekers are only given a glimpse, and then must pay $59.99 for the magazine. Positions listed are in IL, MI, MO and WI.
Resumes: **No** Cost to post resumes: N/A Cost to see resumes: N/A	
E-mail Alert (Push): N/A	
Specialty: **Law Enforcement**	
Industry: **Law Enforcement**	
Feature: N/A	
Location: **US/MW/IL/MI/MO/WI**	

Boldface Jobs

www.boldfacejobs.com

Tom Martinell
8033 N. 3rd Place, Phoenix, AZ 95020
Ph: 602-861-8982   Fax: 602-861-8992   E-mail: jobs@boldfacejobs.com

Jobs: **Yes** Cost to post jobs: **Fee** Cost to see jobs: **Free**	**Boldface Jobs** is charging $50 for employers to post up to 25 jobs, and their self-service capability allows adding or deleting positions at any time. Initial postings are free for 30 days. All jobs and resumes are dated. A well-designed home page and search engine facilitates navigation for even novice job seekers. Nearly a free site, recruiters are taking notice.
Resumes: **Yes** Cost to post resumes: **Free** Cost to see resumes: **Free**	
E-mail Alert (Push): N/A	
Specialty: **All**	
Industry: N/A	
Feature: N/A	
Location: **US**	

Boston Globe

www.boston.com

Walter Coffey, Boston Globe Electronic Publishing
320 Congress Street, Boston, MA 02210
Ph: 617-929-3107   Fax: 617-929-7026   E-mail: wcoffey@boston.com

Jobs: **Yes** Cost to post jobs: **Fee** Cost to see jobs: **Free**	Job seekers can search help-wanted classifieds for this major Northeastern paper the prior three Sundays. This publisher also participates in CareerPath. com (see CareerPath. com)
Resumes: **Yes** Cost to post resumes: **Free** Cost to see resumes: **Fee**	
E-mail Alert (Push): N/A	
Specialty: **All**	
Industry: **All**	
Feature: N/A	
Location: **US/NE/MA/Boston**	

Boston Herald JobFind

www.jobfind.com

Herald Interactive Advertising Inc.
300 Harrison Avenue, Boston, MA 02109
Ph: 617-426-4545   Fax: 617-426-1208   E-mail: jobfind@jobfind.com

Jobs: **Yes** Cost to post jobs: **Fee** Cost to see jobs: **Free**	
Resumes: **Yes** Cost to post resumes: **Free** Cost to see resumes: **Fee**	
E-mail Alert (Push): **N/A**	
Specialty: **All**	
Industry: **All**	
Feature: **N/A**	
Location: **US/NE**	

The Boston Herald continues to provide an interesting option in the Boston marketplace with their **Jobfind** service. This site offers to store candidate resumes on a confidential database and let you respond to selected jobs. Employers pay $100 for 1–3 postings and $75 for each additional position without requiring an ad in their publication's print edition. Crazy move long term—but while they do it, use it. Recruiters can view their resume database for $750/month or $1,500/quarter. An interesting resume search feature is that once a recruiter selects their criterion, they can save it and retrieve it on another visit. A weekly career-related newsletter is available via e-mail if you choose to subscribe.

Boston Job Bank

www.bostonjobs.com

Charles Jukiewicz, Jr., Information Unlimited
110 Church Street, Westwood, MA 02090
E-mail: info@bostonjobs.com

Jobs: **Yes** Cost to post jobs: **Fee** Cost to see jobs: **Free**	
Resumes: **Yes** Cost to post resumes: **Free** Cost to see resumes: **Free**	
E-mail Alert (Push): **N/A**	
Specialty: **All**	
Industry: **All**	
Feature: **N/A**	
Location: **US/NE/MA/Boston**	

Several years ago, the site owner simply asked for $20 from each employer to post a job for four weeks, and in good faith, posted the openings he received prior to getting paid. He's still doing it! Use the self-service form, and don't forget to send a check. Job seekers can post their resumes and recruiters can view them—all for free. This is the job site version of shareware.

Boston Search.com

www.bostonseach.com

Thomas McGoldrick, 221 W. Newton Street
Boston, MA 02116
Ph: 617-266-2707   Fax: 617-266-0939   E-mail: tom@bostonsearch.com

Jobs: **Yes** Cost to post jobs: **Fee** Cost to see jobs: **Free**	
Resumes: **Yes** Cost to post resumes: **Free** Cost to see resumes: **Fee**	
E-mail Alert (Push): **Employer**	
Specialty: **All**	
Industry: **All**	
Feature: N/A	
Location: **US/E/MA/Boston**	

BostonSearch.com is a regional site that will post employer openings for 45 days for $70 each. For an additional fee of $750 the site's owners will review all resumes in their online database, utilize their "specialized recruitment strategies" (whatever that is), and forward all candidates that match for 30 days. Recruiter "agents" will soon enjoy their day in the sun, but it will have to cover more than a single site.

Branch Out

www.branchout.com

David Ronick, Brainstorm Interactive
150 Fifth Avenue, Suite 216, New York, NY 10011
Ph: 212-627-0059   Fax: 212-208-4453   E-mail: feedback@branchout.com

Jobs: **Yes** Cost to post jobs: **Fee** Cost to see jobs: **Free**	
Resumes: **No** Cost to post resumes: N/A Cost to see resumes: N/A	
E-mail Alert (Push): **Job Seeker**	
Specialty: **All**	
Industry: **All**	
Feature: N/A	
Location: **US**	

Branch Out is a unique site. For individuals who have attended either, Brown, Yale, Duke, Stanford, Harvard, MIT, Dartmouth, Penn, Columbia, U. of Chicago, Berkeley, Cornell, Princeton, Michigan or Northwestern, this is a place where these colleges' graduates can connect and share information. From **Branch Out**, you can find jobs and other classifieds for buying/selling just about anything. A yellow pages for finding people in areas of common interest (that are alumni/ae of course) is a great tool for networking. Employers can post jobs for a $100 each (two free postings). Positions are kept on the site for four weeks. This is a brilliant "community" model that others will emulate and has powerful possibilities for the future.

Brave New Work World

www.newwork.com

Gary Johnson
New York News
E-mail: gjohnson@pclink.com

Jobs: **Yes** Cost to post jobs: N/A Cost to see jobs: N/A	
Resumes: **No** Cost to post resumes: N/A Cost to see resumes: N/A	
E-mail Alert (Push): N/A	
Specialty: **All**	
Industry: **All**	
Feature: N/A	
Location: **US**	

Brave New Work World collects articles from major publications all over the world on work-related issues. The information is updated on a daily basis with a synopsis of each article and a link to the document. Some very challenging ideas and concepts are addressed—from "discrimination in the workforce" to "where have all the hi-tech workers gone?." A career management site with a difference.

BridgePath Employment Services

www.bridgepath.com

Auren Hoffman
2560 Bancroft Way, Suite 209, Berkeley, CA 94704
Ph: 415-512-1900   Fax: 415-512-1961   E-mail: auren@bridgepath.com

Jobs: **Yes** Cost to post jobs: **Fee** Cost to see jobs: **Free**	
Resumes: **Yes** Cost to post resumes: **Free** Cost to see resumes: **Fee**	
E-mail Alert (Push): **Job Seeker**	
Specialty: **College**	
Industry: **All**	
Feature: N/A	
Location: **US**	

BridgePath has collected thousands of e-mail addresses of college students and experienced professionals with up to ten years of experience. For $225 per posting, employers can post job announcements which are then sent within 24 hours via e-mail to matching applicants. **BridgePath** will also pre-screen candidates for $1,200 and submit a slate of 7–15 candidates.

BRINT (@BRINT)

www.brint.com

US Government

E-mail: feedback@brint.con

Jobs: **No** Cost to post jobs: N/A Cost to see jobs: N/A	Job seekers and recruiters use the Knowledge Management Think Tank to find links to any business subject you could imagine. An online Q&A allows individuals to ask questions and pose answers. Search engine allows you to get right to the issue you want. All information is dated. Well-done and worth a visit.

Jobs: **No**
Cost to post jobs: N/A
Cost to see jobs: N/A

Resumes: **No**
Cost to post resumes: N/A
Cost to see resumes: N/A

E-mail Alert (Push): N/A

Specialty: N/A

Industry: **All**

Feature: **Research**

Location: **US**

Job seekers and recruiters use the Knowledge Management Think Tank to find links to any business subject you could imagine. An online Q&A allows individuals to ask questions and pose answers. Search engine allows you to get right to the issue you want. All information is dated. Well-done and worth a visit.

Bullseye Job Shop

interoz.com/usr/gcbristow

E-mail: gcbristow@interoz.com

Jobs: **No**
Cost to post jobs: N/A
Cost to see jobs: N/A

Resumes: **No**
Cost to post resumes: N/A
Cost to see resumes: N/A

E-mail Alert (Push): N/A

Specialty: N/A

Industry: N/A

Feature: **Meta-links**

Location: **US**

Links, links and more links. Usenet resources and listservs are also available.

BusinessWeek Online Career Center

www.businessweek.com/careers/index.html

BusinessWeek Magazine
New York, NY
Ph: 888-841-8013

Jobs: **Yes**	
Cost to post jobs: **Fee**	
Cost to see jobs: **Free**	
Resumes: **No**	
Cost to post resumes: N/A	
Cost to see resumes: N/A	
E-mail Alert (Push): **Job Seeker**	
Specialty: **Executive**	
Industry: **All**	
Feature: N/A	
Location: **US**	

BusinessWeek Online Career Center allows employers to post positions for a fee to this site, although we are not sure if there is a print version. Job seekers can view positions through the site's search engine, which includes many options for search criterion. Registering skills and e-mailing the site will "push" opportunities to the job seeker. Hundreds of jobs were listed, and a map helped to pinpoint their locations. We especially liked the section "who's hiring," which shows links to hundreds of corporations. Slick and easy.

Cal State Univ. Employ. Board Job Hunt

csueb.sfsu.edu/jobs.html

San Francisco State Career Center
E-mail: csujobs@sfsu.edu

Jobs: **No**	
Cost to post jobs: N/A	
Cost to see jobs: N/A	
Resumes: **No**	
Cost to post resumes: N/A	
Cost to see resumes: N/A	
E-mail Alert (Push): N/A	
Specialty: College	
Industry: **All**	
Feature: **Meta-links**	
Location: **US**	

California State University Employment Board Job Hunt (formerly webdog's Job Hunt) includes a meta-list of links for job and career information for graduating students. We especially liked the link list for the San Francisco Bay Area. We wonder why they changed their name?

California Journalism Job Bank

www.cxne.org/csne/postingfees.html

Becky Day, California Society of Newspaper Editors

Ph: 510-337-1832   E-mail: beckyday@csne.org

Jobs: **Yes** Cost to post jobs: **Fee** Cost to see jobs: **Free**	
Resumes: **No** Cost to post resumes: N/A Cost to see resumes: N/A	
E-mail Alert (Push): N/A	
Specialty: **Communications/ Journalism**	
Industry: **All**	
Feature: N/A	
Location: **US/MW/CA**	

California Journalism Job Bank posts jobs for its members for free while non-members pay $25/$60 if outside California and Nevada. There were several dozen positions posted from associate editors to reporters. All jobs have posting dates and direct contact data.

Career Action Center

www.csne.org/jobs/postings.html

10420 Bubb Road, Suite 100, Cupertino, CA 95014
Ph: 408-253-3200   Fax: 408-257-6400   E-mail: info_request@careeraction.org

Jobs: **No** Cost to post jobs: N/A Cost to see jobs: N/A	
Resumes: **No** Cost to post resumes: N/A Cost to see resumes: N/A	
E-mail Alert (Push): N/A	
Specialty: **All**	
Industry: **All**	
Feature: N/A	
Location: **US/W/CA**	

Career Action Center has been providing first-class services in career counseling for the last 24 years. Online activities include: career self-assessment, marketing, career fitness etc. The center posts a listing of workshops. If you need help in getting your career back on track, visit CAC. Annual memberships are $145 which includes a 50-minute counseling session.

Career America

www.careeramerica.com

Cheryl Wayne, Phoenix Professionals
P.O. Box 4081, Mammouth Lakes, CA 93546
Ph: 619-934-3566   Fax: 619-934-1838   E-mail: technet@qnet.com

Jobs: **Yes** Cost to post jobs: **Fee** Cost to see jobs: **Free**
Resumes: **Yes** Cost to post resumes: **Fee** Cost to see resumes: N/A
E-mail Alert (Push): N/A
Specialty: **All**
Industry: **All**
Feature: **Yes**
Location: **US**

This site is owned by a recruitment agency that charges job seekers $25 to post a resume. They also charge employers $15 to post a position for three months. You can search jobs by state or employers.

Career Avenue

www.careeravenue.com

Internet Advertising, Inc.
1H 10 West, Suite 291, San Antonio, TX 78230
Ph: 800-279-6540   Fax: 210-979-6540   E-mail: info@iads.com

Jobs: **Yes** Cost to post jobs: **Fee** Cost to see jobs: **Free**
Resumes: **Yes** Cost to post resumes: **Free** Cost to see resumes: **Fee**
E-mail Alert (Push): N/A
Specialty: **All**
Industry: **All**
Feature: N/A
Location: **US**

Career Avenue is worth a stroll as an inexpensive ($30) buy for three months of unlimited job postings, especially because only "members" can search the resume database. K's Resume Service is an excellent added feature with career articles. Job seekers can post their resume for six months for free. Search engine works well for finding jobs, but the site needs help formatting job information text. Date of job posting is listed.

Career Babe

www.careerbabe.com

Fran Quittel, P.O. Box 8668
Emeryville, CA 94608
Ph: 415-281-5981   Fax: 510-653-0260   E-mail: careerbabe@msn.com

Jobs: **No** Cost to post jobs: N/A Cost to see jobs: N/A	Fran Quittel's **Career Babe** is one of the sites that will woo more job seekers into carefully thinking about their future and provide them with solid career advice through the articles at the site. Fran writes for major publications (*Washington Post, Fast Co. Magazine* etc). She provides free e-mail advice to all who ask for help. A great piece on writing your resume comes with excellent recommendations.
Resumes: **No** Cost to post resumes: N/A Cost to see resumes: N/A	
E-mail Alert (Push): N/A	
Specialty: **All**	
Industry: **All**	
Feature: N/A	
Location: **US**	

Career Board

www.careerboard.com

Denise P. Geisler, Career Board
27600 Chagrin Blvd, Cleveland, Ohio 44122
Ph: 216-595-2200   Fax: 216-595-2227   E-mail: dgeisler@careerboard.com

Jobs: **Yes** Cost to post jobs: **Fee** Cost to see jobs: **Free**	**Career Board** is a regional niche job site showcasing opportunities in the Cleveland and Akron Ohio areas. Jobs are posted with direct contact information which is unique for a placement agency. Employer cost to post a job is $75 or $350 per month for unlimited postings and access to the resume database. Employers receive e-mail reports on hit volume. Date of posting is also listed. If you place your resume on the site you can e-mail it to any web site of your choosing. Job seekers can elect to have openings Pushed to their e-mail address. Owned by a placement agency who seems to be positively playing both sides of the fence.
Resumes: **Yes** Cost to post resumes: **Free** Cost to see resumes: **Fee**	
E-mail Alert (Push): **Job Seeker**	
Specialty: **All**	
Industry: **All**	
Feature: N/A	
Location: **US/MW/OH**	

Career Bridge

www.careerbridge.com

Josef Raffai, CareerBridge Corporation
360 Albert St, Ottawa, Ontario, Canada
Ph: 613-236-2263   Fax: 613-236-9819   E-mail: gerrys@careerbridge.com

Jobs: **Yes** Cost to post jobs: **Fee** Cost to see jobs: **Free**	
Resumes: **Yes** Cost to post resumes: **Yes** Cost to see resumes: **Fee**	
E-mail Alert (Push): N/A	
Specialty: **All**	
Industry: **All**	
Feature: N/A	
Location: **Int'l/Canada**	

Canadian-based site that states it has web-based software for global job posting, resume handling and workflow management. We found some difficulty in finding information here on what the products can actually do or what they cost. Typical of sites raising high expectations with minimal disclosure.

CareerBuilder

www.careerbuilder.com

Jennifer Giles, CareerBuilder, Inc.
11495 Sunset Hills Road, Reston, VA 20190
Ph: 703-709-1001   Fax: 703-471-4596   E-mail: info@netstartinc.com

Jobs: **Yes**	
Cost to post jobs: **Fee**	
Cost to see jobs: **Free**	
Resumes: **Yes**	
Cost to post resumes: **Free**	
Cost to see resumes: **N/A**	
E-mail Alert (Push): **Job Seeker**	
Specialty: **All**	
Industry: **All**	
Feature: **N/A**	
Location: **US/Int'l/Europe/ Asia/Canada**	

CareerBuilder is a much more than a job and resume posting site. Employers using **CareerBuilder's** system have access to a set of web-enabled recruiting tools that begins with company Intranet and Internet Templates, provides multiple posting options to nearly two dozen web sites in addition to **CareerBuilder,** and manages the resume search and applicant tracking for resumes that come in through the site. Job seekers who visit **CareerBuilder** complete a short online form specifying areas of interest, location, salary etc. When new jobs are posted that fit specific requirements, job seekers are notified via e-mail. When we registered though, we selected specific salary levels, but the jobs received ranged well beyond what we specified. Allied with a powerful marketing engine, ADP, **CareerBuilder** has significant potential. We think their price for multiple posting services needs reworking to be competitive.

Career Buzz

www.careerbuzz.com

Kurt Schwartz, Success Advertising
3 Regent Street, Suite 304, Livingston, NJ 07039
Ph: 888-784-6487   E-mail: info@careerbuzz.com

Jobs: **Yes** Cost to post jobs: **Fee** Cost to see jobs: **Free**	
Resumes: **Yes** Cost to post resumes: **Free** Cost to see resumes: N/A	
E-mail Alert (Push): **Job Seeker**	
Specialty: **All**	
Industry: **All**	
Feature: N/A	
Location: **US**	

Want to have some fun while you are looking for your next opportunity? Trivia contests, complete with prizes awarded by corporate sponsors, make this site fun to visit. **Career Buzz** will Push jobs to you via e-mail when you register your field of interest. You can also use their search engine to go directly to your job of choice. Jobs are posted for 60 days for $25 each. Other packages are available.

CareerCast

www.careercast.com

Rick Miller
Ph: 760-431-9641   E-mail: rick@careercast.com

Jobs: **Yes** Cost to post jobs: **Fee** Cost to see jobs: **Free**	
Resumes: **Yes** Cost to post resumes: **Free** Cost to see resumes: **Fee**	
E-mail Alert (Push): N/A	
Specialty: **All**	
Industry: **All**	
Feature: N/A	
Location: **US**	

CareerCast's technology is a major convenience to employers who post all their openings on their corporate web site. For a reasonable monthly or annual fee, **CareerCast** will "copy" all of the corporate openings and include them in their database. Job seekers who are targeting multiple companies using **CareerCast**, can conduct a thorough search from this single site. Candidates link directly to the job description page. Fast, easy to navigate and targeted, **CareerCast** provides a viable solution. The site also allows jobs in newsgroups to be searched. Participating employers can search the resume database.

Career Center for Workforce Diversity

www.eop.com

John Miller, EOP, Inc.
150 Motor Pkwy, Hauppauge, NY 11788
Ph: 516-421-9421   E-mail: eopub@aol.com

Jobs: **Yes**	
Cost to post jobs: **Fee**	
Cost to see jobs: **Free**	
Resumes: **No**	
Cost to post resumes: N/A	
Cost to see resumes: N/A	
E-mail Alert (Push): N/A	
Specialty: **All**	
Industry: **All**	
Feature: **Diversity**	
Location: **US**	

Owner publishes *Equal Opportunity, Women Engineer, Minority Engineer, Careers and the Disabled* and *Workforce Diversity* magazines. All help-wanted advertisers are supplied free links to their site. Solid, helpful articles regarding the world of workforce diversity. A listing of diversity career fairs across the country is available.

CareerCentral

www.careercentral.com

Jeffrey Hyman, Career Central Corporation
3500 West Bayshore, Palo Alto, CA 94303
Ph: 800-932-4668   Fax: 888-671-8159   E-mail: jeff@careercentral.com

Jobs: **Yes**	
Cost to post jobs: **Fee**	
Cost to see jobs: **Free**	
Resumes: **Yes**	
Cost to post resumes: **Free**	
Cost to see resumes: **Fee**	
E-mail Alert (Push): **Yes**	
Specialty: **College/MBAs/IT**	
Industry: **All**	
Feature: N/A	
Location: **US/Europe/ Latin America/Asia**	

CareerCentral is expanding beyond its beginning as a niche site for MBAs. Employers post their requirements, and job seekers are then sent an e-mail when there is a match. If the candidate is interested, they can then send their resume via e-mail (or snail mail). **Career-Central** does not store resumes, but they have collected thousands of e-mails. Recruiters pay $1,995 for an initial search of MBA graduates or $2,995 for experienced professionals. Candidates are presented in five business days. Site guarantees ten interested candidates who match your specifications, or no fee is charged. Recent alliance with CareerMosaic should make things interesting for the future.

Career City

www.careercity.com

Richard Ashidian, Adams Media Corporation
260 Center Street, Holbrook, MA 02343
Ph: 800-872-5627   Fax: 617-767-2055   E-mail: info@careercity.com

Jobs: **Yes**
Cost to post jobs: **Fee**
Cost to see jobs: **Free**
Resumes: **Yes**
Cost to post resumes: **Free**
Cost to see resumes: **Fee**
E-mail Alert (Push): N/A
Specialty: **All/College**
Industry: **All**
Feature: N/A
Location: **US**

Career City is a "Career Hub" with a full array of services for the job seeker and employer. The site search engine is fast and effective, providing multiple search options. **Career City** claims over 3,500 companies have posted jobs. Searches can be split between corporations and third party recruitment organizations. Resumes can be posted electronically and are kept for four months. Career articles are helpful, and an HR Center includes examples of employment letters. Content adds real value. Recruiters pay $150 to post a job for 90 days, and other pricing packages are available. Resumes can be viewed for $490 a quarter or $1,390 per year.

Career Connect

www.theglobeandmail.com/careerconnect

Toronto Globe and Mail
444 Front Street West, Toronto, Ontario, Canada M5V 2S9
E-mail: careerconnect@globeandmail.ca

Jobs: **Yes**	
Cost to post jobs: **Fee**	
Cost to see jobs: **Free**	
Resumes: **Yes**	
Cost to post resumes: **Free**	
Cost to see resumes: **Fee**	
E-mail Alert (Push): **Job Seeker**	
Specialty: **All**	
Industry: **All**	
Feature: N/A	
Location: **Int'l/Canada**	

Career Connect is a Canadian site from the publisher of *The Globe and Mail*, Canada's national newspaper. Costs to post or see resumes run from $550 to $1,375 per month depending on the package you select. Site's search engine makes it easy to navigate. You can view all of the ads from the newspaper by date of publication or title. Interesting career articles can also be viewed from the web site. With the job seeker's ability to register for jobs to be "Pushed" to them via e-mail, this is one place in Canada we would automatically visit.

The Career Connection

www.connectme.com

David Garther, Getwork Network, Inc.
1094 Cudahy Street, Suite 206, San Diego, CA 92110
Ph: 800-780-7810   Fax: 619-275-0099   E-mail: david@connectme.com

Jobs: **Yes**	
Cost to post jobs: **Free**	
Cost to see jobs:	
Resumes: **No**	
Cost to post resumes: N/A	
Cost to see resumes: N/A	
E-mail Alert (Push): N/A	
Specialty: **All**	
Industry: **All**	
Feature: N/A	
Location: **US**	

The Career Connection is a labor of love, as the site's owner allows job seekers and recruiters to post and view jobs for free. The site's search engine allows job seekers to view all positions by topic or state. Hundreds of opportunities are listed with direct contact information in an easy-to-read format. All are date posted.

Career Espresso/Emory University

www.sph.emory.edu/studentservice/Career.html

John Youngblood Jr.
Emory University Career Services
E-mail: jyoungb@sph.emory.edu

Jobs: **Yes**	
Cost to post jobs: **Free**	
Cost to see jobs: **Free**	
Resumes: **No**	
Cost to post resumes: N/A	
Cost to see resumes: N/A	
E-mail Alert (Push): N/A	
Specialty: **HC/Public Health**	
Industry: **Government**	
Feature: **Meta-links**	
Location: **US/Int'l**	

Career Espresso is a finely-brewed cyberdrink that stands out from the standard fare on most college campuses. The owner has added a jobs page for public-sector healthcare graduates and professionals. You can find jobs by country, state, city, title, organization, date etc. When you find what you want, all have complete descriptions and contact information. Link from here to other potential public health sites and to the Internship Exchange. A satisfying niche web site with a distinctive flavor.

CAREER ESPRESSO!

The Absolute Hottest Public Health Career Search Website Anywhere!

CAREER ESPRESSO is proudly served by:
The Career Action Center
The Rollins School of Public Health

Check out what they're saying about us!

"Simply the finest. Great taste, good froth...who could want more?" - **Juan Valdez**

"Something for everyone. Rich & delightful. White mugs but no white water." - **Hillary**

"A brief visit to this site helped me decide baseball was a bad career move." - **Michael**

CareerExchange

www.careerexchange.com/

Jason Moreau, CorpNet InfoHub Ltd.
Unit E-7950 Huston Road, Delta, B.C., Canada V4G 1C2
Ph: 604-940-2754   Fax: 604-940-2840   E-mail: jobs@careerexchange.com

Jobs: **Yes** Cost to post jobs: **Fee** Cost to see jobs: **Free**	
Resumes: **Yes** Cost to post resumes: **Free** Cost to see resumes: **Fee**	
E-mail Alert (Push): **Job Seeker**	
Specialty: **IT**	
Industry: **All**	
Feature: N/A	
Location: **Int'l/Canada/US**	

CareerExchange lists positions in Canada and the US. Several thousand positions are listed, and their search engine is fast and on target. Job seekers can send their online resume directly to recruiters who advertise here. Positions are primarily in IT areas, but many jobs in other specialties are also available. Employer cost to post jobs is $60 for one job for two months or ten jobs per month for $195. A career chatroom is also available for those who register. New features make this a site that continues to compete.

Career Exposure

www.careerexposure.com

Jan Donnelly, Career Exposure, Inc.
1881 SW Front Avenue, Portland, OR 97201
Ph: 503-525-8498   Fax: 503-525-8497   E-mail: bizmail@careerexposure.com

Jobs: **Yes** Cost to post jobs: **Fee** Cost to see jobs: **Free**	
Resumes: **Yes** Cost to post resumes: **Free** Cost to see resumes: **Fee**	
E-mail Alert (Push): N/A	
Specialty: **All**	
Industry: **All**	
Feature: N/A	
Location: **US/Int'l**	

Career Exposure has job openings from all over the world. Candidates can search by position, company, state or country. Once you find position of interest it is easy to apply online. Recruiters post positions for free. The resume database costs $299 per quarter to view. Interesting business articles can also be found. Site has a career counselor who selects interesting questions and posts answers. Long list of college career center links for information. Lots of added features make this a site to watch. Check out www.careerwomen. com and www.mbacareers. com which are sister sites.

CareerFile

www.careerfile.com

Cynthia Welch
55 A Hurlburt Road, Great Barrington, MA 01230
Ph: 413-528-4769   Fax: 413-528-4735   E-mail: info@careerfile.com

Jobs: **Yes**
Cost to post jobs: **Fee**
Cost to see jobs: **Free**
Resumes: **Yes**
Cost to post resumes: **Free**
Cost to see resumes: **Fee**
E-mail Alert (Push): **Both**
Specialty: **All/Executive**
Industry: N/A
Feature: **N/A**
Location: **US**

CareerFile is a resume library of executive, managerial and technical talent. Employers can browse the site and search through resumes (contact information costs employers $6. 95 each). Job seekers who post their resume will have their skills matched to all positions that have been listed for the last 30 days for free. Great use of technology if you are in the resume hunt. This is another search firm that is utilizing their "excess resume" database.

CareeRGuide

www.careerguide.com

Jared Greenwald, Rich/Gardner Advertising
8215 Roswell Road Building 800, Atlanta, GA 30350
Ph: 770-392-0340   Fax: 770-353-2773   E-mail: jgreenwald@rgadv.com

Jobs: **Yes**
Cost to post jobs: **Fee**
Cost to see jobs: **Free**
Resumes: **Yes**
Cost to post resumes: **Free**
Cost to see resumes: **Fee**
E-mail Alert (Push): N/A
Specialty: **All**
Industry: **All**
Feature: N/A
Location: **US/SE/GA/Atlanta**

CareeRGuide is an online employment resource that focuses on opportunities and companies in Atlanta and the southeast. Search engine allowed us to view their 784 posted jobs with ease. Date of posting and direct contact information are available. Recruiters pay $60 per posting which are up for 30 days. When searching for corporate information the site could find a better way to advise candidates which corporations they have in their database. CareeRGuide claims Atlanta as its hub. Unfortunately, only two corporate profiles were online to view. Applicants can create their resume online, but with limited disclosure about where it will go or how employers will view it.

Career Index

www.careerindex.com

Brian Wachter, Westech
4701 Patrick Henry Drive, #1901, Santa Clara, CA 95054
Ph: 408-970-8800   Fax: 408-980-5103   E-mail: webmaster@vjf.com

Jobs: **Yes** Cost to post jobs: N/A Cost to see jobs: **Free**
Resumes: **No** Cost to post resumes: N/A Cost to see resumes: N/A
E-mail Alert (Push): N/A
Specialty: **All**
Industry: **All**
Feature: N/A
Location: **US/Int'l**

Career Index is a tool to provide job seekers and a selected group of web sites with the potential "end game" in recruiting. Owned by Westech, The Virtual Job Fair folks, job seekers can select as many or as few sites that are listed (20 as of this writing with three search engines), put in their search criteria, and the search engine will take you to a list of direct links to the position selected. The job seeker has to understand that whatever "words" they choose will be reflected in the jobs that come up. The results appear to have no ranking, and the job seeker still has to go through a lot of scrolling and searching. A listing of job sites by country and profession is also available. Good attempt to make life easier for the job seeker.

CareerIndia

www.careerindia.com

Shirley Premsingh, NetKraft
#5 Cornwell Road, Langford Gardens, Bangalore, India 560 025
Ph: 918-022-78845   E-mail: response@careerindia.com

Jobs: **Yes** Cost to post jobs: **Fee** Cost to see jobs: **Free** (See **No**tes)
Resumes: **Yes** Cost to post resumes: **Free** Cost to see resumes: **Fee**
E-mail Alert (Push): **Job Seeker**
Specialty: **IT**
Industry: **All**
Feature: N/A
Location: **Int'l/India**

The **CareerIndia** policy is that you must be a member (post your resume and get an ID) to see jobs. All of this is free for the job seeker who can also have positions "Pushed" to their desktop by registering their e-mail. Employers pay a membership fee of $475 per year to see resumes and post positions. Recruiters can see a profile on candidates without the fee, but must be a member to get the contact information.

CareerIndia concentrates on IT opportunities. The look and feel is a generation behind.

Career Internetworking

www.careerkey.com

Career Internetworking
5255 Yonge Street, Suite 711 P.O. Box 17, North York, Ontario, Canada M2N 6P4
Ph: 416-229-2666   Fax: 416-229-2943   E-mail: career@ican.net

Jobs: **Yes** Cost to post jobs: **Fee** Cost to see jobs: **Free**	
Resumes: **No** Cost to post resumes: N/A Cost to see resumes: N/A	
E-mail Alert (Push): N/A	
Specialty: **All**	
Industry: **All**	
Feature: N/A	
Location: **Int'l/Canada/(US)**	

Career Internetworking provides Canadian-based job opportunities. Recruiters pay $100 to post a position for one month. Other packages are available. Site lists "hot jobs" in a separate page. Search engine needs help as its capability limits you to some provinces and not others. Many links for obtaining information on working in Canada.

CareerLab

www.careerlab.com

William Frank
304 Inverness Way South, Suite 465, Englewood, CO 80112
Ph: 303-790-0505   Fax: 303-790-0606   E-mail: comments@careerlab.com

Jobs: **No** Cost to post jobs: N/A Cost to see jobs: N/A	
Resumes: **No** Cost to post resumes: **Fee** Cost to see resumes: N/A	
E-mail Alert (Push): N/A	
Specialty: **All**	
Industry: **All**	
Feature: N/A	
Location: **US**	

CareerLab claims it will Push your mini-resume to 2,400 employers and 600 executive search firms for $95. Several interesting career articles are here even though the site's emphasis is on selling the owner's cover letter book. Sample letters can be found for free which makes this visit worthwhile.

Career Link

www.penton.com/corp/classifieds

Michelle Hardy, Penton Media, Inc
1100 Superior Avenue, Cleveland, OH 44136
Ph: 216-696-7000   Fax: 216-696-8206   E-mail: careerlink@penton.com

Jobs: **Yes** Cost to post jobs: **Fee** Cost to see jobs: **Free**	
Resumes: **No** Cost to post resumes: N/A Cost to see resumes: N/A	
E-mail Alert (Push): N/A	
Specialty: **Eng/Mfg/** **Hospitality/Airline** **Aviation/Sales**	
Industry: **All**	
Feature: N/A	
Location: **US/England/Germany** **Middle East**	

Career Link provides job postings from Penton Publishing's magazine roster. These include positions in: engineering, management, manufacturing, hospitality, airline/aviation, sales and electronics. Simple site, a few openings at each link, and you have to place an ad in print to get the web component.

Career Link USA

www.careerlinkusa.com

Mickey Tyler, Career Link USA, Inc.
2239 Charles Street, Rockford, IL 61104
Ph: 800-667-465   Fax: 815-227-5482   E-mail: hrlinks@aol.com

Jobs: **Yes** Cost to post jobs: **Fee** Cost to see jobs: **Free**	
Resumes: **Yes** Cost to post resumes: **Fee** Cost to see resumes: **Free**	
E-mail Alert (Push): **No**	
Specialty: **All**	
Industry: **All**	
Feature: N/A	
Location: **US/MW**	

Career Link USA concentrates on the midwest. Recruiters can view the resume database for free while paying $175 to post a position. Job seekers pay $35 to post their resume which will stay in the database for one year. Search engine allows you to browse the database or be specific by location or job category. The name of the employer is listed for each position, but you have to go through the site to post your resume. Slow process.

CareerMagazine

www.careermag.com

Gary Resnikoff, NCSJobline, Inc.
4775 Walnut Street, Suite 2A, Boulder, CO 80301
Ph: 888-440-5110   Fax: 303-440-3386   E-mail: sales@careermag.com

Jobs: **Yes**	
Cost to post jobs: **Fee**	
Cost to see jobs: **Free**	
Resumes: **Yes**	
Cost to post resumes: **Free**	
Cost to see resumes: **Free**	
E-mail Alert (Push): **Job Seeker**	
Specialty: **All**	
Industry: **All**	
Feature: **Diversity**	
Location: **US**	

CareerMagazine allows the job seeker to search via their engine or go to an employers information page which has either a link to their web site or a direct contact. Job seekers register and the site Pushes matching positions out to them. Excellent career articles complement the online magazine design. Employers can still search resumes for free and post a job $95 for four weeks (an entire range of packages for multiple posting, banners, tiles etc. are available). The site career forum allows professionals to post articles as well as Q&As. A headhunter directory by specialty, college and diversity sections with interesting articles offers useful alternatives. Career Magazine's venture into a video/audio PC to PC interviewing service can be reviewed by clicking on SearchLINC. This turnkey process for recruiters is ahead of its time. Job seekers may soon be advised to go to a local hotel for screening interviews with companies a continent away. One of the best.

CareerMart

www.careermart.com

Darren Grant, BSA Advertising
360 Lexington Avenue, New York, NY 10017
Ph: 212-907-9300   Fax: 212-907-9312   E-mail: darren@careermart.com

Jobs: **Yes**	
Cost to post jobs: **Fee**	
Cost to see jobs: **Free**	
Resumes: **Yes**	
Cost to post resumes: **Free**	
Cost to see resumes: **Fee**	
E-mail Alert (Push): **Job Seeker**	
Specialty: **All**	
Industry: N/A	
Feature: N/A	
Location: **US**	

CareerMart is a "Career Hub" that has a wide range of recruiter tools. Site Pushes job openings to applicants for free, makes a chatroom available for discussions, includes a search engine that offers great choices, and has great graphics. Employers pay in the $100 range to post job opportunities on the BSA recruitment advertising agency's site. Graphics are beautiful, but you may want to look at this site by hitting the text only button as even on our cable modem made it a slow ride. You can post your resume for free, but recruiters must pay to see them. Long list of corporate links. If they would only change the graphics as communication is key. Limited visibility among job seekers due to limited marketing.

Career Match

www.careermatch.com

Philip Quarles
Ph: 516-754-7655   Fax: 516-754-1990   E-mail: marketing@careermatch.com

Jobs: **Yes**	
Cost to post jobs: **Free**	
Cost to see jobs: **Free**	
Resumes: **Yes**	
Cost to post resumes: **Free**	
Cost to see resumes: **Fee**	
E-mail Alert (Push): N/A	
Specialty: **IT/**	
Industry: **All**	
Feature: N/A	
Location: **US/E/NY**	

Career Match is a newly-designed site for computer professionals, recent college graduates and interns for the NY metropolitan marketplace. Site matches the job seeker's skills to the employer's specifications. Job seeker cannot see the employer's contact information. The employer pays $95 for the candidate's contact information after reviewing the profiles that have been received via e-mail. No other subscription costs at this time, although that may change.

CareerMosaic

www.careermosaic.com

Jeffrey Hodes, Bernard Hodes Advertising
555 Madison Avenue, NY, NY 10022
Ph: 800-624-7744   Fax: 212-486-4049   E-mail: sales@careermosaic.com

Jobs: **Yes**	
Cost to post jobs: **Fee**	
Cost to see jobs: **Free**	
Resumes: **Yes**	
Cost to post resumes: **Free**	
Cost to see resumes: **Fee**	
E-mail Alert (Push): **N/A**	
Specialty: **All**	
Industry: **All**	
Feature: **Diversity**	
Location: **US/Int'l**	

CareerMosaic's extensive marketing capability extends its lead among the "career hubs" on the net. Creating alliances with more than a dozen associations, industry specific sites, radio and TV stations, and as a gateway to nine continent/country sites, CM is living up to its name as a "mosaic" of opportunity. Employers' cost to post individual positions is in the $160 range for a 30-day run. Many other packages are available. A new feature allows the job seeker to search within 50 miles of their zip code for their next opportunity. To stay close to their advertisers, CM has created the HR Plaza where professionals can look for jobs or post resumes. Still avoiding a job alert service for visitors in favor of a high traffic model, we think CM may have to eventually re-evalute, but for now they sit on top. Site continues to be an aggressive leader in the marketplace, and should be considered as a place to visit.

Career NET (Career/NET)

www.careernet.com

Laura Buccellati
1320 South Dixie Hwy., Suite 761, Coral Gables, FL 33146
Ph: 305-665-8219   Fax: 305-665-5633   E-mail: jennifer@careernet.com

Jobs: **Yes** Cost to post jobs: **Fee** Cost to see jobs: **Free**	For an annual fee of $2,295 ($295 for individual postings or $395 per month to search the resume database) recruiters can post unlimited jobs and search their resume database. Positions are easy to find—the search engine allows you to hunt by title, company or industry. Site states they have an advanced search tool that allows applicants to select positions by industry, location and experience level, but on several tries, we came up empty.
Resumes: **Yes** Cost to post resumes: **Free** Cost to see resumes: **Fee**	
E-mail Alert (Push): N/A	
Specialty: **IT**	
Industry: **All**	
Feature: N/A	
Location: **US**	

Career Opportunities in Singapore

www.singapore-careers.com

Singapore Econ. Dev. Board, Int'l Manpower Programme
210 Twin Dolphin Drive, Redwood City, CA 94065
Fax: 415-591-1328   E-mail: joboffer@newsserver.technet.sg

Jobs: **Yes** Cost to post jobs: **Fee** Cost to see jobs: **Free**	Local and international corporations post jobs here. Candidates can use a resume form to apply directly. Site gives you general information about the openings (all jobs we were able to get to see were all coded). Site's approach limits visitors to industry and title search. Positions posted were in many different fields. Additional information on the cost of living in Singapore is also available.
Resumes: **No** Cost to post resumes: **Free** Cost to see resumes: N/A	
E-mail Alert (Push): N/A	
Specialty: **All**	
Industry: **All**	
Feature: N/A	
Location: **Int'l/Singapore**	

CareerPath.com

www.careerpath.com

Delia Patel
523 W. Sixth Street, Suite 515, Los Angeles, CA 90014
Ph: 213-623-0200   Fax: 213-623-0244   E-mail: delia@careerpath.com

Jobs: **Yes**	
Cost to post jobs: **Fee**	
Cost to see jobs: **Free**	
Resumes: **Yes**	
Cost to post resumes: **Free**	
Cost to see resumes: **Fee**	
E-mail Alert (Push): N/A	
Specialty: **All**	
Industry: **All**	
Feature: N/A	
Location: **US**	

CareerPath.com has over 58 major newspaper partners posting jobs to this site from all over the U.S. You no longer have to call your maiden aunt across the country to see what job openings there are in the local paper. Recent alliances with major high traffic sites will increase the traffic here measurably. With over 268,000 jobs posted on our recent visit this is a "must stop" for the job seeker. Site this year started collecting resumes and,for a fee,will search it's database and have professional recruiters go over the resumes to provide you with (on average) 10 – 15 qualified candidates. For $1,500 we feel they should provide employers with a self-service web-based tool to do it yourself. **CareerPath.com** has enormous potential if they weigh in with their member papers to collect resumes. They have also collected hundreds of thousands of e-mails and if they learn to communicate with them to the benefit of the newspapers, they could really add value to print help-wanted ads. However, plans to charge $175 for directly placing ads on **CareerPath.com** will dilute that connection. This is one of the few sites that asks for voluntary gender/race of it's readership. A top site that can truly impact the web if it finds the right formula.

CareerPro

www.career-pro.com

7825 Midlothian Turnpike
Suite 220, Richmond, VA 23235
Ph: 804-323-0120   E-mail: service@careerpro.com

Jobs: **Yes** Cost to post jobs: **Free** Cost to see jobs: **Free**	
Resumes: **Yes** Cost to post resumes: **Free** Cost to see resumes: **Free**	
E-mail Alert (Push): N/A	
Specialty: **All**	
Industry: **All**	
Feature: N/A	
Location: **US/E/VA**	

CareerPro's real business is to provide customized career counseling and resume services. Recruiters can post jobs and view resumes for free. Job seekers can post their resume and see job opportunities for free. Not a well-organized site, but you get what you pay for. Hundreds of jobs and resumes were available for viewing.

Career Resource Center

www.careers.org

Marc D. Snyder, Career Resource Center
2508 Fifth Avenue, Suite 147, Seattle, WA 98121
Ph: 206-233-8672   Fax: 206-727-7970   E-mail: marcds@careers.org

Jobs: **No** Cost to post jobs: N/A Cost to see jobs: N/A	
Resumes: **No** Cost to post resumes: N/A Cost to see resumes: N/A	
E-mail Alert (Push): N/A	
Specialty: **All**	
Industry: **All**	
Feature: **Meta-links**	
Location: **US**	

Links, links and more links to all your career needs. From career "gems" (best sites), employer sites, job sites, education, reference sites and career management sites. Easy to view and well-categorized.

Career Search

www.careersearch.net

Career Search
21 Highland Circle, Needham, MA 02194
Ph: 781-449-0312   Fax: 781-449-4657   E-mail: info@carersearch.net

Jobs: **No**	
Cost to post jobs: N/A	
Cost to see jobs: N/A	
Resumes: **No**	
Cost to post resumes: N/A	
Cost to see resumes: N/A	
E-mail Alert (Push): N/A	
Specialty: **All**	
Industry: **All**	
Feature: **Research Tools**	
Location: **US/Int'l**	

Career Search's Internet product allows job seekers and others to search out companies by industry, specialty and location and then link directly to the company's web site. This is one of the best, focused career managment tools we've seen yet. Recruiters need to ensure that their company comes up on the appropriate search parameters. A real winner. Perfect accessory for career planning professionals to offer their clients.

Career Shop

www.careershop.com

Bill Boyer, Tenkey Interactive Inc.
6355 Metrowest Blvd, Suite 260, Orlando, FL 32835
Ph: 800-639-2060   Fax: 407-352-1462   E-mail: bill@careershop.com

Jobs: **Yes**	
Cost to post jobs: **Fee**	
Cost to see jobs: **Free**	
Resumes: **Yes**	
Cost to post resumes: **Free**	
Cost to see resumes: **Fee**	
E-mail Alert (Push): **Employer**	
Specialty: **All**	
Industry: **All**	
Feature: N/A	
Location: **US**	

Career Shop provides extensive services for job seekers and recruiters. Jobs posted will also be distributed to Yahoo, Headhunter.Net and numerous newsgroups. Candidates resumes and employers openings are matched and information e-mailed to recruiters. Jobs can easily be exported from the company site to **Career Shop** for easy posting. Unlimited jobs can be posted for $295 per month (60 days). The online "job fair" is, in reality, links to corporations who post jobs on this site. A link to an IT salary survey is also available. Job search engine works well and displays date of posting. Site claims over 10,000 resumes in their database 3,000 new ones a month (they expire after 120 days). Site continues to improve its traffic, but needs more marketing to make the first tier.

CareerSite

www.careersite.com

Seth Peets, Virtual Resources Corporation
310 Miller Avenue, Ann Arbor, MI 48103
Ph: 734-213-9500   Fax: 734-213-9011   E-mail: seth@careersite.com

Jobs: **Yes** Cost to post jobs: **Fee** Cost to see jobs: **Free**	
Resumes: **Yes** Cost to post resumes: **Free** Cost to see resumes: **Fee**	
E-mail Alert (Push): **Job Seeker**	
Specialty: **All**	
Industry: **All**	
Feature: N/A	
Location: **US**	

CareerSite is one of the web's best "career hubs." Applicants who register will have job openings automatically searched by keywords and forwarded via e-mail. Job seekers can maintain confidentiality (employers simply see a snapshot of the applicant). Job seekers can also apply directly to positions once they have posted their resume and gotten their password. Cost to post jobs is around $100. The site can also integrate its technology with a corporation's HR management system to handle electronic responses. We like the ease with which job seekers and recruiters can navigate this site. Other than having to contact the site for cost information and minimal career information, this is a well-designed site.

The Career Spot

www.careerspot.com

Catherine Daley, Ft. Lauderdale Sun Sentinel
200 East Las Olas Blvd., Fort Lauderdale, FL 33301
Ph: 945-425-1529   E-mail: cdaley@tribune.com

Jobs: **Yes** Cost to post jobs: **Fee** Cost to see jobs: **Free**	
Resumes: **No** Cost to post resumes: N/A Cost to see resumes: N/A	
E-mail Alert (Push): N/A	
Specialty: **All**	
Industry: **All**	
Feature: N/A	
Location: **US/SE/FL/** **Ft. Lauderdale**	

Ft. Lauderdale Sentinel which is one of the few newspapers we know that posts print job classifieds to the web on a daily basis at **The Career Spot.** A "checklist" allows you to search under many categories and then guides you to refining your search for greater accuracy. A newly created "resume connection" has been added to help visitors create or edit their resume. Site belongs to the CareerPath.com network (and this is where your resume will reside).

Career Talk

www.careertalk.com

Joe Stimac, Seaton Corp.
P.O. Box 3096, Lawrence, KS 66047
Ph: 913-522-1144   E-mail: webmaster@careertalk.com

Jobs: **No**	
Cost to post jobs: N/A	
Cost to see jobs: N/A	
Resumes: **No**	
Cost to post resumes: N/A	
Cost to see resumes: N/A	
E-mail Alert (Push): N/A	
Specialty: **All**	
Industry: N/A	
Feature: **Meta-links**	
Location: **US**	

Career Talk has just been updated with career management tips for the job seeker and recruiting tips for the hiring manager. Interesting real life situations are online with advice on how to handle different situations. Owner will respond to all e-mails regarding career questions. Site sells "The Ultimate Job Search Kit" which helps the job seeker with interviewing skills

Career Tech.com

www.careertech.com

Peter Fuhrman, Peterson's Magazine Group
202 Carnegie Center, Princeton, NJ 08540
Ph: 609-243-9111   Fax: 609-243-9150   E-mail: peterf@petersons.com

Jobs: **Yes**	
Cost to post jobs: **Fee**	
Cost to see jobs: **Free**	
Resumes: **No**	
Cost to post resumes: N/A	
Cost to see resumes: N/A	
E-mail Alert (Push): N/A	
Specialty: **College/Eng/IT**	
Industry: **All**	
Feature: N/A	
Location: **US**	

Numerous college centers have already created links to the Peterson Group's new site. CareerTech has excellent content from its college publications including their flagship, Graduating Engineer and Computer Careers Magazine. Technical entry level students will be well advised to take a look.

Career Toolbox

www.careertoolbox.com

Chivas Regal

Ph: 800-244-8271

Jobs: **No**	
Cost to post jobs: N/A	
Cost to see jobs: N/A	
Resumes: **No**	
Cost to post resumes: N/A	
Cost to see resumes: N/A	
E-mail Alert (Push): N/A	
Specialty: **All**	
Industry: **All**	
Feature: N/A	
Location: **US**	

Career Toolbox is a site promoted by Chivas Regal(scotch). Career articles range from tips on handling conflict to how to become an entrepreneur. The "Virtual Mentor" provides case study Q&As where you can select a response and see the advised correct answer. Worth a visit as the content is kept fresh.

CareerWeb

www.cweb.com

Jennifer Ruffin, Landmark Communications, Inc.
150 W. Brambleton Avenue, Norfolk, VA 23510
Ph: 800-871-0800   Fax: 757-623-5942   E-mail: jruffin@cweb.com

Jobs: **Yes** Cost to post jobs: **Fee** Cost to see jobs: **Free**
Resumes: **Yes** Cost to post resumes: **Free** Cost to see resumes: **Fee**
E-mail Alert (Push): **Job Seeker**
Specialty: **All**
Industry: **All**
Feature: N/A
Location: **US/Int'l**

CareerWeb is a vastly improved "career hub" from our '97 edition. The site provides multiple features for the job seeker and recruiter. A revitalized job alert Pushes new jobs to candidates via e-mail. **CareerWeb** claims over 18,000 job openings via hundreds of client employers. Jobs are posted for $135 to a geographical region ($15 for each additional region). Postings are also reposted on Yahoo classifieds. Employer menu assists tracking responses. Resume database costs $2,000 for employers to see or comes at a discount with several packages. Resumes are kept for 90 days. Sister web sites include:
www.healthcarerweb.com
http: //carolinas.carerweb.com
http: //belgium.careerweb.com
www.greentogray.com.
A solid list of articles and links to help the job seeker rounds out this top site.

Career Women

www.careerwomen.com

J. Donnelly, Career Exposure, Inc.
1881 SW Avenue, Portland, OR 97201
Ph: 503-525-8498   Fax: 503-525-8497   E-mail: bizmail@careerwomen.com

Jobs: **Yes** Cost to post jobs: **Fee** Cost to see jobs: **Free**	**Career Women** is a sister site to Career Exposure. Cost to post is $89 per job for a 30-day run. Resumes bank can be reviewed for $299 per quarter. Long list of links for gender issues.
Resumes: **Yes** Cost to post resumes: **Free** Cost to see resumes: **Fee**	
E-mail Alert (Push): N/A	
Specialty: **All**	
Industry: **All**	
Feature: **Diversity**	
Location: **US/Int'l**	

Careers and Jobs

www.starthere.com/jobs

Ray Holt, Internet Information Associates
1009 E. Capitol Expwy, Suite 304, San Jose, Ca 95121
Ph: 408-227-1620   E-mail: starthere@usa.net

Jobs: **No** Cost to post jobs: N/A Cost to see jobs:	**Careers and Jobs** is web altruism at its best. Meta-list of links to job and resume services. Owners request that if you gain an interview from using this list that you donate $5 for each interview and $25 when you get a new job. To top it off you are not requested to pay the $25 until you get your first paycheck. Only on the web!
Resumes: **No** Cost to post resumes: N/A Cost to see resumes: N/A	
E-mail Alert (Push): N/A	
Specialty: **All**	
Industry: **All**	
Feature: **Meta-links**	
Location: **US**	

Careers Online

disserv3.stu.umn.edu/COL/

Tim Fitzgerald, U. of Minnesota, Disability Services
12 Johnston Hall, 101 Pleasant St., SE, Minneapolis, MN 55455
Ph: 612-626-9649   E-mail: careers@disserv.stu.umn.edu

Jobs: **Yes**
Cost to post jobs: **Free**
Cost to see jobs: **Free**
Resumes: **Yes**
Cost to post resumes: **Free**
Cost to see resumes: **Free**
E-mail Alert (Push): N/A
Specialty: **All**
Industry: **All**
Feature: **Diversity**
Location: **US/MW/MN**

Careers Online provides jobs and internship information for people with disabilities. This is a cooperative effort of University of Minnesota's Disability Services and the U.S. Department of Education. Site has not been updated since March 1998 and we wonder why? Links to many other sites and a listing of job hotlines are also available.

CAREERXROADS

www.careerxroads.com

Mark Mehler/Gerry Crispin, MMC Group
P.O. Box 253, Kendall Park, NJ 08824
Ph: 908-821-6652   Fax: 908-821-1343   E-mail: mmc@careerxroads.com

Jobs: **No**
Cost to post jobs: N/A
Cost to see jobs: N/A
Resumes: **No**
Cost to post resumes: N/A
Cost to see resumes: N/A
E-mail Alert (Push): **Both**
Specialty: N/A
Industry: N/A
Feature: N/A
Location: **US/Int'l**

CAREERXROADS is now in its fourth edition. If you've read this far and haven't registered at our site for updates—*DO IT NOW*. We won't be sending you anything other than our updates— no spamming, no strange e-mail challenges or opportunities, no advertising.

*"Where Talent & Opportunity
Connect on the Internet."*

Carolina Career Center

www.webcom.com/~nccareer/

Rich Schreyer,
243 Chattaroy Drive, Charlotte, NC 28214
Ph: 704-399-7888   Fax: 704-399-8190   E-mail: nccareer@bellsouth.net

Jobs: **Yes** Cost to post jobs: **Fee** Cost to see jobs: **Free**	
Resumes: **Yes** Cost to post resumes: **Free** Cost to see resumes: **Free**	
E-mail Alert (Push): N/A	
Specialty: **All**	
Industry: **All**	
Feature: N/A	
Location: **US/SE/NC**	

Carolina Career Center provides resume and job information for the North and South Carolina areas. Resumes can be posted and seen for free. Employers can receive resumes on a continuous basis for $200 a month or $1,200 a year. As an extra service for $75 job seekers can have their e-mail sent to over 1,500 companies, databases and executive recruiters. We would like to hear from readers who have used this service.

Carolinas Career Web

www.carolinascareerweb.com

Jennifer Ruffin, Career Web
150 W. Brambleton Avenue, Norfolk, VA 23510
Ph: 800-871-0800   Fax: 757-623-0166   E-mail: jruffin@cweb.com

Jobs: **Yes** Cost to post jobs: **Fee** Cost to see jobs: **Free**	
Resumes: **Yes** Cost to post resumes: **Free** Cost to see resumes: **Fee**	
E-mail Alert (Push): N/A	
Specialty: **All**	
Industry: **All**	
Feature: N/A	
Location: **US/SE/NC/SC**	

Carolinas Career Web is a sister site to CareerWeb, and unfortunately on our visit, did not "Push" information out to the job seeker. Dozens of links to employers home pages are here. Recruiters have to purchase the CareerWeb package to post jobs and see resumes.

Casino Careers Online

www.casinocareers.com

Beth Deighan
1873 Route 70 East, Suite 107, Cherry Hill, NJ 08003
Ph: 609-489-8950   E-mail: info@casinocareers.com

Jobs: **Yes** Cost to post jobs: **Fee** Cost to see jobs: N/A	
Resumes: **Yes** Cost to post resumes: **Free** Cost to see resumes: **Fee**	
E-mail Alert (Push): **Employer**	
Specialty: **Hospitality**	
Industry: **Hospitality/Casinos**	
Feature: N/A	
Location: **US**	

Visitors to **Casino Careers Online** can post their resume in an "open access" format or confidentially. Employers post position profiles, and the site provides a resume matching service to their specifications. Recruiters can have resumes e-mailed to them and request that any new resumes that come into the system and match the job profile be sent to them as well. Cost to access the resume database is based on the number of employees in a corporation (under 1,000 employees is $5,000 per year per). This is an awkward model for job seekers who cannot see job specs and must rely on the site to match their resumes and job profiles. This makes **Casino Careers Online** a bit of a gamble.

Casting Net

www.castingnet.com

The Casting Net
333 Washington Blvd, Suite 121, Marina Del Rey, CA 90292
Ph: 701-420-1069   E-mail: questions@castingnet.com

Jobs: **Yes** Cost to post jobs: **Free** Cost to see jobs: **Fee**	
Resumes: **No** Cost to post resumes: N/A Cost to see resumes: N/A	
E-mail Alert (Push): N/A	
Specialty: **Entertainment/Actor**	
Industry: **Entertainment**	
Feature: N/A	
Location: **US/Int'l**	

Actors and actresses pay $19.95 to become a member of the site and view positions listed by posting date, location and role. Jobs are posted for free and listings are from all over the world. The site tried "Pushing" acting jobs to their members and they did not like it. Jobs are posted daily.

CATIA Job Network

www.catjn.com

Josh Rothman, Mercury Enterprises
P.O. Box 1983, Tustin, CA 92781
Ph: 714-648-2261   Fax: 714-242-1406   E-mail: admin@catjn.com

Jobs: **Yes**	
Cost to post jobs: **Fee**	
Cost to see jobs: **Free**	
Resumes: **No**	
Cost to post resumes: N/A	
Cost to see resumes: N/A	
E-mail Alert (Push): **Job Seeker**	
Specialty: **IT/CATIA/CAD/ CAM/AutoCAD**	
Industry: **IT**	
Feature: N/A	
Location: **Int'l/Eur./S.A./US**	

Niche site requiring knowledge of CATIA software (cad/cam/cae skills). Employers post jobs for $100 per 30-day run. Jobs on this site are also advertised in the following magazines and newsletters: *Design News, Machine Design, Product Design & Development, Computer Aided Engineering, ASME and SAE UPdate* etc. Jobs can be searched by region through a site link map while also being Pushed to an applicants e-mail address. Entrepreneurs who own this site also manage: Pro/E Job Network www.pejn.com; Ideas Job Network (SDRC CAD/CAM/CAE) www.ideasjn. com; UG Job Network (Unigraphics CAD/CAD/ CAE) www.ugjn. com; SolidWorks Job Network (SolidWorks Cad Skills) www.swjn. com; AutoCad Job Network (AutoCad skills) www.acjn. com

Cell Press

server.cell.com

Keith Wollman, 1050 Massachusetts Ave
Cambridge, Mass 02138
Ph: 617-661-7057   Fax: 617-661-7061   E-mail: kwollman@cell.com

Jobs: **Yes**	
Cost to post jobs: **Fee**	
Cost to see jobs: **Free**	
Resumes: **No**	
Cost to post resumes: N/A	
Cost to see resumes: N/A	
E-mail Alert (Push): N/A	
Specialty: **Science/Biology**	
Industry: **All**	
Feature: N/A	
Location: **US/Int'l**	

Cell Press and its sister publications, *Immunity, Molecular Cell* and *Neuron* use this site. They used to allow job seekers to post their resume for free, but that service has disappeared. All jobs have direct contact information for related scientific positions.

CFO Magazine

www.cfonet.com/html/cfojobs.html

Jason Sciarillo, CFO Publishing
253 Summer Street, Boston, MA 02210
Ph: 617-345-9700   Fax: 617-951-4090   E-mail: (See Notes)

Jobs: **Yes** Cost to post jobs: **Free** Cost to see jobs: **Free**	**CFO Magazine** allows recruiters to post jobs for free, typically high-level finance positions (CFOs, treasurers etc.) A CFO salary survey is available, with perks by industry. Jobs can be sent via e-mail to: jasonsciarillo@cfopub.com.
Resumes: **No** Cost to post resumes: N/A Cost to see resumes: N/A	
E-mail Alert (Push): N/A	
Specialty: **Finance/Accounting**	
Industry: **All**	
Feature: N/A	
Location: **US**	

Changing Times

www.lmcia.bc.ca

JudyLynn Archer, Labour Market & Career Information Association
Suite 600, 5050 Kingway, Burnaby, BC, Canaada V5H 4C3
Ph: 604-436-5624   Fax: 604-435-5548   E-mail: jlarcher@helix.net

Jobs: **No** Cost to post jobs: N/A Cost to see jobs: N/A	**Changing Times (LMCIA) Labour Market and Career Information Association of British Columbia** is a nonprofit organization dedicated to enhancing career information in Canada. Numerous articles from their monthly publication *"Changing Times"* can be viewed on this web site. Check out the article on "Electronic Job Banks" as many Canadian links are available.
Resumes: **No** Cost to post resumes: N/A Cost to see resumes: N/A	
E-mail Alert (Push): N/A	
Specialty: **All**	
Industry: **All**	
Feature: N/A	
Location: **Int'l/Canada**	

Chemistry & Industry Magazine

pharma.mond.org

Society of Chemical Industry
15 Belgrave Square, London, UK SW1X 8PS
Ph: 441-712-353681   Fax: 441-712-359410   E-mail: (See Notes)

Jobs: **Yes**
Cost to post jobs: **Free**
Cost to see jobs: **Free**

Resumes: N/A
Cost to post resumes: N/A
Cost to see resumes: N/A

E-mail Alert (Push): **Job Seeker**

Specialty: **Science/Pharm/ Food**

Industry: **All**

Feature: N/A

Location: **Int'l/US**

Chemistry & industry Magazine is part of the Society of the Chemical industry, and reaches 30,000 readers worldwide. Their target market includes research managers, senior executives and scientists in the chemical, pharmaceutical and food industries. Recruiters can post jobs online for free. This UK-based site is viewed all over the world. Job seekers who register and complete a profile are e-mailed positions that fit their interests. Site's e-mail address is: advertising@chemind. demon. co. uk Price is right so give it a try.

Chicago Software Newspaper CareerCat

www.chisoft.com

Jeffrey Hunt, Chicago Software Newspaper, 108 Walter Street, Watertown, MA 02472
Ph: 617-926-1900   Fax: 617-926-1919   E-mail: info@chisoft.com

Jobs: **Yes**
Cost to post jobs: **Fee**
Cost to see jobs: **Free**

Resumes: **No**
Cost to post resumes: N/A
Cost to see resumes: N/A

E-mail Alert (Push): N/A

Specialty: **IT/Software**

Industry: **IT**

Feature: N/A

Location: **US/MW/IL/Chicago**

Chicago Software Newspaper classified section is searchable on this site. If you do not want to go into the paper you can post on the site for $50. 688 jobs were posted on our last visit by date/title or you can use the search engine. Listing of area search firms can also be found.

Chicago Tribune

www.chicago.tribune.com

Randy White, Chicago Tribune
401 N. Michigan Ave., Chicago, IL 60611
Ph: 312-222-4211   E-mail: rcwhite@tribune.com

Jobs: **Yes** Cost to post jobs: **Fee** Cost to see jobs: **Free**
Resumes: **No** Cost to post resumes: N/A Cost to see resumes: N/A
E-mail Alert (Push): N/A
Specialty: **All**
Industry: N/A
Feature: N/A
Location: **US/MW/IL/Chicago**

Chicago Tribune classifieds are searchable from the previous three Sundays. Job seekers can save interested positions in a "note pad" for further review. All help-wanted categories and display ads are included at no extra cost. The Tribune participates in CareerPath.

CHIME

www.chime-net.org/crc/job/job.htm

Cristine Przykucki, College of Healthcare Infor. Mgmt. Executives
3300 Washtenaw Avenue #255, Ann Arbor, MI 48104
Ph: 734-665-4922   E-mail: christina@chime-office.org

Jobs: **Yes** Cost to post jobs: **Fee** Cost to see jobs: **Free**
Resumes: **Yes** Cost to post resumes: **Free** Cost to see resumes: **Fee**
E-mail Alert (Push): **Job Seeker**
Specialty: **IT/CIO**
Industry: **All**
Feature: N/A
Location: **US**

The College of Healthcare Information Management Executives has developed this site to help their membership. Job postings can only be seen by members, and contact information on resumes posted can be coded or open (the members choice). All jobs are "Pushed" on a weekly basis, and the cost to post a job is $500. Why one would have to be a member to see jobs is a restrictive, but typical, traditional thinking. For many of the services offered you have to e-mail for more information. Participants can have their resume mailed to 50 healthcare/IT executive recruiters by this organization. Lots of services, but awkward set up.

Christian Jobs Online

www.christianjobs.com

Neal H. Jacobs, Christian Jobs Online
P.O. Box 69, Girard, PA 16417-0069
Ph: 814-774-7029   Fax: 814-774-7330   E-mail: webmaster@christianjobs.com

Jobs: **Yes**	
Cost to post jobs: **Fee**	
Cost to see jobs: **Free**	
Resumes: **Yes**	
Cost to post resumes: **Fee**	
Cost to see resumes: **Fee**	
E-mail Alert (Push): **Job Seeker**	
Specialty: **All**	
Industry: **All**	
Feature: N/A	
Location: **US**	

Christian Jobs Online asks recruiters to make a statement of faith (not mandatory) before they post positions so you can receive a special logo (cross) next to your job. Job seekers are asked to pay $10 to post their resume, and recruiters pay $75 per job. Site also has "Push" for sending postings to job seekers. We saw two positions wanted, and three jobs posted on our visit. Need to say a prayer for this one.

Chronicle of Higher Education

www.chronicle.com

Christopher Sheppard, The Chronicle of Higher Education
1255 23rd Street NW, Washington, DC 20037
Ph: 202-466-1050   Fax: 202-296-2691   E-mail: jobs@chronicle.com

Jobs: **Yes**	
Cost to post jobs: **Fee**	
Cost to see jobs: **Fee** (Subscribe)	
Resumes: **No**	
Cost to post resumes: N/A	
Cost to see resumes: N/A	
E-mail Alert (Push): N/A	
Specialty: **Teaching/Admin.**	
Industry: **Education/University**	
Feature: N/A	
Location: **US**	

All current positions listed are those published weekly in the **Chronicle of Higher Education**. A broad range of faculty, research, administration and executive positions. 540 current job openings with 670 posted for the prior week that you could see for free. You must be a subscriber to the *Chronicle* to see the current open positions ($75). Employers must pay for the print and internet combination.

City Surf

www.citysurf.com

Randy Jo Wilcox, CitySurf
7170 S. Braden, Suite 140, Tulsa, OK 74136
Ph: 918-492-1170   Fax: 918-492-6676   E-mail: info@citysurf.com

Jobs: **No**	
Cost to post jobs: N/A	
Cost to see jobs: N/A	
Resumes: **No**	
Cost to post resumes: N/A	
Cost to see resumes: N/A	
E-mail Alert (Push): N/A	
Specialty: N/A	
Industry: N/A	
Feature: **Research Tools**	
Location: **US**	

City Surf will give you all the relocation information you will need about major cities across the US. We especially liked their e-mail directory—we never knew there were six Mark Mehlers in different parts of the country. Using their search engine you will find major attractions from museums to baseball parks. The one issue we have with this site is that the businesses that are mentioned are not linked.

Classified Employment Web Site (CLEWS)

www.yourinfosource.com

Ken Cunningham, Info Source & Services
P.O. Box 67032, St. Pete Beach, FL 33736
Ph:727-360-8728   Fax:727-360-4544   E-mail:(See Notes)

Jobs:**Yes** Cost to post jobs:**Fee** Cost to see jobs:**Free**
Resumes: **Yes** Cost to post resumes: **Free** Cost to see resumes: **Fee**
E-mail Alert (Push): N/A
Specialty: **All**
Industry: **All**
Feature: **Security Clearance**
Location: **US**

Infosource has created a new (7/2/98) site for employers looking for candidates with U.S. top security clearances. Employers can access the site for $10 a month or $100 a year. To see resume contact information, it will cost recruiters either $25 per resume or $195 per month for unlimited access. Job posting is either $5.00 per posting and $2.50 per response or $95 per month for unlimited postings. E-mail: feedback.clews@ yourinfosource.com for more information as the tour for the site also keeps you in the dark. If you haven't heard about this one before it is because it's Top Secret.

Classified Warehouse

www.adone.com

Carolyn LoGalbo, AdOne Classified Network, Inc.
361 Broadway, Suite 100, New York, NY 10013
Ph: 212-965-2900   Fax: 212-334-3307   E-mail: sales@classifiedwarehouse.com

Jobs: **Yes** Cost to post jobs: **Fee** Cost to see jobs: **Free**
Resumes: **No** Cost to post resumes: N/A Cost to see resumes: N/A
E-mail Alert (Push): **Job Seeker**
Specialty: **All**
Industry: **All**
Feature: N/A
Location: **Int'l/Canada/US**

Classified Warehouse (AdOne) serves as the classified site for over 400 small market newspapers throughout the U.S. and Canada. Most are small daily and weekly papers that have help-wanted advertising. Job seekers can use an agent (Ad Hound) to identify job categories/ regions and seat for their next opportunity. After registering, applicants will receive e-mails listing opportunities that match their requirements. For the job seeker whose desired location can be narrowed to an area covered by several of these small papers, this site is worth the trip.

Classifieds2000

www.classifieds2000.com

William Chen
617 Palomar Avenue, Sunnyvale, CA 94086
Ph: 408-773-2028   Fax: 408-773-2001

Jobs: **Yes**	
Cost to post jobs: **Fee**	
Cost to see jobs: **Free**	
Resumes: **Yes**	
Cost to post resumes: **Free**	
Cost to see resumes: N/A	
E-mail Alert (Push): N/A	
Specialty: **All**	
Industry: **All**	
Feature: N/A	
Location: **US**	

Classifieds2000 will post employer positions on their network of 100+ web sites. Cost to post jobs is $50 for a four-week run, and satisfaction is guaranteed. For employers with multiple listings, the length of job posting periods depends on you. All jobs get refreshed on a weekly basis. If the job has been filled it will disappear, if it hasn't been filled then the employer can leave it or replace it with another position. RESUME CENTRAL, was recently launched, but on our visits just collects resumes as it does not have a way for employers to view at this time. Site also uses Junglee technology to mirror all of the employer's positions. "Cool Notify" will Push business services to you, but for some unknown reason will not Push job listings.

CLNET

latino.sscnet.ucla.edu/

Richard Chabran, Chicano Studies Research Center
54 Haines Hall, University of Calif., Los Angeles, CA 90024
E-mail: salinas@latino.sscnet.ucla.edu

Jobs: **Yes**	
Cost to post jobs: **Free**	
Cost to see jobs: **Free**	
Resumes: **No**	
Cost to post resumes: N/A	
Cost to see resumes: N/A	
E-mail Alert (Push): N/A	
Specialty: **All**	
Industry: **All**	
Feature: **Diversity/Meta-links**	
Location: **US/W/CA**	

CLNet provides information about Hispanic communities of southern California. A dozen jobs were posted with direct contact information. This site has local content about Latino organizations and educational resources. A long list of diversity sites is also available.

Coach Online Service

www.coachhelp.com/jobs.htm

Warren Swann, COACH
1025 North Central Expressway, #300-343, Plano, TX 75075
Ph: 800-339-9652   E-mail: wbswann@mymail.net

Jobs: **Yes**	
Cost to post jobs: **Free**	
Cost to see jobs: **Free**	
Resumes: **Yes**	
Cost to post resumes: **Fee**	
Cost to see resumes: **Free**	
E-mail Alert (Push): N/A	
Specialty: **Ed./High School Sports Coaching**	
Industry: **Ed./HS & College**	
Feature: N/A	
Location: **US/Int'l**	

Coach Online Service maintains job listings from all 50 states and many foreign countries. A new resume bank is planned, and will charge the job seeker $30 for three months. Football coaching jobs are posted for free (other sports are also covered). Employers can view resumes for free. A new online football coaches association operates here to provide the latest information on the profession for ($40 a year). An online Q&A also is available. This one is right between the uprights.

College Central Network

www.collegecentral.com

Stuart Nachbar, College Central Network
141 West 28th Street, 9th Fl, NY, NY 10001
Ph: 800-044-3614   Fax: 212-714-1688   E-mail: info@collegecentral.com

Jobs: **Yes**	
Cost to post jobs: **Fee**	
Cost to see jobs: **Free**	
Resumes: **Yes**	
Cost to post resumes: **Free**	
Cost to see resumes: **Fee**	
E-mail Alert (Push): **Job Seeker**	
Specialty: **College/Entry-level**	
Industry: **All**	
Feature: N/A	
Location: **US**	

College Central Network has geographic focus in the Northeast and concentrates on college and alumni services. Unique feature of this college site is that the posted positions are e-mailed to school career service centers. Employers pay $15 for 30 days of regionalized postings (no fee for government and nonprofit organizations). Student and alumni resumes are available at a cost of $30 for 30 resumes. Employers can preview the resumes for free and then pay for the contact information. **College Central's** additional services include a resume database that students can modify and export to other sites. We also like the fact that students and alumni merely log on and declare their school without having to go to their school's career services department to obtain a special password. Some of the advertisers who flash "in-your-face ads" are not our cup of tea, but that is web business.

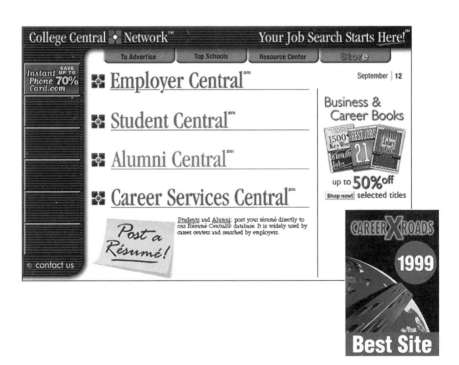

College Connection

www.careermosaic.com/cm/cc/cc1.html

Bernard Hodes Advertising
555 Madison Avenue, New York, NY 10022
Ph: 212-758-2600

Jobs: **Yes**	
Cost to post jobs: **Fee**	
Cost to see jobs: **Free**	
Resumes: **Yes**	
Cost to post resumes: **Free**	
Cost to see resumes: **Free**	
E-mail Alert (Push): N/A	
Specialty: **College/Entry-level**	
Industry: **All**	
Feature: **C/M**	
Location: **US**	

College Connection is part of the CareerMosaic connection. Career articles, and links to other sites are interesting and useful. Employers are listed with links to their openings instead of a search engine. Dozens of links to internships. The **College Connection** is not as competitive as one would expect. C+.

College Grad Job Hunter

www.collegegrad.com

Brian Kreuger, College Grad Job Hunter
1629 N Summit Drive, Suite 200, Cedarburg, WI 53012-9399
Ph: 414-376-1000   Fax: 414-376-1030   E-mail: info@collegegrad.com

Jobs: **Yes**	
Cost to post jobs: **Fee**	
Cost to see jobs: **Free**	
Resumes: **No**	
Cost to post resumes: N/A	
Cost to see resumes: N/A	
E-mail Alert (Push): N/A	
Specialty: **College/Entry-level**	
Industry: **All**	
Feature: N/A	
Location: **US**	

Visitors to **College Grad Job Hunter** can see all positions posted and respond directly. Job postings cost employers $250 for 90 days ($550 for one year). E-mail and hyperlinks are included in those prices. Articles geared to help entry-level job seekers abound. A salary calculator gives the college grad an idea of what they are worth in different parts of the country. A new internship section has recently been added. Well-organized, **Job Hunter** is on the right track.

College Net

www.collegenet.com

Mary Nisbet, Universal Algorithms, Inc.
One SW Columbia, Suite 100, Portland, OR 97258
Ph: 503-973-5200   E-mail: webadmin@collegenet.com

Jobs: **No**	
Cost to post jobs: N/A	
Cost to see jobs: N/A	
Resumes: **No**	
Cost to post resumes: N/A	
Cost to see resumes: N/A	
E-mail Alert (Push): N/A	
Specialty: N/A	
Industry: **Education**	
Feature: **College Admissions**	
Location: **US**	

College Net is the grad school equivalent of a job database. A U.S. map enables graduating seniors find colleges in every location. Law schools, MBA programs, medical schools and many other programs can be found here. Potential applicants can review cost information and then link to a school's application form or e-mail admissions department is a nice touch. The site has comprehensive information on scholarships and financial aid. For $9 students can create a profile that is viewed by admissions directors—we love this idea. Advanced ideas for advanced degrees.

College News Online

www.collegenews.com/jobs.htm

Chris Brannen, Central Newspaper, Inc.
The Willoughby Tower St.1616, 8 South Michigan Avenue, Chicago, IL 60603
Ph: 312-263-5388   Fax: 312-263-6095   E-mail: webteam@collegenews.com

Jobs: **Yes**	
Cost to post jobs: **Fee**	
Cost to see jobs: **Free**	
Resumes: **Yes**	
Cost to post resumes: **Free**	
Cost to see resumes: N/A	
E-mail Alert (Push): N/A	
Specialty: **College/Entry-level**	
Industry: **All**	
Feature: **N/A**	
Location: **US/IL/Chicago**	

College News is a print publication with an online component complete with articles, and job postings. A College Talk chatroom has been created so students can discuss anything having to do with college. The cost to post jobs starts at $150 for 30 days. Job seekers can post their resume for free. Sites strength lies mainly in the upper midwest. Resumes are collected, but we have not been advised if they can be searched. **College News** is a work in progress.

Colorado Jobs Online

www.coloradojobs.com/about/html

Randy Rose
2110 Hollow Brook Drive, Colorado Springs, CO 80918
Ph: 719-590-7400   E-mail: rroses@jobdigest.om

Jobs: **Yes**	
Cost to post jobs: **Fee**	
Cost to see jobs: **Free**	
Resumes: **Yes**	
Cost to post resumes: **Free**	
Cost to see resumes: **Free**	
E-mail Alert (Push): N/A	
Specialty: **All**	
Industry: **All**	
Feature: N/A	
Location: **US/W/CO**	

Colorado Jobs Online was up for sale at the time of our review. Positions are posted in real time with their online form. Many different disciplines can be found for jobs and resumes. Employer cost to post a job is $25 for a 30-day listing. Job seekers pay $5 and up to post their resume. Interesting search engine asks questions when you do your initial search (you are asked if you want to look under a subheading for more detailed content). Nice concepts kept this site in the directory, but results are marginal (we conducted over a half dozen searches for jobs, and were not impressed). Needs some marketing to get this one out of the corral. Owner has other sites that are also up for sale: www.southernjobs.com, www.jobdigest.com and more.

Columbia-Williamette Compensation Group

www.cwcg.org

Ellen Roney, P.O. Box 1114, Portland, OR 97207-1114
Ph: 503-578-5432   E-mail: sysadmin@cwcg.org

Jobs: **Yes**	
Cost to post jobs: **Free**	
Cost to see jobs: **Free**	
Resumes: **No**	
Cost to post resumes: N/A	
Cost to see resumes: N/A	
E-mail Alert (Push): **No**	
Specialty: **HR Compensation**	
Industry: **All**	
Feature: N/A	
Location: **US/W/WA/Vancouver OR/Portland**	

Columbia-Williamette Compensaton Group is a nonprofit professional organization providing education and networking opportunities in compansation and benefits for their members. Jobs can be posted for free (there were only two listed on our visit).

Columbus Dispatch

www.dispatch.com

Pam Coffman, The Columbus Dispatch
5300 Crosswind Drive, Columbus, OH 43228
Ph: 614-461-8803   Fax: 614-461-8525   E-mail: pcoffman@dispatch.com

Jobs: **Yes** Cost to post jobs: **Fee** Cost to see jobs: **Free**	
Resumes: **No** Cost to post resumes: N/A Cost to see resumes: N/A	
E-mail Alert (Push): N/A	
Specialty: **All**	
Industry: N/A	
Feature: N/A	
Location: **US/MW/OH/Columbus**	

Nice design element—a classified button at the top right side of this Ohio newspaper's home page. Help-wanted ads (just not the display ads) are available seven days a week. A resume builder is included to help job seekers put their best foot forward. Job hunting tips are helpful. A simple search engine gets the job done. This site also participates in CareerPath.com

Community Career Center (nonprofit jobs)

www.nonprofitjobs.org/

Gino Maini, Enterprise Inc
2160 W. Charleston, Suite L345, Las Vegas, NV 89102
Ph: 702-259-9580   Fax: 702-259-0244   E-mail: info@nonprofitjobs.org

Jobs: **Yes** Cost to post jobs: **Fee** Cost to see jobs: **Free**	
Resumes: **Yes** Cost to post resumes: **Fee** Cost to see resumes: **Fee**	
E-mail Alert (Push): N/A	
Specialty: **All**	
Industry: **Nonprofit**	
Feature: N/A	
Location: **US**	

Community Career Center (nonprofit jobs) claims St. Jude Children's Hospital, The American Cancer Society, Junior Achievement, and several other well-known charities are members. Job seekers pay $25 to post their resume for six months while recruiters pay $125 per job (or become members). Resumes posted to the site can only be seen by member companies. There were 268 jobs posted on our visit so job seekers can use the site's search engine to scroll through the openings. Jobs are listed in reverse date order (oldest posted job is first), which we find extremely awkward. This for-profit site with its emphasis on nonprofit work is worth the visit if only for the cool audio when you enter.

Comprehensive Career Ministries

eab.datastar.net/eab.html

Multimedia Resume Services
P.O. Box 1911, Picayune, MS 39466
E-mail: newellrn@datastar.net

Jobs: **No**	
Cost to post jobs: N/A	
Cost to see jobs: N/A	
Resumes: **Yes**	
Cost to post resumes: **Free**	
Cost to see resumes: **Free**	
E-mail Alert (Push): **Employer**	
Specialty: **All**	
Industry: **All**	
Feature: N/A	
Location: **US**	

Comprehensive Career Ministries brings church and employer just a little too close for us. Job seekers can post their resume, and gain spiritual guidance along the way. Recruiters can see resumes for free with all direct contact data. This is not a site for individuals interested in a religious career. Instead, the site focuses on giving religious advice to job seekers. Either we have spent too many hours behind a PC or we are missing something. The site's salutation suggests visitors e-mail prayer requests, questions, testimonies and comments.

The ComputerJobs Store

www.computerjobs.com

Michael K. Gilfillan, The Computer Jobs Store, Inc.
2000 Powers Ferry Road, Suite 300, Atlanta, GA 30067
Ph: 770-850-0045   E-mail: info@computerjobs.com

Jobs: **Yes** Cost to post jobs: **Fee** Cost to see jobs: **Free**
Resumes: **Yes** Cost to post resumes: **Free** Cost to see resumes: **Fee**
E-mail Alert (Push): N/A
Specialty: **IT**
Industry: **IT**
Feature: N/A
Location: **US/SE/Atlanta/ Carolina/IL/Chicago/TX**

The ComputerJobs Store is one of the better niche concepts for IT recruiting. New state sites have been added, and more are planned. These geographically focused centers allow job seekers and employers better control and wider choice. Added features such as listings of local and regional professional associations is a great networking tool for someone looking for a job or professional connections. Recruiters can post a job for $30 a week, but must advertise on a monthly basis to access the resume database. Sites objective is to have a store in all 50 states.

CStores are now in:

www.atlanta.computerjobs.com • *3,204 jobs listed*
www.carolina.computerjobs.com • *1,250 jobs listed*
www.chicago.computerjobs.com • *1,147 jobs listed*
www.florida.computerjobs.com • *754 jobs listed*
www.texas.computerjobs.com • *2,279 jobs listed*
www.national.computerjobs.com • *1,153 jobs listed*

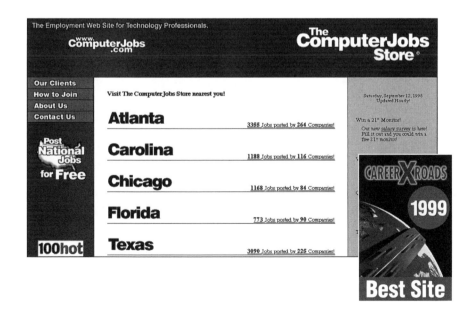

Computer Work

www.computerwork.com

Lynn Rachal, Internet Associaton Group
P.O. Box 4266, Greensboro, NC 27404
Ph: 800-691-8413 Fax: 904-296-1993 E-mail: lynn_rachal@resourcecenter.com

Jobs: **Yes**	
Cost to post jobs: **Fee**	
Cost to see jobs: **Free**	
Resumes: **Yes**	
Cost to post resumes: **Free**	
Cost to see resumes: **Fee**	
E-mail Alert (Push): **Job Seeker**	
Specialty: **IT**	
Industry: **All**	
Feature: N/A	
Location: **US**	

Computer Work specializes in providing jobs and resumes for the IT/IS industry. This online job board and resume bank specializes in computer industry consultants and contractors. Site claims approximately 7,000 jobs and 8,500 resumes. Search engine works well and quickly returns links to text with complete contact information and link back to the employer's site as well. Recruiters are invited to post jobs for free for 30 days. **Computer Work** has a network of mirror regional sites similar to The ComputerJobs Store. Well worth a look, especially for contract workers.

Computer World's IT Careers

www.computerworld.com

Nikki Wilson, Computerworld
500 Old Connecticut Path, Framingham, MA 01701
Ph: 508-879-0700 Fax: 508-875-6310 E-mail: nikki_wilson@cw.com

Jobs: **Yes**	
Cost to post jobs: **Fee**	
Cost to see jobs: **Free**	
Resumes: **Yes**	
Cost to post resumes: **Free**	
Cost to see resumes: N/A	
E-mail Alert (Push): **Job Seeker**	
Specialty: **IT**	
Industry: **IT**	
Feature: N/A	
Location: **US**	

Computer World's site includes an abundance of career advice and job postings from their magazine. Job seekers "register" their skills in a database and the publication's Push agent, "Career Central," will e-mail any positions that match the applicant's background on a daily basis. An extensive listing of career related articles can be keyword searched. Employer packages are available for corporate advertisers. Numerous links to employers are setup on a U.S. map by region for ease of access- very nice idea. Several hundred employers and thousands of jobs are posted here.

Computerwork.com

computerwork.com

National Association of Computer Consultants
Ph: 800-313-1920   E-mail: sales@computerwork.com

Jobs: **Yes**	
Cost to post jobs: **Fee**	
Cost to see jobs: **Free**	
Resumes: **Yes**	
Cost to post resumes: **Free**	
Cost to see resumes: **Fee**	
E-mail Alert (Push): **Employer**	
Specialty: **IT**	
Industry: **Computer**	
Feature: N/A	
Location: **US**	

The National Association of Computer Consulting Businesses gives recruiters a 30-day free membership to post jobs and review resumes. Site matches job seekers skills with open positions and e-mails resumes directly to recruiters. Recruiters can also select 10 states from which candidate resumes will be e-mailed to them as well. All company positions have direct contact information and are date posted. This site has sister sites in Toronto and 34 others states in the U.S. A resume bank is free for job seekers, but employers, must become a member of the organization in order to regularly post jobs and search the resume bank. In addition, there is a monthly charge to corporations who utilize the site.

Connect to Jobs

www.cabrillo.cc.ca.us/affiliate/

Debra Jones, Cabrillo College
6500 Soquel Dr., Aptos, CA 95003
Ph: 408-479-6540   E-mail: dejones@cabrillo.cc.ca.us

Jobs: **No**	
Cost to post jobs: **Fee**	
Cost to see jobs: N/A	
Resumes: **No**	
Cost to post resumes: N/A	
Cost to see resumes: N/A	
E-mail Alert (Push): N/A	
Specialty: **All**	
Industry: **All**	
Feature: **Meta-links**	
Location: **US/W/CA**	

Connect to Jobs is sponsored by Cabrillo College and is essentially a lengthy descriptive list of links to some very interesting job sites. Click on "Job Boards" and you will find links by profession. This list is well-done and worth checking.

Consumer Net

consumer.net/tracert/

P.O. Box 44232, Washington, DC 20026
Ph: 703-567-2375   Fax: 703-567-2375   E-mail: web@consumer.net

Jobs: N/A
Cost to post jobs: N/A
Cost to see jobs: N/A
Resumes: N/A
Cost to post resumes: N/A
Cost to see resumes: N/A
E-mail Alert (Push): N/A
Specialty: **IT/Research**
Industry: **All**
Feature: N/A
Location: **US**

If you've ever used LOOKUP, WHOIS, PING, TRACERT, and other such utilities to locate information on domains, web site owners etc., you'll appreciate having all these web look-up tools in one place.

Contract Employment Connection

www.ntes.com

Jack Nadelman, National Technical Employment Services Association
309 Taylor Street, Scottsboro, AL 35768
Ph: 205-259-6837   E-mail: info@ntes.com

Jobs: **Yes**
Cost to post jobs: **Fee**
Cost to see jobs: **Free**
Resumes: **Yes**
Cost to post resumes: **Free**
Cost to see resumes: **Fee**
E-mail Alert (Push): N/A
Specialty: **IT**
Industry: **All**
Feature: N/A
Location: **US**

Contract Employment Connection advertises contract employment opportunities through their weekly newspaper and on this web site. CEC claims if you e-mail your resume in ASCII or mail it on a floppy, they'll make it available to every technical service firm in the US. IT/IS positions are listed from their *Hotflash* magazine. Contract recruiters can be searched alphabetically and also through a state listing. This is a no-brainer.

Contract Employment Weekly

www.ceweekly.com

Jerry Erickson, C.E.Publications
P.O.Box 3006, Bothell, WA 98041
Ph: 425-806-5200   Fax: 425-806-5585   E-mail: publisher@ceweekly.com

Jobs: **Yes**
Cost to post jobs: **Fee**
Cost to see jobs: **Free**

Resumes: **Yes**
Cost to post resumes: **Free**
Cost to see resumes: **Fee**

E-mail Alert (Push): **Job Seeker**

Specialty: **IT/Engineering**

Industry: **All**

Feature: N/A

Location: **US**

Contract Employment Weekly is published for computer contract service firms. Approximately 40-50% of the posted jobs can be seen for free, but you must subscribe to see them all. Employers pay print advertising costs plus $5 to place their opportunity on this web site. Resumes that are submitted to the site are mailed each Friday to all who advertise jobs during that week. New job postings are searched each day, and matches are e-mailed to all job seekers who register their pre-set keywords on this site. A live chat room is also available.

Cool Works

www.coolworks.com

Bill Berg, Cool Works
P.O. Box 272, Gardiner, MT 59030
Ph: 406-848-2380   Fax: 404-685-0919   E-mail: greatjobs@coolworks.com

Jobs: **Yes**	
Cost to post jobs: **Fee**	
Cost to see jobs: **Free**	
Resumes: **No**	
Cost to post resumes: **N/A**	
Cost to see resumes: **N/A**	
E-mail Alert (Push): **N/A**	
Specialty: **Sports/Outdoors College**	
Industry: **Hospitality/Recreation**	
Feature: **N/A**	
Location: **US/Int'l**	

When it is time to get out of the corporate rat race go to **Cool Works** and check out the 40,000 positions from national parks, ski resorts, cruise lines and every other outdoor activity you can think of. Jobs can be searched by most states, type of job or organization. Employers pay $50 per month to post a job. Site has recently conducted a chat event co-sponsored with studentcenter.com. Job seekers connected with the HR Mgr. for Yellowstone Park Lodges. CWorks is an inspiration to all the baby boomers that talked about taking a job in a national park, on a cruise ship, at camp and resorts—even jobs for RVers. If it's not too late, go for it.

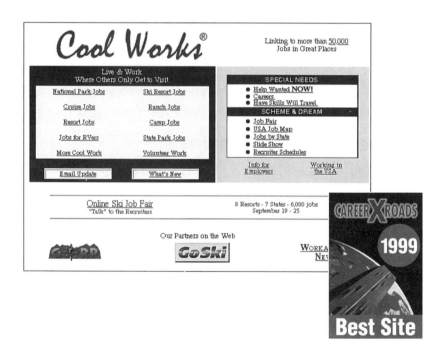

Corporate Aviation Resume Exchange

scendtek.com/care

ScendTek Internet Corp.
804 Park Hill Drive, Euless, TX 76040
Ph: 800-611-3565   E-mail: sti@scendtek.com

Jobs: **No** Cost to post jobs: N/A Cost to see jobs: N/A	
Resumes: **Yes** Cost to post resumes: **Free** Cost to see resumes: **Free**	
E-mail Alert (Push): N/A	
Specialty: **Aviation/Airline Pilots**	
Industry: **Aviation**	
Feature: N/A	
Location: **US**	

Corporation Aviation Resume Exchange explains it all. Check sheet format is designed to make it easy for pilots to fill in information and post their resume (or take off). Hundreds of pilots' are listed, and resumes can be viewed for free. Links to other aviation sites are also included.

Corporate Gray Online

www.greentogray.com

Jennifer Ruffin, Career Web
150 W. Brambleton Avenue, Norfolk, VA 23510
Ph: 800-871-0800   Fax: 757-623-0166   E-mail: Jruffin@cweb

Jobs: **Yes** Cost to post jobs: **Fee** Cost to see jobs: **Free**	
Resumes: **Yes** Cost to post resumes: **Free** Cost to see resumes: **Fee**	
E-mail Alert (Push): **Both**	
Specialty: **All**	
Industry: **All**	
Feature: **Military Outplacement**	
Location: **US**	

Corporate Gray Online is a CareerWeb site that provides individuals leaving the military a look into the business world. A long list of articles and advice on transition from the services is provided by Ron Krannich, an expert career counselor. Jobs can be posted for $135 for a geographic area ($15 for each additional posting). Employer cost for resumes is $2,000 for a year.

Cowley Job Centre

www.cowleys.com/au/public/jobs.htm

Scott Williams, Cowley Online
P.O. Box 341, Armidale 2350, Australia
E-mail: cowleys@cowleys.com.au

Jobs: **Yes**	
Cost to post jobs: **Free**	
Cost to see jobs: **Free**	
Resumes: **Yes**	
Cost to post resumes: **Free**	
Cost to see resumes: **Free**	
E-mail Alert (Push): **N/A**	
Specialty: **All**	
Industry: **All**	
Feature: **N/A**	
Location: **Int'l/Australia**	

Cowley Job Centre may be the site to post a position wanted or a job opening if Australia is your country of choice. Job seekers can e-mail responses to employers after reviewing a short "brief" about the position. Job listings are broken down into numerous categories (a search engine would be a big help). Lots of general information on Australia can also be found.

Creative Freelancers Online

www.freelancers.com

Marilyn Howard, Creative Freelancers
99 Park Avenue #210A, New York, NY 10016
Ph: 212-344-7067   E-mail: cfonline@freelancers.com

Jobs: **Yes**	
Cost to post jobs: **Fee**	
Cost to see jobs: **Free**	
Resumes: **Yes**	
Cost to post resumes: **Free**	
Cost to see resumes: **Fee**	
E-mail Alert (Push): **N/A**	
Specialty: **Graphic Arts/ Freelancers**	
Industry: **Entertainment**	
Feature: **N/A**	
Location: **US**	

Creative Freelancers connects designers, illustrators, writers, editors and photographers to their next assignment. Employers can view resumes, but contact information will cost you $50. Other packages are available. Resumes can be posted for free (site is owned by a temporary employment agency). More and more agencies are parlaying their resume database into a cash cow. A sister site, www.illustratorsonline.com was added.

Crystallography Worldwide

www.iucr.ac.uk/crystal_index.html

Lachlan Cranswick
University of Geneva
E-mail: cww.editor@iucr.org

Jobs: **Yes** Cost to post jobs: **Free** Cost to see jobs: **Free**	
Resumes: **No** Cost to post resumes: N/A Cost to see resumes: N/A	
E-mail Alert (Push): N/A	
Specialty: **Sci./Crystallography**	
Industry: **Education/University**	
Feature: N/A	
Location: **Int'l/US**	

Positions are listed first by individual employer and then by country (keep scrolling on the right side or you will miss this). Date of posting is included. Extensive content on the subject is available.

Cyber India Online

www.ciol.com

Meenal Gupta, Cyber Media India Limited
D 126 Panchsheel Enclave, New Delhi, India 110017
Ph: 911-164-33999   Fax: 911-164-75765   E-mail: editorial@ciol.com

Jobs: **Yes** Cost to post jobs: **Fee** Cost to see jobs: **Free**	
Resumes: **No** Cost to post resumes: N/A Cost to see resumes: N/A	
E-mail Alert (Push): N/A	
Specialty: **IT**	
Industry: **IT**	
Feature: N/A	
Location: **Int'l/India/US**	

This IT site targets professionals in India and many of the openings listed are for U.S. openings. Site search engine allows you to see openings all over the world. Career articles were limited, and many had broken links. A chatroom was available. Sites like these will really explode when they facilitate screening and selection interviews via video and audio.

daVinci Times

www.daVinciTimes.org

Tom Mushow, The daVinci Project of Central NY
Greater Syracuse Eco. Council, 572 South Salina Street, Syracuse, NY 13202
Ph: 315-445-5845   E-mail: davinciads@davincitimes.org

Jobs: **Yes**	
Cost to post jobs: **Fee**	
Cost to see jobs: **Free**	
Resumes: **Yes**	
Cost to post resumes: **Free**	
Cost to see resumes: **Fee**	
E-mail Alert (Push): **Job Seeker**	
Specialty: **Engineer**	
Industry: **All**	
Feature: N/A	
Location: **US/NY/Syracuse**	

daVinci Times was designed as a collaboration of engineering companies who felt that collaborating to draw more talent to Syracuse was better than competing for the scarce resources already there. The area expects over 1,000 openings in the next three years, and if you like the snow, this is the place to go. This 1998 site was designed for its appeal to engineers. We like its look and the creative toys, tools and resources it is trying to develop to appeal to engineers—and hopefully draw repeat traffic. A resume wizard will assist you in formatting your perfect profile, and visitors can check out real estate or spousal job hunting assistance from here as well. Member corporations can be lifetime patrons for $5,000 – $10,000. Included are unlimited job postings, a site profile, resume/job matching service (job seekers can post skills, and the site will e-mail the information to employers for follow up). To top it off, they have online technical forums (chatroom) to draw the job seekers in, and members can publish white papers. If they can successfully market the site, it will be an outstanding benchmark for other areas of the country.

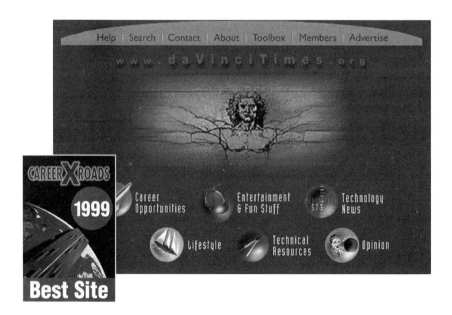

Defense Outplacement Referral System

www.dmdc.osd.mil/dors

E-mail: dorshelp@osd.pentagon.mil

Jobs: **Yes** Cost to post jobs: **Free** Cost to see jobs: **Free**
Resumes: **Yes** Cost to post resumes: N/A Cost to see resumes: **Free**
E-mail Alert (Push): N/A
Specialty: **All**
Industry: **All**
Feature: **Military Outplacement**
Location: **US/Int'l**

Show up at the **DORS** home page, and you will learn that it is sponsored by the Department of Defense. This is a "resume" registry and referral system that provides resumes of military and federal civilian personnel and their spouses to potential employers—for free. More than 2 million resumes were sent to employers in the last twelve months. Over 100,000 job ads representing 20,000 jobs can be seen here every day. A no-brainer for any recruiter.

The Definitive Internet Career Guide

phoenix.placement.oakland.edu/career/Guide.htm

Oakland University
E-mail: placement@oakland.edu

Jobs: **No** Cost to post jobs: N/A Cost to see jobs: N/A
Resumes: **No** Cost to post resumes: N/A Cost to see resumes: N/A
E-mail Alert (Push): N/A
Specialty: **All**
Industry: **All**
Feature: **Meta-links**
Location: **US**

The Definitive Internet Career Guide has one of the longest and best lists of links to job, resume and career management sites on the web. Site will only accept links which do not charge for their services. This is somewhat of an open statement based on the links here, but we believe it means—no headhunters.

Design Sphere Online

www.dsphere.net/comm/jobs.html

Irene Woerner, Cogent Software, Inc.
234 E. Colorado Blvd., Suite 725, Pasadena, CA 91101
Ph: 800-733-3380   Fax: 626-585-2785   E-mail: webmaster@dsphere.com

Jobs: **Yes** Cost to post jobs: **Free** Cost to see jobs: **Free**	
Resumes: **Yes** Cost to post resumes: **Free** Cost to see resumes: **Free**	
E-mail Alert (Push): N/A	
Specialty: **IT/Communications** **Graphic Arts**	
Industry: **All**	
Feature: N/A	
Location: **US**	

DesignSphere Online posts jobs and resumes for free in the communication and graphic arts fields. Positions and resumes are posted by date for freshness. All contact information is included. Altruistic endeavor, simple to view.

Developers.net

www.developers.net

Dayle Bowen, TapestryNet
111 Mission Street, Santa Cruz, CA 95060
Ph: 408-469-0700   E-mail: info@developers.net

Jobs: **Yes** Cost to post jobs: **Fee** Cost to see jobs: **Free**	
Resumes: **Yes** Cost to post resumes: **Free** Cost to see resumes: N/A	
E-mail Alert (Push): **Job Seeker**	
Specialty: **IT**	
Industry: **IT**	
Feature: N/A	
Location: **US/Int'l**	

Developers.net is a brand new "community" being built by the folks who brought us AsiaNet (see review). Employers pay $1,595 to have an opening e-mailed to interested candidates. Employers who participate can post openings at the site for free (50,000 were posted on our visit). Developers with specialties in DBMS, Web, UNIX and Windows register their e-mail and select the part of the country that they want to see positions from to reduce the overload. Owners have the right idea and enough marketing "moxie" to create another winner.

DICE High Tech Jobs Online

www.dice.com

William Schultz, D & L Online
P.O. Box 7070, Des Moines, IA 50309
Ph: 515-280-1144   Fax: 515-280-1452   E-mail: william@dlinc.com

Jobs: **Yes**
Cost to post jobs: **Fee**
Cost to see jobs: **Free**

Resumes: **Yes**
Cost to post resumes: **Free**
Cost to see resumes: **Fee**

E-mail Alert (Push): **Job Seeker**

Specialty: **IT**

Industry: **All**

Feature: N/A

Location: **US/Canada**

DICE continues to be a top site for IT, engineering and technical fields. Site claims thousands of jobs, and over 6,000 people have registered their e-mail to view job postings. All jobs have direct contact information. Base price for unlimited job postings is $550 per month, but are relegated to a specific state depending on the package you select. Job seekers can post their profile for 30 days, and then they need to reenter the site to keep it active. Profiles are sent to member employers on a daily basis. Employers can also search the profile database by keywords. Hundreds of links to member employer sites which includes a search of the U.S. by region. Niche site that does a good job, and even more important, knows how to promote its services.

Digital Cat

human.javaresource.com

Digital Cat, LLC
953 Industrial Avenue, Palo Alto, CA 94303
Ph: 650-493-3929   Fax: 650-843-1151   E-mail: hrc@javacats.com

Jobs: **Yes**
Cost to post jobs: **Fee** (See Notes)
Cost to see jobs: **Free**
Resumes: **Yes**
Cost to post resumes: **Free**
Cost to see resumes: **Fee**
E-mail Alert (Push): N/A
Specialty: **IT/Java**
Industry: **All**
Feature: N/A
Location: **US/Int'l/Japan**

Digital Cat specializes in Internet services for the Java community, and has built a small, but targeted, online service for matching Java professionals with world-wide related jobs. The site's human resource center has two components—one for the professional seeking employment, and the other for companies seeking employees. Recruiters pay $300 for three months of job postings (normally $700). On our last visit, there were free promotions.

Direct Marketing World Job Center

www.dmworld.com

Mainsafe Marketing Information
1113 Channing Way, Suite 11, Berkeley, CA 94702
E-mail: editor@web.mainsail.com

Jobs: **Yes**   Cost to post jobs: **Free**   Cost to see jobs: **Free**
Resumes: **Yes**   Cost to post resumes: **Free**   Cost to see resumes: **Free**
E-mail Alert (Push): N/A
Specialty: **Marketing**
Industry: **All**
Feature: N/A
Location: **US**

Direct Marketing World Job Center allows companies to post jobs and resumes for free. There were 72 new jobs and 17 new resumes posted on our last visit. Resumes were not only for marketing jobs, but IT and other areas as well. Their search engine is simple and effective.

direct-jobs.com

www.direct-jobs.com

John Bell, Direct-Jobs, LLC
Suite 300, 130 Cockeysville Road, Cockeysville, MD 21030
Ph: 888-491-8833   E-mail: jbell@direct-jobs.com

Jobs: **Yes**   Cost to post jobs: **Fee**   Cost to see jobs: **Free**
Resumes: **Yes**   Cost to post resumes: **Free**   Cost to see resumes: **Fee**
E-mail Alert (Push): N/A
Specialty: **All**
Industry: **All**
Feature: N/A
Location: **US**

direct-Jobs is a new site that posts jobs for employees and contractors in all fields. Site is owned by a headhunter who is playing both sides of the street. Employers pay $150 to post a position, and candidates send their resumes through the site to recruiters (employers pay only if qualified applicants respond). Job seekers can post a resume and their confidential information will only be sent if they OK it to employers. Site has the ability to pull jobs off your site and post them to other sites. Pricing is still open on this product. Title, location, salary range, and hiring organization are shown on all postings.

Discovery Place Oil & Gas

www.discoveryplace.com

World Web Technologies
410, 1010-1 St. S.W., Calgary, Alberta, Canada T2R 1K4
Ph: 403-777-9300   E-mail: webmaster@discoveryplace.com

Jobs: **Yes** Cost to post jobs: **Free** Cost to see jobs: **Free**	
Resumes: **Yes** Cost to post resumes: **Free** Cost to see resumes: **Free**	
E-mail Alert (Push): N/A	
Specialty: **Engineering/Chemical**	
Industry: **Oil/Petroleum/Gas**	
Feature: N/A	
Location: **Int'l/Canada (US)**	

Discovery Place Oil & Gas displays jobs by date of receipt. Corporations who have purchased banners are at the top of the listings. Hundreds of jobs and resumes were free to see with direct contact information. Jobs/resumes are a small piece of this petroleum industry site.

Diversilink

www.diversilink.com

Pedro Medrano, IHRS
801 W. El Camino Real, Suite 360, Mountain View, CA 94043
Ph: 650-962-0235   E-mail: sales@diversilink.com

Jobs: **Yes** Cost to post jobs: **Fee** Cost to see jobs: **Free**	
Resumes: **Yes** Cost to post resumes: **Free** Cost to see resumes: **Fee**	
E-mail Alert (Push): **Job Seeker**	
Specialty: **Engineering/PE**	
Industry: **All**	
Feature: **Diversity**	
Location: **US/Int'l**	

The DiversiLink web site is the official online job posting medium for the Society of Hispanic Professional Engineers (SHPE). A map of the U.S. allows job seekers to first select their region of choice, and then type in the position of interest. Takes a minute to get used to this two-step process, but it works well. Cost to post a job is $50, and another $15 for each additional job. Packages are available for banners and multiple postings. A virtual job fair is advertised, but in reality there are companies posting banners with links to their opportunities—no live chat, no interviews. Cost to view resumes is $150 per month. We have had positive feedback from recruiters using this site. Give it a try.

Diversity Careers Online

www.diversitycareers.com

Janet Penn, Diversity/Careers in Eng. & Information
P.O. Box 557, Springfield, NJ 07081
Ph: 973-912-8555   Fax: 973-912-8599   E-mail: sales@diversitycareers.com

Jobs: **Yes** Cost to post jobs: **Fee** Cost to see jobs: **Free**	**Diversity Careers Online** is a publication that comes out in print six times a year for minority technical professionals. Online, **Diversity Careers** provides links to those companies advertising in their publication. Resumes can be posted for free, and are then sent to the companies that advertise.
Resumes: **Yes** Cost to post resumes: **Free** Cost to see resumes: **Fee**	
E-mail Alert (Push): N/A	
Specialty: **Engineering/IT**	
Industry: **All**	
Feature: **Diversity**	
Location: **US**	

DiversityLink

www.diversitylink.com

Milton Spain
P.O. Box 5151, Incline Village, NV 89450
Ph: 702-831-7493   Fax: 702-831-1460   E-mail: diversity@diversitylink.com

Jobs: **Yes** Cost to post jobs: **Fee** Cost to see jobs: **Free**	**DiversityLink's** message is to "bring together females, minorities and other diversity professionals with proactive employers and search firms offering outstanding career opportunities." This is a new site that is trying hard to carve out its niche. Employers can post a job for $100 for 60 days. Recruiters can access the resume database for $1,500 a year. Jobs can be seen with full contact information, and are date posted. Some major corporations are sponsors. Watch for continued growth.
Resumes: **Yes** Cost to post resumes: **Free** Cost to see resumes: **Fee**	
E-mail Alert (Push): N/A	
Specialty: **All**	
Industry: **All**	
Feature: **Diversity**	
Location: **US**	

Donohue's RS/6000 Employment Page

www.s6000.com

Susan Donohue, Donohue Consulting, Inc.
P.O. Box 42046, Washington, DC 20015
Ph: 800-324-4749   Fax: 202-364-2249   E-mail: dci@s6000.com

Jobs: **Yes**	
Cost to post jobs: **Fee**	
Cost to see jobs: **Free**	
Resumes: **Yes**	
Cost to post resumes: **Free**	
Cost to see resumes: **Free**	
E-mail Alert (Push): N/A	
Specialty: **IT/IBM RS6000**	
Industry: **All**	
Feature: N/A	
Location: **US/England/Europe**	

Donohue's RS/6000 allows employers to go after this niche area in a simple way. Jobs listings are posted for 90 days for $50 ($200 for five positions). Resume profiles can be seen for free. Service provided by this Internet consulting company whose expertise is UNIX system administration. Simple site for recruiting that gets it done.

Drake Beam Morin

www.dbm.com/dbm.html

Steve Hoffman
100 Park Avenue, Third Floor, New York, NY 10017
Ph: 800-326-0033   E-mail: feedback@dbm.com

Jobs: **Yes**	
Cost to post jobs: **Free**	
Cost to see jobs: **Free** (See Note)	
Resumes: **Yes**	
Cost to post resumes: **Fee**	
Cost to see resumes: **Free**	
E-mail Alert (Push): N/A	
Specialty: **All**	
Industry: **All**	
Feature: N/A	
Location: **US**	

Drake Beam Morin allows recruiters to register at their site and receive resumes of their outplaced clients. Employers are invited to post their jobs, but, DBM only makes them available to their "clients." We can't blame them, but it does mean responses will be restricted. Job seekers can send career questions to a DBM featured consultant who may place your Q&A on their site. DBM hosts the Riley Guide reviewed in this edition.

Drilling Research Institute

www.drillers.com/classifi.htm

Steve Deveraux, DRI
E-mail: dm@techwrights.com

Jobs: **Yes**	
Cost to post jobs: **Free**	
Cost to see jobs: **Free**	
Resumes: **Yes**	
Cost to post resumes: **Free**	
Cost to see resumes: **Free**	
E-mail Alert (Push): **N/A**	
Specialty: **Engineering/Chemical**	
Industry: **Oil/Gas/Petroleum**	
Feature: N/A	
Location: **US/Int'l**	

Drilling Research Institute provides free job posting. The resumes are also free to see. There were several dozen applicant profiles with direct contact information. Jobs run for four weeks, and profiles for two to three weeks. Listings that are removed are saved in an archive text file that can be downloaded from the site. Simple, but effective site in the oil and gas industry.

Dr. Dobb's Journal

www.ddj.com

Stephen Bach
411 Borel Avenue, Suite 100, San Mateo, CA 94402
Ph: 650-358-9500   Fax: 650-358-9749   E-mail: sbach@well.com

Jobs: **Yes**	
Cost to post jobs: **Fee**	
Cost to see jobs: **Free**	
Resumes: N/A	
Cost to post resumes: N/A	
Cost to see resumes: N/A	
E-mail Alert (Push): N/A	
Specialty: **IT**	
Industry: **IT**	
Feature: **Research**	
Location: **US/Int'l**	

Dr. Dobb's Journal is a monthly publication going back to the early days of the PC that covers the practical side of technology for software developers. The programming community uses this publication to revise proposed standards, explore new technologies, argue over programming style, and share tricks of the trade. DDJ states that it prints more code examples than any other publication. Hundreds of IT positions can be viewed at this site that have been advertised in the magazine. The best and the brightest shop here. Not a place to find cut rate talent.

Dubuque Iowa

www.dubuque-ia.com/jobs.cfm

Michelle Rios, Greater Dubuque Development Corp.
Ph: 888-584-1931   E-mail: dubuqueia@wcinet.com

Jobs: **Yes** Cost to post jobs: **Fee** Cost to see jobs: **Free**
Resumes: **Yes** Cost to post resumes: **Free** Cost to see resumes: **Fee**
E-mail Alert (Push): **Job Seeker**
Specialty: **All**
Industry: **All**
Feature: N/A
Location: **US/IA/Dubuque**

Dubuque Iowa has definitely acknowledged the "power" of the web by forming a consortium of corporations to post their jobs and receive resumes via the web. Several hundred area employers have signed on to post positions. Job seekers can select the area or employer of choice, use the site's "note pad" to select the position of choice, and respond online. Site will also "push" jobs to you for future interest. All the local information you could want can be obtained at this site. Their "search engine" could use some work as you must select by employer or from limited categories. You cannot do a key word search. Great community concept that is ready to explode everywhere.

e-Math

www.ams.org/employment

American Mathematical Society
P.O. Box 6248, Providence, RI 02940
Ph: 800-321-4267   Fax: 401-455-4000   E-mail: emp-info@ams.org

Jobs: **Yes** Cost to post jobs: **Fee** Cost to see jobs: **Free**
Resumes: **Yes** Cost to post resumes: **Free** (See Note) Cost to see resumes: **Free** (See Note)
E-mail Alert (Push): N/A
Specialty: **Science/Math**
Industry: **Education**
Feature: N/A
Location: **US**

e-Math is the home of the American Mathematical Society. Ph.D. job opportunities in the academic world are posted here. Candidates post their e-mail addresses, and interested employers can send additional information to the applicants. No profiles of skills are posted at this site. Cost to post jobs is $120 for two months.

Eagleview

www.eagleview.com

Ed Alexander, SelectCandidate Network
1601 Trapelo Road, Waltham, MA 02154
Ph: 800-528-7380   Fax: 781-672-6019   E-mail: Evi@mail.eagleview.com

Jobs: **Yes**	
Cost to post jobs: **Fee**	
Cost to see jobs: **Free**	
Resumes: **Yes**	
Cost to post resumes: **Free**	
Cost to see resumes: **Fee**	
E-mail Alert (Push): **Job Seeker**	
Specialty: **All**	
Industry: **N/A**	
Feature: **N/A**	
Location: **US**	

Eagleview matches company jobs with a job seeker's background, and e-mails the results. Pricing has been modified to reflect the size of the corporate client. Site claims over 10,000 IT resumes in their database; they are deleted every 90 days.

Eagleview offers all the recruiting services an HR department needs. Executive search, providing recruiting contractors for those peaks and valley periods in recruiting, is all part of their service.

Eagleview is successful at being your outsourcing arm. Currently focused in the Northeast, but a recent merger with Management Process will give them more overall presence. Job seekers can post a complete profile for employers to view. Now that pricing is more in line with the marketplace, **Eagleview** should soar to new heights in the continued hunt for IT talent.

Eastern & European Job Bank

www.ecejobbank.com

Philip Atkinson, Scala ECE, Budapest
Ph: 361-327-5805   Fax: 361-266-5701   E-mail: job-bank@isys.hu

Jobs: **Yes**	
Cost to post jobs: **Free**	
Cost to see jobs: **Free**	
Resumes: **Yes**	
Cost to post resumes: **Free**	
Cost to see resumes: **Free**	
E-mail Alert (Push): **N/A**	
Specialty: **All**	
Industry: **All**	
Feature: **N/A**	
Location: **Int'l/Europe**	

Eastern & European Job Bank is as altruistic as it gets. This Budapest company allows employers and job seekers to meet for free via the web. They advise that they expect to grow their own workforce by 100 this year, so they are taking the cream-of-the-crop, and leaving the rest for anyone to view. There were 26 job postings and over 200 resumes, from many former communist countries, on our last visit.

Ed Physician

www.edphysician.com/

Ralph Single
P.O. Box 1361, Derry, New Hampshire 03038
Ph: 603-437-2989   Fax: 603-437-2989   E-mail: info@edphysician.com

Jobs: **Yes** Cost to post jobs: **Free** Cost to see jobs: **Free**	
Resumes: **No** Cost to post resumes: N/A Cost to see resumes: N/A	
E-mail Alert (Push): N/A	
Specialty: **Health Care/MD** **Emergency Room**	
Industry: **Health Care**	
Feature: N/A	
Location: **US**	

Ed Physician allows employers to post jobs for emergency physician openings for free. Job seekers view 100 openings organized by state. Direct contact information with a "New ", button to designate freshness of posting is a good idea. There was also an opening for an MD in Saudia Arabia and Canada.

Education JobSite

www.edjobsite.com

2037 W. Butler
Suite 107, Phoenix, AZ 85021
Ph: 602-242-0058   Fax: 602-841-8628   E-mail: webmaster@edjobsite.com

Jobs: **Yes** Cost to post jobs: **Fee** Cost to see jobs: **Free**	
Resumes: **No** Cost to post resumes: N/A Cost to see resumes: N/A	
E-mail Alert (Push): N/A	
Specialty: **Ed/K-12**	
Industry: **Ed/K-12**	
Feature: N/A	
Location: **US**	

Education JobSite is for those interested in teaching K-12. School districts can post unlimited positions for $50 for 30 days. A great buy. The site's search engine allows job seekers to view the U.S., search by specialty/certification, and obtain direct contact information.

Educator's Network EDNET

pages.prodigy.com/CA/luca52a/

Karla Freedman, Educator's Network-EDNET
5426 Woodlake Avenue, Woodland Hills, CA 91367
Ph: 818-999-9432   Fax: 818-999-5134   E-mail: luca52a@prodigy.com

Jobs: **Yes** Cost to post jobs: **Fee** Cost to see jobs: **Free**	There were over 285 teaching positions vacant in Southern California listed here when we visited, and **EDNET** plans to expand to the rest of the state (21 other postings). Jobs are posted within 48 hours, and you can place your initial openings for three months for free. If you want to continue, the cost is $300 for the next 12-month period. Good Q&A regarding how to get a job in the CA school system. Search results show the type of position and the school district. You have to do the rest. Long list of links to school districts.
Resumes: **No** Cost to post resumes: N/A Cost to see resumes: N/A	
E-mail Alert (Push): N/A	
Specialty: **Ed/K-12**	
Industry: **Higher Education**	
Feature: N/A	
Location: **US/W/CA**	

Electra a Women's View on Careers

electra.com

Joy Every, American Online Inc.
E-mail: electraghn@aol.com

Jobs: **Yes** Cost to post jobs: **Fee** Cost to see jobs: **Free**	**Electra** is owned by American Online, but is powered by the Monster Board. Q&A for career questions, and interesting gender-based articles are here. The rest is a channel to Monster Board.
Resumes: **Yes** Cost to post resumes: **Free** Cost to see resumes: **Fee**	
E-mail Alert (Push): **Job Seeker**	
Specialty: **All**	
Industry: **All**	
Feature: Diversity	
Location: **US**	

Electric Power NewsLink

www.powermag.com

Melissa Kansa, McGraw-Hill/Power
11 West 19th Street, 2nd Floor, New York, NY 10011
Ph: 330-478-4037   E-mail: powermag@mindspring.com

Jobs: **Yes** Cost to post jobs: **Fee** Cost to see jobs: **Free**	
Resumes: **No** Cost to post resumes: N/A Cost to see resumes: N/A	
E-mail Alert (Push): N/A	
Specialty: **Engineering/Power**	
Industry: **Power**	
Feature: N/A	
Location: **US**	

Electric Power magazine publishes it's employment opportunities on this site. Positions cover nuclear power engineers and related disciplines...even CEOs. Dozens of positions are listed in an easy-to-read format. Employment opportunities link is on the left side of the home page. Very easy to navigate.

Electronic Engineering Times

www.eet.com

Lynette McGill Hodge, CMP Media Group
(See TechWeb)
Ph: 800-598-7689   E-mail: lhodge@cmp.com

Jobs: **Yes** Cost to post jobs: **Fee** Cost to see jobs: **Free**	
Resumes: **Yes** Cost to post resumes: **Free** Cost to see resumes: **Fee**	
E-mail Alert (Push): N/A	
Specialty: **Engineering/IT**	
Industry: **IT**	
Feature: N/A	
Location: **US**	

EE Times has collaborated with Career-Mosaic for job and resume features for their site. An interesting salary survey can be viewed for engineers in an area set aside for career articles. Our favorite section is their Q&A with "Ask the Headhunter" author Nick Corcodilos. Recruiters pay $150 to post a position on **EE Times**, which is then posted to CareerMosaic for 30 days.

Electronic News OnLine

www.electronicnews.com

John Caggiano, Cahners Publishing Company
475 Park Avenue South, 2nd Floor, New York, NY 10016
Ph: 212-545-5454   Fax: 212-545-5460   E-mail: enews@cahners.com

Jobs: **Yes** Cost to post jobs: **Fee** Cost to see jobs: **Free**	
Resumes: **No** Cost to post resumes: N/A Cost to see resumes: N/A	
E-mail Alert (Push): N/A	
Specialty: **Engineering/** **Electronics**	
Industry: **Electronics**	
Feature: N/A	
Location: **US**	

Electronic News Online posts its weekly classified section on the web. All types of openings were listed from the very technical to VP of Operations. This site caused us problems with its layout as the design did not fit our screen. Great niche, but needs more work to capitalize on the web.

Emergency Medicine Practice Opportunity

www.embbs.com/job/jobs.html

Ash Nashed, Triple Star Systems
10 Swackhamer Road, Whitehouse Station, NJ 08889
E-mail: ashrafn@aol.com

Jobs: **Yes** Cost to post jobs: **Fee** Cost to see jobs: **Free**	
Resumes: **No** Cost to post resumes: N/A Cost to see resumes: N/A	
E-mail Alert (Push): N/A	
Specialty: **Health Care/MD**	
Industry: **Health Care**	
Feature: **Yes**	
Location: **US**	

In addition to job postings (employer cost is $25), this site also has interesting medical questions to challenge doctors (engaging idea) who visit. Individuals must register to see the articles and other content.

Employment Channel

www.employ.com

Broderick Byers, The Employment Channel
152 Madison Avenue, 22nd Floor, New York, NY 10016
Ph: 212-843-8585   Fax: 212-843-9093   E-mail: broderick@employ.com

Jobs: **Yes**	
Cost to post jobs: **Fee**	
Cost to see jobs: **Free**	
Resumes: **Yes**	
Cost to post resumes: N/A	
Cost to see resumes: N/A	
E-mail Alert (Push): N/A	
Specialty: **All**	
Industry: **All**	
Feature: N/A	
Location: **US/NJ**	

Calling all couch potatoes. If you are free Mondays at 7 PM, and live in NJ, you can see open positions throughout the state posted on this sponsor supported station (NJN). Outside the viewing area, the same jobs can be linked from NJ Department of Labor.

Employment of People with Disabilities

www.pcepd.gov

Dina Dorich, U.S. Government
1331 F Street N.W. Suite 300, Washington, DC 20004
Ph: 202-376-6200   Fax: 202-376-6219   E-mail: ddorich@pcepd.gov

Jobs: **No**	
Cost to post jobs: N/A	
Cost to see jobs: N/A	
Resumes: **No**	
Cost to post resumes: N/A	
Cost to see resumes: N/A	
E-mail Alert (Push): N/A	
Specialty: **Jobs for Disabled**	
Industry: **All**	
Feature: **Diversity**	
Location: **US**	

The President's Committee on Employment of People with Disabilities provides free links to over 60 organizations, and corporations who are committed to hiring and helping the disabled. Corporations can post their name and address and site will link directly back to their jobs page for free. Every employer NOT reaching out to the disabled ought to be considered "workforce challenged."

Employment Weekly

www.employment-weekly.com

P.O. Box 26499, Rochester, NY 14626
Ph: 716-227-7296   Fax: 716-227-7296

Jobs: **Yes** Cost to post jobs: **Fee** Cost to see jobs: **Free**	
Resumes: **No** Cost to post resumes: N/A Cost to see resumes: N/A	
E-mail Alert (Push): N/A	
Specialty: **All**	
Industry: **All**	
Feature: N/A	
Location: **US/NE/NY/Rochester**	

Employment Weekly lists jobs in the Rochester, NY area (this is the online version of a biweekly paper). Information about local job fairs can also be viewed

Employnet

employnet-inc.ksi.com/index.htm

Jim Chrisholm, 111 Broadway
Floor 8, New York, NY 10006
Ph: 212-634-0604   Fax: 212-634-0611   E-mail: resume@employnet-inc.com

Jobs: **No** Cost to post jobs: N/A Cost to see jobs: N/A	
Resumes: **Yes** Cost to post resumes: **Fee** Cost to see resumes: **Free**	
E-mail Alert (Push): N/A	
Specialty: **All**	
Industry: N/A	
Feature: N/A	
Location: **US**	

Employnet claims over 600 recruitment firms use their resume database (resumes are scanned). Recruiters use a dial-up system to get to the database. Site also has a resume writing service for $149. The cost to see resumes is $29 per month or $279 per year. Interesting career articles.

Engineering Job Source

www.engineerjobs.com

Jean Eggertsen
2016 Manchester #24, Ann Arbor, MI 48104
Ph: 734-971-6995   Fax: 734-677-4386   E-mail: advertise@engineerjobs.com

Jobs: **Yes** Cost to post jobs: **Fee** Cost to see jobs: **Free**	
Resumes: **Yes** Cost to post resumes: **Free** Cost to see resumes: **Fee**	
E-mail Alert (Push): **Job Seeker**	
Specialty: **Engineering**	
Industry: **All**	
Feature: N/A	
Location: **US/MW/MI**	

Engineering Job Source posts positions in engineering primarily in Michigan and Illinois, but is expanding throughout the U.S. Job seekers register at this site, and positions are "pushed" to them on a weekly basis for free. Employers pay $20 to post a position for 60 days. A simple search engine allows candidates to view all 50 states for jobs. Searches can be restricted to the last seven to 60 days. A simple site that Midwest engineers should visit.

Engineering Jobs.com

www.EngineeringJobs.com

Wayne Black
P.O. Box 1195 El Cerrito, CA 94530
E-mail: info@EngineeringJobs.com

Jobs: **Yes** Cost to post jobs: **Free** Cost to see jobs: **Free**	
Resumes: **Yes** Cost to post resumes: **Free** Cost to see resumes: **Free**	
E-mail Alert (Push): N/A	
Specialty: **Engineering**	
Industry: **All**	
Feature: N/A	
Location: **US/Int'l**	

Many corporations have links to their openings for engineering positions from **Engineering Jobs.com.** Applicants can have a link to their full resume from a short one. Resumes are sorted by specialty, and there are dozens from which to choose. Corporations pay for placing banner ads.

Engineering News Record

www.enr.com

Mark Barreca, The McGraw-Hill Companies
1221 Avenue of the Americas, 41st Floor, New York, NY 10020
Ph: 800-458-3842   Fax: 212-512-2074   E-mail: mark_barreca@mcgraw-hill.com

Jobs: **Yes** Cost to post jobs: **Fee** Cost to see jobs: **Free**
Resumes: **No** Cost to post resumes: N/A Cost to see resumes: N/A
E-mail Alert (Push): N/A
Specialty: **Engineering/Civil/ Construction**
Industry: **Construction**
Feature: N/A
Location: **US/Int'l**

Engineering News Record, a weekly publication devoted to the engineering, design, environmental and construction industries, posts its print help-wanted classifieds here. Ads can be seen from the prior four weeks issues. Their search engine allows you to view the information by title, keyword or state. Interesting banner opportunities for intrusive advertising.

Entry Level Job Seeker Assistant

members.aol.com/Dylander/jobhome.html

Joseph E. Schmalhofer III
E-mail: Dylander@aol.com

Jobs: **No** Cost to post jobs: N/A Cost to see jobs: N/A
Resumes: **Yes** Cost to post resumes: **Free** Cost to see resumes: **Free**
E-mail Alert (Push): N/A
Specialty: **College**
Industry: **All**
Feature: **Meta-links**
Location: **US**

Entry Level Job Seeker Assistant lists links to corporate job sites, newsgroups and numerous websites. The best feature is that graduating students can post their resumes for free, and they can be seen by all who visit. Resumes can be searched by field of interest.

Environmental Careers Org. (Eco.org)

www.eco.org

Kim Hibbard, The Environmental Careers Organization
179 South Street, Boston, MA 02111
Ph: 617-426-4375   Fax: 617-423-0998

Jobs: **Yes**	
Cost to post jobs: **Fee**	
Cost to see jobs: **Free**	
Resumes: **No**	
Cost to post resumes: N/A	
Cost to see resumes: N/A	
E-mail Alert (Push): **No**	
Specialty: **Science/ Environmental**	
Industry: **All**	
Feature: **Diversity**	
Location: **US**	

The Environmental Careers Organization posts internships for its member corporations for free. Students can search by region of the U.S., but all interested candidates have to send their resume through ECO. A diversity initiative asks all minorities who apply for positions to type "diversity initiative" in the upper right hand corner of their resume, and send it back to ECO.

Environmental Careers World

www.environmental-jobs.com

Ph: 757-727-7895   Fax: 757-727-7904   E-mail: ecwo@environmental-jobs.com

Jobs: **Yes**	
Cost to post jobs: **Fee**	
Cost to see jobs: **Free**	
Resumes: **No**	
Cost to post resumes: N/A	
Cost to see resumes: N/A	
E-mail Alert (Push): N/A	
Specialty: **Science/ Environmental**	
Industry: **All**	
Feature: N/A	
Location: **US**	

Environmental Careers World is a recruitment consulting firm in the environmental field. Recruiters pay $69 for a 30-day run, and if you are a nonprofit organization, you pay only $39. A link is an additional $25 to your homepage. Positions here are also included in the organization's *National Environmental Employment Report* newspaper.

Equipment Leasing Association Online

www.elaonline.com

Denise L. James, Equipment Leasing Association
1300 N. 17th Street, Suite 1010, Arlington, VA 22209
Ph: 703-527-8655   Fax: 703-527-2649   E-mail: djames@elamail.com

Jobs: **Yes** Cost to post jobs: **Fee** Cost to see jobs: **Free**	
Resumes: **No** Cost to post resumes: N/A Cost to see resumes: N/A	
E-mail Alert (Push): N/A	
Specialty: **Business/Leasing**	
Industry: **Equipment Leasing**	
Feature: N/A	
Location: **US**	

The Equipment Leasing Association allows ELA members to post openings for $295 (nonmembers pay $495) for a six-week run. All types of positions are listed for this industry, with direct contact information available on the web. Jobs are in all fields and are posted in alphabetical order with date of posting. There were about 20 jobs here on our last visit, ranging from CFO/VP to a university designer.

Escoffier On Line - Employment Resources

www.escoffier.com/nonscape/employ.shtml

George Cook, Escoffier On Line
P.O. Box 483, Point Lookout, NY 11569
Ph: 516-676-8507   E-mail: george@escoffier.com

Jobs: **Yes** Cost to post jobs: **Free** Cost to see jobs: **Free**	
Resumes: **Yes** Cost to post resumes: **Free** Cost to see resumes: **Free**	
E-mail Alert (Push): N/A	
Specialty: **Hospitality/ Food/Chefs**	
Industry: **Hospitality**	
Feature: **Meta-links**	
Location: **US/Int'l**	

Escoffier On Line is a wonderful addition to *Careerxroads*. It is run by the New York Institute of Technology Culinary Arts Program. Site lists positions all over the world for chefs ("working", executive, pastry, baker, food & beverage managers or any food service employment). A search engine has been added to the resume side of the house, but not on the jobs side. You can respond directly online through the job seeker's e-mail. All things to see and post are free. A long list of food career links is also available. This site is always being improved, and we truly wish them well.

Exec-U-Net

www.execunet.com

Dave Opton, Exec-U-Net, Inc.
25 Van Zant Street, Norwalk, CT 06855
Ph: 800-637-3126   Fax: 203-851-5177   E-mail: execunet@execunet.com

Jobs: **Yes**	
Cost to post jobs: **Free**	
Cost to see jobs: **Fee**	
Resumes: **No**	
Cost to post resumes: N/A	
Cost to see resumes: N/A	
E-mail Alert (Push): N/A	
Specialty: **Executive**	
Industry: **All**	
Feature:	
Location: **US/Int'l/Canada**	

Exec-U-Net is one of the best networking publications for executive job leads (over $100K). Position information is generated from members, search firms and corporations who can submit their openings for free. Members pay $125 a quarter to be able to access leads via the web or receive hard copy. Originally, **Exec-U-Net** was a human resource professional network, but rapidly grew to cover all fields and specialties. This organization also has monthly networking meetings all over the country, and recently, Canada as well. Site has interesting security features—subscribing members are not permitted to share job leads.

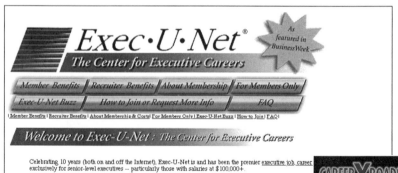

Federal Jobs Digest

www.jobsfed.com

FJD Hotline
310 North Highland Avenue, Ossining, NY 10562
Ph: 914-762-5111   Fax: 914-762-4818   E-mail: bobc@jobsfed.com

Jobs: **Yes** Cost to post jobs: **Free** (See Note) Cost to see jobs: **Free**
Resumes: **Yes** Cost to post resumes: **Free** (See Note) Cost to see resumes: **Fee**
E-mail Alert (Push): N/A
Specialty: **All**
Industry: **Government**
Feature: N/A
Location: **US**

Federal Jobs Digest claims more federal vacancies than any other source. Indications are that 6,810 vacancies were listed at the site on our last visit. They will soon launch job postings from private employers. Site provides a fee service, where for $40 it will advise you which federal jobs will match your qualifications. You send them your resume via the web, and they do a search of the federal job database to match your skills with current openings. Still takes three to four weeks to get back to you. Site advises that they get 800,000 visitors a month, and tells employers that they have 800,000 high-quality candidates. Hmmm. Would a private employer post jobs on a site named **Federal Jobs**? We wonder why.

FedWorld Federal Job Announcement Search

www.fedworld.gov

National Technical Information Service, U.S. Dept. of Commerce, Springfield, VA 22161
Ph: 703-487-4650   E-mail: webmaster@fedworld.gov

Jobs: **Yes** Cost to post jobs: N/A Cost to see jobs: **Free**
Resumes: **No** Cost to post resumes: N/A Cost to see resumes: N/A
E-mail Alert (Push): **Job Seeker**
Specialty: **All**
Industry: **Government**
Feature: N/A
Location: **US**

FedWorld Federal Job Announcement Search is an excellent site to browse for government openings. Site's search engine will allow you to view positions by state, summer jobs, Atlantic and Pacific overseas openings, as well as key word search. Sign up to get openings "pushed" to your PC for free. The database is updated twice a week. This is one of the few sites that post the salary range for all positions.

Feminist Career Center

www.feminist.org/911/911jobs.html

Jyotsna Srrenivasan, Feministy Majority Foundation
1600 Wilson Blvd., Suite 801, Arlington, VA 22209
E-mail: jyotsna@feminist.org

Jobs: **Yes**	
Cost to post jobs: **Free**	
Cost to see jobs: **Free**	
Resumes: **Yes**	
Cost to post resumes: **Free**	
Cost to see resumes: **Free**	
E-mail Alert (Push): **N/A**	
Specialty: **All**	
Industry: **All**	
Feature: **Diversity**	
Location: **US**	

The Feminist Career Center is managed by the Feminist Majority Foundation which is supported by more than 10,000 members. Recruiters can post positions for free as well as review resumes. Job seekers have access to several dozen positions listed by region and title of the posting organization or company. Over 100 internship positions are also listed in company alpha order.

FinCareer Global Financial Careers

www.fincareer.com

John Chetelat, Domine & Partners
75 Cannon Street, London, England 5BN
Ph: 441-719-290101   E-mail: mail@fincareer.com

Jobs: **Yes**	
Cost to post jobs: **Fee**	
Cost to see jobs: **Free**	
Resumes: **Yes**	
Cost to post resumes: **Free**	
Cost to see resumes: **Fee**	
E-mail Alert (Push): **N/A**	
Specialty: **Finance/Executive**	
Industry: **Finance**	
Feature: N/A	
Location: **Int'l/US**	

FinCareer places people in top level finance positions throughout the world. What makes this site unique is that they link to home pages for some of the largest corporations to help them fill entry- and mid-level positions. Job seekers can see this information for free. Several profiles of job seekers can be viewed with contact information. Company deals with global and investment banks and insurance and asset management firms. Site provides interesting data on the top firms in these fields.

Finishing.com

www.finishing.com

Ted Mooney
503 Brick Blvd., Brick, NJ 08723
Ph: 732-477-1447   Fax: 732-477-1974   E-mail: mooney@finishing.com

Jobs: Yes	
Cost to post jobs: **Free**	
Cost to see jobs: **Free**	
Resumes: **Yes**	
Cost to post resumes: **Free**	
Cost to see resumes: **Free**	
E-mail Alert (Push): N/A	
Specialty: **Manuf'g/Finishing**	
Industry: **Manufacturing**	
Feature: N/A	
Location: **US**	

Finishing.com continues to improve its internet commerce niche. Job seekers can post brief profiles with date of posting and include their contact information. Positions can be posted via the sites online form, and postings "scroll down" in no particular order. Date of posting is shown. Industry information includes links to many finishing associations and publications throughout the world. If anodizing, plating or powder coating is your field this is the place to shop for your next job.

Five O'Clock Club

www.fiveoclockclub.com

Max Zaretsky
300 East 40th Street, Suite 6L, New York, NY 10016
Ph: 212-286-9332   Fax: 212-286-9571   E-mail: 5occ@bway.net

Jobs: No	
Cost to post jobs: N/A	
Cost to see jobs: N/A	
Resumes: **No**	
Cost to post resumes: N/A	
Cost to see resumes: N/A	
E-mail Alert (Push): N/A	
Specialty: **All**	
Industry: **All**	
Feature: N/A	
Location: **US**	

The Five O'Clock Club is a national career counseling network offering affordable individual and group counseling. This site is not about job listings, but about career counseling. Membership is $35 per year, and counseling fees can run from $40 to $150 an hour. These are in-person meetings—not over the web. They will also provide a battery of tests if you so choose for an upfront fee of $500.

Florida Career Link

www.floridacareerlink.com

Pamela Kauten
Peak Consultants, Inc.
E-mail: peak@digital.net

Jobs: **Yes**	
Cost to post jobs: **Fee**	
Cost to see jobs: **Free**	
Resumes: **Yes**	
Cost to post resumes: **Free**	
Cost to see resumes: **Fee**	
E-mail Alert (Push): **Job Seeker**	
Specialty: **All**	
Industry: **All**	
Feature: N/A	
Location: **US/SE/FL**	

The Florida Career Link posts hundreds of jobs for corporations in this state. Positions can be searched by topic using the site's engine or by scrolling down the jobs page in alpha order. Site has a $295 set up fee to post jobs. Pricing runs from $75 per week with other packages available. There is also an e-mail "Push" service to job seekers at a cost of $50 per week. Needless to say we doubt if many job seekers pay to use this feature.

Food and Drug Packaging Online

www.fdp.com

Carol Young Orlando, Food & Drug Packaging
18724 W. Osage, Mundelein, IL 60060
Ph: 847-949-9604   Fax: 847-949-9686   E-mail: fdp@fdp.com

Jobs: **Yes**	
Cost to post jobs: **Fee**	
Cost to see jobs: **Free**	
Resumes: **No**	
Cost to post resumes: N/A	
Cost to see resumes: N/A	
E-mail Alert (Push): N/A	
Specialty: **Eng/Packaging**	
Industry: **Manufacturing**	
Feature: N/A	
Location: **US**	

Food and Drug Packaging Online requires you to register (free) before you can access the classified section of their publication. On our last visit there were only three jobs. A "chatroom" allows packaging individuals to share industry information. Cost to post is $100 per 250 words per month.

Forty Plus (Northern California)

web.sirius.com/~40plus/#contact

Forty Plus
7440 Earhart Road, Oakland, CA 94603
Ph: 510-430-2400   Fax: 510-430-1750   E-mail: 40plus@fortyplus.org

Jobs: **No** Cost to post jobs: N/A Cost to see jobs: N/A
Resumes: **Yes** Cost to post resumes: **Fee** Cost to see resumes: **Free**
E-mail Alert (Push): N/A
Specialty: **All**
Industry: N/A
Feature: **Diversity**
Location: **US/W/CA**

Forty Plus provides their members with free resume posting and allows employers to e-mail their openings to their office (but they do not post them on the web). Site has not really improved in the last year. Too bad—some of us are prospects for this club—and the rest of us eventually will be. Job seeker must be a member to post their resume. Site has links to other 40+ groups and job sites. Their primary mission is to help each other with career advice and guidance. They may want to consider investing more in their web site so they can broaden their services.

Frasernet

www.frasernet.com

George Fraser
Success Guide
E-mail: fraser@frasernet

Jobs: **Yes** Cost to post jobs: **Fee** Cost to see jobs: **Free**
Resumes: **Yes** Cost to post resumes: **Free** Cost to see resumes: **Fee**
E-mail Alert (Push): N/A
Specialty: **All**
Industry: N/A
Feature: **Diversity**
Location: **US**

Frasernet would like to connect the African community using the web. Chatroom, posted positions, a resume bank could all be the keys to success. Unfortunately, this site disappoints. Recruiters can post positions for $59 for six months. When we tried to view them, the links were no longer working. We did several searches of the resume database, and came up empty every time. To join the site (which is free) you are asked to agree with the goals and principles of **Frasernet's** philosophy (no matter if it is positive) and sign an agreement. Something is missing here.

Funeral Net

www.funeralnet.com/classifieds/index.html

Michael Turkiewicz, FuneralNet
6902 SE 18th Street, Portland, OR 97202
Ph: 800-721-8166   Fax: 800-943-5552   E-mail: turk@funeralnet.com

Jobs: **Yes** Cost to post jobs: **Free** Cost to see jobs: **Free**	
Resumes: **Yes** Cost to post resumes: **Free** Cost to see resumes: **Free**	
E-mail Alert (Push): **Job Seeker**	
Specialty: **Funeral Indusry**	
Industry: **Funeral**	
Feature: N/A	
Location: **US/Int'l/Canada**	

Funeral Net. Can you believe it? Here's a site with jobs you could just die for (sorry, Mark made me do it). Owner provides all job/resume services for free. We saw numerous internships and resumes of experienced individuals as well as those looking for their first opportunity. All resumes and positions are date posted. We did not see any jobs listed which tells us that either this industry is in serious decline (ohhh) or (you fill in the pun). Michael, the site's owner, advised us that it is just slow at the present time. Sure, we're all putting off the inevitable until a more convenient time.

Future Access Employment Guide

futureaccess.com: 80/employ.html

Bill Havlice, Future Access
P.O. Box 584, Saratoga, CA 95070
Ph: 916-767-1868   E-mail: webmaster@futureaccess.com

Jobs: **Yes** Cost to post jobs: **Fee** Cost to see jobs: **Free**	
Resumes: **Yes** Cost to post resumes: **Free** Cost to see resumes: **Free**	
E-mail Alert (Push): N/A	
Specialty: **Engineering**	
Industry: **All**	
Feature: N/A	
Location: **US**	

Future Access is a simple site where you can post your resume and see jobs for free. All of the job postings we saw were for engineers. Employers pay $10 per month to post positions. Jobs are date posted. Employer contact information and a search engine that allows you to view openings by state is available.

The (San Francisco Chronicle) Gate

www.sfgate.com/classifieds/

San Francisco Chronicle/Examiner
925 Mission Street, San Francisco, CA 94103
Ph: 415-447-6302   E-mail: whoshiring@sfgate.com

Jobs: **Yes**
Cost to post jobs: **Fee**
Cost to see jobs: **Free**

Resumes: **No**
Cost to post resumes: N/A
Cost to see resumes: N/A

E-mail Alert (Push): **Job Seeker**

Specialty: **All**

Industry: **All**

Feature: N/A

Location: **US/W/CA/**
San Francisco

The San Francisco Chronicle and Examiner classifieds are posted here daily. Employers can post to the "Hot Jobs" section for $300 per month per position and $95 for each additional position. Despite the **Gate** competing with its print, you can also post to their main classified web section for $95 for 30 days. No display ads are on the web. An e-mail feature takes this site a step above other newspaper publications. The newspaper allows job seekers to register their job search keywords and receive e-mail of those jobs that match their requirements. Positions wanted are also posted on the web.

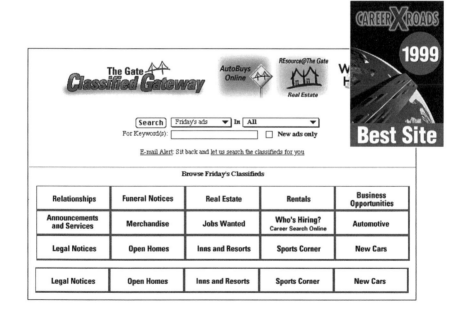

GeoWeb Interactive

www.ggrweb.com

Henry Hoffman, GeoWeb
2339 Plantation Bend Dr., Houston, TX 77478
Ph: 713-994-9903   Fax: 281-565-8583   E-mail: info@ggrweb.com

Jobs: **Yes** Cost to post jobs: **Fee** Cost to see jobs: **Free** (See Note)	
Resumes: **Yes** Cost to post resumes: **Free** (See Note) Cost to see resumes: **Free**	
E-mail Alert (Push): **Both**	
Specialty: **IT/Geographic Systems**	
Industry: **All**	
Feature: N/A	
Location: **US/Int'l/Europe/** **UK/Canada**	

GeoWeb Interactive is specifically for IT, Geo Science and Engineering professionals. Employers can post jobs for $199 each for two months which will be e-mailed to their 20,000 subscribers. Jobs will also be posted to other job sites/newsgroups. Site guarantees response or they will continue to run the ad for an additonal 30 days for free. Job Seekers can become members, post their resume, have it sent to agencies and potential employers, and see open positions for $49.99 for six months (and see all the jobs). They will distribute job seeker resumes to agencies and potential employers free, but limit access to the recent postings to the members. A newsletter is e-mailed to all who register. Recruiters can see several dozen resumes on the site or have them e-mailed for free.

Get a Job!

www.getajob.com

1031 Southwood Drive
San Louis Obispo, CA 93401
Ph: 805-546-0265

Jobs: **Yes** Cost to post jobs: **Fee** Cost to see jobs: **Free**	
Resumes: **No** Cost to post resumes: N/A Cost to see resumes: N/A	
E-mail Alert (Push): N/A	
Specialty: **All**	
Industry: **All**	
Feature: N/A	
Location: **US**	

Get a Job was reviewed in our last directory, and problems we found then with their search engine still persist. We tried, on several occasions, to view job postings, but could not get in. Different rate packages range from $1,000 a year for unlimited postings to monthly memberships or, simply pay $15 a job. An interesting list of links to newsgroups. Look into their free trial job posting.

GetMeAJob

www.getmeajob.com

Wayne Diu, WDP
1229 Walkley Road, Ottawa, ON, Canaada K1V6P9
E-mail: webmaster@getmeajob.com

Jobs: **Yes** Cost to post jobs: **Free** Cost to see jobs: **Free**	
Resumes: **Yes** Cost to post resumes: **Free** Cost to see resumes: **Free**	
E-mail Alert (Push): N/A	
Specialty: **All**	
Industry: **All**	
Feature: N/A	
Location: **Int'l/Canada/US**	

Getmeajob has remained true-to-form. keeping all services free. Resumes (date posted) and jobs can be posted and seen for free You can purchase a banner for $50 which will link to your site. A search engine has been added to help you on your voyage. Easy, simple, but needs a focus.

Getting A Job

www.americanexpress.com/student/

American Express University

Jobs: **Yes** Cost to post jobs: N/A Cost to see jobs: **Free**	
Resumes: **No** Cost to post resumes: N/A Cost to see resumes: N/A	
E-mail Alert (Push): N/A	
Specialty: **College/Internships**	
Industry: N/A	
Feature: N/A	
Location: **US**	

Getting A Job provides a long list of corporate and nonprofit internship programs. Some interesting career articles are available. The "Money Pit" still remains our favorite, advising parents how poor they will be no matter how much they save. A budget calculator will instantly explain how much all this education will cost you. Well-done, even though it is just a large advertisement for American Express Financial Assistance.

Getting Past Go:
A Survival Guide for College and Beyond

www.mongen.com/getgo

Chris Webb, Monumental General Insurance Group
1111 N. Charles St., Baltimore, MD 21201
Ph: 410-685-5500   Fax: 410-347-8693   E-mail: mongen@monlife.com

Jobs: **No**
Cost to post jobs: N/A
Cost to see jobs: N/A
Resumes: **No**
Cost to post resumes: N/A
Cost to see resumes: N/A
E-mail Alert (Push): N/A
Specialty: **College**
Industry: N/A
Feature: N/A
Location: **US**

Getting Past Go is a true survival guide for college and beyond. Practical advice worth bookmarking as you never know where you'll land when you are rolling those career dice. Not much different from a year ago, but these basics never go out of style.

GIS Jobs Clearinghouse

www.gjc.org

E-mail: adlime@gis.umn.edu

Jobs: **Yes**
Cost to post jobs: **Free**
Cost to see jobs: **Free**
Resumes: **No**
Cost to post resumes: N/A
Cost to see resumes: N/A
E-mail Alert (Push): N/A
Specialty: **IT/GIS**
Industry: **All**
Feature: N/A
Location: **US/Int'l**

GIS Jobs Clearinghouse (General Information Systems) is a free job-posting site. Simple, hundreds of jobs in text format by month of posting, and all have direct contact information. Links to associations and other IT topics are available. Some niche.

Global Careers

www.globalcareers.com

Global Career Services, Inc.
555 Fifth Avenue, 8th Floor, NY, NY 10017
Ph: 888-323-3066   Fax: 212-599-4684   E-mail: info@globalcareers.com

Jobs: **Yes**	
Cost to post jobs: **Fee**	
Cost to see jobs: **Free**	
Resumes: **Yes**	
Cost to post resumes: **Free**	
Cost to see resumes: **Free**	
E-mail Alert (Push): N/A	
Specialty: **All**	
Industry: **Business/ Transportation**	
Feature: N/A	
Location: **Int'l/US**	

Global Careers specializes in transportation, finance and international business careers. Recruiters pay $100 for 30 days to post a job. Also available is a 90-day trial for $300 including ten job postings or one-year membership for$900/30 job postings. You must be a subscriber to see the contact information on the resumes. A solid online resume form makes it easy to record skills data.

Global Job Net

riceinfo.rice.edu/projects/careers

Michael Breu, Rice CSC - MS 521
6100 Main, Houston, TX 77054
Ph: 713-527-4055   E-mail: breu@rice.edu

Jobs: **No**	
Cost to post jobs: N/A	
Cost to see jobs: N/A	
Resumes: **No**	
Cost to post resumes: N/A	
Cost to see resumes: N/A	
E-mail Alert (Push): N/A	
Specialty: **College**	
Industry: N/A	
Feature: N/A	
Location: **US**	

Global JobNet is set up like a TV studio with content at different "channels." Despite the fact that the content is a little thin, it is an engaging theme with many design ideas. Internships are posted, and several career links are available.

GO Jobs: The Guide to Online Jobs

www.gojobs.com

Jonathon Duarte, GO Jobs, Inc.
1439 Sea Ridge, Newport Beach, CA 92660
Ph: 949-720-3848   Fax: 949-760-9428   E-mail: jduarte@gojobs.com

Jobs: **Yes** Cost to post jobs: **Fee** Cost to see jobs: **Free**	
Resumes: **Yes** Cost to post resumes: **Free** Cost to see resumes: **Fee**	
E-mail Alert (Push): **N/A**	
Specialty: **All**	
Industry: **All**	
Feature: N/A	
Location: **US**	

Go Jobs will post a job for $65 or $400 for unlimited postings per month. Easy-to-use and view, as employers can see resumes if they go for the $400 monthly package. Contract as well as full-time positions are posted. Hundreds of links to job sites are broken into region, industry and occupation to make this a user-friendly site. Owners are promising software allowing recruiters to post jobs to multiple sites.

Good Works

www.essential.org/goodworks/

Charles Bennington, Good Works
P.O. Box 19405, Washington, DC 20036
E-mail: ei@essential.org

Jobs: **Yes** Cost to post jobs: **Free** Cost to see jobs: **Free**	
Resumes: **No** Cost to post resumes: N/A Cost to see resumes: N/A	
E-mail Alert (Push): N/A	
Specialty: **Nonprofit**	
Industry: **Nonprofit**	
Feature: N/A	
Location: **US**	

Good Works is a national directory for social change organizations and public interest careers. Jobs can be posted by e-mailing them to goodjobs@essential.org. A map of the U.S. makes it easy to select a state for your next job opportunity. Site is broadening its scope to include jobs in Canada.

Great Summer Jobs

www.gsj.petersons.com

Susan Greenberg, Peterson's
202 Carnegie Center, Princeton, NJ 08543
Ph: 800-338-3282   Fax: 609-243-9150   E-mail: crism@petersons.com

Jobs: **Yes**
Cost to post jobs: **Fee**
Cost to see jobs: **Free**
Resumes: **No**
Cost to post resumes: N/A
Cost to see resumes: N /A
E-mail Alert (Push): N/A
Specialty: **College/Summer**
Industry: **Recreation**
Feature: N/A
Location: **US**

Great Summer Jobs lists summer camp openings across the U.S. Cost to post is $399 for four jobs for six months. You need to list positions early in the winter prior to the upcoming summer season, as the site claims it gets thousands of job listings. Also listed is information on the types of jobs, what you can expect in salary from these positions, and a well-written piece on what camp directors are looking for in prospective counselors. Site is well-maintained, but get there early because when the summer months come, there are no jobs listed. We love it.

Hard@Work

www.hardatwork.com

Dennis Murphy, Hard@Work, Inc.
210 Commerce Boulevard, Round Rock, TX 78664
Ph: 800-580-5421   Fax: 512-255-7523   E-mail: demwit@hardatwork.com

Jobs: **No**	
Cost to post jobs: N/A	
Cost to see jobs: N/A	
Resumes: **No**	
Cost to post resumes: N/A	
Cost to see resumes: N/A	
E-mail Alert (Push): **Job Seeker**	
Specialty: **All**	
Industry: **All**	
Feature: N/A	
Location: **US**	

Hard@Work continues to be our favorite watercooler. It's a human resource and career management site that's a little different, run by owners who continue to keep it fresh. Day-to-day employer/employee problems are discussed, and readers can send in their comments. Check out any of the sections from "Stump the Mentor" to "Sisyphus Unwound." Check out the question of the day, often with unusual opinions.

Hard@Work Pushes an online newsletter to its readers. Take a break.

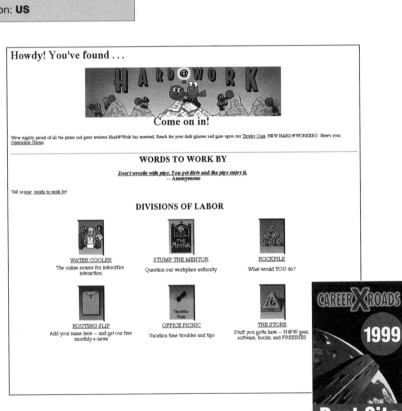

Hartford Courant

www.courant.com

285 Broad Street
Hartford, CT 06115
Ph: 800-524-4242   Fax: 860-241-3864

Jobs: **Yes**	
Cost to post jobs: **Fee**	
Cost to see jobs: **Free**	
Resumes: **No**	
Cost to post resumes: N/A	
Cost to see resumes: N/A	
E-mail Alert (Push): N/A	
Specialty: **All**	
Industry: **All**	
Feature: N/A	
Location: **US/NE/CT**	

We always like it when a newspaper puts their classified help-wanted link right up front on the home page so it is easy to find. **Hartford Courant** participates in CareerPath.

HeadHunter.NET

www.headhunter.net

Warren Bare, Software Technology Corp
1430 Boundary Blvd., Suwanee, GA 30174
Ph: 770-300-8892   Fax: 770-495-6363   E-mail: feedback@headhunter.net

Jobs: **Yes**
Cost to post jobs: **Free** (See Note)
Cost to see jobs: **Free**
Resumes: **Yes**
Cost to post resumes: **Free**
Cost to see resumes: **Free**
E-mail Alert (Push): **Job Seeker**
Specialty: **IT**
Industry: **All**
Feature: N/A
Location: **US**

HeadHunter.NET is as creative as anyone when it comes to ramping up a business model with a twist. All jobs are posted for free, but if employers would like a higher position in the list (so your job is seen first), you need to pay $900 per month to join their Friends Corporate Plus Program. This gets your company unlimited postings, and your jobs are upgraded for $.08 per day + other site marketing programs. For $495 per month + $.05 per day you also get unlimited postings minus a few marketing promotions. Positions are dated. This is one of the hottest sites on the web for IT professionals. As a job seeker you can still keep your identity confidential and openings that match your interests will be e-mailed to you. Jobs listed on **HeadHunter** are also posted to more than 75 newsgroups. Salary ranges for open positions are also available at the employer's option. Site claims 177,000 + jobs, 89,000 were updated last week and they get 44,000 visitors per day. Those are impressive numbers that they show on their homepage. Headley the helper has been added to guide you through this site.

HealthBank USA

www.healthbankusa.com

395 South End Avenue
Suite 15-D, New York, NY 10280
Ph: 212-912-0175   E-mail: careers@healthbankusa.com

Jobs: **Yes** Cost to post jobs: **Free** Cost to see jobs: **Free**
Resumes: **Yes** Cost to post resumes: **Free** Cost to see resumes: **Fee**
E-mail Alert (Push): N/A
Specialty: **Health Care**
Industry: **All**
Feature: N/A
Location: **US/Int'l**

HealthBank USA allows employers to post jobs for free for 60 days. For access to the resume database, recruiters pay an annual fee of $499. Other packages are available. Candidates can have a confidential profile listed for free. Job seekers should post their resume online because it will cost you $25 to mail it.

Health Care Jobs Online

www.hcjobsonline.om

Paul Erickson, Erickson & Assoc., Inc
338 Winnebago Rod, Lake Winnebago, MO 64034
Ph: 816-537-5511   Fax: 816-537-8493   E-mail: Paul@qni.com

Jobs: **Yes** Cost to post jobs: **Fee** Cost to see jobs: **Free**
Resumes: **No** Cost to post resumes: N/A Cost to see resumes: N/A
E-mail Alert (Push): N/A
Specialty: **Health Care**
Industry: **Health Care**
Feature: N/A
Location: **US**

Health Care Jobs emphasizes opportunities with hospitals, healthcare corporations and long term care facilities. Positions in nursing, ancillary health care professionals, physicians and administration are all date posted. The cost to post jobs is $50 for a 30-day run. Continuing improvements during the last year are paying off.

Health Care Recruitment Online

www.healthcarerecruitment.com

Richard Sierra, Sierra Recruitment Service, Inc.
9000 W. Sheridan St. 151, Pembroke Pines, FL 33054
Ph: 954-435-0093   Fax: 954-435-9040   E-mail: rsierra@interpoint.net

Jobs: **Yes** Cost to post jobs: **Fee** Cost to see jobs: **Free**	
Resumes: **No** Cost to post resumes: **Free** Cost to see resumes: N/A	
E-mail Alert (Push): N/A	
Specialty: **Health Care/Nursing**	
Industry: **Health Care**	
Feature: N/A	
Location: **US/Saudi Arabia/UK**	

Health Care Recruitment Online specializes in openings for nurses and allied health professionals. Site's search engine allows you to view jobs by state or specialty. Recruiters pay $150 for a 30-day job posting. An added feature is a listing of state licensure information centers across the U.S. Active for several years, this site has continually improved.

Health Career Web

www.HealthCareerWeb.com

Jennifer Ruffin, Career Web
150 W. Brambleton Avenue, Norfolk, VA 23510
Ph: 800-871-0800   Fax: 757-623-5942   E-mail: jruffin@cweb.com

Jobs: **Yes** Cost to post jobs: **Fee** Cost to see jobs: **Free**	
Resumes: **Yes** Cost to post resumes: **Free** Cost to see resumes: **Fee**	
E-mail Alert (Push): **Job Seeker**	
Specialty: **Health Care/Nursing** **Physician/Allied Health**	
Industry: **Health Care**	
Feature: N/A	
Location: **US/Int'l**	

Health Career Web is another of the sister sites in the Career Web chain. Cost to post a position is $80 per month. Recruiters can search the site's resume database for $1,500 per month. Resumes are posted for 90 days, and on the 80th day, the job seeker is advised to update or leave the system. Good move. Over 100 corporations have their jobs page linked to this site so candidates can go direct as well. We believe CareerWeb's strategy to build niche sites like these will pay off.

HealthOpps

www.healthopps.com

Michele Groutage, HealthOpps
17150 Sawyer Street SE, Monroe, WA 98272
Ph: 800-293-2700   Fax: 425-481-6488   E-mail: mgroutage@careermosaic.com

Jobs: **Yes**	
Cost to post jobs: **Fee**	
Cost to see jobs: **Free**	
Resumes: **Yes**	
Cost to post resumes: **Free**	
Cost to see resumes: **Fee**	
E-mail Alert (Push): N/A	
Specialty: **Health Care/ Physician/Nursing**	
Industry: **Health Care**	
Feature: N/A	
Location: **US**	

HealthOpps is now a part of CareerMosaic. Cost to post jobs is $160 for 30 days. Resumes can be seen if you purchase a standard package (see Career Mosaic). Jobs are listed with direct links to the corporation's jobs. Links to several hundred employer sites may also be viewed.

Heart

www.career.com

Sandhya Dave, Heart Advertising Network, Inc.
4546 El Camino Real, Suite 247, Los Altos, CA 94022
Ph: 650-917-510   Fax: 650-917-5515   E-mail: sales@careers.com

Jobs: **Yes**	
Cost to post jobs: **Fee**	
Cost to see jobs: **Free**	
Resumes: **Yes**	
Cost to post resumes: **Free**	
Cost to see resumes: **Fee**	
E-mail Alert (Push): **Job Seeker**	
Specialty: **All**	
Industry: **All**	
Feature: **Virtual Job Fair**	
Location: **US/Int'l**	

Heart offers online "Virtual Job Fairs," with real-time interviews for job seekers and recruiters. We suggest that you check this out before you buy, but you would be hard pressed to find a better job site design. Heart continues to be creative and should be part of your recruiting strategy. Cost to post individual jobs is $150 for a one-month posting. Jobs are posted with direct contact information and can be viewed in several different ways. Job seekers post their resumes for free. Resumes are e-mailed to the corporations that post jobs. **Heart** has added an international component to the site.

Help Wanted

www.helpwanted.com

Recruitment On_Line, Inc.
771 Boston Post Road, Marlboro, MA 01752
Ph: 508-485-1230   Fax: 508-481-9616   E-mail: info@helpwanted.com

Jobs: **Yes** Cost to post jobs: **Free** Cost to see jobs: **Free**	**Help Wanted** has changed their business model, and all job postings and resumes are free to view. Job seekers can also post their resume at no charge. Split screen to view resumes is a pet peeve with us as "scrolling" is not our forte. However, direct contact information can be viewed, and the price is right. An example of an increasing trend toward income models from banners rather than posting.
Resumes: **Yes** Cost to post resumes: **Free** Cost to see resumes: **Free**	
E-mail Alert (Push): **N/A**	
Specialty: **All**	
Industry: **All**	
Feature: **N/A**	
Location: **US**	

Help-Wanted USA

www.iccweb.com

James Gonyea, Gonyea and Associates, Inc.
1151 Maravista Drive, New Port Richey, FL 34655
Ph: 813-372-1333   Fax: 813-372-0394   E-mail: gonyeaasoc@aol.com

Jobs: **Yes** Cost to post jobs: **Fee** Cost to see jobs: **Free**	**Help-Wanted USA** is one of the pioneers in this industry, and with its sister site—Internet Career Connection, still offers a good value. Their database is built through a network of independent sites in cities throughout the country. Jobs can be posted for $75 each for a two-week run. A "super volume discount" allows employers (or other sites that represent their services) to use a software program to prepare ads offline, and then upload them to their service. When you send the file you will be invoiced $50 for each 100 ads you place ($.50 per ad). A long list of information and links to working for Uncle Sam is also included. HW-USA can also be viewed through AOL. The charge to post your resume is $25 for six months.
Resumes: **Yes** Cost to post resumes: **Fee** Cost to see resumes: **Free**	
E-mail Alert (Push): **N/A**	
Specialty: **All**	
Industry: **All**	
Feature: **N/A**	
Location: **US**	

Hi Tech Career Centre

www.hitechcareer.com

Debbie McGrath, The CEO Group - Washington Post
355 Harry Walker Parkway, Newmarket, Ontario, Canada L3Y 7B3
Ph: 905-830-1990   Fax: 905-830-0062   E-mail: dmcgrath@ceogroup.com

Jobs: **Yes** Cost to post jobs: **Fee** Cost to see jobs: **Free**	**Hi Tech Career Centre** is owned by a job fair organization recently acquired by the *Washington Post*. Recruiters who participate in their programs can obtain resumes and post jobs on the site. Candidates can submit their resume online, and they will be matched with posted positions. When job seekers register, they will be sent e-mail high-tech career job alerts twice a month. Job seekers have to send their resume directly through the site to the employer. No direct contact information is available. Schedule of Canadian job fair dates is posted.
Resumes: **Yes** Cost to post resumes: **Free** Cost to see resumes: **Fee**	
E-mail Alert (Push): **Job Seeker**	
Specialty: **All**	
Industry: **All**	
Feature: **Job Fair**	
Location: **Int'l/Canada**	

Hire Wire

www.hirewire.com

Barbara Gorla, Cass Communications
3880 Murphy Canyon Road, San Diego, CA 92123
Ph: 800-378-3700   Fax: 619-505-8290   E-mail: membersupport@college.com

Jobs: **No** Cost to post jobs: N/A Cost to see jobs: N/A	**Hire Wire** has been around now for about a year and focuses on the college market. The articles that we saw last year haven't been improved. Site is limited in scope as it has not added significantly to its original goal connecting to schools all over the country.
Resumes: **No** Cost to post resumes: N/A Cost to see resumes: N/A	
E-mail Alert (Push): N/A	
Specialty: **College**	
Industry: **All**	
Feature: N/A	
Location: **US**	

Hispanic Online Magazine

www.hisp.com

Enrique Gonzales, Olive Tree Publications
5928 Broaway, Suite 305, San Antonio, TX 78209
Ph: 888-841-9786   Fax: 909-924-1139   E-mail: webmaster@hisp.com

Jobs: **Yes** Cost to post jobs: **Fee** Cost to see jobs: **Free**
Resumes: **Yes** Cost to post resumes: **Free** Cost to see resumes: **Fee**
E-mail Alert (Push): **Job Seeker**
Specialty: **All**
Industry: **All**
Feature: **Diversity/Chatroom**
Location: **US**

Hispanic Online Magazine has created an interesting model for the publishing industry. Recruiters can have candidates fill out an online resume and e-mail it directly to them with the job ID identified. Job seekers can register for their "Personal Search Agent" which asks for a skills profile and e-mails positions that fit to your desktop. The site's search engine will allow job seekers to search by major cities and advises which have open positions. It can also be searched by job function or salary level. Recruiters pay $200 to post a position. Other packages are available.

Hollywood Web

www.hollywoodweb.com

Brett Crosby, HOLLYWOODWEB
555 Rose Suite 1, Venice, CA 90291
Ph: 310-392-3636   E-mail: bc@hollywoodweb.com

Jobs: **Yes** Cost to post jobs: **Free** Cost to see jobs: **Free**
Resumes: **Yes** Cost to post resumes: **Free** Cost to see resumes: **Free**
E-mail Alert (Push): N/A
Specialty: **Entertainment/** **All Areas**
Industry: **Entertainment**
Feature: N/A
Location: **US**

HollywoodWeb provides actors and actresses a "stage" for free. Directors, writers, technicians, models and extras can also be part of this cyberaudition. All union members can register their area of interest, scan in a headshot, and send it to the site via e-mail (snail will cost you $15). Casting directors provide audition information, which the site verifies, afterwhich they receive a password to view the backgrounds of the candidates.

Hong Kong Standard

www.hkstandard.com

Hong Kong Standard Newspapers Ltd.
Hong Kong
Ph: 852-279-98833   E-mail: jobmarket@hkstandard.com

Jobs: **Yes** Cost to post jobs: **Fee** Cost to see jobs: **Free**	This Hong Kong newspaper has a search engine allowing access to its classified help-wanted positions. Candidates search by company, agency or position title. Site also provides an online
Resumes: **Yes** Cost to post resumes: **Free** Cost to see resumes: N/A	resume form to speed direct replies. We tried and tried to get into the site's resume database (or whatever they do with the resumes they collect) and had no luck. Interesting job-tip articles with
E-mail Alert (Push): N/A	actual examples of problems and professional recommendations.
Specialty: **All**	
Industry: **All**	
Feature: N/A	
Location: **Int'l/Hong Kong**	

Hoover's

www.hoovers.com

Gary Hoover, Hoover's, Inc.
1033 La Posada Drive, Ste. 250, Austin, TX 78752
Ph: 512-374-4563   E-mail: info@hoovers.com

Jobs: **No** Cost to post jobs: N/A Cost to see jobs: N/A	**Hoover's Online** is the place to go when you are looking for company profiles for your next interview. Many parts of this site are free (subscription costs $12.95 per month). A research
Resumes: **No** Cost to post resumes: N/A Cost to see resumes: N/A	treasure trove.
E-mail Alert (Push): N/A	
Specialty: **All**	
Industry: **All**	
Feature: **Research**	
Location: **US/Int'l**	

Hospital-Web

neuro-www.mgh.harvard.edu/hospitalweb.shtml

John Lester

E-mail: lester@helix.mgh.harvard.edu

Jobs: **No**	
Cost to post jobs: N/A	
Cost to see jobs: N/A	
Resumes: **No**	
Cost to post resumes: N/A	
Cost to see resumes: N/A	
E-mail Alert (Push): N/A	
Specialty: **Health Care**	
Industry: **Health Care**	
Feature: **Meta-links**	
Location: **Health Care**	

Hospital-Web is exactly what its name implies—links to U.S. and international hospitals—thousands of facilities by state and country. Great starting point.

Hospitality Net

www.hospitalitynet.nl/

Henri Roelings, Hospitality Net
Akersteenweg 31, Maastricht, Netherlands 6226 HR
Ph: 310-433-626600   Fax: 310-433-626770   E-mail: jobs@hospitalitynet.nl

Jobs: **Yes**	
Cost to post jobs: **Free**	
Cost to see jobs: **Free**	
Resumes: **Yes**	
Cost to post resumes: **Free**	
Cost to see resumes: **Free**	
E-mail Alert (Push): N/A	
Specialty: **All**	
Industry: **Hospitality**	
Feature: N/A	
Location: **Int'l/Netherlands/US**	

Hospitality Net's owner has carved out a well-designed international industry niche where jobs and resumes are posted for free. All resumes and jobs are date posted. Site has grown to the point where a search engine is necessary. Site's main income is from selling banners. All types of positions in the hospitality industry are posted at this site.

Hot Jobs

www.hotjobs.com

Kelly Michaelian, Otec Inc.
24 West 40th Street, 11th floor, New York, NY 10128
Ph: 212-302-0060   Fax: 212-840-0397   E-mail: kelly@hotjobs.com

Jobs: **Yes** Cost to post jobs: **Fee** Cost to see jobs: **Free**	
Resumes: **Yes** Cost to post resumes: **Free** Cost to see resumes: **Fee**	
E-mail Alert (Push): N/A	
Specialty: **IT**	
Industry: **IT**	
Feature: N/A	
Location: **US**	

Hot Jobs connects job seekers to employers who use the site's web-enabled product SoftShoe. Sold to major employers (Lucent Technologies for example), SoftShoe is a staffing template for posting jobs by location, title and date, and links the job seeker to the job description. Applicant tracking and reporting are part of the package. This is all keyword search, and is right up there with some of the best web-based systems products out on the market. (See Tools and Resources). At **Hot Jobs,** job seekers can select hundreds of opportunities by job type, company or location. Companies still have to scan all the paper resumes, but they will help you with the scanning process. The full system is over six figures, but recruiters can purchase pieces of the puzzle, and only companies that buy pieces of the puzzle can post jobs to their site.

Houston Chronicle Interactive

www.chron.com

Houston Chronicle
801 Texas Avenue, Houston, TX 77002
Ph: 713-224-6868   E-mail: classifieds@chron.com

Jobs: **Yes** Cost to post jobs: **Fee** Cost to see jobs: **Free**	
Resumes: **No** Cost to post resumes: N/A Cost to see resumes: N/A	
E-mail Alert (Push): N/A	
Specialty: **All**	
Industry: N/A	
Feature: N/A	
Location: **US/SW/TX/Houston**	

On the **Houston Chronicle** web pages, visitors will find help-wanted ads from the current day's newspaper as well as the prior Sunday. **The Houston Chronicle** participates in CareerPath.com.

HR COMM

www.hrcomm.com

The Human Resource Community Network
P.O. Box 23412, Pleasant Hill, CA
Ph: 510-844-1016   Fax: 510-944-5012   E-mail: support@hrcomm.com

Jobs: **Yes**	
Cost to post jobs: **Fee**	
Cost to see jobs: **Free**	

Resumes: **No**
Cost to post resumes: N/A
Cost to see resumes: N/A

E-mail Alert (Push): N/A

Specialty: **Human Resources**

Industry: **All**

Feature: N/A

Location: **US**

HR Comm posts openings by function or by date of entry. Compensation professionals can participate in their salary surveys by purchasing a membership for $249 per year. Long list of links to HR services is worth a visit.

HR Network

www.hrreport

George Crosby
P.O. Box 225, Coopersville, MI 49404-0225
Ph: 515-837-7857

Jobs: **Yes**
Cost to post jobs: N/A
Cost to see jobs: N/A

Resumes: **No**
Cost to post resumes: N/A
Cost to see resumes: N/a

E-mail Alert (Push): N/A

Specialty: **Human Resources**

Industry: **All**

Feature: N/A

Location: **US**

HR Network is not really a web service—not yet. It is, however, one of the best sources for finding human resource jobs at $80,000 plus. Members pay $105 a quarter to share job leads. If the jobseeker does not share his/her leads, then future leads will not be available Members are warned not to copy or share the leads. Whether you are looking for a position as VP or Director of HR, OD, Compensation or Benefits many unpublished opportunities reside here because the posting for the company is free.

HR Perc Network Job Opps

www.perc.net/hr.html

Doug Kalish
Positive Employee Relations Council
Ph: 770-454-9130   Fax: 770-454-9781   E-mail: dkalish@perc.net

Jobs: **Yes**	
Cost to post jobs: **Free**	
Cost to see jobs: **Free**	
Resumes: **Yes**	
Cost to post resumes: **Free**	
Cost to see resumes: **Free**	
E-mail Alert (Push): N/A	
Specialty: **Human Resources**	
Industry: **All**	
Feature: N/A	
Location: **US**	

HR Positive Employee Relations Council has 1,100 members in professional ER, legal or management jobs in over 800 companies around the world. An HR "question of the day" describes difficult situations and how they are handled. A handful of resumes and jobs were posted. Resumes are coded, and recruiters have to e-mail the individual through the site for contact information. Jobs have direction contact information.

HR Professionals

hrpro.org/main.html

Ph: 513-677-0514   E-mail: dkaiser@hrpro.org

Jobs: **No**	
Cost to post jobs: N/A	
Cost to see jobs: N/A	
Resumes: **No**	
Cost to post resumes: N/A	
Cost to see resumes: N/A	
E-mail Alert (Push): N/A	
Specialty: **All**	
Industry: **All**	
Feature: **Meta-links**	
Location: **US**	

HR Professionals is a listing of information links for human resource professionals trying to keep their head above the water. Check out the long list of employment opportunities links here.

HR Recruiting

hr-recruiting.com

Blaine Campbell, Quantum Business Solutions
1005 Cumberland Drive, Auburn, AL 36830
Ph: 800-899-3277   Fax: 334-821-6497   E-mail: gbs@eapp.com

Jobs: **Yes**	
Cost to post jobs: **Fee**	
Cost to see jobs: **Free**	
Resumes: **Yes**	
Cost to post resumes: **Free**	
Cost to see resumes: **Fee**	
E-mail Alert (Push): N/A	
Specialty: **Human Resources**	
Industry: **All**	
Feature: **N/A**	
Location: **US**	

HR Recruiting is a database of human resource resumes. Candidates are phone screened, and a brief summary is placed in the database for recruiters to view. All are coded. A one-month membership is $250 which allows you to post three jobs for 30 days. Other packages are available. Site guarantees that all candidates have a minimum of three years experience and have completed a written screening assessment. We had real difficulty being able to find job postings as the area requires a password. New site that will need time to grow, and will need to develop a plan to market its service beyond the web to succeed.

HRSites

www.hrsites

Art Koff, HR Sites International
820 North Orleans, Suite 218, Chicago, IL 60610
Ph: 888-921-9400   Fax: 312-202-1818   E-mail: artkoff@enteract.com

Jobs: **Yes**	
Cost to post jobs: **Fee**	
Cost to see jobs: **Free**	
Resumes: N/A	
Cost to post resumes: N/A	
Cost to see resumes: N/A	
E-mail Alert (Push): N/A	
Specialty: **All**	
Industry: **All**	
Feature: **Multiple Site Job Posting**	
Location: **US**	

HRSites has raised the bar when it comes to posting jobs to the Internet. HRSites has developed its service so that recruiters can review hundreds of job sites, choose the most appropriate for the open position, and automatically have their opening posted to everyone. **HRSites** doesn't stop there as they also generate reports which indicate how many resumes have been received from these sites. Additional services that involve private databases and resume ranking strategies. The cost for large corporations is $25,000 or $10,000 for smaller companies (plus any costs from sites that charge fees). **HRSites** has also made agreements with several recruitment advertising firms who use the tool to post jobs for their clients whose budgets won't support membership.

HR World

www.hrworld.com

David Mahal, DGM Associates
P.O.Box 10639, Marina del Rey, CA 90295-6639
E-mail: dgm@hrworld.com

Jobs: **Yes**	
Cost to post jobs: **Free**	
Cost to see jobs: **Free**	
Resumes: **Yes**	
Cost to post resumes: **Free**	
Cost to see resumes: **Free**	
E-mail Alert (Push): N/A	
Specialty: **Human Resources**	
Industry: N/A	
Feature: N/A	
Location: **US**	

HR World requires that you register for access, but once in, you'll find a wealth of information. A Q&A allows visitors to ask questions related to HR planning, compensation and benefits, IS or training. A "Push" feature is being created with a "skills profile" that recruiters can have matched against their openings. Positions are broken into functional groups for viewing. Then, job seekers can "scroll" down the listings posted by date of receipt. This could use improvement.

HRIM Mall

www.hrimmall.com

Jim Morrone, PeoplePros, Inc.
5603-B W. Friendly Ave. #269, Greensboro, NC 27410
Ph: 800-296-3254   Fax: 336-643-9519   E-mail: sales@hrimmall.com

Jobs: **Yes**	
Cost to post jobs: **Free**	
Cost to see jobs: **Free**	
Resumes: **No**	
Cost to post resumes: N/A	
Cost to see resumes: N/A	
E-mail Alert (Push): **Job Seeker**	
Specialty: **Human Resources HRIS**	
Industry: **All**	
Feature: **Meta-links**	
Location: **US**	

HRIM Mall specializes in information for the Human Resource community. Register your e-mail, and the owners will send you updates when new jobs are posted. A new design and an improved search engine makes shopping at the mall much easier. All jobs have posting dates which is a great help. Long lists of links to many human resource products and services.

IACC online

www.iacconline.com/home.cfm

International Association of Conference Centers

Ph: 314-993-8575   Fax: 314-993-8919   E-mail: jwhite@iacconline.com

Jobs: **Yes** Cost to post jobs: **Fee** Cost to see jobs: **Free**	
Resumes: **Yes** Cost to post resumes: **Free** Cost to see resumes: **Free**	
E-mail Alert (Push): **N/A**	
Specialty: **Hospitality/ Conference Center**	
Industry: **Hospitality**	
Feature: N/A	
Location: **US**	

International Association of Conference Centers will post your position ($35 members, $50 nonmembers) for 30 days. Resumes can be posted and viewed for free. They are coded for confidentiality as employers may contact you via an online form keyed to your ID. Employers do not need to register with the site to view your profile. All resumes and jobs are date stamped. A well-designed site that provides tremendous information regarding the industry.

IEEE

www.ieee.org

William R. Anderson, Institute of Electrical and Electronic Engineers
1828 L Street, NW, Suite 1202, Washington, DC 20036
Ph: 202-785-0017   Fax: 202-785-0835   E-mail: rossr@ix.netcom.com

Jobs: **Yes** Cost to post jobs: **Fee** Cost to see jobs: **Free**	
Resumes: **No** Cost to post resumes: **N/A** Cost to see resumes: **N/A**	
E-mail Alert (Push): **N/A**	
Specialty: **Engineering/ Electrical/Electronic**	
Industry: **All**	
Feature: N/A	
Location: **US/Intl**	

Resumes of members go to Resume-link as well as SkillScan, databases of computer professionals that are downloaded each week and sent to subscribing employers on a CD. We heard there are some plans for an internal resume database, but we do not know when they will finalize it. With over 315,000 members and claims it averages 65,000 job searches a month, an organization this well-known and well-respected should have moved further faster. Price to post on their IEEE-U.S. A. site (affiliated, but not a part of the **IEEE**, has increased $50). Additional job listings can be found (only by members) within the pages dedicated to their flagship publication—*The IEEE Spectrum*.

IFEBP Online

www.ifebp.org/jobs

Barb Pamperin, International Foundation of Employee Benefit Plans
Job P.O.sting Service, P.O. Box 69, Brookfield, WI 53008-0069
Ph: 414-786-6710   Fax: 414-786-8780   E-mail: infocntr@ifebp.org

Jobs: **Yes** Cost to post jobs: **Fee** Cost to see jobs: **Free**	
Resumes: **No** Cost to post resumes: N/A Cost to see resumes: N/A	
E-mail Alert (Push): N/A	
Specialty: **Human Resources** **Benefits**	
Industry: **All**	
Feature: N/A	
Location: **US**	

The **International Foundation of Employee Benefit Plans** posts jobs by title, date of posting or geographic location. Limited to 500 words and a single position, rates are $150 for 60 days. Discounts for members. Several hundred benefits and compensation positions are listed with direct contact information. Linking to Hot Topics will give you interesting articles on the latest and greatest goings-on in the benefits world. A long list of links to benefit information sites is also available.

IHRIM

www.ihrim.org

Mat Batt, International Assoc. of HR Info. Mgmt.
401 N. Michigan Avenue, Chicago, IL 60611
Ph: 312-644-6610   Fax: 312-245-1080   E-mail: matthew_batt@sba.com

Jobs: **Yes** Cost to post jobs: **Fee** Cost to see jobs: **Free**	
Resumes: **No** Cost to post resumes: N/A Cost to see resumes: N/A	
E-mail Alert (Push): **No**	
Specialty: **Human Resources/** **HRIS**	
Industry: **All**	
Feature: N/A	
Location: **US/Canada**	

The **International Association of Human Resource Information Management** has redesigned their site into eight effective functional groupings. Easy access for recruiters who pay $200 to post a position for 30 days or $450 for 90 (IHRIM members get a 15% discount). Jobs are posted by region of the U.S. and can be searched or scrolled by order received. Some parts of the site are for IHRIM members only (Bulletin Board, Conference Speaker handouts). Site has a listserve for its members to communicate with each other. Well-designed as you would expect from this group.

IICS NY Job Listings

www.iicsny.org/jobs

Thiery Sansaricq, International Interactive Communications Society
New York
Ph: 212-736-4427   E-mail: theory@walrus.com

Jobs: **Yes**
Cost to post jobs: **Free**
Cost to see jobs: **Free**
Resumes: **No**
Cost to post resumes: N/A
Cost to see resumes: N/A
E-mail Alert (Push): N/A
Specialty: **IT/Graphics/ Communications**
Industry: **All**
Feature: N/A
Location: **US/NE/NY**

The International Interactive Communications Society (IICS) is the nation's oldest professional organization for interactive arts and technology professionals. Positions are posted for free (only a handful were listed). Multimedia project managers, producers and much more. Direct contact information is available. More than 30 chapters and 3,000+ members.

ijob

www.ijob.com

Judy Ward, 13800 Benson Road
Edmond, OK 73034
Ph: 405-936-2600   E-mail: jward@ijob.com

Jobs: N/A
Cost to post jobs: **Fee**
Cost to see jobs: N/A
Resumes: **Yes**
Cost to post resumes: **Free**
Cost to see resumes: **Fee**
E-mail Alert (Push): N/A
Specialty: **All**
Industry: **All**
Feature: **Resume Database**
Location: **US**

ijob provides recruiters with an online staffing system. This site will register candidates, take their job preferences, allow for screening functions, accept resumes, and then allow the recruiter to search against their openings. Site automatically matches recruiters jobs with the resumes they have secured from the web. No jobs can be seen on this site. In Oklahoma, **ijob** is accessible from some malls and other "remote application centers."

Imcor Provides Top-Level Executives

www2.imcor.com/ct/imcor

Laura Copeland
100 Prospect Street, North Tower, Stamford, CT 06901
Ph: 800-468-3746   Fax: 203-975-8199   E-mail: imcor@snet.net

Jobs: **Yes**	
Cost to post jobs: **Fee**	
Cost to see jobs: **Free**	
Resumes: **Yes**	
Cost to post resumes: **Free**	
Cost to see resumes: **Fee**	
E-mail Alert (Push): **N/A**	
Specialty: **All/Executive**	
Industry: **All**	
Feature: N/A	
Location: **US**	

If you earn a minimum of $75,000, have at least ten years of management experience and know your industry, **Imcor** specializes in temporary to permanent executives. Present assignments can be viewed on this site by function. Definitely worth a visit as many high level positions are temporary to permanent and realistically we are all contract employees. **Imcor** was acquired by Norrell, a well-known temporary and permanent placement agency.

Impact Online

www.impactonline.org

Andrea Grindeland
325 B Forest Avenue, Palo Alto, CA 94301
Ph: 650-428-2962   Fax: 650-327-1395   E-mail: Andreagr@infoarts.com

Jobs: **Yes**	
Cost to post jobs: **Free**	
Cost to see jobs: **Free**	
Resumes: **No**	
Cost to post resumes: **N/A**	
Cost to see resumes: **N/A**	
E-mail Alert (Push): **N/A**	
Specialty: **All**	
Industry: **Nonprofit**	
Feature: N/A	
Location: **US/Int'l**	

Impact Online matches prospective volunteers with nonprofit organizations. If it is time to give something back, sign up online and their volunteer match provides suggested assignments in many major cities throughout the U.S. and several foreign countries. Site also has an e-mail newsletter to keep you up-to-date on this organization.

IndoScape

www.indoscape.com/cfo

Indonesia
E-mail: info@indoscape.com

Jobs: **Yes** Cost to post jobs: **Fee** Cost to see jobs: **Free**	
Resumes: **Yes** Cost to post resumes: **Free** Cost to see resumes: **Fee**	
E-mail Alert (Push): **Job Seeker**	
Specialty: **All**	
Industry: **All**	
Feature: N/A	
Location: **Int'l/Indonesia**	

IndoScape posts positions and accepts resumes for openings in Indonesia. Some very large corporations have banners on this site, and on our visit, we found thirty seven job listings. Jobs can be searched via the sites engine or by individual company listing. Several openings had direct contact information while others asked job seekers to send their resume via the site to the employer. Site can be viewed in English or Bahasa Indonesia languages. Q&As can also be placed on this site. Recruiting in this part of the world is hard enough, and if this web site can get it done it should be worth a try.

InformationWeek Career

www.informationweek.com/career

Barbara Kerbel, CMP Publications
600 Community Drive, Manhasset, NY 11030
Ph: 516-562-5218   Fax: 516-562-7830   E-mail: cmppr@techweb.com

Jobs: **Yes** Cost to post jobs: **Fee** Cost to see jobs: **Free**	
Resumes: **Yes** Cost to post resumes: **Free** Cost to see resumes: N/A	
E-mail Alert (Push): **Job Seeker**	
Specialty: **IT**	
Industry: **High Technology**	
Feature: N/A	
Location: **US**	

Let's see if we can get this one straight. TechWeb and **InformationWeek**, both owned by CMP, have teamed up with BestJobsUSA and the MonsterBoard to develop this site.
InformationWeek lists links to some of their top 500 employers (in the top 20 we only found five). You'll have to pay attention to know where you are.

Infoworks, The Computer Job Center

www.IT123.com

Robert Mulcahy, Infoworks USA
750 Broad Street, Shrewsbury, NJ 07702
Ph: 800-288-5153   Fax: 732-219-7199   E-mail: info@infoworksusa.com

Jobs: **Yes** Cost to post jobs: **Fee** Cost to see jobs: **Free**	
Resumes: **Yes** Cost to post resumes: **Free** Cost to see resumes: **Fee**	
E-mail Alert (Push): N/A	
Specialty: **IT**	
Industry: **All**	
Feature: N/A	
Location: **US/NE**	

Infoworks is a recruitment company with a twist. Site collects resumes of IT professionals (claims 37,000) and allows job postings from "members" companies. Resumes are kept for 90 days. Corporations pay a fee to become members and search the resume. **Infoworks** search engine allows the job seeker to hunt by the geographic region and title of his choice. Thousands of jobs were found on our search with the date posted. The keywords job seekers use to search will show up as "bold" in the text of the jobs returned from the search. Member companies have links to their corporation jobs page. This site has improved significantly in the last year and is worth considering. Membership is still a little pricey at $625 a month.

Infoworld

www.infoworld.com

Janice Crowley
P.O. Box 1172, Skokie, IL 60076
Ph: 800-227-8365   Fax: 415-312-0607   E-mail: electric@infoworld.com

Jobs: **No** Cost to post jobs: N/A Cost to see jobs: N/A	
Resumes: **No** Cost to post resumes: N/A Cost to see resumes: N/A	
E-mail Alert (Push): N/A	
Specialty: **IT/Client Server**	
Industry: **All**	
Feature: N/A	
Location: **US/Int'l**	

Infoworld has posted their online magazine. Job seekers can view opportunities from the magazine by region, title or company. Many career articles can also be viewed and we particularly liked "Keep Technology Safe While on the Road" (Gerry travels with a laptop, beeper, cell phone, palm pilot and whatever gadget is on the market).

Institute of Physics

www.iop.org

Paul Guinnessy, IOP Publishing Ltd.
Dirac House, Temple Back, Bristol, UK BS1 6BE
Ph: 440-117-9297481   Fax: 440-117-9294318   E-mail: custserv@ioppublishing.co.uk

Jobs: **Yes**	
Cost to post jobs: **Fee**	
Cost to see jobs: **Free**	
Resumes: **Yes**	
Cost to post resumes: **Free**	
Cost to see resumes: **Free**	
E-mail Alert (Push): **Job Seeker**	
Specialty: **Ed/University/ Science/Physics**	
Industry: **All/Ed/U**	
Feature: N/A	
Location: **Int'l/UK**	

The Institute of Physics site Internet Pilot (TIPTOP) is where scientific and computing jobs reside. If science is in your career plans, the pilot posts jobs for postdoctorals and tenured teaching positions throughout the world. PhysicsWeb has positions in many different fields of science. The Internet Pilot will post jobs and resumes for free. *Scientific* and *PhysicsWeb* are publications whose print ads are included on the web as added value. Site will "push" new job postings to job seekers via e-mail.

Instrument Society of America

www.isa.org/classads

Instrument Society of America
67 Alexander Drive, P.O. Box 12277, Research Triangle Park, NC 27709
Ph: 919-990-9216   Fax: 919-549-8288   E-mail: rburnham@isa.org

Jobs: **Yes**	
Cost to post jobs: **Fee**	
Cost to see jobs: **Free**	
Resumes: **Yes**	
Cost to post resumes: **Fee**	
Cost to see resumes: **Free**	
E-mail Alert (Push): N/A	
Specialty: **Eng/Measurement & Control**	
Industry: **All**	
Feature: N/A	
Location: **US/Int'l**	

ISA classified is the web arm of *INTECH* magazine, which reaches 80,000 measurement and control professionals. Recruiters can place an ad in the print or web version ($165 for both). Job seekers pay to post a resume (no wonder there were no resumes posted on our last visit). Contact information for posting is: Brian Welsh The Waller Co. 716 N. Bethlehem Pike Suite 101, Lower Gwynedd, PA 19002 215-619-4600, fax 215-654-5186, Few jobs listed in this highly-specialized niche.

Insurance Career Center

www.insjobs.com

Jeffrey Hodes, Bernard Hodes Advertising
555 Madison Avenue, New York, NY 10022
Ph: 888-339-8989   E-mail: sales@careermosaic.com

Jobs: **Yes**	
Cost to post jobs: **Fee**	
Cost to see jobs: **Free**	
Resumes: **Yes**	
Cost to post resumes: **Free**	
Cost to see resumes: **Fee**	
E-mail Alert (Push): N/A	
Specialty: **Insurance**	
Industry: **Insurance**	
Feature: N/A	
Location: **US**	

Insurance Career Center provides the job seeker free access to post their resume and see opportunities with direct contact information. Recruiters are charged $150 to post a position which is listed for no longer than 30 days. To access the resume database you will need to pay $595 for six months. See Career Mosaic for more detail as this site now is fully integrated into their system.

Inter Career Net

www.intercareer-com/inder.html

Linda Fleming, International Career Information, Inc.
111 Pavonia Avenue, Jersey City, NJ 07310
Ph: 800-859-8535   E-mail: lfleming@rici.com

Jobs: **Yes**	
Cost to post jobs: **Fee**	
Cost to see jobs: **Free**	
Resumes: **Yes**	
Cost to post resumes: **Free**	
Cost to see resumes: **Fee**	
E-mail Alert (Push): **Job Seeker**	
Specialty: N/A	
Industry: N/A	
Feature: **Diversity**	
Location: **Int'l/US**	

ICI is a Japanese firm with high visibility in the global recruitment. In the U.S., **ICI** conducts specialized job fairs for Asian nationals. Job seekers can have a profile matched against postings, post a resume for review, and register anonymously so that employers cannot see their personal contact information for free. Employers can post positions for $200 for 30 days and search a resume database for $800 for one month. Applicants must register to see open positions.

Interesting Web Sites

www.usbol.com/wjmackey/weblinks.html

W. J. Mackey
Ph: 408-280-7624   E-mail: wjmackey@netcom.com

Jobs: **No** Cost to post jobs: N/A Cost to see jobs: N/A	**Interesting Web Sites** has lists and links to major sites as well as selected diversity sites. Great service.

Jobs: **No** Cost to post jobs: N/A Cost to see jobs: N/A
Resumes: **No** Cost to post resumes: N/A Cost to see resumes: N/A
E-mail Alert (Push): N/A
Specialty: **All**
Industry: **All**
Feature: **Meta-links/Diversity**
Location: **US**

International Jobs

www.internationaljobs.org

International Careers, 1088 Middle River Road, Standardsville, VA 22973
Ph: 800-291-4618   Fax: 804-985-6828

Jobs: **Yes** Cost to post jobs: **Free** (See Notes) Cost to see jobs: **Fee**
Resumes: **No** Cost to post resumes: N/A Cost to see resumes: N/A
E-mail Alert (Push): N/A
Specialty: **All/International**
Industry: **All**
Feature: N/A
Location: **Int'l**

International Career Employment Weekly claims that it has over 30,000 subscribers for this 24 page newspaper, and distributes more than 500 jobs in each issue. If you live outside the U.S., jobs will be e-mailed to you, but, if you are in the U.S., this is a newspaper, so snail mail she goes. Recruiters pay $25 per column inch if they want their jobs posted on the web and in the newspaper. The newspaper is free to post jobs for corporate recruiters (now isn't that a switch). Headhunters pay $25 per column inch to post positions. Job seekers pay $26 for a six-week subscription.

International Personnel Mgmt. Assoc.

www.ipma-hr.org

Eleanor Trice
1617 Duke Street, Alexandria, VA 22314
Ph: 703-549-7100   Fax: 703-684-0948   E-mail: ipma@ipma-hr.org

Jobs: **Yes**	
Cost to post jobs: **Free**	
Cost to see jobs: **Free**	
Resumes: **No**	
Cost to post resumes: **N/A**	
Cost to see resumes: **N/A**	
E-mail Alert (Push): **No**	
Specialty: **Human Resources**	
Industry: **Government**	
Feature: N/A	
Location: **US**	

IPMA is a professional association for public personnel professionals who are in federal, state, or local government. Many links to public sector openings throughout the U.S. and an e-mail discussion group with Q&A related to HR are available. Job posting rates range from $100 to $150 per position. One negative is that the site posts jobs on a monthly basis (not within 48 hours like most do). Jobs listed on the site are also included in a newsletter mailed to all members. Direct contact information and salary range is available for each position posted.

International Pharmajobs

www.pharmajobs.com

Michael Stowe Mamet, R.S.V.P. Personnel Agency
Reuterweg 51-53, 60323 Frankfurt am Main, Germany
Ph: 800-880-1754   Fax: 496-995-966611   E-mail: info@pharmajobs.com

Jobs: **Yes**	
Cost to post jobs: **Free**	
Cost to see jobs: **Free**	
Resumes: **Yes**	
Cost to post resumes: **Free**	
Cost to see resumes: **Free**	
E-mail Alert (Push): **Job Seeker**	
Specialty: **All**	
Industry: **Biotechnology Pharmaceutical**	
Feature: N/A	
Location: **Int'l/Asia/Europe/US**	

International Pharmajobs works with companies that have recruitment needs in Asia and Europe—and now the U.S. Positions cost $295 to post for eight weeks, or until the job is filled. Recruiters with multiple locations can purchase memberships for $1,500 per year for unlimited postings as well as access to their resume database. If you need confidentiality, resumes can be sent to the site and forwarded to the recruiter. Job seekers can have openings e-mailed to them by registering at the site. Corporations can also have jobs posted with their e-mail address and links to their home page. There were dozens of jobs posted in many categories during our visit.

International Seafarers Exchange

www.jobxchange.com/xisetoc.htm

Jack Reynolds, BlueSeas International Inc.
19370 Collins Avenue, Miami Beach, FL 33160
Ph: 954-986-5488   E-mail: webmaster@jobxchange.com

Jobs: **Yes** Cost to post jobs: **Free** Cost to see jobs: **Free**
Resumes: **Yes** Cost to post resumes: **Free** Cost to see resumes: **Free**
E-mail Alert (Push): **Job Seeker**
Specialty: **All**
Industry: **Maritime**
Feature: N/A
Location: **US**

International Seafarers Exchange appeals to the wanderer in all of us. According to the site's owner, cruise and maritime jobs are so highly desirable that the site only allows job seekers to see a preview of the job—not the contact information. Employers can post jobs directly, although most do not. The site has over 1,500 "crew members" registered, each paying $30 to be listed for six months ($40 for a one-year membership). The site claims it reviews resumes and does not accept everyone. Employers pay $275 for unlimited postings per month. The Exchange claims over 55,000 visitors a month from 105 countries and, in their two years on the web, 1,700 hires through the site. Newsletter is pushed to all potential sailors.

International Society for Performance Improvement

www.ispi.org

Megan Spillane, 1300 L Street N.W. #1250, Washington, DC 20005
Ph: 202-408-7969   Fax: 202-408-7972   E-mail: info@ispi.org

Jobs: **Yes** Cost to post jobs: **Free** Cost to see jobs: **Free**
Resumes: **No** Cost to post resumes: N/A Cost to see resumes: N/A
E-mail Alert (Push): N/A
Specialty: **Human Resources/ T&D**
Industry: **All**
Feature: N/A
Location: **US**

The International Society for Performance Improvement (ISPI) posts jobs on its site for all to view. A chatroom allows members to voice their opinion on the latest and greatest in this field. Hundreds of jobs were posted and easy to view with the site's search engine. All direct contact information is listed. Recruiters can obtain a national listing of chapters and send an e-mail with openings to them as well. The ISPI job bank is a free service.

Internet Business Network

www.interbiznet.com

John Sumser, 346 Starling Road
Mill Valley, CA 94914
Ph: 415-380-8244   Fax: 415-383-8676   E-mail: info@interbiznet.com

Jobs: N/A Cost to post jobs: N/A Cost to see jobs: N/A	
Resumes: N/A Cost to post resumes: N/A Cost to see resumes: N/a	
E-mail Alert (Push): N/A	
Specialty: **All**	
Industry: N/A	
Feature: **Research**	
Location: **US**	

The **Internet Business Network (Interbiznet)** provides hundreds of links and information for recruiters to find the niche they need to fill their openings. **IBN** also publishes a directory rating thousands of sites that sells for $997.00. A free newsletter and a subscription-only weekly newsletter are available for those who register. An extensive schedule of training courses for recruiters conducted by the site's owner can also be found here.

Internet Fashion Exchange

www.fashionexch.com

Martin Weitzman, Gilbert Career Resumes Ltd.
275 Madison Avenue, New York, NY 10016
Ph: 800-967-3846   Fax: 212-661-7595   E-mail: gilcareer@aol.com

Jobs: **Yes** Cost to post jobs: **Free** Cost to see jobs: **Free**	
Resumes: **Yes** Cost to post resumes: **Free** Cost to see resumes: **Free**	
E-mail Alert (Push): N/A	
Specialty: **Retail**	
Industry: **Retail/Fashion**	
Feature: N/A	
Location: **US**	

The Internet Fashion Exchange is back and dressed for success. A simple site for the NY clothing designer market, the service is owned by a resume-writing company. Job seekers can post their resume and see all jobs for free. Recruiters can view brief profiles and contact job seekers directly for free. There is a small charge to post jobs.

Internet Job Locator

www.joblocator.com

Brett Tabin, Travelers Online
15242 Clark St., Sherman Oaks, CA 91411
Ph: 818-907-8873   E-mail: supP.O.rt@joblocator.com

Jobs: **Yes** Cost to post jobs: **Free** Cost to see jobs: **Free**	
Resumes: **Yes** Cost to post resumes: **Free** Cost to see resumes: **Free**	
E-mail Alert (Push): **Both**	
Specialty: **All**	
Industry: **All**	
Feature: **N/A**	
Location: **US**	

Internet Job Locator remains one of the top values on the web for recruiting. Employers receive credits (a credit is $1 with minimum purchase of $25), and with a four-month membership, each credit represents one job posting and one resume search for 21 days. Pretty specific. This site does the searching for employers and e-mails the basic info on matching resumes along with a direct e-mail link to the applicant. Site searches its resume database daily. Jobs will also be posted to newsgroups. For job seekers, direct contact information is provided, and the Job Locator will push new, matching jobs via e-mail for free. In speaking with the owners, the site has not changed much in the last year. This site remains a winner lacking only marketing muscle to hit the big time.

The Internet Job Source

statejobs.com

Joseph Shieh, The Internet Job Source
P.O. Box 45, Guilderland, NY 12084
Ph: 518-869-9279   E-mail: jobsource@aol.com

Jobs: **Yes** Cost to post jobs: **Free** Cost to see jobs: **Free**	
Resumes: **N/A** Cost to post resumes: **N/A** Cost to see resumes: **N/A**	
E-mail Alert (Push): **N/A**	
Specialty: **All**	
Industry: **All/Government/** **State/Fed**	
Feature: **N/A**	
Location: **US**	

The Internet Job Source has opportunities for many major U.S. companies as well as state and federal government agencies. Links to over 200 of the Fortune 500 can be seen through this site. Forty three state links for private and government openings. All jobs can be searched by title or company using the site's search engine. Cost to post listings is $50 per job for a 30-day listing. Date of posting and direct contact information are available. A newsletter is also pushed to all who register their e-mail. Well worth a try.

Internet Job Surfer

www.rpi.edu/dept/cdc/jobsurfer/jobw.html

Jasmit Singh Kochhar, Rensselaer P.O.lytechnic Institute
Department of Decision Science, and Engineering Systems, Troy, NY 12180
Ph: 518-276-2952   E-mail: kochhj@rpi.edu

Jobs: **No**	
Cost to post jobs: N/A	
Cost to see jobs: N/A	
Resumes: **No**	
Cost to post resumes: N/A	
Cost to see resumes: N/A	
E-mail Alert (Push): N/A	
Specialty: **All**	
Industry: N/A	
Feature: **Meta-links**	
Location: **US**	

Internet Job Surfer keeps its owner busy as it is one of the longest lists of job related links on the net. Many of the links on the site have seen better days and, from our viewpoint, too many are third-party recruiters.

Internet World

jobs.internet.com

Elisa Narsu, Mecklermedia Corporation
The Internet Media Company, 20 Ketchum Street, Westport, CT 06880
Ph: 203-341-2997   E-mail: enarsu@mecklermedia

Jobs: **Yes**	
Cost to post jobs: **Free**	
Cost to see jobs: **Free**	
Resumes: **Yes**	
Cost to post resumes: **Free**	
Cost to see resumes: **Free**	
E-mail Alert (Push): **Job Seeker**	
Specialty: **All/IT/Internet**	
Industry: **IT**	
Feature: N/A	
Location: **US/Int'l**	

INTERNET WORLD is a weekly industry publication that targets the pure Internet professional and has a circulation nationally of 125,000. Posted positions are worldwide and cover many different technical disciplines. Job seekers register their skills and e-mail address for the site to "push" jobs matches. Recruiters pay $150 for a single job. Well-designed and easy to use.

Irish Jobs

www.exp.ie

John Feeley, Software Expressions
Carraig Court, Georges Ave., Blackrock, Co., Dublin, Ireland
Ph: 353-128-83732   E-mail: info@exp.ie

Jobs: **Yes**	
Cost to post jobs: **Fee**	
Cost to see jobs: **Free**	
Resumes: **Yes**	
Cost to post resumes: **Free**	
Cost to see resumes: **Fee**	
E-mail Alert (Push): **Job Seeker**	
Specialty: **IT**	
Industry: **All**	
Feature: N/A	
Location: **Int'l/Ireland**	

Irish Jobs provides a great service for overseas job seekers. If candidates provide their e-mail, **Irish Jobs** will send via a monthly listing of opportunities that match their interests. Positions as well as resumes are all date posted. Jobs are split by employer or agency listings—good idea. Recruiters search resume database for free, but the contact information is coded to protect confidentiality— that's when you might consider the subscription cost of $2,000. Jobs are categorized "IT" and "non-IT," and can be posted for 140 pounds for one month (resumes directly to the employer). The bottom line is the site also charges 950 pounds if you hire a candidate from the resume database. **Irish Jobs** has accountancy, engineering and recent graduate sites as well, which can be linked from here.

ITTA

www.it-ta.com

Tom Murray, ITTA LLC
5759 E. Acoma Drive, Scottsdale, AZ 85253
Ph: 602-953-4870   Fax: 602-953-2038   E-mail: tmurray@it-ta.com

Jobs: **Yes**	
Cost to post jobs: **Fee** (See Notes)	
Cost to see jobs: **Free**	
Resumes: **Yes**	
Cost to post resumes: **Free**	
Cost to see resumes: **Fee**	
E-mail Alert (Push): N/A	
Specialty: **IT**	
Industry: N/A	
Feature: **Resume Robot**	
Location: **US/Int'l**	

ITTA's resume robot, ProRecruiter, is used by employers to search for resumes (up to four queries per night). The ITTA resume retrieval software searches public resume databases (private databases can be included for a fee if you are a subscriber), and returns resumes based on a wide range of criteria for $500 per month The site also allows for job and resume postings. One of the best tools we've seen.

Jaeger's Interactive Career Center

www.jaegerinc.com/jaeger2.html

Phil Brindley, Jaeger Advertising
Cleveland, OH
Ph: 216-243-8700   Fax: 216-243-1888   E-mail: info@jaegerinc.com

Jobs: **Yes** Cost to post jobs: **Fee** Cost to see jobs: **Free**	
Resumes: **No** Cost to post resumes: N/A Cost to see resumes: N/A	
E-mail Alert (Push): N/A	
Specialty: **All**	
Industry: **All**	
Feature: N/A	
Location: **US**	

Jaeger's Interactive Career Center posts jobs for its clients who place ads through this recruitment advertising firm. Jobs can be searched by function from accounting through technicians. Simple site with direct contact information.

Java World

www.javaworld.com

Tony Hunt
Web Publishing Inc.
Ph: 415-974-7443   Fax: 415-974-4570   E-mail: tony.hunt@javaworld.com

Jobs: **Yes** Cost to post jobs: **Fee** Cost to see jobs: **Free**	
Resumes: **No** Cost to post resumes: N/A Cost to see resumes: N/A	
E-mail Alert (Push): **Job Seeker**	
Specialty: **IT/JAVA**	
Industry: **All**	
Feature: N/A	
Location: **US**	

Java World has formed a partnership with Career Central for job seekers to find their next opportunity. Positions posted on *Java World* magazine are now at Career Central, and can be accessed from either site. Job seekers who register their e-mail and skill profile can have openings "pushed" to them. If you have an interest, you can return an electronic version of your resume which will be forwarded to the employer. High degree of confidentiality for the job seeker. Lots of IT jobs from all over the world.

Jewish Vocational Services

www.jvsjobs.com

105 Chauncy Street
6th Floor, Boston, MA 02111
Ph: 617-451-8147   E-mail: jvs@tiac.net

Jobs: **Yes** Cost to post jobs: **Free** Cost to see jobs: **Free**	
Resumes: **Yes** Cost to post resumes: **Free** Cost to see resumes: **Free**	
E-mail Alert (Push): **N/A**	
Specialty: **All**	
Industry: **All**	
Feature: **N/A**	
Location: **US/E/MA**	

Jewish Vocational Services (JVS) is a nonprofit organization sponsored by Combined Jewish Philanthropies and the United Way of Masachusetts Bay. Recruiters need to obtain a password to view candidate profiles and post jobs for free. They must advise the site of their interest by e-mail. Job seekers can post their profiles for free. Awkward model. Dozens of company profiles were available for view. Site should consider giving corporations links to their sites.

JobAssistant.com

www.jobassistant.com

Bill Reilly, JobAssistant.com
781 Creek Road, Bellmawr, NJ 08031
Ph: 609-933-3942   Fax: 609-933-1042   E-mail: info@jobassistant.com

Jobs: **Yes** Cost to post jobs: **Fee** Cost to see jobs: **Free**	
Resumes: **Yes** Cost to post resumes: **Free** Cost to see resumes: **Free**	
E-mail Alert (Push): **N/A**	
Specialty: **All**	
Industry: **All**	
Feature: **N/A**	
Location: **US**	

JobAssistant.com allows recruiters to post unlimited jobs per year for $100 (90 days) . Company profiles are free. Employers can try a listing for $50 for 30 days. Jobs are also placed on major search engines and on AOL's employment bulletin board. This site's search engine is designed to view jobs and resumes by selected category and state. A little restrictive. Resumes can be viewed for free, and all include direct contact information.

Job Bank USA

www.jobbankusa.com

Brett Warner
3232 Cobb Parkway, Suite 611, Atlanta, GA 30339
Ph: 770-971-1971   Fax: 770-971-7788   E-mail: webmaster@jobbankusa.com

Jobs: **Yes**	
Cost to post jobs: **Fee**	
Cost to see jobs: **Free**	
Resumes: **Yes**	
Cost to post resumes: **Free**	
Cost to see resumes: **Fee**	
E-mail Alert (Push): **Job Seeker** (See Notes)	
Specialty: **All**	
Industry: **All**	
Feature: N/A	
Location: **US**	

Job Bank USA has changed their format, providing more information for the job seeker. Contact data, date of posting and years of experience needed to apply are some of the added features. Recruiters can post a position for $125, and the site claims it will soon "push" matched positions to the job seeker. (fourth quarter of 1998) Resumes can be viewed for $595 per quarter, and this comes with unlimited job postings. There is now "no cost" to the job seeker to post their resume. A meta-list of job newsgroups by function and location is available to view as an added bonus.

JobCenter Employment Services, Inc.

www.jobcenter.com/

Christopher McQueeney
2 Fennell Street, P.O. Box 125, Skaneateles, NY 13152
Ph: 800-562-236837   Fax: 315-673-1820   E-mail: service@jobcenter.com

Jobs: **Yes**	
Cost to post jobs: **Fee**	
Cost to see jobs: **Free**	
Resumes: **Yes**	
Cost to post resumes: **Free** (See Notes)	
Cost to see resumes: **Free**	
E-mail Alert (Push): **Both**	
Specialty: **All**	
Industry: N/A	
Feature: N/A	
Location: **US**	

JobCenter has matching capability for the employer as well as the job seeker. Recruiters can post positions for $30 per job for a two-week run. Job seekers can post their resume for free, but if they want jobs "pushed" to them there is a $5 fee for a six-month service. Site reposts resumes to newsgroups.

JobDirect.com

www.jobdirect.com

Rob Ford, JobDirect
201 Summer Street, Stamford, CT 06901
Ph: 203-327-2201   Fax: 203-327-2261   E-mail: sales@jobdirect.com

Jobs: **Yes**	
Cost to post jobs: **Fee**	
Cost to see jobs: **Free**	
Resumes: **Yes**	
Cost to post resumes: **Free**	
Cost to see resumes: **Fee**	
E-mail Alert (Push): N/A	
Specialty: **College**	
Industry: **All**	
Feature: N/A	
Location: **US**	

JobDirect.com's tag line could read "take the bus and leave the driving to U.S."
JobDirect.com literally goes on the road to collect college and student resumes across the country for their database. Employers pay $500 for an initial subscription to view the students resume. Web matching features for student skills/interests with the employers openings is excellent, and extensive matches are "pushed" to the employer. Recruiters can also post jobs, and many packages are available. New features allow member companies to track candidates through the hiring process. Site claims over 100,000 active students have registered, which gives **JobDirect.com** a powerful database .
Originally founded by two women with a great idea, **JobDirect.com** is a professionally-managed business model with creative marketing strategies and solid technology. Give them two years, and they will have a unique capability to expand beyond the college market.

JobExchange

www.jobexchange.com

The JobExchange
23461 South Pointe Drive, Suite 375, Laguna Hills, CA 92653
Ph: 800-562-7030   E-mail: jobex@jobexchange.com

Jobs: **Yes** Cost to post jobs: **Fee** Cost to see jobs: **Free**	
Resumes: **Yes** Cost to post resumes: **Fee** Cost to see resumes: **Free**	
E-mail Alert (Push): N/A	
Specialty: **All**	
Industry: **All**	
Feature: N/A	
Location: **US/CA**	

JobExchange is a registry that gives job seekers the ability to post their resume, a video. Audio clip, a still photo—even letters of recommendation—for $200 a year. Recruiters can search this database for free. Strange and confusing is that you can also search the classified sections of six newspapers from different parts of the country. Papers such as the *Pittsburgh Post-Gazette* to the *Wisconsin State Journal.*

Job Farm

www.jobfarm.com

24315 E Gage, Liberty Lake, WA 99019
Ph: 509-255-5989   Fax: 509-255-5989   E-mail: jeffb@jobfarm.com

Jobs: **Yes** Cost to post jobs: **Fee** Cost to see jobs: **Free**	
Resumes: **No** Cost to post resumes: N/A Cost to see resumes: N/A	
E-mail Alert (Push): N/A	
Specialty: **Science/Agriculture**	
Industry: **Agriculture**	
Feature: N/A	
Location: **US**	

Job Farm is a new site where recruiters post a job for $2 a day + a $25 one-time set up fee. If you really need "Old MacDonald," recruiters can post unlimited positions for $450 per month. Job seekers can see all direct contact information, and can apply online. Ei-Ei-O.

JobFest

www.jobfest.com

Mike Temkin, Shaker Advertising Agency, Inc.
1100 Lake Street, Oak Park, IL 60301
Ph: 800-323-5170   E-mail: mike_temkin@shaker.com

Jobs: **Yes**
Cost to post jobs: **Fee** (See Notes)
Cost to see jobs: **Free**
Resumes: **No**
Cost to post resumes: N/A
Cost to see resumes: N/A
E-mail Alert (Push): N/A
Specialty: **All**
Industry: **All**
Feature: N/A
Location: **US**

JobFest is the job warehouse for the thousands of ads placed in various media by this recruitment advertising agency. Provided as a service to the agency's clients, job seekers can register and view tens of thousands of openings. Helpful information about the recruiting activity of companies, links to clients and much more can be found here.

JobHunt: On-Line Job Meta-List

www.job-hunt.org

Dane Spearing
Stanford University
E-mail: dave@job-hunt.org

Jobs: **No**
Cost to post jobs: N/A
Cost to see jobs: N/A
Resumes: **No**
Cost to post resumes: N/A
Cost to see resumes: N/A
E-mail Alert (Push): N/A
Specialty: **All**
Industry: **All**
Feature: **Meta-links**
Location: **US**

JobHunt gives new meaning to the term "meta-list" although, it looks like the owner has had enough of the web (his site is now for sale). Links are classified as academic, classified ads, companies, general, newsgroups, recruiting agencies, science, engineering , medicine, and other services such as commercial services, other meta-lists, reference material, resume banks and university career resource centers. All links are in alpha order with a mini-review.

JobKeys

www.jobkeys.com

Doug Berg, JobKeys, A division of RIT Systems
6505 City West Parkway, Eden Prairie, MN 55344
Ph: 800-829-3424   Fax: 612-944-8919   E-mail: dberg@jobkeys.com

Jobs: **Yes** Cost to post jobs: **Fee** Cost to see jobs: **Free**	
Resumes: **Yes** Cost to post resumes: **Free** Cost to see resumes: **Fee**	
E-mail Alert (Push): **Job Seeker**	
Specialty: **IT/Engineering**	
Industry: **All**	
Feature: N/A	
Location: **US/MW/MN-US/ NW/OR**	

JobKeys currently has its strength in Minneapolis, MN, and their new site in Portland, OR (www.channel6000.jobkeys.com), and emphasizes IT and Engineering opportunities. Recruiters can post jobs for three months for $2,000. Job seekers can register their e-mail, and if a company has an interest, the site will send an e-mail message to let you about the job match. The job seeker has a choice of receiving e-mail messages about career opportunities or not. All who visit the site have to register to view job information.

Job Lynx

joblynx.com

Andrea Hoover, JobLynx
2797 Candle Lane, Green Bay, WI 54304
Ph: 920-496-2001   Fax: 920-499-2001   E-mail: success@joblynx.com

Jobs: **No** Cost to post jobs: N/A Cost to see jobs: N/A	
Resumes: **Yes** Cost to post resumes: **Fee** Cost to see resumes: **Free**	
E-mail Alert (Push): N/A	
Specialty: N/A	
Industry: **Staffing**	
Feature: **Resume Service**	
Location: **US/Europe**	

Job Lynx claims to have 9,600 links to the wonderful world of headhunters. Job seekers are pitched to have their resume shopped (confidentially) for $19.95 for one month (other packages available for longer periods of time). While this site states it keeps resumes confidential, we still wonder how 9,600 recruiters can keep a top IT prospect secret. A new feature for '98/'99 offers the job seeker the opportunity to view the top 20 job hunting resources on the Internet for $7.99. That's about $7.97 more than its worth. We've kept this site listed in *Careerxroads* as representative of the 500 we wouldn't recommend

The JobMarket

www.thejobmarket.com

Marc Hatton
411 Laguna Street, Coral Gables, FL 33146
Ph: 305-663-3563   Fax: 305-663-4979   E-mail: corpsales@thejobmarket.com

Jobs: **Yes**	
Cost to post jobs: **Fee**	
Cost to see jobs: **Free**	
Resumes: **Yes**	
Cost to post resumes: **Free**	
Cost to see resumes: **Fee**	
E-mail Alert (Push): N/A	
Specialty: **All**	
Industry: **All**	
Feature: N/A	
Location: **US/SW/FL**	

Visitors to the **JobMarket** site can take advantage of a full line of job seeking and recruitment tools aimed at putting qualified candidates in touch with potential employers. Services includes a database of online classified ads in areas as sales/marketing, financial and high-tech oriented jobs and a resume builder. Members can take advantage of a resume and correspondence library that enables the user to download resume and cover letter templates and merge them with corporate contact information found in The **JobMarket's** databases. A useful array of relocation information ranging from apartment locators to moving services is available. Employer profiles: $1000 for a year; a resume database: $150 to search; a job database: $50 to post; and links: $125. We had difficulty using these services despite repeated visits.

Job Navigator

www.jobs.co.za

Fiona Buchner, Systems Publishers
372 Smuts Avenue, Craighall, South Africa 20204
Ph: 271-178-91808   Fax: 271-178-94725   E-mail: gionae@systems.co.za

Jobs: **Yes**	
Cost to post jobs: **Fee**	
Cost to see jobs: **Free**	
Resumes: **Yes**	
Cost to post resumes: **Free**	
Cost to see resumes: **Fee**	
E-mail Alert (Push): N/A	
Specialty: **IT**	
Industry: **All**	
Feature: N/A	
Location: **Int'l/South Africa (US)**	

Job Navigator posts positions for IT professionals all over the world. This site advises the reader when the job was last modified. Employers pay $800 to post jobs for one month (unlimited), but you must take a three-month minimum. Over 1,200 jobs were posted on our last visit. Usually a site's "career center" is a place for articles. No career information here. Instead, **Job Navigator** posts employer profiles. Search engine was a snap using the site's categories or key words. Candidates who post their resume can use the site's "Fuzzy Find" search engine to match with positions. Nice feature.

JobNet

www.jobnet.com

Ward Christman, Online Opportunities
205 E. King Street, Malvern, PA 19355
Ph: 888-562-6382   Fax: 610-296-9181   E-mail: sales@jobnet.com

Jobs: **Yes**	
Cost to post jobs: **Fee**	
Cost to see jobs: **Free**	
Resumes: **Yes**	
Cost to post resumes: **Free**	
Cost to see resumes: **Fee**	
E-mail Alert (Push): **Employer**	
Specialty: **All**	
Industry: **All**	
Feature: N/A	
Location: **US/E/PA/NJ**	

JobNET continues to give the Delaware Valley a vital source for recruitment via the web. Recruiters can post positions for $50 (other packages and services are available). All postings have direct contact information. The resume database claims 37,000 resumes are warehoused, and can be searched for $700 per quarter. All new resumes are Pushed to subscribing employers, but this is not a skills matching service. A monthly newsletter is mailed to recruiters and can be also be found on the site. At a candidate's request the site will distribute their resume to 1,300 web sites for $49. 95. Regional information on living in and around the city of brotherly love can also be found. Solid value in the Philadelphia, New Jersey area. Experience pays off. The owner has been building credibility in this community for many years.

JobOptions

www.joboptions.com

Tom Flood,
8440 Woodfield Crossing, Suite 170, Indianapolis, IN 46240
Ph: 800-682-2901   Fax: 317-469-4518   E-mail: tom@joboptions.com

Jobs: **Yes**	
Cost to post jobs: **Fee**	
Cost to see jobs: **Free**	
Resumes: **Yes**	
Cost to post resumes: **Free**	
Cost to see resumes: **Fee**	
E-mail Alert (Push): **Employer**	
Specialty: **All**	
Industry: **All**	
Feature: N/A	
Location: **US**	

JobOptions has replaced E-Span as new management has created innovative tools to remain one of the top career sites on the net. Alliances with CompuServe and AltaVista's CareerZone drive job seekers/traffic to this site—more to come. A new navigation tool allows job seekers to hone in on exactly the position they want from over 6,000 employers' web sites. A built-in resume and e-mail forwarding mechanism makes it easier to reach your targets. Job Alert will send open positions directly to candidates who do not have to return to the site. Job specs are matched with incoming resumes and forwarded to employers. Employers who pay will have their positions at the top of the charts. Initial pricing is $150 per post for a 60-day run. Unlimited job posting, use of the resume database, and matching service is $5,370 per year, but lower cost packages will provide almost the same result. Creative, cutting edge technology will keep **JobOptions** as a CXR Best…just in time.

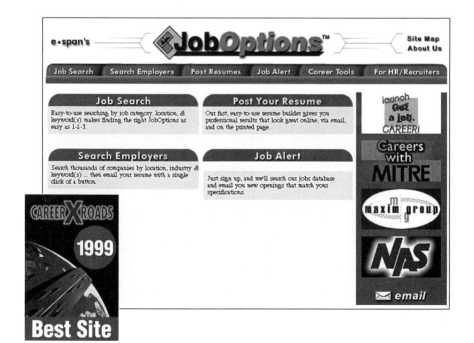

The Job Resource

www.thejobresource.com

Roberto Angulo

E-mail: angulo@thejobresource.com

Jobs: **Yes**
Cost to post jobs: **Free**
Cost to see jobs: **Free**
Resumes: **Yes**
Cost to post resumes: **Free**
Cost to see resumes: **Free**
E-mail Alert (Push): N/A
Specialty: **College/Entry-level**
Industry: **All**
Feature: N/A
Location: **US/W/CA**

The Job Resource was started by students from Stanford University, and is a totally free site. Resumes are posted with contact information. Resumes are collected from college and university students. There were over 650 jobs posted on our last visit, and they can be searched by job type, company type or type of work as well as by state. Several career articles can also be found, and one, "Is your Resume 'Byte-Able'"? caught our eye. They originally refused positions from third-party recruiters, but now accept them. Price is right.

Job Resources by US Region

www.wm.edu/csrv/career/stualum/jregion.html

College of William & Mary
Williamsburg, VA 23187
Ph: 757-221-3329   Fax: 757-221-3240   E-mail: career@facstaff.wm.edu

Jobs: **No**
Cost to post jobs: N/A
Cost to see jobs: N/A
Resumes: **No**
Cost to post resumes: N/A
Cost to see resumes: N/A
E-mail Alert (Push): N/A
Specialty: **All**
Industry: **All**
Feature: **Meta-links**
Location: **US**

Job Resources by U.S. Region is a meta-list of links to jobs throughout the U.S. From the creator of Catapult you can search by Internet job bank, education, government, summer, postgraduate and internship positions. Each link is briefly described.

Job Searching - Mining Co.

jobsearchtech.miningco.com

Steven Niznik
The Mining Co.
E-mail: (See Notes)

Jobs: N/A	
Cost to post jobs: N/A	
Cost to see jobs: N/A	
Resumes: N/A	
Cost to post resumes: N/A	
Cost to see resumes: N/A	
E-mail Alert (Push): N/A	
Specialty: **All**	
Industry: **All**	
Feature: **Meta-links**	
Location: **US**	

The Mining Company which is a search engine with an extensive career center. A career "chatroom" and bulletin board are available for all to use. Numerous career articles and links to many job sites are also available. For more information you can e-mail the management at: jobsearchtech. guide@miningco. com

Job Serve: IT Vacancies in the UK

www.jobserve.com

Hannah Smith, JobServe Ltd.
Freepost CL3872, Tiptree, Colchester, England CO5 0BR
Ph: 016-218-17335   Fax: 016-218-17336   E-mail: hannah@jobserve.com

Jobs: **Yes**	
Cost to post jobs: **Fee**	
Cost to see jobs: **Free**	
Resumes: **Yes**	
Cost to post resumes: **Free**	
Cost to see resumes: **Fee**	
E-mail Alert (Push): **Job Seeker**	
Specialty: **IT**	
Industry: **All**	
Feature: N/A	
Location: **Int'l/Europe/UK**	

Job Serve is a listserv that claims it "pushes" 95,000 new contract and permanent IT vacancies a month. These positions are e-mailed daily to 57,000 subscribers. To register: send a blank e-mail message to: subscribe@jobserve.com. Jobs are posted for over 20 countries including the U.S. You can browse using the site's search engine to check postings that are date stamped within the last five days. All assignments have salary ranges listed and direct contact information. Recruiters pay (5 pounds) per CV with a 20-pound per month minimum.

JobSmart California Job Search Guide

www.jobsmart.org

Brent Fraser, Bay Area Library & Information System
KPIX
Ph: 415-765-8737   E-mail: fraserb@kpix.cbs.com

Jobs: **No**	
Cost to post jobs: N/A	
Cost to see jobs: N/A	
Resumes: **No**	
Cost to post resumes: N/A	
Cost to see resumes: N/A	
E-mail Alert (Push): N/A	
Specialty: **All**	
Industry: **All**	
Feature: N/A	
Location: **US/W/CA**	

JobSmart: the California Job Search Guide is located within the local library system in the Bay Area. All candidates have to do is "point and click" to find one of the best career information sites on the web. This site is broken down by regions in California (S.F. Bay, Sacramento, L.A., and San Diego) for ease of access. 170 links to salary surveys guarantees that this address is popular. The site also contains links to 350 local area job banks, 1,250 job hotlines, 95 job fair sites, 120 online libraries and 300 career centers. The career articles are extensive. You can contact the library system directly for more information by e-mailing Mary-Ellen Mort (known as "Electra") electra@jobsmart.org. Take note all as this is the community model that will dominate the local scene.

JobSpan

www.jobspan.com

Eve Stern, Etho Solutions Inc.
15815 SE 37th Street, Suite 104, Bellevue, Washington 98006
Ph: 888-562-7726   Fax: 425-957-7133   E-mail: webmaster@jobspan.com

Jobs: **Yes**	
Cost to post jobs: **Fee**	
Cost to see jobs: **Free**	
Resumes: **Yes**	
Cost to post resumes: **Free**	
Cost to see resumes: **Fee**	
E-mail Alert (Push): N/A	
Specialty: N/A	
Industry: N/A	
Feature: N/A	
Location: **US**	

Job seekers can post their resume in a confidential or open mode. Employers can post positions with direct contact information, but applicants have to remember a job code in order to submit their resume online. Recruiters can have **JobSpan** search its database for applicants that match their criterion. Other human resource services are advertised, but costs were not available, and e-mails went unanswered. Independent articles describing **JobSpan** suggest that it has a suite of tools to automate the recruitment process from the desktop to the web with applicant profiling/tracking and skills-based screening processes.

JobStreet

Mark Chang, 1 Ground Floor Office
Equatorial Hotel, Penang, Malasia 11900
Ph: 011-604-6445912   Fax: 011-604-6428653   E-mail: mark@jobstreet.com.my

Jobs: **Yes** Cost to post jobs: **Fee** Cost to see jobs: **Free**
Resumes: **Yes** Cost to post resumes: **Free** Cost to see resumes: **Fee** (See Notes)
E-mail Alert (Push): **Job Seeker**
Specialty: **All**
Industry: **All**
Feature: N/A
Location: **Int'l/Malaysia/** **Singapore**

JobStreet is a sister site to Malaysia Online. Jobs are listed by date of entry, company, location, industry or position. Job seekers can register to have selected openings e-mailed to their desktop. Site has a matching agent called "LiNa" that brings together the employers requirements and the candidates resumes. Employers only see resumes if the candidates release them. Confidentiality is a major issue on this site. Recruiters pay $200 per job posting for a one-month run. When you enter the jobs area, a survey asks your opinion of the job market in Malaysia as well as your age and sex—then you can view current results. There were over 90 jobs posted in all occupations.

CareerXroads conducts seminars on Human Resources staffing and the Internet.

Check our web site for a schedule of events.

CAREERXROADS

www.careerxroads.com
Ph: 732-821-6652 • E-mail: mmc@careerxroads.com

Where Talent and Opportunity Connect on the Internet.

CAREERXROADS® The 1999 Directory of Job, Resume & Career Management Sites on the World Wide Web   **261**

JOBTRAK

www.jobtrak.com

Ken Ramberg, Jobtrak Corporation
1964 Westwood Blvd,, 3rd Floor, Los Angeles, CA 90025
Ph: 800-999-8725   Fax: 310-475-7912   E-mail: kramberg@jobtrak.com

Jobs: **Yes**	
Cost to post jobs: **Fee**	
Cost to see jobs: **Free**	
Resumes: **Yes**	
Cost to post resumes: **Free**	
Cost to see resumes: **Fee**	
E-mail Alert (Push): N/A	
Specialty: **College**	
Industry: **All**	
Feature: N/A	
Location: **US**	

JOBTRAK has taken a great idea and built an edge in the college marketplace by having agreements with over 700 career counseling offices. The site provides students and alumni with a password, and offers companies the ability to reach just their target schools' students and alumni. This makes eminent sense if the students are graduates of programs that a company wants to target, but misses the mark if the company is looking to recruit nationally.

JOBTRAK has done an outstanding marketing job, and has garnered a tremendous amount of visibility, which keeps student traffic and advertisers active. In addition to the cost of job postings, which range from $15 for one college to $395 for all 700 colleges (the most popular is a six-pack of colleges for $75), **JOBTRACK** offers banners and links that range as high as $10,000. A new software product, InterviewTrak, allows recruiters self-service management of their on-campus interviews, view resumes to pre-select students and coordinate their schedules.

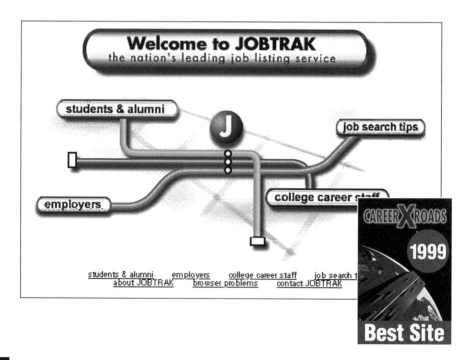

JobWarehouse

www.jobwarehouse.com

Patrick Novick, E.T.I.
2457 A South Hiawassee Road, #245, Orlando, FL 32835
Ph: 407-660-8385   Fax: 407-650-2607   E-mail: patrick@jobwarehouse.com

Jobs: **Yes**	
Cost to post jobs: **Fee**	
Cost to see jobs: **Free**	
Resumes: **Yes**	
Cost to post resumes: **Free**	
Cost to see resumes: **Fee**	
E-mail Alert (Push): N/A	
Specialty: **IT/Programmers Software Engineers**	
Industry: **All**	
Feature: N/A	
Location: **US/Int'l/UK/France**	

JobWarehouse specializes in IT professionals for the U.S. and several foreign countries. Jobs can be searched by specific company, or keyword. Site claims over 2,800 jobs posted from over 100 corporations, and will provide a resume CD of 42,000+ resumes of IT candidates. Site is organized so that if a candidate selects all jobs, they then see a listing of companies, which they will then drill down by clicking to see the client's banner, then clicking to see jobs, then clicking on the job to see job detail and contact information. Long process. Job seekers who input their resume can have the site "Quick-Search" their skills against current openings (solution). Register an e-mail address, and **JobWarehouse** will push jobs that match the candidate's skills.

JobWeb

www.jobweb.org/

Norita Rehrig, National Association of Colleges and Employers
62 Highland Avenue, Bethlehem, PA 18017
Ph: 800-544-5272   Fax: 610-868-0208   E-mail: norita@jobweb.org

Jobs: **Yes**	
Cost to post jobs: **Fee**	
Cost to see jobs: **Free**	
Resumes: **No**	
Cost to post resumes: N/A	
Cost to see resumes: N/A	
E-mail Alert (Push): N/A	
Specialty: College	
Industry: **All**	
Feature: **Diversity/Meta-links**	
Location: **US**	

JobWeb has created a new look, and hopes to build its presence among college students. A creation of the National Association of Colleges and Employers (NACE), **JobWeb** has outstanding content to compliment its efficient, self-service postings and searchable profiles. Banners and links are also available, and at reasonable prices (a link from your profile goes for just $100/month added to the annual profile cost of $300). Recruiters pay $80 to post a job for a month, and direct contact information is available on all jobs posted. Also, check out Catapult (a meta-link site), which is on **JobWeb,** for additional information about the college career market, diversity and much more.

Jobs 4 HR

www.jobs4hr.com

Brian Weis, CityCom Marketing
5464 N. Port Washington Road, Suite 196, Milwaukee, WI 53217
E-mail: info@jobs4hr.com

Jobs: **Yes**	
Cost to post jobs: **Fee**	
Cost to see jobs: **Free**	
Resumes: **Yes**	
Cost to post resumes: **Free**	
Cost to see resumes: **Fee** (See Notes)	
E-mail Alert (Push): **Job Seeker**	
Specialty: **Human Resources**	
Industry: **All**	
Feature: N/A	
Location: **US**	

Jobs 4 HR is a new site set up to serve human resource professionals. Job seekers can register their e-mail and have positions sent to them for free in their particular area of expertise. Recruiters pay $100 per posting. On our visit about a dozen positions were listed for all levels and types of HR positions. Easy to view and get what you need. Site also hosts a listserv for recruiters.

Jobs Careers

www.jobs-careers.com

David Graham, Internet Today
6830 Eastland Road, Cleveland, OH 44130
Ph: 440-816-1540 Fax: 440-816-1548 E-mail: david@ww2.itoday.com

Jobs: **Yes**	
Cost to post jobs: **Fee**	
Cost to see jobs: **Free**	
Resumes: **Yes**	
Cost to post resumes: **Free**	
Cost to see resumes: **Fee**	
E-mail Alert (Push): **No**	
Specialty: **All**	
Industry: **All**	
Feature: N/A	
Location: **US/Europe/UK/Asia**	

Jobs Careers is an unique new web recruiting model. Up for less than a year, the site takes customized, interactive content to a new level. When job seekers pick from 33 discipline categories, a frame allows them to see a customized section with a live chatroom, listings of recruiters with openings, links to other sites and a Q&A—all customized to the chosen field. This is well-presented and it even works! Recruiters are charged $495 to post unlimited jobs and view resumes for one year. Owners are web site developers who do this as a side business. We wish them well, and congratulate them on their effort. With a few more needed items (push, job date posting), and a little marketing, this site could be a big winner in the future.

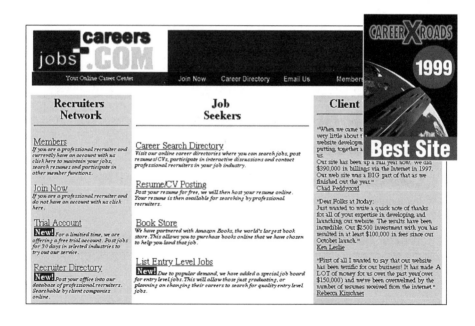

Jobs for Bankers

www.bankjobs.com

P.O. Box 23915, Nashville, TN 37202
Ph: 800-999-6497   E-mail: comment@bankjobs.com

Jobs: **Yes** Cost to post jobs: **Free** Cost to see jobs: **Fee** (See Notes)	
Resumes: **Yes** Cost to post resumes: **Free** Cost to see resumes: **Fee**	
E-mail Alert (Push): **Job Seeker**	
Specialty: **Finance/Banking**	
Industry: **Finance/Banking**	
Feature: N/A	
Location: **US**	

Jobs for Bankers seems to have been set up for corporations that are downsizing and willing to pay to help their employees seek their next postion. Must be, because we can't imagine anyone paying to see these job leads. Job seekers can only see a "short" list of openings for free, and on our visits, there were none posted. Job locator will match your skills and e-mail job opportunities for those who pay $249 for this 26-week service, or $99 to search the job database only. Resumes can be posted for free, and several major banks had job links posted. We list this site because it goes against the grain.

Jobs for Programmers

www.prgjobs.com

JFP Resources
1085 South 124th Street, Brookfield, WI 53005
Ph: 414-782-0072   E-mail: webmaster@jfpresources.com

Jobs: **Yes**	
Cost to post jobs: **Fee**	
Cost to see jobs: **Free**	
Resumes: **Yes**	
Cost to post resumes: **Free**	
Cost to see resumes: **Fee**	
E-mail Alert (Push): **Employer**	
Specialty: **IT/Programmers**	
Industry: **All**	
Feature: N/A	
Location: **US**	

Jobs for Programmers continues to provide an excellent service for the IT/programming community. Site claims over 25,000 resumes, and provides recruiters with a 30-day free trial to post up to 100 jobs or view their resume database. What have you got to lose? Interesting articles, and we especially liked "Tips for Effective Job Postings," which explains why web ads succeed or fail. Recruiters can have a report "pushed" to them on a daily basis which summarizes the day's resumes received by the site. Cost to see resumes and post jobs runs from $450-$600 a quarter. The higher-end package includes a "resume spider" that searches numerous sites to bring you back all the IT folks it can find. A resume matching service is also available, and the site will match employer specs against its database, and e-mail recruiters only the resumes that hit the mark. JFP has developed a cult following, and has earned our top rating.

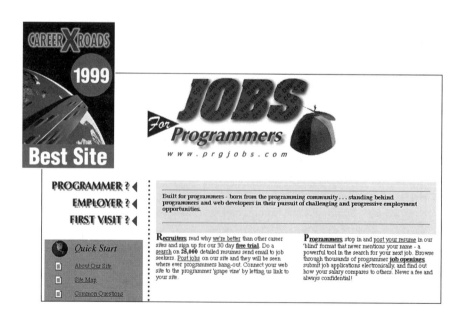

Jobs in Government

www.jobsingovernment.com

P.O. Box 1436
Agoura Hills, CA 91376
Ph: 818-991-3335   Fax: 818-991-9673   E-mail: info@jobsingovernment.com

Jobs: **Yes** Cost to post jobs: **Fee** Cost to see jobs: **Free**
Resumes: **Yes** Cost to post resumes: **Free** Cost to see resumes: **Fee**
E-mail Alert (Push): **Job Seeker**
Specialty: **All**
Industry: **Government**
Feature: N/A
Location: **US/**

Jobs in Government is primarily a subscription-based job posting service targeting state agency employers. Modest employer subscription costs are $225 for five job postings. Intern and summer positions can be posted free of charge. Nice site for job seekers to check out. A resume database is available which protects confidentiality, as well as an e-mail notification of job opportunities. Public sector employers are invited to post as well.

Jobs in Higher Education

volvo.gslis.utexas.edu: 80~acadres/jobs/index.html

Dan Knauft, National Academic Advising Association
University of Texas, Austin, TX
E-mail: dknauft@gslis.utexas.edu

Jobs: **Yes** Cost to post jobs: **Free** Cost to see jobs: **Free**
Resumes: **No** Cost to post resumes: N/A Cost to see resumes: N/A
E-mail Alert (Push): N/A
Specialty: **Teaching**
Industry: **Education**
Feature: **Meta-links**
Location: **US/Int'l**

Jobs in Higher Education is the list of links to jobs in the education field. Links are listed by individual colleges and universities, faculty and administration in the U.S., Canada, Australia and the UK. Maintained by the University of Texas, this is a great place to research academic positions. You can also search universities in alpha order (most link directly to their job opening pages).

Jobs in Journalism

eb.journ.latech.edu/jobs.html

Paul Grabowicz
Louisiana Tech
E-mail: grabs@uclink.berkeley.edu

Jobs: **Yes** Cost to post jobs: **Free** Cost to see jobs: **Free**	
Resumes: **No** Cost to post resumes: N/A Cost to see resumes: N/A	
E-mail Alert (Push): N/A	
Specialty: **Journalism**	
Industry: **Journalism**	
Feature: N/A	
Location: **US**	

Jobs in Journalism is a volunteer effort by its owner to compile listings of journalism jobs or internships that he has either been sent or found on the web. Jobs are listed by date of posting, and there are dozens posted each week. A free service, and obviously a labor of love.

Jobs Jobs Jobs

www.jobsjobsjobs.com

Margaret Cooley, Coolware Inc.
385 Forest, Palo Alto, CA 94301
Ph: 415-322-4722   Fax: 415-326-2479   E-mail: mcooley@coolware.com

Jobs: **Yes** Cost to post jobs: **Fee** Cost to see jobs: **Free**	
Resumes: **No** Cost to post resumes: N/A Cost to see resumes: N/A	
E-mail Alert (Push): N/A	
Specialty: **IT**	
Industry: **All**	
Feature: N/A	
Location: **US/W/CA/** **San Francisco**	

Jobs Jobs Jobs is a Bay Area job site that claims over 6,000 jobs listed. Easy-to-use search engine, and date stamped openings with direct contact information made this visit a pleasure. Job openings cost employers $49 a month to post and banners cost $295 a month. Jobs are primarily in the IT/IS area.

Jobs & Career Links

www.owt.com/jobsinfo/jobsinfo.htm

Bob Gordon, Partenariat CanWorkNet Partnership
4th Floor, Place du Portage, Ottawa, Ontario, Canaada K1A0J9
Ph: 819-994-3556   E-mail: gordons@owt.com

Jobs: **No** Cost to post jobs: N/A Cost to see jobs: N/A	Gordon's Group home page provides a long list of links to jobs and career information. Site provides links to major search engines. We like the way they are broken into groups for ease of use.
Resumes: **No** Cost to post resumes: N/A Cost to see resumes: N/A	
E-mail Alert (Push): N/A	
Specialty: **All**	
Industry: **All**	
Feature: **Meta-links**	
Location: **US**	

Jobvertise

www.jobvertise.com

Sam Roseman
2102 Rodney Drive, Champaign, IL 61821
E-mail: samr@cu-online.com

Jobs: **Yes** Cost to post jobs: **Free** Cost to see jobs: **Free**	**Jobvertise** is what makes the web a space that everyone can use. Sam, a software engineer, created this site so that companies could advertise positions for free. He developed individual company career/job pages that employers can maintain themselves. Practical approach. All jobs are date posted, and there were over 500 listed on our last visit. Simple site, and price is right.
Resumes: **No** Cost to post resumes: N/A Cost to see resumes: N/A	
E-mail Alert (Push): N/A	
Specialty: **All**	
Industry: **All**	
Feature: N/A	
Location: **US**	

Kansas Careers

www-personal.ksu.edu/~dangle/

Kansas State University
Kansas Careers, 2323 Anderson Avenue Suite 248, Manhattan, KS 66502
Ph: 913-532-6540   Fax: 913-532-7732   E-mail: dangle@ksu.edu

Jobs: **No**
Cost to post jobs: N/A
Cost to see jobs: N/A
Resumes: **No**
Cost to post resumes: N/A
Cost to see resumes: N/A
E-mail Alert (Push): N/A
Specialty: **All**
Industry: N/A
Feature: **Diversity**
Location: **US/MW/KS**

The web address may not look correct, but it is. **Kansas Careers** has value added content for women looking for career advice. Check out their internet assessment. Many gender-oriented career articles. We especially liked their internet career & educational links for students of color.

Kelly Services

www.kellyservices.com

Kelly
999 West Big Beaver Road, Troy, MI 48084
Ph: 888-465-3559   Fax: 810-522-9819   E-mail: staffing@kellyservices.com

Jobs: **Yes**
Cost to post jobs: N/A
Cost to see jobs: **Free**
Resumes: **Yes**
Cost to post resumes: **Free**
Cost to see resumes: N/A
E-mail Alert (Push): N/A
Specialty: **All**
Industry: **All**
Feature: N/A
Location: **US**

Kelly Services is one of the largest temporary corporations in the world. Job seekers can post their resume on this site or find a local Kelly office. Jobs are posted with location and date of posting only. Candidates can reply online. Many corporations have outsourced their technical, and in some cases temporary, managerial needs to this agency.

LatinoWeb

www.latinoweb.com/jobs/jobs.htm

P.O. Box 3877
Montebello, CA 90640
Ph: 626-440-0476   Fax: 626-440-0418   E-mail: info@@latinoweb.com

Jobs: **Yes** Cost to post jobs: **Fee** Cost to see jobs: **Free**	
Resumes: **No** Cost to post resumes: N/A Cost to see resumes: N/A	
E-mail Alert (Push): N/A	
Specialty: **All**	
Industry: **All**	
Feature: **Diversity**	
Location: **US/W/CA**	

LatinoWeb is geared for the west coast Latino community. We scrolled through dozens of positions that were posted at all levels and in various occupations. Direct contact information and e-mail access were provided for each position. Recruiters pay $60 to post a position. **LatinoWeb** chat and many other interesting features make this a good value for recruiters.

LATPRO

www.latpro.com

Eric Shannon, Latin America's Professional Network
Section 3403, P.O. Box 02-5339, Miami, FL 33102
E-mail: ejs@latpro.com

Jobs: **Yes** Cost to post jobs: **Free** Cost to see jobs: **Free**	
Resumes: **Yes** Cost to post resumes: **Fee** Cost to see resumes: **Fee**	
E-mail Alert (Push): **Job Seeker**	
Specialty: **All**	
Industry: **All**	
Feature: **Diversity**	
Location: **US/Int'l**	

LATPRO is dedicated to bilingual professionals who speak English and Spanish or Portuguese. Career management tools provided include news, networking and employment. Recruiters can post unlimited jobs during a 30-day free trial. The site publishes jobs in Spanish and Portuguese. Job seekers pay $29 to post their resume for three months. Site also has a free online newsletter and a moderated discussion forum covering career issues.

Law Employment Center

www.lawjobs.com/

Barbara Lamm, New York Law Publishing Company
345 Park Avenue South, New York, NY 10010
Ph: 800-888-8300   Fax: 212-481-8110   E-mail: blamm@ljextra.com

Jobs: **Yes**	
Cost to post jobs: **Fee**	
Cost to see jobs: **Free**	
Resumes: **No**	
Cost to post resumes: N/A	
Cost to see resumes: N/A	
E-mail Alert (Push): N/A	
Specialty: **Law**	
Industry: **Legal**	
Feature: N/A	
Location: **US/E/NY**	

The Law Employment Center is maintained by the *National Law Journal* as a classified web service. Recruiters can place ads in print as well as online for a fee. We have always enjoyed Ann Israel's Q&A on employment advice. The site also has a "job goddess" who answers questions on careers. We especially liked the question "Should I take my wedding ring off before I go for an interview?" (hmmm). Salary surveys and a listing of recruiters who place lawyers is also available. Hundreds of legal openings can be viewed by category, region or simply by scrolling through the listings.

Layover

www.layover.com

Bruce Martin, Layover.com
872 East Main Street, Ephrata, PA 17522
Ph: 800-361-3081   Fax: 717-859-1524   E-mail: info@layover.com

Jobs: **Yes**	
Cost to post jobs: **Fee**	
Cost to see jobs: **Free**	
Resumes: **Yes**	
Cost to post resumes: **Free**	
Cost to see resumes: **Fee**	
E-mail Alert (Push): N/A	
Specialty: **Truck Driver**	
Industry: **Trucking**	
Feature: N/A	
Location: **US**	

Layover is proof-positive that everyone is traveling the cyberhighway. Dozens of trucker jobs are posted, and 18-wheeler jockeys can fill out an online application from a rest stop, learn where to pick up their next load or read well-written articles on what is happening in the trucking industry— even find out what it is like to be a female trucker. In the layover lounge you can post messages to find your next pickup, say goodnight to your spouse and kids or learn about new products. This site will be around for a long time.

Lee Hecht Harrison

www.careerlhh.com

Claudia Gentner, Lee Hecht Harrison
50 Tice Boulevard, Woodcliff Lake, NJ 07675
Ph: 800-611-4544   Fax: 201-505-1439   E-mail: claudia_gentner@lhh.com

Jobs: **No** Cost to post jobs: **Free** (See Notes) Cost to see jobs: N/A	
Resumes: **Yes** Cost to post resumes: **Fee** (See Notes) Cost to see resumes: **Free**	
E-mail Alert (Push): N/A	
Specialty: **All**	
Industry: **All**	
Feature: N/A	
Location: **US**	

Lee Hecht Harrison provides employers access to their clients' outplaced employees. Recruiters can register and be able to view candidate profiles in 72 hours. What criterion LHH uses to give access to the resume database would be interesting to know. At the HR Center we found several interesting career articles. We recommend "Reacting to Job Loss" as one everyone should read. A new service "Lead Link" allows employers to post jobs for free (they can only be seen by LHH clients).

Lendman Group Job Fairs

www.lendman.com

The Lendman Group
141 Business Park Drive, Virginia Beach, VA 23462
Ph: 888-765-4473   Fax: 757-490-7448   E-mail: comments@lendman.com

Jobs: **Yes** Cost to post jobs: **Fee** Cost to see jobs: **Free**	
Resumes: **Yes** Cost to post resumes: **Free** Cost to see resumes: **Fee**	
E-mail Alert (Push): N/A	
Specialty: **All**	
Industry: **All**	
Feature: **Job Fairs**	
Location: **US**	

This career fair pioneer continues to publish a strong schedule of career fairs throughout the U.S. Currently **Lendman** is owned by the *Washington Post*. Employers who participate in **Lendman** job fairs can also have their positions posted on this site. The split screen design of this site is awkward and very frustrating. If you check out their career magazine, read the "Lendman Top 10." It will leave you with a chuckle.

Los Angeles Times

www.latimes.com

Nancy Massa, Los Angeles Times
145 S. Spring Street, Los Angeles, CA 90012
Fax: 213-237-3181   E-mail: classifieds@@latimes.com

Jobs: **Yes** Cost to post jobs: **Fee** Cost to see jobs: **Free**	
Resumes: **No** Cost to post resumes: N/A Cost to see resumes: N/A	
E-mail Alert (Push): N/A	
Specialty: **All**	
Industry: N/A	
Feature: N/A	
Location: **US/W/CA/LA**	

Los Angeles Times search engine makes it easy to view either Sunday or daily advertisements. Paper also participates in CareerPath. com (See CareerPath. com).

MacTalent.com

www.mactalent.com

Doug Noble, MacTalent
15321 S. Dixie Highway, Suite 309, Miami, FL 33137
Ph: 305-259-7920   Fax: 305-378-4703   E-mail: info@mactalent.com

Jobs: **Yes** Cost to post jobs: **Free** Cost to see jobs: **Free**	
Resumes: **Yes** Cost to post resumes: **Fee** Cost to see resumes: **Free**	
E-mail Alert (Push): **Job Seeker**	
Specialty: **IT/Macintosh**	
Industry: **All**	
Feature: N/A	
Location: **US**	

MacTalent. com is one of the few sites we know that caters to the Apple. Recruiters can post jobs and view resumes for free. Job seekers pay $49 to post their profile for six months or $89 to post their full CV. Site "Pushes" all job opportunities to the job seeker. Site claims its membership is over 1,000 Macintosh professionals and rising at a rapid pace. Well-designed and easy to navigate.

Manpower

www.manpower.com

Manpower, Inc.
5301 North Ironwood Road, Milwaukee, WI 53217
Fax: 414-906-7908   E-mail: jobs@manpower.com

Jobs: **Yes** Cost to post jobs: **Fee** Cost to see jobs: **Free**	
Resumes: **Yes** Cost to post resumes: **Free** Cost to see resumes: N/A	
E-mail Alert (Push): N/A	
Specialty: **All**	
Industry: **All**	
Feature: N/A	
Location: **US/Int'l**	

Manpower is one of the largest staffing and employment services in the world with over 2,200 offices in 43 countries, a technical division specializing in professional. Site's search engine allows job seekers to explore openings in any state or country they choose. Many companies are using the contractor route to fill in positions that may eventually become regular jobs. Job seekers should not forget the temporary arena in their job search. Many regular positions are also posted here.

Manufacturing Job Search

www.manufacturing.net/resources/jobs/default.htm

Monster Board
Ph: 800-606-7837   E-mail: feedback@manufacturing.net

Jobs: **Yes** Cost to post jobs: **Fee** Cost to see jobs: **Free**	
Resumes: **Yes** Cost to post resumes: **Free** Cost to see resumes: **Fee**	
E-mail Alert (Push): N/A	
Specialty: **Manufacturing**	
Industry: **All**	
Feature: **Salary Surveys**	
Location: **US**	

Manufacturing Job Search is part of Cahners Business Information, and now has partnered with the Monster Board. Standard Monster packages for posting jobs and seeing resumes (see Monster Board). Interesting articles and salary surveys on life in manufacturing. We still wonder what the job seeker feels when they think they are sending their resume to one location and, in reality, it winds up on another site.

MarketingJobs.com

www.marketingjobs.com

Woody Haskins, Marketing Classifieds
P.O. Box 1055, Brighton, MI 48116
Ph: 810-225-0225   E-mail: whaskins@marketingjobs.com

Jobs: **Yes** Cost to post jobs: **Fee** Cost to see jobs: **Free**	
Resumes: **Yes** Cost to post resumes: **Free** Cost to see resumes: **Fee**	
E-mail Alert (Push): **Job Seeker**	
Specialty: **Marketing**	
Industry: **All**	
Feature: N/A	
Location: **US**	

MarketingJobs.com is trying to fill a difficult niche. Site has an executive marketing recruiter directory that can be searched by state. Jobs are viewed through the site's search engine and are date posted with direct contact information. Easy to view and works well. Recruiters pay $75 to post a position for two months. The resume database can be searched for $50 a month. Useful tips for preparing your resume are also available. The big question is how (other than word-of-mouth) a site like this reaches marketing job seekers.

MBA Careers

www.mbacareers.com

J. Donnelly, Career Exposure, Inc.
1881 SW Front Avenue, Portland, OR 97201
Ph: 503-525-8498   Fax: 503-525-8497   E-mail: bizmail@mbacareers.com

Jobs: **Yes** Cost to post jobs: **Free** (See Notes) Cost to see jobs: **Free**	
Resumes: **Yes** Cost to post resumes: **Fee** Cost to see resumes: **Fee**	
E-mail Alert (Push): **No**	
Specialty: **Business/MBA**	
Industry: **All**	
Feature: N/A	
Location: **US/Int'l/Canada/ Europe**	

MBA Careers is a new site created by the owner of Career Exposure. Recruiters can post jobs for free (at some point it will cost $89 per job). Resumes cost $299 per quarter to view. All jobs have direct contact information. The site's search engine allows the job seeker to search by function, company, state, country or keyword. We like the fact that the designers allowed us to search all jobs.

MBA Employment Connection Assoc.

www.mbanetwork.com

Brian Chase, MECA
P.O. Box 415, Palmyra, VA 22963
Ph: 804-286-3866   Fax: 804-286-3866   E-mail: meca@mbanetwork.com

Jobs: **Yes** Cost to post jobs: **Fee** Cost to see jobs: **Free**
Resumes: **Yes** Cost to post resumes: **Free** Cost to see resumes: **Free**
E-mail Alert (Push): **Employer**
Specialty: **Business/MBA**
Industry: **All**
Feature: N/A
Location: **US**

MBA Employment Connection Association (MECA) tells you right on their home page that they have nine jobs posted, 228 registered recruiters and 1,011 MBA profiles that can be viewed. We like this kind of full disclosure, and believe job seekers will as well. Recruiters pay $45 to post a position for one month. They can also receive periodic notices of new resumes that are added to the database via e-mail (resumes can be seen on the site for free). Jobs are posted by date. Job seekers can post their profile for free with or without direct contact information. If candidates prefer, they can just leave their e-mail for recruiters to contact them. Great design.

MBA Free Agents.com

www.mbafreeagents.com

Rob Steir
2124 Broadway, Suite 233, New York, New York 10023
Ph: 212-579-1781   Fax: 212-877-1276   E-mail: rob@mbafreeagents.com

Jobs: **Yes** Cost to post jobs: **Fee** Cost to see jobs: **Fee**
Resumes: **Yes** Cost to post resumes: **Free** (See Notes) Cost to see resumes: **Fee**
E-mail Alert (Push): **Job Seeker**
Specialty: **Business/MBA**
Industry: **All**
Feature: N/A
Location: **US/Int'l**

MBA Free Agents. com is a niche site going after students and alumni from major universities. Site charges $495 to post a job for 45 days. All jobs are "pushed" to enrolled job seekers on a biweekly basis. For $1,995 recruiters can post a position and it will be immediately e-mailed to qualified and currently available candidates with your direct contact information. Job seekers can register for free, but soon will be asked to pay $25 for a six-month registration. Jobs can only be seen by registered members. Owners of the site state they want to only deal directly with employers—no headhunters allowed.

MBAjob.com

www.mbajob.com

MBAjob
P.O. Box 15861, Nashville, TN 37215
Ph: 615-298-4369   Fax: 615-298-4369   E-mail: mba@mbajob.com

Jobs: **Yes** Cost to post jobs: **Free** Cost to see jobs: **Free**	
Resumes: **Yes** Cost to post resumes: **Fee** Cost to see resumes: **Free**	
E-mail Alert (Push): N/A	
Specialty: **Business/MBA**	
Industry: **All**	
Feature: N/A	
Location: **US**	

MBAjob. com was created by students to help applicants find jobs in major corporations. You would think students would not charge their own a fee and, instead, go after recruiters who have the $$$. But n-o-o-o...MBAs pay $15 for six months or $25 to post their resume for a year. Recruiters can post jobs for free. Banners and tiles are available for a fee. Recruiters can view resumes with direct contact information for free.

Med Connect

www.medconnect.com

Medical Network,Inc.
Princeton, NJ
E-mail: reply@medconnect.com

Jobs: **Yes** Cost to post jobs: **Fee** Cost to see jobs: **Free**	
Resumes: **No** Cost to post resumes: N/A Cost to see resumes: N/A	
E-mail Alert (Push): N/A	
Specialty: **Health Care/MD**	
Industry: **Health Care**	
Feature: N/A	
Location: **US**	

Med Connect posts positions for doctors in many specialties. Jobs can be searched by functional area and then by state. Employer contact information can be seen. You must register with the site to use it (they want to keep track of visitors).

MedHunters

www.medhunters.com/scripts/mh.py

Robin Kerr, MedHunters
180 Dundas Street West, Suite 2403, Toronto, ON, Canaada M5G 1Z8
Ph: 800-664-0278   Fax: 416-977-6128   E-mail: info@medhunters.com

Jobs: **Yes** Cost to post jobs: **Fee** Cost to see jobs: **Free**	**MedHunters** appeals to all manner of medical professionals, and although the site is owned by a recruitment firm, employers can post a job for $150 (unlimited positions for a year for $3,000). All jobs are posted for 60 days provide the jobseeker with contact information. Employers can view posted resume profiles, but must return to the site for contact information. Search engine is interactive, and asks recruiters specific questions to help narrow their search. Nicely done.
Resumes: **Yes** Cost to post resumes: **Free** Cost to see resumes: **Fee**	
E-mail Alert (Push): N/A	
Specialty: **Health Care**	
Industry: **Health Care**	
Feature: N/A	
Location: **Int'l/Canada/US**	

MedSearch

www.medsearch.com

Pati Galloway, 2780 Waterfront Parkway
E Drive, Suite 100, Indianapolis, IN 46214
Ph: 800-899-7058   Fax: 317-293-6692   E-mail: patricia@occ.com

Jobs: **Yes** Cost to post jobs: **Fee** Cost to see jobs: **Free**	**Medsearch** is now fully integrated into the TMP lineup. The first item viewed on our visit was a large banner touting the Online Career Center. Recruiters can post an ad for $150 (which can include up to three jobs) for a 60-day run. Unlimited resumes can be viewed for $2,900 per year. Site map allows job seekers to search the U.S. for their position of choice. Date posted job listings are in the biomedical, biotechnology, research or other scientific fields. All job seekers can e-mail their resume direct or apply online. When you do so online your resume goes through OCC. Thousands of jobs in this field were posted on our visit. A special section has been created for cultural diversity programs with links to numerous organizations.
Resumes: **Yes** Cost to post resumes: **Free** (See Notes) Cost to see resumes: **Fee**	
E-mail Alert (Push): N/A	
Specialty: **Science/Biomedical**	
Industry: **Health Care**	
Feature: N/A	
Location: **US**	

Medical Device Link

www.devicelink.com/career

Rebecca Bermudez, Canon Communications, Inc.
3340 Ocean Park Blvd., Suite 1000, Santa Monica, CA 90405
Ph: 310-392-8839   Fax: 310-392-4920   E-mail: feedback@canon.com

Jobs: **Yes** Cost to post jobs: **Fee** Cost to see jobs: **Free**
Resumes: **No** Cost to post resumes: N/A Cost to see resumes: N/A
E-mail Alert (Push): N/A
Specialty: **Science/** **Medical Device**
Industry: **Health Care**
Feature: N/A
Location: **US**

Medical Device Link provides interesting articles from the *Medical Device and Diagnostic Industry* magazine. Recruiters pay $50 for a 100-word ad that is posted for 30 days. A salary survey and a salary estimator are an added bonus.

Medzilla

www.medzilla.com

Frank Heasley, Ph.D., Franklin Search Group
4522 54th Place West, Redmonds, WA 98026
Ph: 425-742-4292   Fax: 425-742-2172   E-mail: info@medzilla.com

Jobs: **Yes** Cost to post jobs: **Fee** Cost to see jobs: **Free**
Resumes: **Yes** Cost to post resumes: **Free** Cost to see resumes: **Fee**
E-mail Alert (Push): **Employer**
Specialty: **Sci/Chem/Pharm** **Health Care**
Industry: **Biotech/Pharm**
Feature: N/A
Location: **US/Int'l**

Medzilla (Franklin Search Group) Online is designed for biotechnology, medicine, healthcare and pharmaceutical candidates. Extensive job listings and a resume database are available. Candidates can post their resume and search jobs in U.S. and internationally for free. Employers may query the candidate database at no charge, but there is a fee to obtain contact information. Recruiters can list a job for $95 ($250 per month for unlimited postings). Resumes that match the employers job specs are "Pushed" to recruiters via e-mail for an additional fee. Academic postings for postdoctorals and faculty are free for employers to list. Career management articles can also be found.

Mercury Center Web

www.sjmercury.com

Greg Aarons, San Jose Mercury News
750 Ridder Park Drive, San Jose, CA 95190
Ph: 408-920-5585 E-mail: gaarons@sjmercury.com

Jobs: **Yes**	
Cost to post jobs: **Fee**	
Cost to see jobs: **Free**	
Resumes: **No**	
Cost to post resumes: **Free**	
Cost to see resumes: N/A	
E-mail Alert (Push): **Job Seeker**	
Specialty: **All**	
Industry: N/A	
Feature: N/A	
Location: **US/W/CA/San Jose**	

Mercury Center Web wins our prize for one of the best job & career centers from a newspaper. Continuing to improve, this site Pushes jobs out via e-mail to job seekers. Their search tool "Talent Scout Job Search" allows those looking for work to hone in on a particular company or area of California. Select the position you want, and then see a brief profile about the corporation. "Job Hound" advises when area business organizations and network meetings are being held. "Talent Scout" provides career articles for those new to the job market. Career articles have an audio component. A pioneer in this industry, **Mercury Center** is still on top. Participates in CareerPath. com (see CareerPath. com)

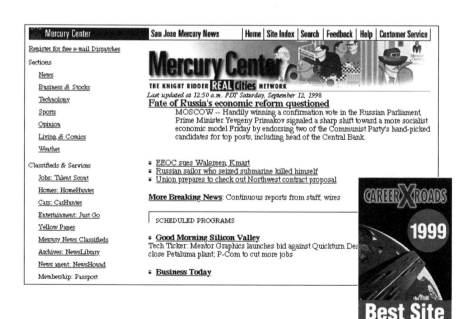

Midrange Computing

midrangecomputing.com

Fern Sheinman, ILR Publications Inc.
5650 El Camino Real, Suite 225, Carlsbad, CA 92008
Ph: 800-477-5665   Fax: 760-931-9935   E-mail: (See Notes)

Jobs: **Yes** Cost to post jobs: **Fee** Cost to see jobs: **Free**
Resumes: **Yes** Cost to post resumes: **Fee** Cost to see resumes: **Free**
E-mail Alert (Push): **Job Seeker**
Specialty: **IT/AS400 dev. (BPCS, PRMS, LANSA, EDI, etc.)**
Industry: **All**
Feature: N/A
Location: **US**

Midrange Computing concentrates on AS400. Dozens of positions are listed with direct e-mail and other contact information. A tough market for talent (we viewed only one resume on our visit). Recruiters pay $200 to post a position for 30 days. An AS400 discussion forum is also available, and is a great place for companies to network for candidates. Site faxes a weekly newsletter to over 25,000 subscribers. Imagine candidates drinking their Monday morning coffee and reading about your opening.

Milwaukee Journal Sentinel

www.onwis.com

Milwaukee Journal
333 W. State Street, Milwaukee, WI 53203
Ph: 888-886-6947   E-mail: onwis@onwis.com

Jobs: **Yes** Cost to post jobs: **Fee** Cost to see jobs: **Free**
Resumes: **No** Cost to post resumes: N/A Cost to see resumes: N/A
E-mail Alert (Push): N/A
Specialty: **All**
Industry: N/A
Feature: N/A
Location: **US/MW/WI/Milwaukee**

Help-wanted classified advertisements are posted on this site. Paper participates in CareerPath. com (See CareerPath. com).

MinistryConnect

ministryconnect.org

Bernadette Dougherty, Ministry Resource Center
1600 Martine Avenue, Scotch Plains, NJ 07076
Ph: 908-889-6425   Fax: 908-889-5270   E-mail: director@ministryconnect.org

Jobs: **Yes** Cost to post jobs: **Fee** Cost to see jobs: **Free**	
Resumes: **Yes** Cost to post resumes: **Fee** Cost to see resumes: **Free**	
E-mail Alert (Push): **N/A**	
Specialty: **All**	
Industry: **Religion**	
Feature: N/A	
Location: **US**	

MinistryConnect was founded as a collaborative venture of 14 congregations of Catholic Sisters. Jobs posted are categorized by: administration, education, health care, parish/pastoral/spiritual, social service or volunteerism. Positions are date posted and cost $25. Resumes are $20 for a one-month run. Jobs can be searched by profession or by region of the U.S. We wonder if the benefits include spiritual intervention.

Minorities' Job Bank

www.minorities-jb.com

Penny Duet Francis, Black Collegian Services, Inc.
140 Carondelet Street, New Orleans, LA 70130
Ph: 504-523-4616   Fax: 504-523-0271   E-mail: penny@black-collegian.com

Jobs: **Yes** Cost to post jobs: **Fee** Cost to see jobs: **Free**	
Resumes: **Yes** Cost to post resumes: **Free** Cost to see resumes: **Fee**	
E-mail Alert (Push): **No**	
Specialty: **All**	
Industry: **All**	
Feature: **Diversity**	
Location: **US**	

The owners of *Black Collegian* magazine, a well-known college publication, provide career opportunities for the all the world's "villages" at **Minorities' Job Bank**. Site's search engine enhances the process of finding jobs, and the jobs themselves include direct contact information and date of posting "Villages " have been created for African, Asian, Hispanic, Native American and other global minorities. A women's village is on the horizon. In these content areas, there are interesting articles on career management and other topics affecting minorities. Recruiters pay $150 per job posting, and can view the resume database for an annual charge of $3,900. Resumes can be posted for free using the sites resume builder or simply cutting and pasting. Candidates can keep their contact information confidential if they choose. Any national company with a serious college strategy would be deficient without including this site.

MMWire.com

www.mmwire.com

Angela Duff, Phillips Business Information
1201 Seven Locks Road, Suite 300, Potomac, MD 20854
Ph: 888-707-5814   Fax: 301-309-3847   E-mail: snance@phillips.com

Jobs: **Yes** Cost to post jobs: **Fee** Cost to see jobs: **Free**	
Resumes: **Yes** Cost to post resumes: **Free** Cost to see resumes: **Free**	
E-mail Alert (Push): N/A	
Specialty: **IT/Multimedia**	
Industry: **All**	
Feature: N/A	
Location: **US**	

MMWire is the web site for an daily interactive entertainment industry publication that is e-mailed to 5,700. Primarily for publishers and developers, this site was under construction on our visit, but we do note that jobs can be posted $49. 95 (each) for one month.

The Monster Board

www.monster.com

Christina Pickle
5 Clocktower Place, Suite 500, Maynard, MA 01754
Ph: 800-666-7837   Fax: 508-879-4651   E-mail: cpickle@monster.com

Jobs: **Yes**	
Cost to post jobs: **Fee**	
Cost to see jobs: **Free**	
Resumes: **Yes**	
Cost to post resumes: **Free**	
Cost to see resumes: **Fee**	
E-mail Alert (Push): **Both**	
Specialty: **All**	
Industry: **All**	
Feature: **N/A**	
Location: **US/Int'l**	

The **Monster Board** grew tremendously in the past year, and continues to be one of the top choices among recruiting professionals. Alliances with Yahoo, Excite, AOL, Medscape, Workforce Online, PlanetAll and the American Society for Quality (to name a few) helps to drive traffic and keep its name in the forefront. Sixty day job postings are $175, and are listed by location and/or a category. Many other packages are available. The **Monster Board** claims to have over 75,000 job seekers visit each day as well as 50,000 job openings and 250,000 or 350,000 resumes depending on the page you read. Recruiters can view the site's resume database for $4,900 per year. They can also have "Cruiter" search the database weekly and e-mail candidate matches back to your office. For job seekers "Swoop" is your personal agent. When you register your profile you will then receive e-mail messages of positions that match your interest. Resume contact data can be kept confidential. Several hundred companies have links/banners to their job pages for applicants to view. Site is owned by TAMP, a recruitment advertising firm.

MTS Group

www.mtsboston.com

235 Bear Hill Road, Waltham, MA 02451
Ph: 781-890-9888   Fax: 781-890-4888   E-mail: webmaster@mtsboston.com

Jobs: **Yes** Cost to post jobs: **Fee** Cost to see jobs: **Free**	
Resumes: **Yes** Cost to post resumes: **Free** Cost to see resumes: **Fee**	
E-mail Alert (Push): N/A	
Specialty: **IT**	
Industry: **All**	
Feature: N/A	
Location: **US/East**	

MTS Group is a recruiting firm with a unique approach that allows corporations to pay a set fee for accessing their resume database. Internal "resume miners" go through the database to provide qualified candidates on a weekly basis. Recruiters can now search their resume database. Jobs are posted with direct contact information available, and most have links back to the employer's web site. Site has a regional focus with office locations in New England, Mid-Atlantic, and the Carolinas. Jobs are posted from all over the U.S. Resumes are only kept for sixty days. Site claims over 2,000 jobs from 500 hiring companies.

Music Pages

www.musicpages.com/index.htm

The Internet Music Pages
Fax: 817-685-9536   E-mail: bobm1@musicpages.com

Jobs: **Yes** Cost to post jobs: **Free** Cost to see jobs: **Free**	
Resumes: **No** Cost to post resumes: N/A Cost to see resumes: N/A	
E-mail Alert (Push): N/A	
Specialty: **All**	
Industry: **Music**	
Feature: N/A	
Location: **US**	

The Internet Music Pages can give you the latest "buzz" about what is "happening" in the music world. Jobs for recording engineers to studio technicians and music teachers can be found here for free. We like sites that give back to their industry.

My Future

www.myfuture.com

Stu Cowan
E-mail: thebrains@myfuture.com

Jobs: **No**	
Cost to post jobs: N/A	
Cost to see jobs: N/A	
Resumes: **No**	
Cost to post resumes: N/A	
Cost to see resumes: N/A	
E-mail Alert (Push): N/A	
Specialty: **College/High School**	
Industry: **All**	
Feature: N/A	
Location: **US**	

My Future is geared to high school graduates who are not sure what they want to do when they grow up. The site includes: a resume work sheet to help you put your best foot forward; a cover letter; a step-by-step interviewing guide and financial aid information with links to directories. A "money game" leads you through actual career situations and scores your answers. Information on joining the Peace Corp or considering the military is also available. Nice site for parents as well as students.

NACUBO

www.nacubo.org

Pierce McManus, Nat'l. Assoc. of College & University Business Officers
2501 M Street NW, Suite 400, Washington, DC 20037
Ph: 202-861-2500   Fax: 202-861-2583   E-mail: pmcmanus@nacubo.nche.edu

Jobs: **Yes**	
Cost to post jobs: **Fee**	
Cost to see jobs: **Free**	
Resumes: **No**	
Cost to post resumes: N/A	
Cost to see resumes: N/A	
E-mail Alert (Push): N/A	
Specialty: **Ed/Executive**	
Industry: **Education**	
Feature: N/A	
Location: **US**	

NACUBO posts employment opportunities in higher education administration at their web site. Applicants will need to drill into the "resouce directory", and then click "employment opportunities" to find them. This is the web component of the association's monthly magazine. Several dozen positions can be scrolled with direct contact information.

NationJob Network

www.nationjob.com

Bob Levinstein, NationJob, Inc.
601 SW 9th Street, Suite J&K, Des Moines, IA 50309
Ph: 800-292-7731   Fax: 515-965-6737   E-mail: njsales@nationjob.com

Jobs: **Yes**
Cost to post jobs: **Fee**
Cost to see jobs: **Free**

Resumes: **Yes**
Cost to post resumes: **Free**
Cost to see resumes: **N/A**

E-mail Alert (Push): **Job Seeker**

Specialty: **All**

Industry: **All**

Feature: N/A

Location: **US**

We used to think of the **NationJob Network** as a national site with a Midwest focus, but, more and more, they are reaching out to every corner of the U.S. This site's agent, "PJ Scout," can "push" job information matching the interests of nearly 300,000 registered job seekers. **NationJob** will post employer openings for 30 days for $95 or $125 with a one-page company profile. Think of the posting price as a potential "direct e-mail" (which includes all the job content and contact information) to a subset of their subscribers, and you can begin to see the added value here. Many specialty areas from aerospace to marketing also make this an easy site to navigate. **NationJob** claims over 20,000 jobs. **NationJob** has also developed hosting relationships with a number of communities throughout the U.S. Ease of access, push capability that really works, and thousands of jobs with direct contact information, would make this a top site in any case, but, we also have a high regard for the owner's business acumen, commitment to customer value, full disclosure, and understanding of the direction the web will take. Try it.

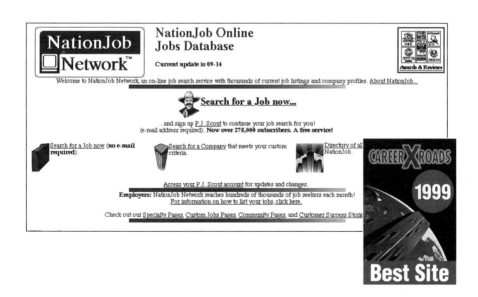

National Alumni Placement Association

www.careers.com

NAPA Inc.
P.O. Box 974, Sausalito, CA 94966
Ph: 415-331-2800   Fax: 415-331-2844   E-mail: napaserv@aol.com

Jobs: **Yes**	
Cost to post jobs: **Fee**	
Cost to see jobs: **Free**	
Resumes: **Yes**	
Cost to post resumes: **Free**	
Cost to see resumes: N/A	
E-mail Alert (Push): N/A	
Specialty: **All/College/ Entry-level**	
Industry: **All**	
Feature: N/A	
Location: **US**	

NAPA provides job listings from their national publication which serves the needs of Career Placement offices and job hunters across the country. You can search open positions by industry or field of interest from their web site. Job seekers can post their resume, and the association states they will send it out to member companies. Site will soon have a full resume service for employers.

The National Assembly

www.nassembly.org

David Holmes
1319 F Street, Suite 601, Washington, DC 20004
Ph: 202-347-2080   Fax: 202-393-4517   E-mail: nassembly@nassembly.org

Jobs: **Yes**	
Cost to post jobs: **Free** (See Notes)	
Cost to see jobs: **Free**	
Resumes: **No**	
Cost to post resumes: N/A	
Cost to see resumes: N/A	
E-mail Alert (Push): N/A	
Specialty: **Nonprofit**	
Industry: **Nonprofit**	
Feature: N/A	
Location: **US**	

The National Assembly is an association of national nonprofit health and human service organizations. Some of the members are the American Cancer Society, Boy Scouts of America and the YM/YWCA. Site has over 2,000 paid and unpaid internship listings that can be searched. Also listed are several dozen permanent positions which are posted for members.

National Business Employment Weekly

www.nbew.com

NBEW
P.O. Box 300, Princeton, NJ 08543
Ph: 800-323-6239   Fax: 609-520-7315

Jobs: **No** Cost to post jobs: **Fee** Cost to see jobs: **Fee**
Resumes: **No** Cost to post resumes: N/A Cost to see resumes: N/A
E-mail Alert (Push): N/A
Specialty: N/A
Industry: N/A
Feature: N/A
Location: **US**

The National Business Employment Weekly publishes all of the *Wall Street Journal's* regional employment opportunities for an introductory price of $19 for six weeks. The jobs can only be seen in the print version. This site contains career management articles.

National Diversity Newspaper Job Bank

www.newsjobs.com

Zandria Jacobs, Florida Times-Union
1 Riverside Ave., Jacksonville, FL 32202
Ph: 904-359-4079   Fax: 904-359-4478   E-mail: newsjobs@newsjobs.com

Jobs: **Yes** Cost to post jobs: **Free** Cost to see jobs: **Free**
Resumes: **Yes** Cost to post resumes: **Free** Cost to see resumes: N/A
E-mail Alert (Push): N/A
Specialty: **Communications** **Journalism**
Industry: **Publishing**
Feature: **Diversity**
Location: **US**

National Diversity Newspaper Job Bank allows recruiters to post jobs for free to attract minority candidates to the journalism field. To see positions you will need to enter your resume or send an e-mail for a password to view open jobs. Passwords are received immediately, and once in, applicants can search on specific functions or titles. Direct contact information and job posting dates have been added this year. Only issue we have is that the resumes job seekers submit appear to go nowhere. They are used for statistical purposes by the site and are not seen by employers. Great effort by owner, *The Florida Times-Union*, make this a top niche site.

National Educators Employment Review

www.teacherjobs.com/

P.O. Box 60309, Colorado Springs, CO 80960
Ph: 719-632-5877   Fax: 800-377-1146

Jobs: **Yes** Cost to post jobs: **Free** Cost to see jobs: **Fee**	
Resumes: **Yes** Cost to post resumes: **Free** Cost to see resumes: **Free**	
E-mail Alert (Push): N/A	
Specialty: **Teaching**	
Industry: **Ed/K-12**	
Feature: N/A	
Location: **US**	

The National Educators Employment Review is a monthly publication, and the intent of this site is to get you to spend $52 to subscribe. Recruiters can post positions and see resumes for free, but job seekers can only see a few samples of the positions available. To see the rest, job seekers have to subscribe to the publication. A search engine includes jobs by state.

National Society of Black Engineers

www.nsbe.org

Robert Ingram, NSBE
1454 Duke Street, Alexandria, VA 22314
Ph: 703-549-2207   Fax: 703-683-5312

Jobs: **Yes** Cost to post jobs: **Fee** Cost to see jobs: **Free**	
Resumes: **No** Cost to post resumes: N/A Cost to see resumes: N/A	
E-mail Alert (Push): N/A	
Specialty: **Engineering**	
Industry: **All**	
Feature: **Diversity**	
Location: **US**	

NSBE provides classified advertisements from their monthly publication on their web site. The objective is to reach out to African American engineering students and professionals. Recruiters pay $50 to post a position for one month. Site's search engine allows the job seeker to view all states and select specific jobs of interest. Note pad concept allows the job seeker to "check" positions and view them in order of selection. Very nice feature. Resumes can be saved to the site and sent directly to each employer. A resume database is under construction. Job fairs and convention information are also available.

National Society of Professional Engineers

www.nspe.org

NSPE, 1420 King Street, Alexandria, VA 22314
Ph: 888-285-6773   E-mail: customer.service@nspe.org

Jobs: **Yes** Cost to post jobs: **Fee** Cost to see jobs: **Free**	
Resumes: **No** Cost to post resumes: N/A Cost to see resumes: N/A	
E-mail Alert (Push): N/A	
Specialty: **Engineering/PE**	
Industry: **Construction**	
Feature: N/A	
Location: **US**	

NSPE provides positions for professional certified engineers in many disciplines. Recruiters pay $50 – $80 per posting depending on size of ad. Nice thing about **NSPE's** job listings is that the states that have positions are highlighted to make it easier to target location, and with no search engine, that is an important feature. Approach is still a bit cumbersome though. Some content is only available to members of the association.

Nature Biotechnology

www.nature.com

Nature America Inc.
345 Park Avenue South, NY, NY 10010
Ph: 212-726-9200   Fax: 212-696-9006   E-mail: classifed@natureny.com

Jobs: **Yes** Cost to post jobs: **Fee** Cost to see jobs: **Free**	
Resumes: **No** Cost to post resumes: N/A Cost to see resumes: N/A	
E-mail Alert (Push): N/A	
Specialty: **Science/BioTech**	
Industry: **All**	
Feature: N/A	
Location: **US/Int'l**	

Nature Magazine is a weekly journal of biotechnology that services the pharmaceutical and chemical products industries. All of their classified ads are published on the web. The site's search engine indexes jobs by subject, country, organization or job title, and positions are updated weekly. Hundreds of jobs can be viewed here. Recruiters and job seekers should also check out www.medicine. nature. com which is their monthly international journal of biomedical research.

Nat'l. Council of Teachers of Math Jobs

www.nctm.org/jobs

National Council of Teachers of Mathematics
1906 Association Drive, Reston, VA 20191
Ph: 703-620-9840   Fax: 703-476-2970   E-mail: jobs@nctm.org

Jobs: **Yes**	
Cost to post jobs: **Fee**	
Cost to see jobs: **Free**	
Resumes: **Yes**	
Cost to post resumes: **Free** (See Notes)	
Cost to see resumes: **Free**	
E-mail Alert (Push): N/A	
Specialty: **Ed./Science/Math**	
Industry: **Education**	
Feature: N/A	
Location: **US**	

The **NCTM** has over 117,000 members devoted to mathematics, the teaching of mathematics, and the discovery of new approaches to improve the teaching of mathematics. Grades Pre-K through 12 and post secondary are represented. Recruiters' costs range $100-$250 for job postings depending on the number of words (30-day listing). Members can list positions wanted for free.

Navy

www.navyjobs.com

Ph: 800-872-6289

Jobs: **Yes**	
Cost to post jobs: N/A (See Notes)	
Cost to see jobs: **Free**	
Resumes: **Yes**	
Cost to post resumes: **Free**	
Cost to see resumes: N/A (See Notes)	
E-mail Alert (Push): N/A	
Specialty: **All**	
Industry: **Military**	
Feature: **Military**	
Location: **US**	

The Navy has kept their site simple by asking visitors about their area of job interest, and then responding with additional information through the U.S. Mail. We think they dropped the anchor on this one.

Needle in a Cyberstack

home.revealed.net/albee

John Albee, Davenport Community Schools
736 Westfield Road, Davenport, IA 52806
Ph: 319-386-2171   E-mail: albee@revealed.net

Jobs: **No** Cost to post jobs: **Free** Cost to see jobs: **Free**	
Resumes: **No** Cost to post resumes: N/A Cost to see resumes: N/A	
E-mail Alert (Push): N/A	
Specialty: **All**	
Industry: **All**	
Feature: **Meta-links/ Research**	
Location: **US**	

Needle in a Cyberstack continues to provide interesting links to help make the internet easier for us all. Click on "Business" and "Career Tools" to find 24 links to the owner's picks for the 24 best sites. Interesting content to help job seekers refine their job research skills.

Nerd World

www.nerdworld.com

David Stein, Nerd World Media
E-mail: nerds@nerdworld.com

Jobs: **No** Cost to post jobs: N/A Cost to see jobs: N/A	
Resumes: **No** Cost to post resumes: N/A Cost to see resumes: N/A	
E-mail Alert (Push): N/A	
Specialty: **IT**	
Industry: **All**	
Feature: **User Groups**	
Location: **US**	

Nerd World has hundreds of annotated links to job sites. It also has a unique list of technical user groups and information on when they meet throughout the U.S. If you want to network with "techies" this is the place to find out "where" and "when. " Submitting a link is free, but recruiters can also purchase preferred links for $180 per year to get near the top of the page. They have recently made an arrangement with Classifieds 2000.

Net Cruiting

www.netcruiting.com

George Zambos, Recruitment Technologies
153 Shelley Avenue, Campbell, CA 95008
Ph: 408-278-7837   E-mail: info@netcruiting.com

Jobs: **Yes** Cost to post jobs: **Free** Cost to see jobs: **Free**	Recruitment Technologies works with CareerBuilder, and the site will post staffing positions for two months for free. All positions have direct contact information. Owner, George Zambos, conducts Internet training for HR professionals, and has also published in 1998 *A Human Resources Guide to Global Sourcing* available through Simon & Schuster for $49. 95.
Resumes: **No** Cost to post resumes: N/A Cost to see resumes: N/A	
E-mail Alert (Push): N/A	
Specialty: **Human Resources Staffing**	
Industry: **All**	
Feature: N/A	
Location: **US**	

Net Jobs Information Services

www.netjobs.com

103 Wright Street, Richmond Hill, ON, LAC, Canaada L4C 4A3
Ph: 800-367-6563   Fax: 905-770-0829   E-mail: info@netjobs.com

Jobs: **Yes** Cost to post jobs: **Fee** Cost to see jobs: **Free**	**Netjobs** is a Canadian-based site that lists dozens of position. Recruiters pay $100 to post a job and can consider other packages as well. Resumes can be searched in alpha or subject order. Contact information is available. Positions are posted by company name, and job seekers then click to find direct contact information.
Resumes: **Yes** Cost to post resumes: **Fee** Cost to see resumes: **Free**	
E-mail Alert (Push): N/A	
Specialty: **All**	
Industry: **All**	
Feature: N/A	
Location: **Int'l/Canada**	

Net Temps

www.net-temps.com

Gregg Booth, Net-Temps Inc.
130 Middlesex Road, Tyngsboro, MA 01879
Ph: 978-649-8575   E-mail: sales@net-temps.com

Jobs: **Yes**	
Cost to post jobs: **Fee**	
Cost to see jobs: **Free**	
Resumes: **Yes**	
Cost to post resumes: **Free**	
Cost to see resumes: **Fee**	
E-mail Alert (Push): N/A	
Specialty: **All**	
Industry: **Computer**	
Feature: N/A	
Location: **US/Int'l/Canada**	

Net-Temps is a third-party staffing industry cybercenter that claims over 80,000 active job openings updated on a daily basis. Add in over 225,000 resumes, and you have one of the larger players the game. **Net-Temps** has a strong following in the placement/staffing community. Job openings are automatically posted to hundreds of locations on the web, and resumes are acquired through the use of spiders from dozens of sources. A 30-day free trial period is offered with confidence. New feature will assist third party recruiters by adding a candidate profiles that employers can view for a fee. Headhunters can buy a basic package for $395 per month. Site continues to grow with fresh ideas.

Netshare

www.netshare.com

Kathy Simmons, Netshare, Inc.
2 Commercial Boulevard, Suite 200, Novato, CA 94949
Ph: 800-241-5642   Fax: 415-883-1799   E-mail: netshare@netshare.com

Jobs: **Yes**
Cost to post jobs: **Free**
Cost to see jobs: **Fee**
Resumes: **Yes**
Cost to post resumes: **Fee** (See Notes)
Cost to see resumes: **Fee**
E-mail Alert (Push): **Job Seeker**
Specialty: **Executive**
Industry: **All**
Feature: N/A
Location: **US/Int'l/Europe/China**

Netshare is an executive networking organization. If you are a $100,000 job seeker or recruiter/employer—particularly on the west coast—you need to be aware of this service. Job seekers pay $195 for six months depending on the level of report desired. **Netshare** sends leads via e-mail or snail mail. Job seekers can search the web site for new leads on a daily basis. Senior positions from $100K to $500K are listed. Sample positions can be viewed at this site, but only members get full access. Companies can post openings at no cost. Employers can search their database of candidates for a fee. A new job matching service has been added.

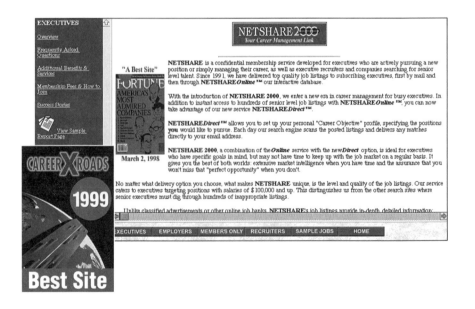

NetworkWorld Fusion

www.nwfusion.com

Ann Roskey, Network World
The Meadows, 161 Worcester Rd., Framingham, MA 01701
Ph: 800-622-1108   Fax: 508-820-1283   E-mail: aroskey@nww.com

Jobs: **Yes** Cost to post jobs: **Fee** Cost to see jobs: **Free**	**NetworkWorld Fusion** is a weekly publication that focuses on Network IS management issues, analysis and news. Job seekers who register their e-mail can receive their twice weekly newsletter with job alerts. Positions can be viewed by U.S. region, title and date of posting. All direct contact information is present. Dozens of helpful management and career articles for the recruiter and job seeker.
Resumes: **No** Cost to post resumes: N/A Cost to see resumes: N/A	
E-mail Alert (Push): **Job Seeker**	
Specialty: **IT/Network IS Management**	
Industry: **Computers**	
Feature: N/A	
Location: **US**	

New England Journal of Medicine

www.nejm.org/

New England Journal of Medicine
1440 Main Street, Waltham, MA 02451
Ph: 617-734-9800   Fax: 617-734-4457   E-mail: nejmads@massmed.org

Jobs: **Yes** Cost to post jobs: **Fee** Cost to see jobs: **Free**	**New England Journal of Medicine** reaches 200,000 physicians per week through its print publication. Classified ads are placed on this web site. Site's search engine allowed us to view their 735 positions by specialty, region or other classification. It also advises the job seeker how many positions are in each specialty, and in which regions of the U.S. All direct contact information is available.
Resumes: **No** Cost to post resumes: N/A Cost to see resumes: N/A	
E-mail Alert (Push): N/A	
Specialty: **Health Care/MD**	
Industry: **Health Care**	
Feature: N/A	
Location: **US**	

New Jersey Online

www.nj.com

Madhavi Saifee, Advance Internet
Star Ledger, 30 Journal Square, Jersey City, NJ 07306
Ph: 201-459-2871   E-mail: njcareer@nj.com

Jobs: **Yes**	
Cost to post jobs: **Fee**	
Cost to see jobs: **Free**	
Resumes: **No**	
Cost to post resumes: N/A	
Cost to see resumes: N/A	
E-mail Alert (Push): N/A	
Specialty: **All**	
Industry: **All**	
Feature: N/A	
Location: **US**/E/NJ	

New Jersey Online is the web complement of the *Newark Star Ledger* and the *Trenton Times* newspapers, and includes their help-wanted advertising. We've included the site in our directory because the site links to the top 100 corporations in the state which is well worth the visit. Other publications would do well to emulate similar content to help the job seeker find, locate and research employers of choice. Too often this content is buried (unless you know the date it was published). From a technical standpoint the site's frame design makes navigation a breeze.

New Media Association of NJ

www.nmanj.com

Ryan W. Maple, Trien Rosenberg
177 Madison Ave., Morristown, NJ 07962
Ph: 201-267-4200   E-mail: nrwm@electricmedia.com

Jobs: **Yes**	
Cost to post jobs: **Free**	
Cost to see jobs: **Free**	
Resumes: **No**	
Cost to post resumes: N/A	
Cost to see resumes: N/A	
E-mail Alert (Push): N/A	
Specialty: **IT/Multimedia**	
Industry: **All**	
Feature: N/A	
Location: **US/NJ**	

The New Media Association of NJ is one chapter in one state. Similar groups are starting up in nearly every state. The **NJNMA** encompasses all of the disciplines that utilize electronic communication tools for business, cultural and/or educational purposes. Employers can post jobs on this site for free. A handful were present with direct contact information.

New York Times

www.nytimes.com

New York Times
229 W. 43rd Street, New York, NY 10036
Ph: 212-237-3181

Jobs: **Yes** Cost to post jobs: **Fee** Cost to see jobs: **Free**
Resumes: **No** Cost to post resumes: N/A Cost to see resumes: N/A
E-mail Alert (Push): N/A
Specialty: **All**
Industry: **All**
Feature: N/A
Location: **US/E/NY/NYC**

The **NYTimes** offers plenty to do and see at a site that is constantly changing. Most major newspapers are beginning to wake up to the net's possibilities, and **NYTimes** is no exception. Register here to keep up on developments, and eventually you may be informed about possibilities that will enhance your career Classifieds are available although not all the help-wanted ads you'll find in print are online as employers must pay an additional fee for the online component to their display ads. **NYTimes** is a member of CareerPath. com

News Page

www.newspage.com

Client Services, NewsEdge Corporation
80 Blanchard Road, Burlington, MA 01803
Ph: 781-229-3000   Fax: 781-229-3030   E-mail: workgroups@newsedge.com

Jobs: N/A Cost to post jobs: N/A Cost to see jobs: N/A
Resumes: N/A Cost to post resumes: N/A Cost to see resumes: N/A
E-mail Alert (Push): **Both**
Specialty: **All**
Industry: **All**
Feature: **Research**
Location: **US/Int'l**

News Page provides the latest information on right sizings, down sizings, major hirings in corporations, major restructuring or whatever subject you could possibly ask for. So imagine, you are a recruiter, and via e-mail you select the topics that we stated above. In your mornings e-mails you receive information on who is laying off, who has shutdown a facility, who is merging throughout the world. This is a very powerful recruiting tool. For job seekers it works the same way. For $3. 00 a month this is a no-brainer. Some articles do have an extra charge.

News Rover

www.newsrover.com/interest.htm

S&H Computer Systems
1027 17th Avenue South, Nashville, TN 37212
Ph: 615-327-3670   Fax: 615-321-5929   E-mail: info@sandh.com

Jobs: N/A	
Cost to post jobs: N/A	
Cost to see jobs: N/A	
Resumes: N/A	
Cost to post resumes: N/A	
Cost to see resumes: N/A	
E-mail Alert (Push): N/A	
Specialty: **All**	
Industry: **All**	
Feature: **Research/Newsgroups**	
Location: **US**	

News Rover will allow recruiters and job seekers to extract information from Usenet groups. This will allow you to find thousands of contacts in your area of interest. Download a demonstration copy for Windows '95/'98, and let us know what you think.

Newspaperlinks

www.newspaperlinks.com

Dreama Taylor, Newspaper Assoc. of America
1921 Gallows Road, Vienna, VA 22182
Ph: 703-902-1600   E-mail: tayld@naa.org

Jobs: **No**	
Cost to post jobs: N/A	
Cost to see jobs: N/A	
Resumes: **No**	
Cost to post resumes: N/A	
Cost to see resumes: N/A	
E-mail Alert (Push): N/A	
Specialty: **Newspapers**	
Industry: **All**	
Feature: **Meta-links**	
Location: **US**	

Links to almost every newspaper in the United States can be found at this site. A map of the U.S. is your introduction where you can select a site which then contains links to the world of print. You can also search by state or city or newspaper. Interesting start to a site that has potential to provide many other products for recruiters and job seekers.

NJ Job Search

nj.jobsearch.org

Fred Cantwell
State of New Jersey
Ph: 609-530-3481

Jobs: **Yes**	
Cost to post jobs: **Free**	
Cost to see jobs: **Free**	
Resumes: **No**	
Cost to post resumes: N/A	
Cost to see resumes: N/A	
E-mail Alert (Push): N/A	
Specialty: **All**	
Industry: **All**	
Feature: N/A	
Location: **US/NJ**	

A state employment service that finally gets it, and it happens to be our home state. **NJ Job Search** allows employers to post positions for free. When the applicant clicks on the job of their choice they get "direct contact with the employer" either through e-mail which they go to directly to from the site or phone, address or fax. Simple, easy to use, and numerous professional and nontechnical positions were posted on our visit. We include this site to remind employers and job seekers to check out the employment offices in your locale.

NJ JOBS

www.njjobs.com

Robert Peters, Advanced Interactive Communications
Ph: 732-303-9333   Fax: 732-303-8614   E-mail: info@njjobs.com

Jobs: **Yes**	
Cost to post jobs: **Fee**	
Cost to see jobs: **Free**	
Resumes: **Yes**	
Cost to post resumes: **Fee**	
Cost to see resumes: **Free**	
E-mail Alert (Push): N/A	
Specialty: **All**	
Industry: **All**	
Feature: N/A	
Location: **US/E/NJ**	

NJ Jobs keeps it simple. With the site's new search engine, job seekers can review hundreds of positions, and find direct contact data for free. Cost to post your resume is $20 for 30 days. Recruiters pay $25 for each posting for a 30-day run. Many positions were in highly technical areas.

NOICC

www.noicc.gov

Jim Woods, Nat'l. Occupational Coordinating Committee
2100 M Street NW, Suite 156, Washington, DC 20037
Ph: 202-653-5665

Jobs: **No**
Cost to post jobs: N/A
Cost to see jobs: N/A
Resumes: **No**
Cost to post resumes: N/A
Cost to see resumes: N/A
E-mail Alert (Push): N/A
Specialty: **All**
Industry: **All**
Feature: N/A
Location: **US**

NOICC is a potential key to governement-related services for the job seeker as well as recruiters. Career information includes career management content, links to labor market information and a meta-list of links to government sites.

Nursing Spectrum

www.nursingspectrum.com

Eric Brown, 5071 Shoreline Road
Barrington, IL 60010
Ph: 847-304-9889   Fax: 847-304-1966   E-mail: natsales@nursingspectrum.com

Jobs: **Yes**	
Cost to post jobs: **Fee**	
Cost to see jobs: **Free**	
Resumes: **No**	
Cost to post resumes: N/A	
Cost to see resumes: N/A	
E-mail Alert (Push): **Job Seeker**	
Specialty: **Health Care/Nursing**	
Industry: **Health Care**	
Feature: N/A	
Location: **US/NE/MW/S/FL**	

Nursing Spectrum's weekly print circulation is 450,000 RNs. Its web site has 742 jobs listed in alpha order with direct contact information provided. Site's search engine allows the job seeker to view the U.S., but most jobs reflect the publication's strength which is concentrated in the NE, MW and Florida regions. Chatroom is open from 7 – 10 PM EST. Many career articles and a guest weekly technical lecture round out a healthcare niche that's bound to grow as health care professionals gain access.

NYC Headhunter's Mall

jobs-nyc.com

Kevin McIntyre
175 West 4th Street, New York, NY 10014
Ph: 212-242-2191   E-mail: kevin@jobs-nyc.com

Jobs: **Yes** Cost to post jobs: **Free** (See Notes) Cost to see jobs: **Free**
Resumes: **Yes** Cost to post resumes: **Free** Cost to see resumes: **Fee**
E-mail Alert (Push): N/A
Specialty: **All**
Industry: **All**
Feature: N/A
Location: **US**

NYC **Headhunter's Mall** was under construction on our last visit. The site makes so much sense we have decided to take a chance and leave it in our directory. Dozens of NYC recruitment agencies have banded together to form this site. Headhunter information for contact is available on all jobs. The positions that are posted are restricted to members firms. Simple and easy to use.

O Hayo Sensei

www.ohayosensei.com/classified.html

1032 Irving Street
Suite 508, San Francisco, CA 94122
Ph: 800-367-5457   E-mail: editor@ohayosensei.com

Jobs: **Yes** Cost to post jobs: **Fee** Cost to see jobs: **Free**
Resumes: **Yes** Cost to post resumes: **Free** Cost to see resumes: **Free**
E-mail Alert (Push): N/A
Specialty: **Education**
Industry: **Education**
Feature: N/A
Location: **Int'l/Japan/US**

O Hayo Sensei, a biweekly newsletter that lists teaching positions in Japan for public schools, colleges and universities. Employer cost to post a job is $50 for two issues. Resume profile can be posted for free. Direct contact information for all postings is available. Ads are in English.

OASYS Network

www.oasysnet.com/home.html

Ph: 800-367-5457   E-mail: info@oasysnet.com

Jobs: **No**
Cost to post jobs: N/A
Cost to see jobs: N/A
Resumes: **Yes**
Cost to post resumes: **Free**
Cost to see resumes: **Fee**
E-mail Alert (Push): N/A
Specialty: **Advertising/ Graphic Arts**
Industry: **Advertising**
Feature: N/A
Location: **US**

OASYS Network is a niche for graphic designers, advertising artists, writers and illustrators to post their resumes for free. They must have a minimum of five years experience or three years in freelancing (it is interesting to note that web developers do not have to meet this criterion). Recruiters pay $200 a month to be able to search the site's resume database. A ten-day free trial is available. Site has a 60-day money back guarantee if recruiters are not satisfied. There are no jobs posted. We always like a commitment. This one is in writing.

Oil Link

www.oillink.com

Kris Erlewine,
7346 South Elm Court, Littleton, CO 80122
Ph: 303-220-7867   E-mail: info@oillink.com

Jobs: **Yes**
Cost to post jobs: **Free**
Cost to see jobs: **Free**
Resumes: **Yes**
Cost to post resumes: **Free**
Cost to see resumes: **Free**
E-mail Alert (Push): N/A
Specialty: **Engineering/Chemical**
Industry: **Oil/Petroleum**
Feature: N/A
Location: **Int'l/US**

Oil Link services include free job posting and resume listing to help corporations in this industry. Resumes and jobs are posted by date of entry, and there were hundreds on our last visit with direct contact information. Site claims over 33,000 visitors per month from 80 different countries. Banners and tiles are available for a fee to give employers broader exposure. An interesting salary survey is also available.

Omicron Personal Career Center

www.omicronet.com/career/resume.htm#top

James Webber
115 Route 46, Suite D-31, Mountain Lakes, NJ 07046
Ph: 888-664-2766 Fax: 973-335-0289 E-mail: resumes@omicr1t.com

Jobs: **No** Cost to post jobs: N/A Cost to see jobs: N/A
Resumes: **Yes** Cost to post resumes: **Free** Cost to see resumes: **Free**
E-mail Alert (Push): N/A
Specialty: **IT**
Industry: **High Technology**
Feature: N/A
Location: **US**

Omicron is an association of major corporations attempting to improve information technology for their businesses. They share experiences, information and buying power. In their career center they allow professionals to post their resumes, and recruiters can view them for free. On our last visit about two dozen resumes were.

Online Career Center

www.occ.com

Craig Besant, Online Career Center
2780 Waterfront Pkwy. E. Dr., Suite 100, Indianapolis, IN 46214
Ph: 800-899-7058   Fax: 800-486-6402   E-mail: webmaster@occ.com

Jobs: **Yes**	
Cost to post jobs: **Fee**	
Cost to see jobs: **Free**	
Resumes: **Yes**	
Cost to post resumes: **Free**	
Cost to see resumes: **Fee**	
E-mail Alert (Push): **N/A**	
Specialty: **All**	
Industry: **N/A**	
Feature: **N/A**	
Location: **US/Int'l**	

OCC was a pioneering web site in the online recruiting field. With the site's new look, job seekers can view openings via a U.S. map by state or by region. International jobs can be viewed by country. Openings can be searched via the site's engine or by company in alpha order. All positions list date of posting, location, title, company and direct contact information. Topical sections (engineering, human resources, healthcare etc.) can also be seen. Site has established relationships with the Society of Women Engineers and WITI as well as other women's career and minority career resource organizations. These associations create important supplementary traffic for the site. College resume links to dozens of universities. Uniquely positioned as a member sponsored association of 400+ companies, new members are charged an annual subscription of $3,900 for unlimited posting and access to the resume database. Viewing resumes alone is $2,200. Other packages were also available as were banners, profiles and hosting services. Well designed and executed, this site offers job applicants an outstanding array of information about job fairs, conferences, links to 800 colleges, and career related articles from well known authors. Career and College Forums allow the job seeker to ask questions and get answers from people all over the world. Joyce Lain Kennedy publishes career information and tips on this site. Jobs to post are $150 for a 60-day run.

Online Sports Career Center

www.onlinesports.com: 80/pages/careercenter.html

Online Sports
9070 Rotherham Avenue, San Diego, CA 92129
Ph: 800-856-2638   Fax: 800-856-2632   E-mail: jobopening@onlinesports.com

Jobs: **Yes**	
Cost to post jobs: **Free**	
Cost to see jobs: **Free**	
Resumes: **Yes**	
Cost to post resumes: **Free**	
Cost to see resumes: N/A	
E-mail Alert (Push): N/A	
Specialty: **Retail/Recreation**	
Industry: **Retail/Recreation**	
Feature: N/A	
Location: **US**	

Online Sports Career Center now posts jobs for free with direct contact information. Owners have gone into the subscription business. For $79 they will sell you the *National Employment Newsletter* (12 issues for six months) which they state has the latest sports employment opportunities. Jobs on this site must be samples of the newsletter. Sports buffs can check out their memorabilia for sale.

Opportunity Nocs

www.opportunitynocs.org/home.html

The Management Center
870 Market Street, Suite #800, San Francisco, CA 94102
Ph: 415-362-9735   Fax: 415-362-4603   E-mail: tmc@tmcenter.org

Jobs: **Yes**	
Cost to post jobs: **Fee**	
Cost to see jobs: **Free**	
Resumes: **No**	
Cost to post resumes: **Free**	
Cost to see resumes: N/A	
E-mail Alert (Push): N/A	
Specialty: **Nonprofit**	
Industry: **Nonprofit**	
Feature: N/A	
Location: **US**	

National **Opportunity Nocs** has an online newsletter that mirrors its print cousin. Nonprofit organizations post positions for $40 per month on the web site. Job seekers need to click on the title of the position of interest to obtain contact information. There were 377 jobs posted in 27 states our visit. A long list of links to career articles is also available.

OPTICS.ORG Job Search

optics.org/employment/employment.html

Mark Mugittroyd, Society of Photo-Optical Instrumentation
1000 20th Street, Bellingham, WA 98225
Ph: 360-676-3290   Fax: 360-647-1445   E-mail: info@optics.org

Jobs: **Yes** Cost to post jobs: **Fee** Cost to see jobs: **Free**	The International Society for Photo-Optical Instrumentation Engineering allows professionals to post their resume for free for 30 days (there were over 156 present on our last visit). Recruiters can see resumes for free, and post jobs for $300 for a four-week run. There were 44 jobs with direct contact information and the date of posting. All transactions can be conducted through the web site. From hands-on engineers to VPs, it is all here.
Resumes: **Yes** Cost to post resumes: **Free** Cost to see resumes: **Free**	
E-mail Alert (Push): N/A	
Specialty: **Science/** **Optical Physics**	
Industry: **All**	
Feature: N/A	
Location: **US**	

ORAsearch

www.orasearch.com

Advanced Data, Inc.
E-mail: adi@orasearch.com

Jobs: **Yes** Cost to post jobs: **Fee** Cost to see jobs: **Free**	**ORASearch** provides jobs and resumes for the Oracle world. Recruiters can join for $695 per month or $1,850 for six months. All positions are coded, and job seekers must reply by cutting and pasting their resume to the site. Recruiters can view resumes, but have to return to the site for contact information. Site has sisters on the web at: http: //www.JVsearch. com for Java professionals and http: //www.WindowsNTsearch. com.
Resumes: **Yes** Cost to post resumes: **Free** Cost to see resumes: **Fee**	
E-mail Alert (Push): **Employer**	
Specialty: **IT/Oracle**	
Industry: **IT**	
Feature: N/A	
Location: **US**	

Orlando Sentinel

www.orlandosentinel.com

Orlando Sentinel Online
633 N. Orange Avenue, Orlando, FL 32801
Ph: 407-420-5179

Jobs: **Yes** Cost to post jobs: **Fee** Cost to see jobs: **Free**	
Resumes: **No** Cost to post resumes: N/A Cost to see resumes: N/A	
E-mail Alert (Push): N/A	
Specialty: **All**	
Industry: N/A	
Feature: **No**	
Location: **US/SE/FL/Orlando**	

Here's an idea ahead of its time. Of all the daily newspapers in the U.S., only the *Orlando Sentinel* consistently posts the their Sunday help-wanted print ads on their web site as they are received. So, if the employer and their advertising agency gets Sunday's ad in by Monday or Tuesday, job seekers who come along in the middle of the week will get an edge, and the employer will get more rapid response.

Overseas Jobs Web

www.overseasjobs.com

Jeff Allen
1050 Cemetery Lane, Aspen, CO 81611
Ph: 970-544-5461   Fax: 970-920-3071   E-mail: jeff@overseasjobs.com

Jobs: **Yes** Cost to post jobs: **Fee** Cost to see jobs: **Free**	
Resumes: **Yes** Cost to post resumes: **Free** Cost to see resumes: **Fee** (See Notes)	
E-mail Alert (Push): N/A	
Specialty: **All**	
Industry: **All**	
Feature: **Meta-links**	
Location: **Int'l**	

Overseas Jobs Web lists hundreds of positions in many different disciplines through-out the world (but especially Europe). Recruiters may list positions for free, but pay to get their jobs to the top of the listings. Fees range from $50 to $150 to get to the front of the line. Many of the jobs listed on this site can also be found in the *Overseas Job Express* newspaper. Positions have direct contact information for job seekers to review. Visitors can view a meta list of over 750 job links to other job sites from around the world arranged by country—worth the trip. Site is currently soliciting resumes, and will have a pricing structure in place in 1999 for recruiters to view resumes.

Oya's Directory of Recruiters

www.fence-post.com/drecruiters.htm

Art Opiela-Young, Fence-Post Technology
5117 NE 31st Ave., Portland, OR 97211
Ph: 503-287-5244   E-mail: oya@fence-post.com

Jobs: **No**	
Cost to post jobs: N/A	
Cost to see jobs: N/A	
Resumes: **No**	
Cost to post resumes: N/A	
Cost to see resumes: N/A	
E-mail Alert (Push): N/A	
Specialty: **All**	
Industry: **All**	
Feature: **Recruiter Directory**	
Location: **US/Int'l**	

Oya's Recruiter Directory is a listing of third-party recruitment firms. Headhunters can be viewed by country or specialty. Site will take job seekers to their recruiter of choice and then link to their site for additional information. Oya's main company, Fence-Post Technology, creates systems for recruiters. Search firms who wish to place a link to this site can do so for free. Nice marketing move by **Oya**, we thank her for it.

Paralegal.org

www.paralegals.com

Bryan Stevenson, National Federation of Paralegal Association
P.O. Box 33108, Kansas City, MO 64114
Ph: 816-941-4000   Fax: 816-941-2725   E-mail: bryanfstevenson@paralegals.org

Jobs: **Yes**	
Cost to post jobs: **Fee**	
Cost to see jobs: **Free** (See Notes)	
Resumes: **Yes**	
Cost to post resumes: **Fee**	
Cost to see resumes: **Free**	
E-mail Alert (Push): N/A	
Specialty: **Law/Paralegal**	
Industry: **Legal**	
Feature: N/A	
Location: **US/Int'l**	

NFPA has 17,000 members in the U.S. and Canada. Posting of positions costs $1. 50 per word. With a $50 minimum. Click on a map of the U.S. to select by. Jobs are listed by date posted. No search engine exists, and only association members can obtain the contact data for some of the openings. Articles on professional advancement and career guidance are also available.

Passport Access

www.passportaccess.com

John Malone, Passport Access
2010 Crow Canyon Place, #100, San Ramon, CA 94583
Ph: 925-552-1000   Fax: 925-552-1010   E-mail: john@passportaccess.com

Jobs: **Yes**	
Cost to post jobs: **Fee**	
Cost to see jobs: **Free**	
Resumes: **Yes**	
Cost to post resumes: **Free**	
Cost to see resumes: **Fee**	
E-mail Alert (Push): **N/A**	
Specialty: **All**	
Industry: **All**	
Feature: **Resume Database**	
Location: **US**	

Passport Access is one of the original resume databases on the web. Site claims over 200,000 resumes in their database (all date stamped). Passport continues to explore alliances with highly trafficked sites to increase their flow. Recruiters pay $1,000 per year to post unlimited jobs, and $500 per year when purchasing their resume database package (this is normally $800). New features abound as recruiters can now make personal notes on resumes in their database and send broadcast e-mails to candidates. Site branched out from the west coast and is now national in scope. Take a test drive.

Perioperative Online Employment Opps.

www.aorn.org

Deb Smith, Association of Operating Room Nurses
2170 South Parker Road, Suite 300, Denver, CO 80231
Ph: 800-755-2676   Fax: 303-750-3462   E-mail: website@aorn.org

Jobs: **Yes**	
Cost to post jobs: **Fee**	
Cost to see jobs: **Free**	
Resumes: **Yes**	
Cost to post resumes: **Fee** (See Notes)	
Cost to see resumes: **Fee**	
E-mail Alert (Push): **N/A**	
Specialty: **Health Care/ Nursing/OR**	
Industry: **Health Care**	
Feature: **N/A**	
Location: **US**	

Perioperative Online Employment Opportunities is what the Association of Operating Room Nurses has named their jobs page. With 43,000 members (from over 340 chapters) recruiters can post jobs for $25 (AORN members) $65 nonmembers. Job seekers can search the U.S. by state or specialty. The association has a referral service that warehouses candidate resume, and when recruiters post positions, they can also conduct a database search. Cost to job seekers is $25 for members.

Peterson's Education Center

www.petersons.com

Mark Fisher, Peterson's
202 Carnegie Center, Princeton, NJ 08543
Ph: 609-243-9111   Fax: 609-243-9150   E-mail: info@petersons.com

Jobs: **Yes**	
Cost to post jobs: **Fee**	
Cost to see jobs: **Free**	
Resumes: **No**	
Cost to post resumes: N/A	
Cost to see resumes: N/A	
E-mail Alert (Push): N/A	
Specialty: **College**	
Industry: **All**	
Feature: **College Admissions**	
Location: **US**	

Peterson's Education Center has extensive career content covering just about every field. Also a great starting point for educational assistance. Recruiters pay $250 to post a position. Alphabetical listing of all employers who have openings posted links to an overview of the corporation. One click and you are at the open posted positions. Applicants can also search for jobs by type, category or geographic location. A sister site reviewed earlier, Great Summer Jobs, is an excellent complement to the Educational Center. Both are well done.

Philanthropy Journal Online

www.philanthropy-journal.org

Marilyn Rose
2 W Hargett Street, Suite 805, Raleigh, NC 27601
Ph: 919-899-3756   Fax: 919-832-2369   E-mail: marilynrose@mindspring.com

Jobs: **Yes**	
Cost to post jobs: **Fee**	
Cost to see jobs: **Free**	
Resumes: **No**	
Cost to post resumes: N/A	
Cost to see resumes: N/A	
E-mail Alert (Push): N/A	
Specialty: **Nonprofit**	
Industry: **Nonprofit**	
Feature: N/A	
Location: **US**	

Philanthropy Journal Online posts information and jobs in nonprofit organizations. A free newsletter will be sent via e-mail to all who register: pjalert-on@mail-list. com. Job seekers can search the U.S. by clicking on their region of choice from a map. Jobs can be viewed by "development," "executive" or "other nonprofit positions." Recruiters pay a $65 setup fee and $5 a day to post a job online.

Planet Jobs

www.phillynews.com/programs/ads/SUNHLP

Dennis Wichterman, Philadelphia Inquirer
400 N. Broad Street, Philadelphia, PA 19101
Ph: 215-563-5000   E-mail: online.staff@phillynews.com

Jobs: **Yes** Cost to post jobs: **Fee** Cost to see jobs: **Free**	
Resumes: **No** Cost to post resumes: N/A Cost to see resumes: N/A	
E-mail Alert (Push): N/A	
Specialty: **All**	
Industry: N/A	
Feature: N/A	
Location: **US/E/PA/Phil.**	

Help-wanted Sunday classifieds of the **Philadelphia Inquirer** are posted to the web. When you enter your name the site will keep a running list of positions you have selected and will then print a listing for you. This notepad concept is a growing trend among newspapers. **Philadelphia Inquirer** participates in CareerPath. com.

Plasma Gate

plasma-gate.weizmann.ac.il/Jobs.html

Yuri Ralchenko
Plasma Laboratory of Weizman Institute
Ph: 972-893-44055   Fax: 972-893-44106   E-mail: (See Notes)

Jobs: **Yes** Cost to post jobs: **Free** Cost to see jobs: **Free**	
Resumes: **No** Cost to post resumes: N/A Cost to see resumes: N/A	
E-mail Alert (Push): N/A	
Specialty: **Science/Physics**	
Industry: **Higher Ed/Research**	
Feature: **N/A**	
Location: **Int'l/US**	

If you think Avogadro's number is a California specialty salad, you'll get lost between the electrons at **Plasma Gate** where jobs in atomic and plasma physics are posted. Site can be contacted via e-mail: fnralch@plasma-gate. weizmann. ac. il All postings have date of site entry, and recruiters can now cut and paste their openings right to the site. We only saw postdoctoral positions listed, but this is a real niche site.

PolySort

www.polysort.com

Janie Campbell
4040 Embassy Parkway, Suite 180, Akron, OH 44333
Ph: 800-326-8666   Fax: 330-665-5152   E-mail: polysort@polysort.com

Jobs: **Yes** Cost to post jobs: **Fee** Cost to see jobs: **Free**	**PolySort** is for those who recruit people in the plastics or rubber industries. This well-run site has been around since the early days of the web and will bend over backwards for their clients (or stretch depending on…oh well). Only a few positions are posted, but over a dozen companies now have links to their jobs page. Recruiters pay $99 per month for a help-wanted ad. PolySort will soon change to a Virtual Job Fair approach with direct postings. These will cost $50 for a 30-day run or $30 for 15 days. Site also distributes a monthly industry newsletter. Expect the owners to launch a new site http: // www.packagingbusiness. com in 99.

Jobs: **Yes**
Cost to post jobs: **Fee**
Cost to see jobs: **Free**

Resumes: **No**
Cost to post resumes: N/A
Cost to see resumes: N/A

E-mail Alert (Push): N/A

Specialty: **Science/Chemistry**

Industry: **Rubber and Plastics**

Feature: N/A

Location: **US**

PositionWatch

www.positionwatch.com

John Granger, Positionwatch Limited
60 Bloor St. West, Suite 1400, Toronto, Canada M4W 3B8
Ph: 888-345-5562   Fax: 416-929-7999   E-mail: jgranger@positionwatch.com

Jobs: **Yes**
Cost to post jobs: **Fee**
Cost to see jobs: **Free**

Resumes: **Yes**
Cost to post resumes: **Free**
Cost to see resumes: N/A

E-mail Alert (Push): **Job Seeker**

Specialty: **IT**

Industry: **All**

Feature: N/A

Location: **Int'l/Canada/US**

PositionWatch now has hundreds of IT jobs posted, and its search engine leaps tall buildings in a single bound. It is fast! Over 195 jobs were posted in the last ten days. Job seekers can register their skills and have e-mail alerts of posted positions. All jobs have date of posting and direct contact information. Site's positions are mainly Canadian, but is trying to crack the U.S. market. New site that we reviewed in May of 1998. **PositionWatch** is growing fast.

Power Magazine

www.powermag.com

Jeff Chufar, McGraw-Hill/Power
4445 20th Street NW, Suite D, Canton, OH 44708
Ph: 330-478-4037   Fax: 330-478-4036   E-mail: chufar@neo.irun.com

Jobs: **Yes** Cost to post jobs: **Fee** Cost to see jobs: **Free**	
Resumes: **No** Cost to post resumes: N/A Cost to see resumes: N/A	
E-mail Alert (Push): N/A	
Specialty: **Engineering/Power**	
Industry: **Utility/Power**	
Feature: N/A	
Location: **US**	

Power Magazine lists their print recruitment positions on the web site. Recruiters who pay for the print ads get the web for free. Several dozen positions are listed with complete contact information. If power is your industry, this is the place to be. Site has sisters in the utility world—www.electricalworld.com www.itforutilities.com Same formats, only different positions.

PrincetonInfo

www.princetoninfo.com

Barbara Figge Fox, U.S. 1 Newspapers
12 Roszel Road, Princeton, NJ 08540
Ph: 609-452-0038   Fax: 609-452-0033   E-mail: info@princetoninfo.com

Jobs: **Yes** Cost to post jobs: **Fee** Cost to see jobs: **Free**	
Resumes: **Yes** Cost to post resumes: **Free** Cost to see resumes: **Free**	
E-mail Alert (Push): N/A	
Specialty: **All**	
Industry: **All**	
Feature: N/A	
Location: **US/E/NJ**	

PrincetonInfo, *U.S. 1* is a local, central NJ weekly newspaper that we enjoy reading. Good local information on living in the area. Job seekers can post positions wanted for free. All positions have direct contact information. Reach out in your community.

Private School Employment Network

www.privateschooljobs.com

Mary-Kay Rath, 17641 College Road
Hagerstown, MD 21740
Ph: 301-766-0349   Fax: 301-766-0349   E-mail: schooljobs@aol.com

Jobs: **Yes** Cost to post jobs: **Fee** Cost to see jobs: **Free**	
Resumes: **Yes** Cost to post resumes: **Fee** Cost to see resumes: **Free**	
E-mail Alert (Push): N/A	
Specialty: **Ed/K-12**	
Industry: **Ed/K-12**	
Feature: N/A	
Location: **US/Int'l**	

The Private School Employment Network posts vacancies in administration and teaching in private and independent schools. Positions and resumes can be viewed for free as most have direct contact information. Coded jobs or resumes have an asterisk next to their title, and you need to go back to the site for the contact data. Recruiters pay $75 – $125 to post openings while job seekers pay $25 to list their resume.

Produce Job Exchange

www.producejobs.com

The Produce Job Exchange
P.O. Box 424, Grover Beach, CA 93438
E-mail: info@producejobs.com

Jobs: **Yes** Cost to post jobs: **Fee** Cost to see jobs: **Free**	
Resumes: **Yes** Cost to post resumes: **Free** Cost to see resumes: **Fee**	
E-mail Alert (Push): N/A	
Specialty: **Retail/Food**	
Industry: **Agriculture**	
Feature: N/A	
Location: **US**	

Produce Job Exchange will list your resume on its site for $20 per year, which employers can see for free. Employers are charged $50 to post a position for three months. An online resume/job form with a search engine makes this an easy site to navigate.

Professionals On-Line

www.webcom.com/wordimg/pro

Words & Images
Brisbane, Australia
Ph: 617-320-27573   Fax: 617-320-27514   E-mail: ian@wordsimages.com

Jobs: No	
Cost to post jobs: N/A	
Cost to see jobs: N/A	
Resumes: **Yes**	
Cost to post resumes: **Free**	
Cost to see resumes: **Free**	
E-mail Alert (Push): N/A	
Specialty: **IT**	
Industry: **IT**	
Feature: N/A	
Location: **Int'l/Australia**	

Professionals On-Line is a free international site set up for IT professionals. Using the site's search engine, candidates select the skill and location (Australia) and up comes the match with direct contact information. This is a headhunters dream as there are over 700 professionals listed. If you need a techie in Australia this is the site to see.

Project Connect

careers.soemadison.wisc.edu/projcon.htm

Steve Head
University of Wisconsin-Madison
Ph: 608-262-1755   E-mail: (See notes)

Jobs: **Yes**	
Cost to post jobs: **Free**	
Cost to see jobs: **Free**	
Resumes: **No**	
Cost to post resumes: N/A	
Cost to see resumes: N/A	
E-mail Alert (Push): N/A	
Specialty: **Teaching**	
Industry: **Education**	
Feature: N/A	
Location: **US**	

Project Connect is a national cooperative between school districts and universities to get educational staffing on the Internet. This program began in 1992 to set standards for vacancy and candidate information. Job openings are transmitted via an online database that teachers can search. You can e-mail your openings to: projectconnect@uw-epcs. soemadison. wisc. edu. To get access information to jobs, teachers need to contact their college career office or school district.

Purchasing NAPM

www.napm.org

Carolyn Pye, National Assoc. of Purchasing Mgmt.
P.O. Box 22160, Tempe, AZ 85285
Ph: 800-888-6276   E-mail: cpye@napm.org

Jobs: **Yes**	
Cost to post jobs: **Free**	
Cost to see jobs: **Fee** (See Notes)	
Resumes: **Yes**	
Cost to post resumes: **Fee** (See Notes)	
Cost to see resumes: **Free**	
E-mail Alert (Push): N/A	
Specialty: Purchasing	
Industry: **All**	
Feature: N/A	
Location: **US/W**	

National Association of Purchasing Management (NAPM) Has 44,000 members in its 180 affiliated associations. It allows anyone to post a position or search their resume database for free. Jobs are listed for 30 days and are then automatically deleted. Only members can view listed positions or post their resumes.

Purdue's Job List

www.ups.purdue.edu/student/jobsites.htm

Stuart Jones, Purdue University
Center of Career Opportunities, 1094 Stewart Center, West Lafayette, IN 47907
E-mail: webmaster@ups.purdue.edu

Jobs: **No**	
Cost to post jobs: N/A	
Cost to see jobs: N/A	

Resumes: **No**	
Cost to post resumes: N/A	
Cost to see resumes: N/A	

E-mail Alert (Push): N/A

Specialty: **All**

Industry: **All**

Feature: **Meta-links**

Location: **US**

Purdue University Center for Career Opportunities provides over 1,000 links to online resources. Categories include: job searching sites, jobs by geographical areas, federal government job listings, international jobs, classifieds, newsgroups, resumes services, researching companies, reference and resource material, professional recruiters and other university placement and career services. The site also advises its viewers of what they consider outstanding job resources and new sites with special annotation. CXR looks at thousands of links to get down to what we consider the 500 best. Purdue's link list is kept up-to-date, and is by far one of the best on the web.

Job Search Sites on the World Wide Web

● *A listing of over 1,000 On-Line Job-Search Resources and Services, brought to you by Purdue University Center for Career Opportunities*

● *Internet awards for this site can be seen at the bottom of this page!*

Purdue's **Center for Career Opportunities**, in *West Lafayette, Indiana*, maintains one of the Internet's **largest** list of job searching web sites with links to each. Many of the sites contain listings of current employment opportunities. In general each one includes opportunities from a number of sources and are not home pages for individual employers. Opportunities are updated regularly. Some sites allow you to provide an on-line resume; thus allowing employers to search for you, rather than the other way around. This alphabetical listing is not an exhaustive list of job-searching sites. Some of these services may charge a fee. Be sure you fully understand the conditions and/or contract terms before agreeing to anything.

Information in the many World Wide Web pages that are linked to Purdue's Center for Career Opportunities "Job Searching Sites on the World Wide Web" comes from a variety of sources. Some of this information comes from official Purdue entities, but much of it comes from unofficial or unaffiliated organizations and individuals, both internal and external to the University. Purdue University and the Center for Career Opportunities does not author, edit, or monitor these unofficial pages and therefore cannot assume responsibility for these contents.

Quintessential Career & Job Hunting Guide

www.stetson.edu/~rhansen/careers.html

Randall Hansen, Stetson University
421 N. Woodland Blvd., Unit 8389, Deland, FL 32720-3771
Ph: 904-822-7495   Fax: 904-822-7393   E-mail: randall.hansen@stetson.edu

Jobs: **No**
Cost to post jobs: N/A
Cost to see jobs: N/A
Resumes: **No**
Cost to post resumes: N/A
Cost to see resumes: N/A
E-mail Alert (Push): N/A
Specialty: N/A
Industry: N/A
Feature: **Meta-links**
Location: **US**

Quintessential Career & Job Hunting Guide includes a meta-list of career links for job seekers. Resume resources, cover letter help, interviewing assistance—are all here. Owner of the site is hawking his books as well, but truly does this as a help for those looking for employment. Links for women and minorities are a recent addition. Particularly helpful for the recent college graduate.

Radio Frame

www.mindspring.com/~coleman/radioframe.html

David Coleman
4180 Triple Creek Court, Atlanta, GA 30319
Ph: 770-936-9131   E-mail: davecol@bellsouth.net

Jobs: **No**
Cost to post jobs: N/A
Cost to see jobs: N/A
Resumes: **No**
Cost to post resumes: N/A
Cost to see resumes: N/A
E-mail Alert (Push): N/A
Specialty: **Entertainment/Radio**
Industry: **Entertainment**
Feature: **Meta-links**
Location: **US**

Radio Frame has now created a separate job link section with a dozen interesting places to sing the blues. Do not get mesmerized by the twirling jukebox. Hundreds of links with brief explanations regarding the music industry.

Real Jobs - Real Estate

www.real-jobs.com

Dr. Norm Miller, University of Cincinnatti
Ph: 513-556-7088   E-mail: norm.miller@uc.edu

Jobs: **Yes**	
Cost to post jobs: **Free**	
Cost to see jobs: **Free**	
Resumes: **Yes**	
Cost to post resumes: **Free**	
Cost to see resumes: **Free**	
E-mail Alert (Push): N/A	
Specialty: **Real Estate**	
Industry: **Real Estate**	
Feature: N/A	
Location: **US**	

At **Real Jobs,** the world of real estate is free to see. Recruiters can post positions for jobs in the real estate profession from sales agents to land barons. This site was initially developed by a professor to support college placement activities, but quickly expanded to assist alumni, professional and trade associations as well.

RealBank

www.realbank.com

Fran Grossman
395 South End Ave., Suite 15-D, New York, NY 10280
Ph: 212-912-0175   E-mail: jobs@realbank.com

Jobs: **Yes**	
Cost to post jobs: **Fee**	
Cost to see jobs: **Free**	
Resumes: **Yes**	
Cost to post resumes: **Free**	
Cost to see resumes: **Fee**	
E-mail Alert (Push): **Job Seeker**	
Specialty: **Real Estate**	
Industry: **Real Estate**	
Feature: N/A	
Location: **US/Int'l**	

RealBank has a new look. Recruiters pay $95 to post an opening. Human Resource positions can be posted for free. There is an additional $75 charge to "push" openings to candidates. Job seekers can now post their resume for free. Recruiters pay to see resumes (several pricing packages). This real estate niche site has grown over the last year. Dozens of employment categories, and several hundred jobs posted.

Recruit Net

recruitnet.guardian.co.uk/

James Burns, The Guardian Media Group
119 Farringdon Road, London, UK EC1R3ER
Ph: 440-171-2399666   Fax: 440-171-8315712   E-mail: james.burns@guardian.co.uk

Jobs: **Yes** Cost to post jobs: **Fee** Cost to see jobs: **Free**
Resumes: **No** Cost to post resumes: N/A Cost to see resumes: N/A
E-mail Alert (Push): **Job Seeker**
Specialty: **All**
Industry: **All**
Feature: N/A
Location: **Int'l/UK**

This publication is doing a great job. Browse the *Guardian* newspaper's help-wanted or post your particular job interests. This UK site will then "push" matching jobs to your desktop. If you want additional job information, click on the "brief," and you'll receive the full text.

Recruiters Online Network

www.ipa.com

Bill Vick
3325 Landershire Lane, kPlano, TX 75023
Ph: 888-821-2490   Fax: 972-612-1924   E-mail: info@recruitersonline.com

Jobs: **Yes** Cost to post jobs: **Fee** Cost to see jobs: **Free**
Resumes: **Yes** Cost to post resumes: **Free** Cost to see resumes: **Fee**
E-mail Alert (Push): N/A
Specialty: **All**
Industry: **All**
Feature: N/A
Location: **US/Int'l**

Recruiter's Online Network (RON) is a worldwide community of recruitment firms. Candidate resumes are shared and commissions split. With 13,000 registered recruiters this is a powerful industry site. Recruiters can join for a 30-day trial membership ($495 per year). This includes posting unlimited positions and viewing resumes. Job seekers can post their resume or view all job postings. Per Bill, "Push" technology and a matching service of resumes and open postings will soon be added.

Recruitex Technologies

www.recruitex.com/

Greg Scott, Recruitex Technologies Inc.
1434 Johnston Road, 2nd Floor, White Rock, BC, Canaada V4B 3Z5
Ph: 604-899-2224   Fax: 604-538-4841   E-mail: gregs@recruitex.com

Jobs: **Yes**	
Cost to post jobs: **Free** (See Notes)	
Cost to see jobs: **Free**	
Resumes: **Yes**	
Cost to post resumes: **Free**	
Cost to see resumes: **Fee**	
E-mail Alert (Push): **N/A**	
Specialty: **All**	
Industry: **All**	
Feature: **N/A**	
Location: **Int'l/Canada/US**	

Recruitex site model is interesting, but a little cumbersome. Recruiters can see profiles of candidates, and then notify the site of their interest to receive the contact information. Job seekers must first submit their resume to one of the agency members of this site before they can search the jobs database. Job seekers can ride for free. Recruiters can place jobs for free, but if they wish to get to the top of the chart, there is a fee. Placement agencies should take a look at this Canada-based site.

Recruiting-Links.com

www.recruiting-links.com/

Al Spencer, Skillsearch Corporation
3354 Perimeter Hill Drive, Suite 235, Nashville, TN 37211-4129
Ph: 800-252-5665   Fax: 615-843-2638   E-mail: moreinfo@recruiting-links.com

Jobs: **No**	
Cost to post jobs: **N/A**	
Cost to see jobs: **N/A**	
Resumes: **No**	
Cost to post resumes: **N/A**	
Cost to see resumes: **N/A**	
E-mail Alert (Push): **N/A**	
Specialty: **All**	
Industry: **All**	
Feature: **Meta-links**	
Location: **US**	

Recruiting-Links.com is technically not a job database nor a resume databank, but it has these features with a wrinkle. Job seekers search against the general skill requirements provided by the employer, and then link to the employers jobs page directly. Recruiters pay $750 for three months or $1,900 for an annual subscription. Site also provides monthly statistics on the site's activity.

Recruitment Extra

www.recruitmentextra.com

Madeline Krazit,
Ph: 201-750-0521   E-mail: jkraz@aol.com

Jobs: **No** Cost to post jobs: N/A Cost to see jobs: N/A	**Recruitment Extra** provides industry information for the savvy recruiter. Layoffs and job fair calendars are only a small part of the information here. The site represents publisher products, and has taken an interesting slant on helping recruiters get their job done. **Recruitment Extra** sells links to vendors such as recruitment advertising agencies. Limited, but worth a visit.
Resumes: **No** Cost to post resumes: N/A Cost to see resumes: N/A	
E-mail Alert (Push): N/A	
Specialty: **All**	
Industry: **All**	
Feature: **Recruiter Research Tools**	
Location: **US**	

Recruit-Net

www.recruit-net.com

Tracy Claybrook
1100 S. Hoover Blvd., Suite 203, Tampa, FL 33609
Ph: 813-282-3005   Fax: 813-282-8852   E-mail: request@recruit-net.com

Jobs: **No** Cost to post jobs: N/A Cost to see jobs: N/A	For recruiters who are tired of posting to one site after another...after another...**Recruit-Net** has developed technology to post at the click of a button. At press time you could place your openings with over 175 different groups, and this could grow rapidly. Cost for this service runs $300-$400 per month for 50 job postings, depending on the number of accounts you require. Recruiters have to negotiate with owners for the fee sites themselves, but jobs can be posted from this site once that is done. Long list of links to free-to-see resume sites is also available. Seminars and a recruiter discussion group are added value.
Resumes: **No** Cost to post resumes: N/A Cost to see resumes: N/A	
E-mail Alert (Push): N/A	
Specialty: **All**	
Industry: N/A	
Feature: **Automated Job Posting**	
Location: N/A	

Red Guide to Temp Agencies

www.panix.com/~grvsmth/redguide/intro.html

Angus B. Grieve-Smith, Angus B. Grieve-Smith
315 Gold Avenue SE, Albuquerque, NM 87102
Ph: 505-767-9916   E-mail: grvsmth@panix.com

Jobs: **No**
Cost to post jobs: N/A
Cost to see jobs: N/A
Resumes: **No**
Cost to post resumes: N/A
Cost to see resumes: N/A
E-mail Alert (Push): N/A
Specialty: **All**
Industry: **All**
Feature: **Meta-links/ Temp Agencies**
Location: **US/E/NY/NYC**

Red Guide to Temp Agencies provides a directory to over 1,000 temporary agencies. New search engine makes it easy if you know what firm you are looking for. Job seekers can still scroll an alphabetical listing. Agencies can now list themselves through Angus' site form. Read his story of how/why he is continuing to keep his site going. A true web tale.

Rehab Options

www.rehaboptions.com

Ken Levinson, Rehab Options USA
6617 W. Boynton Beach Blvd., Suite 202, Boynton, FL 33437
Ph: 800-863-8314   Fax: 800-357-8684   E-mail: ken@rehaboptions.com

Jobs: **Yes**
Cost to post jobs: **Fee**
Cost to see jobs: **Free** (See Notes)
Resumes: **Yes**
Cost to post resumes: **Free**
Cost to see resumes: **Fee**
E-mail Alert (Push): **Both**
Specialty: **Health Care/ Rehab/PT/OT/Speech**
Industry: **Health Care**
Feature: N/A
Location: **US**

Rehab Options provides opportunities for physical therapists, PTs, OTs. COTAs and speech language pathologists. Job seekers who register are e-mailed the sites job postings. They can also post their resumes for free which are then e-mailed to the subscribing employers who pays a fee. Rehab has now spawned sister sites: www.nurseoptions.com and www.medoptions.com. Same premise on all three. Minimal employer cost.

Resort Jobs

www.resortjobs.com

Jeff Allen
1050 Cemetery Lane, Aspen, CO 81611
Ph: 970-544-5461   Fax: 970-020-3071   E-mail: jobs@resortjobs.com

Jobs: **Yes**	
Cost to post jobs: **Free** (See Notes)	
Cost to see jobs: **Free**	
Resumes: **No**	
Cost to post resumes: N/A	
Cost to see resumes: N/A	
E-mail Alert (Push): N/A	
Specialty: **Hospitality/Resort Summer**	
Industry: **Hospitality/Resorts/Hotel**	
Feature: N/A	
Location: **US/Int'l**	

Resort jobs from all over the world can be viewed and posted here for free. This is a sister site to www.summerjobs.com and ww.overseasjobs.com. Recruiters can post jobs for free, but pay to have their job reach the top of the chart. Cost is $150 for worldwide category, $100 for Summer for the top of the USA category, and 450 per Summer for the top of any other category. Only allows top 20 jobs to pay the above fees. All jobs are posted with direct contact information, and the site's search engine gets you to the right resort without even giving it a tip. No resumes are on this site.

Resucom Resume-Network

www.pbgi.com/resucom/search.htm

Blake Swensen, Pyramus Online
P.O. Box 741954, Dallas, TX 75374
Ph: 800-231-0762   Fax: 214-358-1558   E-mail: sales@pyramus.com

Jobs: **Yes**	
Cost to post jobs: N/A	
Cost to see jobs: N/A	
Resumes: **Yes**	
Cost to post resumes: **Fee**	
Cost to see resumes: **Free**	
E-mail Alert (Push): **Employer**	
Specialty: **All**	
Industry: **All**	
Feature: N/A	
Location: **US**	

Resucom Resume-Network is a side business for a web design firm. Corporate recruiters register their e-mail address, and the site will send all of the resumes that they have in their database to the employer on a regular basis. Job seekers pay $49.95 to have their paper listed. We would like to hear a few success stories from people who have used this service.

Resumail Network

www.resumail.com

Steve Rofey, Opportunity Network, Inc.
6309 North O'Connor Road, Suite 216, Irving, TX 75039-3510
Ph: 800-916-7638   E-mail: srofey@resumail.com

Jobs: **Yes**
Cost to post jobs: **Fee**
Cost to see jobs: **Free**
Resumes: **Yes**
Cost to post resumes: **Free**
Cost to see resumes: **Fee**
E-mail Alert (Push): **N/A**
Specialty: **All**
Industry: **All**
Feature: **Resume Software**
Location: **US**

Visitors to **Resumail Network** can download Resumail™ software for free to develop and send resumes to employers. Founded in 1989 by Opportunity Network, Inc. (d.b.a. Resumail Network), employers use Resumail Office to post job openings, company profiles and benefits on the Internet, and to search resumes. Job seekers access the **Resumail Network** site to identify opportunities, and use the software to prepare and send resumes electronically, in formats companies prefer. **Resumail Network** provides a wide range of services in addition to its resume-preparation software. It acts as a clearinghouse, bringing together job seekers and employers looking for qualified candidates. Job seekers can search the database by company name, industry, location or even by benefits such as health plans and on-site child-care facilities. Employers pay $995 for ten job postings, $75 for each additional, and $199 for access to the resume bank. Prices vary depending on the package corporations select. **Resumail** has also made alliances with job fairs.

Resumania On-line

www.umn.edu/ohr/ecep/resume

Eric Schnell, University of Minnesota
Employee Career Program, 1313 5th St. SE, Suite 220, Minneapolis, MN 55414
Ph: 612-626-0774   E-mail: schne050@tc.umn.edu

Jobs: **No**	
Cost to post jobs: N/A	
Cost to see jobs: N/A	
Resumes: **No**	
Cost to post resumes: N/A	
Cost to see resumes: N/A	
E-mail Alert (Push): N/A	
Specialty: N/A	
Industry: **All**	
Feature: **Resume Writing**	
Location: **US**	

At **Resumania Online,** job seekers will find excellent advice on how to prepare a resume. Check out the six steps to the perfect resume— simple and focused. A valuable check sheet is provided to critique your work. Q&As are informative, covering the basics, and then some. Review samples of different styles of resumes. We've recommended that Eric extend his expertise to web resumes, and to add suggestions for adapting a resume for optically scanned systems.

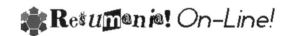

WELCOME TO RESUMANIA!

So, You Want Some Resume Help...

Then you've come to the right place! Resumania On-Line is an award winning (thank you NACE!), and a Lycos Top 5% interactive workbook designed to make resume writing less of a pain in the [ ] , and hopefully a bit more fun!

While Resumania won't actually write a resume for you, it will teach a lot about how to write a resume. However, before you catch a full-blown case of Resumania!, we recommend you click on some of these "Frequently Asked Questions". They are a good introduction to this web site. When you're ready to begin Resumania, scroll to the bottom of this screen and click on one of the six steps! You'll be on your way!

PLEASE NOTE: If you want a web site to assemble and format a resume for you (and I don't advise it), THIS SITE IS NOT FOR YOU! This is a teaching tool, and I hope that you'll print your workbook pages and use them as material from which YOU will assemble and format your resume. **This web site will not save any of your work,** so it's up to you to print out your workbook pages!

Resumania On-Line
Frequently Asked Questions

● What WILL Resumania On-Line do for me?   ● What WON'T Resumania On-Line do for me?

ResumeLink

resume-link.com

Rocque Trem,
5995 Wilcox Place, Dublin, OH 43026
Ph: 614-923-0600   Fax: 614-771-0610   E-mail: rtrem@resume-link.com

Jobs: **No**
Cost to post jobs: N/A
Cost to see jobs: N/A
Resumes: **Yes**
Cost to post resumes: **Free**
Cost to see resumes: **Fee**
E-mail Alert (Push): N/A
Specialty: **All**
Industry: **All**
Feature: N/A
Location: **US**

ResumeLink has developed a model for collecting resumes from colleges, associations and career fairs. Employers select the association of their choice, and send a job description to the site. Within three to five days the recruiter can expect to receive a fax of all matching resumes. If unable to forward six matches, employers are entitled to one free search. Member associations are listed, and there are some great ones that recruiters will want to target. However, if we were the recruiters, we would want to do our own searches. Costs run from $395 and up. With web technology, this needs to be automated. Seems to be an awkward online business model.

Retail JobNet

www.retailjobnet.com

P.O. Box 289, Stafford, VA 22555-2890
Ph: 540-373-2584   Fax: 540-373-3152   E-mail: advsales@retailjobnet.com

Jobs: **Yes**
Cost to post jobs: **Fee**
Cost to see jobs: **Free**
Resumes: **Yes**
Cost to post resumes: **Fee**
Cost to see resumes: **Fee**
E-mail Alert (Push): **Job Seeker**
Specialty: **Retail**
Industry: **Retail**
Feature: N/A
Location: **US**

Retail JobNet has hundreds of industry positions. Site charges job seekers $25 to post their resume for three months to sites within their state and within their job classification. What this really means, we were not able to discover. Recruiters can view resumes for free, but site has advised us that this will soon be for a fee. Recruiters pay $125 to post a position for 30 days. All posted positions and resumes have direct contact information, and the site's search engine allows you to view by state. Searches are fast, and information on jobs and resumes is designed for easy viewing.

Right Management Consultants, Inc.

www.right.com

1818 Market Street, Thirty-third Floor, Philadelphia, PA 19103
Ph: 800-237-4448   Fax: 215-988-0081   E-mail: info@right.com

Jobs: **Yes**	
Cost to post jobs: **Free**	
Cost to see jobs: **Fee** (See Notes)	
Resumes: **Yes**	
Cost to post resumes: **Fee** (See Notes)	
Cost to see resumes: **Free**	
E-mail Alert (Push): N/A	
Specialty: **All**	
Industry: **All**	
Feature: N/A	
Location: **US**	

Right Management Consultants is an outplacement service that provides some interesting web tidbits on its site. Click on the Internet Handbook, and find definitions of web words that are frequently used. An extensive list of links to help job seekers conduct "research" for their next occupation is very useful. Recruiters can post jobs here, but can they can only be seen by Right candidates. Candidate resumes can be viewed by corporations once they register and are approved. Sorry, no headhunters allowed in the resume database.

The Riley Guide

www.dbm.com/jobguide

Margaret F. Dikel (Riley)
11218 Ashley Drive, Rockville, MD 20852
Ph: 301-946-429   Fax: 301-933-6390   E-mail: mfriley@erols.com

Jobs: **No**
Cost to post jobs: N/A
Cost to see jobs: N/A
Resumes: **No**
Cost to post resumes: N/A
Cost to see resumes: N/A
E-mail Alert (Push): N/A
Specialty: **All**
Industry: **All**
Feature: **Meta-links**
Location: **US/Int'l**

The Riley Guide is a meta-list of links to employment opportunities and job resources on the net. Margaret is still the "Queen of Job Links" in our book, and continues to maintain a great list catgegorized in every imaginable way. She is developing an alphabetical listing of links as a work in progress. Brief reviews of each site are available, and if you find a new one, she would appreciate an e-mail. Great work.

The Riley Guide

Employment Opportunities and Job Resources on the Internet

Compiled by Margaret F. Dikel

Dikel?!?!? What happened to Margaret F. Riley?

"This is the best by far. If I could only go to one gateway job site on the Web, this would be it."
-- Richard Bolles, What Color is Your Parachute: The Net Guide

"Margaret Riley Dikel is the preeminent expert on Internet job hunting. And the Riley Guide is an invaluable tool for savvy job hunters."
--Tony Lee, Editor in Chief, Careers.wsj.com
from The Wall Street Journal Interactive Edition.

CAREER X ROADS 1999 Best Site

The RS/6000 Employment Page

www.s6000.com/job.html

Donohue Consulting, Inc.
P.O. Box 42046, Washington, DC 20015
Ph: 202-362-8144   Fax: 202-364-2249   E-mail: dci@s6000.com

Jobs: **Yes** Cost to post jobs: **Fee** Cost to see jobs: **Free**	
Resumes: **Yes** Cost to post resumes: **Free** Cost to see resumes: **Free**	
E-mail Alert (Push): N/A	
Specialty: **IT/RS 6000**	
Industry: **All**	
Feature: N/A	
Location: **US**	

RS/6000 Employment Page provides job listings and resumes for this niche IT area. Job seekers can post their name and e-mail address. Recruiters now pay $50 per posting or $200 for five listings for a 90-day run. Jobs are in alphabetical or date order by title, and there were several dozen listed.

Sales Job.com

www.salesjob.com

Jobs: **Yes** Cost to post jobs: **Fee** Cost to see jobs: **Free**	
Resumes: **No** Cost to post resumes: N/A Cost to see resumes: N/A	
E-mail Alert (Push): N/A	
Specialty: **Sales/Marketing**	
Industry: **All**	
Feature: N/A	
Location: **US**	

Sales Job.com is new. Recruiters can post positions for 60 days for $150. Site's search engine allows the job seeker to select any U.S. state and many sales occupation titles. Unfortunately, ten searches yielded zero jobs. **Salesjob** will need help, but this niche is important, and the address makes sense.

Saludos Web

www.saludos.com

Susan Bryck, Saludos Hispanos
73-121 Fred Waring Drive, Suite 100, Palm Desert, CA 92260
Ph: 760-776-1206   Fax: 760-776-1229   E-mail: info@saludos.com

Jobs: **Yes** Cost to post jobs: **Fee** Cost to see jobs: **Free**	
Resumes: **Yes** Cost to post resumes: **Free** Cost to see resumes: **Free**	
E-mail Alert (Push): N/A	
Specialty: **All**	
Industry: **All**	
Feature: **Diversity**	
Location: **US/W/CA**	

Saludos Web is supported by the *Saludos Hispanos* magazine. Job seekers can post their resumes for free, and search jobs by function or by geographic preference. Several dozen major employers have positions posted. Recruiters pay $89 to post a position. Interesting list of career links and mailing list addresses are also available.

SCWIST Work Pathfinder

www.harbour.sfu.ca/scwist/pathfinder/index.htm.

Society for Canadian Women in Science, Canada
E-mail: scwist@sfu.ca

Jobs: **No** Cost to post jobs: N/A Cost to see jobs: N/A	
Resumes: **No** Cost to post resumes: N/A Cost to see resumes: N/A	
E-mail Alert (Push): N/A	
Specialty: Science	
Industry: **All**	
Feature: **Diversity/Meta-links**	
Location: **Int'l/Canada**	

SCWist Work Pathfinder is a career site for women interested in technology and the sciences. Links to many Canadian companies that have jobs posted. Personal accounts about how careers have grown, and how expectations for the future have changed are great.

Science Professional Network

www.scienceonline.org

Gabrielle Boguslawaki, Science Magazine
1200 NY Avenue N.W., Washington, DC 20005
Ph: 202-326-6400   Fax: 202-682-0816   E-mail: gbogusla@aaas.org

Jobs: **Yes**	
Cost to post jobs: **Fee**	
Cost to see jobs: **Free**	
Resumes: **Yes**	
Cost to post resumes: **Free** (See Notes)	
Cost to see resumes: **Fee**	
E-mail Alert (Push): N/A	
Specialty: **Sci/Pharm/Biotech**	
Industry: **Science**	
Feature: N/A	
Location: **US/Int'l**	

Earlier this year, **The Science Professional Network** launched a "push" e-mail alert announcing advertised positions from their magazine. Within 12 days they had over 2,000 scientists signed up and ready to rock-'n-roll for possible new job opportunities. All of the job ads that are placed in their magazine are posted at this site. Prior issues can also be seen. Career links are advertisers who have purchased banners to their job sites. *Science* typically sponsors four career fairs a year to attract pharmaceutical and biotechnology talent for their advertisers. Employers who are exhibitors can search the sites resume bank. Lots of career content to go along with a well-designed site.

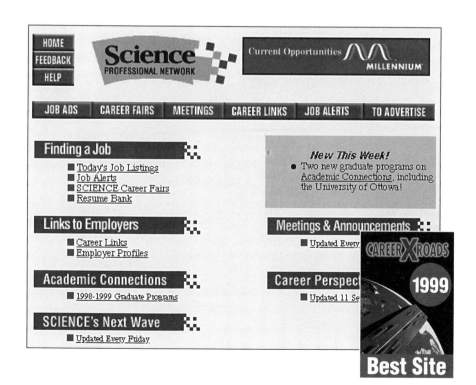

ScitechJobs.Com

www.scitechjobs.com

Stacy Barrett, Scientific American & Nature
345 Park Avenue South, 10th Floor, New York, NY 10010
Ph: 800-653-9923   Fax: 212-696-0769   E-mail: stacy@scitechjobs.com

Jobs: **Yes** Cost to post jobs: **Fee** Cost to see jobs: **Free**	
Resumes: **No** Cost to post resumes: N/A Cost to see resumes: N/A	
E-mail Alert (Push): N/A	
Specialty: **Science**	
Industry: **All**	
Feature: N/A	
Location: **US/Int'l**	

Scitechjobs.com is a joint venture of *Scientific American* and *Nature*, international publications attracting a wide range of scientific talent. Jobs can be searched by position, organization or location, and all have direct contact information. Everything from postdoctorals to senior level research opportunities can be found.

The Seamless Website

www.seamless.com/jobs/

Kevin Lee Thomason, TSW Ltd
300 Montgomery Street, 4th Fl., San Francisco, CA 94104
Ph: 415-732-5600   Fax: 415-732-5606   E-mail: access@seamless.com

Jobs: **Yes** Cost to post jobs: **Free** Cost to see jobs: **Free**	
Resumes: **Yes** Cost to post resumes: **Free** Cost to see resumes: **Free**	
E-mail Alert (Push): N/A	
Specialty: **Law**	
Industry: N/A	
Feature: N/A	
Location: **US/W/CA**	

The legal profession can post resumes, link to jobs for free and share Q&As regarding careers and jobs. Well done and easy to access.

Search Base

www.searchbase.com

Kevin Krantz, Search Systems Corporation
Pembrooke 5, Suite 511, Virginia Beach, VA 23462
Ph: 877-777-3272   E-mail: support@searchbase.com

Jobs: **No**
Cost to post jobs: N/A
Cost to see jobs: N/A
Resumes: **Yes**
Cost to post resumes: **Fee**
Cost to see resumes: N/A
E-mail Alert (Push): N/A
Specialty: **All**
Industry: **All**
Feature: **Resume Service**
Location: **US**

Search Base states it has a listing of over 6,000 executive recruiters, and for $148 will e-mail your resume to them all. We would want to know more about the listings of recruiters. Quantity may be large, but all the recruiters cannot be in one specialty. They may not even be interested in getting your resume if you are not in their field of expertise. Contact information is now on the site, but we would be a little concerned about this one. We've kept this site in the directory because of the questions we've received from job seekers asking about it. Draw your own conclusions.

SelectJOBS

www.selectjobs.com.

Jodi Elam, SelectJobs
7900 Nova Drive, Suite 101, Davie, FL 33329
Ph: 954-424-0563   Fax: 954-424-6626   E-mail: webmaster@selectjobs.com

Jobs: **Yes**
Cost to post jobs: **Fee**
Cost to see jobs: **Free**
Resumes: **Yes**
Cost to post resumes: **Free**
Cost to see resumes: **Fee**
E-mail Alert (Push): **Both**
Specialty: **IT/High Tech**
Industry: **IT**
Feature: N/A
Location: **US/Int'l/Canada England/Japan**

SelectJOBS is geared for the IT/high technology industries across the U.S. Unlimited job postings are $360 per month, a single job posting is $50, and viewing the resume database is $50 per month. Jobs will also be posted to America's Job Bank, Career City, Classifieds 2,000, HeadHunter.NET, Yahoo and related newsgroups. Site's search engine allows job seekers to view the U.S. and plug in the title or job description for their area of interest. They can also maintain their confidentiality on their resume posting. Site e-mails position matches to job seekers. Employer receives resumes via e-mail that match openings as well. This is done on a daily basis. Site states employers are only sent resumes that match their criteria. The right tools are in place.

SenseMedia Surfer Get A Job

sensemedia.net/getajob/

SenseMedia
E-mail: surfer@sensemedia.net

Jobs: **No** Cost to post jobs: N/A Cost to see jobs: N/A	
Resumes: **No** Cost to post resumes: N/A Cost to see resumes: N/A	
E-mail Alert (Push): N/A	
Specialty: **All**	
Industry: **All**	
Feature: **Meta-links**	
Location: **US**	

GETAJOB SenseMedia Surfer provides dozens of links to major and minor web sites. An eclectic list from colleges to water sites. No rhyme to the reason for these link listings.

Shawn's Internet Resume Center

www.inpursuit.com/sirc/

Shawn Spengler, Inpursuit
6405 Paddington Ct., #304, Centreville, CT 20121
E-mail: sirc@claravista.com

Jobs: **Yes** Cost to post jobs: **Fee** Cost to see jobs: **Free**	
Resumes: **Yes** Cost to post resumes: **Free** Cost to see resumes: **Free**	
E-mail Alert (Push): N/A	
Specialty: **Executive**	
Industry: **All**	
Feature: N/A	
Location: **US**	

SIRC—Shawn's Internet Resume Center has changed their model for helping executives find their next career move. Job seekers must first post their resume (for free) to gain access to the job postings. Recruiters can view resumes for free. Job postings cost $75 for a 30-day listing. For an annual fee ($1,500 – $2,500), employers have unlimited job posting capability. Many high tech firms are listed as clients.

ShowBizJobs.com

www.showbizjobs.com

Paul Buss, Entertainment Recruitment Network
7095 Hollywood Blvd., Suite 711, Hollywood, CA 90028
Ph: 972-243-3825   E-mail: paul@showbizjobs.com

Jobs: **Yes**	
Cost to post jobs: **Fee**	
Cost to see jobs: **Free**	
Resumes: **Yes**	
Cost to post resumes: **Fee**	
Cost to see resumes: **Fee**	
E-mail Alert (Push): **Job Seeker**	
Specialty: **Entertainment**	
Industry: **Entertainment**	
Feature: N/A	
Location: **US/Int'l/ Europe/Canada**	

ShowBizJobs.com lists opportunities for the film, television, recording, multimedia and attractions job markets. Site's search engine needs help and a better explanation of how it works. You can select a company, a category, a location or a posting date. Can you select more than one? Do you have to select all four? Confusing. Recruiters pay $100 per posting, and can search resumes for free. Job seekers pay $35 to post their resume to the sites database. Site will send you confirming messages that client companies have reviewed your resume. Thanks…I think.

SHRM HR Jobs

www.shrm.org

Mike Frost, Society for Human Resource Management
1800 Duke Street, Alexandria, VA 22314
Ph: 703-548-3440   Fax: 703-836-0367   E-mail: frost@shrm.org

Jobs: **Yes**	
Cost to post jobs: **Fee**	
Cost to see jobs: **Free**	
Resumes: **No**	
Cost to post resumes: N/A	
Cost to see resumes: N/A	
E-mail Alert (Push): **Job Seeker**	
Specialty: **Human Resources**	
Industry: **All**	
Feature: **Meta-links**	
Location: **US/Int'l**	

The SHRM (Society for Human Resource Management) continues to improve its presence on the web, and is an association benchmark for how to do it right. Job seekers who register on the jobs page receive notification of new positions via e-mail. These listings will eventually see print in the Society's monthly tabloid *HRNews*, but are posted immediately to the Net—an important consideration that most other print publications have yet to understand. Positions can be viewed across the U.S. by location, title, or date of posting. A handful of international openings were also listed. Jobs are also tagged "New" or "Entry Level." At $20+ per line SHRM not only assists members and employers connect, but they've built an excellent business model as well. Job descriptions are brief, to the point, and all contain contact information.

Siam Net

www.siam.net/jobs/

Jobs & Adverts, 4th Floor Cyberia Building
654-8 Sukhumvit 24 Rd., Klongton, Klongtoey, Bangkok, Thailand 10110
Ph: 663-462-15   Fax: 663-462-0   E-mail: info@jobsadverts.com

Jobs: **Yes**
Cost to post jobs: **Fee**
Cost to see jobs: **Free**
Resumes: **Yes**
Cost to post resumes: **Free**
Cost to see resumes: **N/A** (See Notes)
E-mail Alert (Push): **Job Seeker**
Specialty: **All**
Industry: **All**
Feature: N/A
Location: **Int'l/Asia/Thailand**

Siam Net has merged with "Job and Adverts" to give more services to job seekers in Asia and Thailand. Recruiters pay 2,950 Baht to post a position. You might want to check exchange rates if you don't have a few baht in your wallet. A resume search tool is on its way as we went to press. Jobs that we viewed all had direct contact information and date of posting. Jobs can be viewed by using the site's search engine or alphabetically under the corporation's name. Job seekers who register and post their skills will have matching positions e-mailed to them every three, seven or 14 days. Your choice.

Silicon Valley Technical Employment Agency

www.sease.com/jobs.html

Jim Sease, Sease Associates, P.O. Box 390576, Mountain View, CA 94039
Ph: 415-964-3348   E-mail: jim@sease.com

Jobs: **No**
Cost to post jobs: N/A
Cost to see jobs: N/A
Resumes: **No**
Cost to post resumes: N/A
Cost to see resumes: N/A
E-mail Alert (Push): N/A
Specialty: N/A
Industry: N/A
Feature: **Meta-links/ Recruitment Agencies**
Location: **US/W/CA**

Silicon Valley Technical Employment Agency is a listing of over 200 recruitment agencies in this area of California. Jim Sease also provides an e-mail address listing which job seekers can cut and paste to send their resume to all on the list.

Sistahspace

www.sistahspace.com

E-mail: webstasistahspace.com

Jobs: **Yes** Cost to post jobs: **Free** Cost to see jobs: **Fee**
Resumes: **No** Cost to post resumes: N/A Cost to see resumes: N/A
E-mail Alert (Push): N/A
Specialty: **All**
Industry: **All**
Feature: **Diversity**
Location: **US**

Sistahspace is a new site that provides African Americans a place to find a job, discuss common issues or find links to diversity sites on the web. Recruiters can post jobs for free and there were several dozen on our visit. A chatroom and Q&A are available for all to use. Site is much more than a job site, it is a slice of culture. Simple, easy to view and worth a visit.

Skill Scape

www.skillscape.com

Colin Houghton, SkillScape Skills Management Services Ltd.
Suite 19, 3318 Oak Street, Victoria, British Columbia, Canada V8X 1R1
Ph: 888-262-6243   Fax: 250-475-7511   E-mail: info@skillscape.com

Jobs: **Yes** Cost to post jobs: **Free** Cost to see jobs: **Free**
Resumes: **Yes** Cost to post resumes: **Free** Cost to see resumes: **Free** (See Note)
E-mail Alert (Push): **Job Seeker**
Specialty: **All**
Industry: **All**
Feature: N/A
Location: **US**

Skill Scape is free for recruiters to post jobs, and free for them to review candidate profiles and contact information, but only the profiles and contact information of those applicants that are responding to their posting. It will cost an employer $35 to look at the candidate contact information of those folks who are not responding to the posting (profiles, you can always see for free). Completing the site's skill set questionnaire takes 30 minutes. A little excessive.

Smart Dog

www.smartdog.org

Barry Orlando, Industrial Management Council
930 East Avenue, Rochester, NY 14607
Ph: 716-244-1800   Fax: 716-244-4864   E-mail: sitemanager@smartdog.org

Jobs: **Yes** Cost to post jobs: **Fee** Cost to see jobs: **Free**	
Resumes: **Yes** Cost to post resumes: **Free** Cost to see resumes: **Fee**	
E-mail Alert (Push): **Job Seeker**	
Specialty: **IT**	
Industry: **All**	
Feature: N/A	
Location: **US/NE/NY/Rochester**	

Smart Dog lists jobs in the Rochester area. The site's focus is on high tech jobs, and their "hope is to use this site to recruit workers from Silicon Valley to upstate, N.Y." Fat chance, but this is nevertheless a great site, and holds promise for similar ventures elsewhere. **Smart Dog** is clearly a partnership model between local companies with high tech interests who have banded together to put Rochester's best foot forward. Cooperating to attract more talent to the area instead of duking it out over the local talent pool, is a great concept. Any company with a facility in the Rochester area should make a point of looking into this site. Corporate membership starts at $2,000 per year, and is based on the number of employees. Job seekers who register will have jobs e-mailed to them. If you have a trailing spouse, area has career development services to assist in the job search. Site map makes it easy to get around the dog pound.

SmartPOST Network

www.smartpost.com

Stephanie Ralston, The WebDesk, LLC
5813 Wrightsville Avenue, Suite 121, Wilmington, NC 28403
Ph: 254-539-6178   Fax: 254-539-6180   E-mail: eralston@the webdesk.com

Jobs: **No** Cost to post jobs: N/A Cost to see jobs: N/A	
Resumes: **No** Cost to post resumes: N/A Cost to see resumes: N/A	
E-mail Alert (Push): N/A	
Specialty: **All**	
Industry: **All**	
Feature: **Automated Job Posting**	
Location: **US**	

SmartPost is a job posting tool that takes the drudgery out of sending classified copy to a growing number of web sites. The service has some very interesting reports and technical features. As their agreements with job posting sites grow, so will this service.

SocialService.Com

www.socialservice.com

Administrative Technology Services
P.O. Box 7089, Kansas City, MO 64113
E-mail: ats@socialservice.com

Jobs: **Yes** Cost to post jobs: **Fee** Cost to see jobs: **Free**	
Resumes: **No** Cost to post resumes: N/A Cost to see resumes: N/A	
E-mail Alert (Push): **Job Seeker**	
Specialty: **Soc Svcs/Psychology**	
Industry: **All**	
Feature: N/A	
Location: **US**	

SocialService.com includes positions throughout the U.S. Jobs we found listed were for employee assistance consultants and psychologists. Recruiters pay $25 to post a job for two weeks for each state. Additional states are $25 each. Jobs are listed by state.

Society of Women Engineers

www.swe.org

Society of Women Engineers
120 Wall Street, 11th Floor, New York, NY 10005
Ph: 212-509-9577   Fax: 212-509-0224   E-mail: vp-special.services@swe.org

Jobs: **Yes** Cost to post jobs: **Free** Cost to see jobs: **Free**	
Resumes: **No** Cost to post resumes: **N/A** (See Notes) Cost to see resumes: **N/A** (See Notes)	
E-mail Alert (Push): **Job Seeker**	
Specialty: **Engineering**	
Industry: **All**	
Feature: **Diversity**	
Location: **US**	

SWE members registering here are automatically forwarded job information via e-mail received from corporate recruiters. It's amazing that this no-cost service isn't more widely used by companies seeking engineers. SWE recommends that their members in transition use Resume-link's database to store their resume. Recruiters can subscribe and receive a disc with information about each candidate. We like the use of "push" on the job openings, although it would be better if it were more visible on the site. The resume approach is a little behind the curve.

Software Contractors' Guild

www.scguild.com

David Keeney, Keeney Software, Inc.
P.O. Box 267, Nottingham, NH 03290
Ph: 603-895-9975   E-mail: admn@www.scguild.com

Jobs: **No** Cost to post jobs: N/A Cost to see jobs: N/A	
Resumes: **Yes** Cost to post resumes: **Fee** Cost to see resumes: **Free**	
E-mail Alert (Push): N/A	
Specialty: **IT**	
Industry: **Computer**	
Feature: N/A	
Location: **US**	

The Software Contractors' Guild
warehouses resumes of software contractors, and states that it has 1,267 members (August '98). Job seekers pay to post their resume ($12 per year). For employers, resumes are free to see. There are five chapters—four of which are under construction. The chapter in France is up, and the text is in French. Hundreds of IT contract firms have their contact information listed on this site.

Sorkins Job Bank

www.sorkins.com

Sorkins Directories Inc.
1001 Craig Road, Suite 260, St. Louis, MO 63146
Ph: 800-758-3228   Fax: 800-721-5478   E-mail: jobmaster@sorkinsjobbank.com

Jobs: **Yes** Cost to post jobs: **Fee** Cost to see jobs: **Free**
Resumes: **Yes** Cost to post resumes: **Free** Cost to see resumes: **Fee**
E-mail Alert (Push): N/A
Specialty: **All**
Industry: **All**
Feature: N/A
Location: **US/MW/IL/MO/KS**

Sorkins Job Bank is a Midwest site catering to job seekers in Illinois, Missouri and Kansas. Site is known for the research job seekers can acquire for a fee on area corporations. They have now gone into the job posting, resume retrieval business, and are learning as they go. Recruiters pay $95 per month to post unlimited jobs and view the resume database. Search engine allows the job seeker to view positions by company, title or keyword. All positions are date posted for freshness, and direct contact information is available. This site will need some nurturing.

Space Careers

www.spacelinks.com/SpaceCareers/

Pierre Oppetit, SpaceLinks
Springdale House, Wallingford, Oxfordshire, UK 0X10 0HQ
Ph: 441-718-32671   Fax: 441-718-26704   E-mail: webmaster@spacelinks.com

Jobs: **No** Cost to post jobs: N/A Cost to see jobs: N/A
Resumes: **No** Cost to post resumes: N/A Cost to see resumes: N/A
E-mail Alert (Push): N/A
Specialty: **Aviation/Engineering/ Aerospace**
Industry: **Aerospace**
Feature: **Meta-Links**
Location: **Int'l/US**

Space Careers has links to over 350 sites, mostly corporations that make satellites, supply NASA, or other international aerospace organizations. Site will even e-mail updates when it adds new links. Check out the "Space Site of the Week." One place where you can't help taking off.

Space Jobs

www.spacejobs.com

John Criswick
153 St. Andrews St., Suite 205, Ottawa, Ont., Canada K1N5G3
Ph: 613-562-2816   Fax: 613-562-1784   E-mail: info@spacejobs.com

Jobs: **Yes** Cost to post jobs: **Fee** Cost to see jobs: **Free**	
Resumes: **No** Cost to post resumes: N/A Cost to see resumes: N/A	
E-mail Alert (Push): **Job Seeker**	
Specialty: **Engineering/Aerospace**	
Industry: **Aerospace**	
Feature: N/A	
Location: **US/Int'l**	

Space Jobs is for aerospace engineers and others who dream about new worlds to conquer. Some of the biggest players in space are here. Job seekers register their skills and receive e-mails when positions match. Site will e-mail only to U.S. citizens. Jobs are date posted, and direct contact information is available. Positions can be found by country, by corporate alphabetical listing, or through the site's search engine. Recruiters pay $150 to post a position for three months. Opportunities are located all over the world, and the navigation tools are like sitting in the good ship Enterprise. Beam me up Scotty.

Star Chefs

www.starchefs.com

Pat Greaney, Boiling Water, Inc.
270 Lafayete Street, Suite 205, New York, NY 10012
Ph: 212-966-3775   Fax: 212-966-6644   E-mail: greaney@starchefs.com

Jobs: **Yes** Cost to post jobs: **Free** Cost to see jobs: **Free**	
Resumes: **Yes** Cost to post resumes: **Free** Cost to see resumes: **Free**	
E-mail Alert (Push): N/A	
Specialty: **Hospitality/ Restaurant/Chefs**	
Industry: **Hospitality**	
Feature: N/A	
Location: **US/Int'l**	

StarChefs is one of our favorite sites. The site hosts a basketful of opportunities for restaurants all over the world. Sous chefs, executive chefs, pastry chefs, even restaurant positions in sales and marketing can all be seen for free. Job listings are posted by date as are the resumes (109 on our visit). Site uses its search engine to find recipes rather than jobs or resumes—where you must scroll…and scroll. Tells you where their priorities are, but we did find a great soufflé. If you register, they will e-mail you their latest culinary creations. Click on "Culinary Careers," and you will see educational programs from major schools from all over the U.S. Send in your favorite QuickMeal recipe, and win the cookbook of the month. Simple, clean and fun. If you get a job from using this site, we'll be happy to stop by.

Stern Alumni Outreach
Career Resources Online

www.stern.nyu.edu/Alumni/career.html

Wendy Siegel, Stern School of Business, New York University, NY
Fax: 212-995-4007   E-mail: wsiegel@stern.nyu.edu

Jobs: **Yes**	
Cost to post jobs: **Free**	
Cost to see jobs: **Free**	
Resumes: **Yes**	
Cost to post resumes: **Fee** (Alumni only)	
Cost to see resumes: **Free**	
E-mail Alert (Push): N/A	
Specialty: **Executive**	
Industry: **All**	
Feature: N/A	
Location: **US**	

This alumni site for the Stern NYU School of Business is a model example of what can be done on the web. Employer's post jobs for free (eight-week listing), and the school will fax resumes. Dozens of links to executive recruiters and corporations as well as career information are housed here. Anyone can see the positions—from administrative assistant to vice president. Korn Ferry posts positions here. If you are an alumnus/ae they provide services (for a fee) to help you land your next opportunity. **Stern** also has a worldwide alumni advisory network. If other schools are looking for a model, this is a good one to benchmark. We noted that some of the salaries approached the stratosphere.

Leonard N. Stern School of Business
New York University

Alumni Outreach Presents

CAREER RESOURCES ONLINE...
...AT YOUR SERVICE

******* Alumni Outreach has improved our job site page to facilitate your needs! *******
Keep in mind that these services remain only one aspect of your job search, an additional resource to support your efforts.
Stern does not officially endorse any of these sites, but we hope they will be useful to you. Good luck!!

- **Links to Alumni Job Opportunities**
  Referrals to specific opportunities sent to Alumni Outreach from executive search firms, corporations and alumni worldwide.

- **NYU Office of Career Services for Alumni**
  Alumni Services packages, available with proof of graduation and an additional fee, include career counseling, job listings, seminars, and much more. Also call (212) 998-4730 for more information.

- **Links to Career Websites**
  Dozens of job databases and career assistance here for your reference! Search them by field, region, etc. There is no charge to browse most of these services, or to post your resume with them online.

- **Links to Newspapers and Publications**
  Newspapers are a reliable source of updated information, local job listings, and free advice. They are conveniently listed here.

Student Advantage

www.mainquad.com

Kevin Watters, Student Advantage
1770 Union Street, San Francisco, CA 94123
Ph: 415-346-4242   Fax: 415-353-0685   E-mail: kevin@mainquad.com

Jobs: **No**	
Cost to post jobs: N/A	
Cost to see jobs: N/A	
Resumes: **No**	
Cost to post resumes: **Free**	
Cost to see resumes: **Fee**	
E-mail Alert (Push): N/A	
Specialty: **College**	
Industry: **All**	
Feature: N/A	
Location: **US**	

Student Advantage has career information for today's college student. An article about internships, and another about making your resume irresistible made for interesting reading. If you are a high school student, check out the pre-college resource center so you can find the $$$ to enter the big time. Site's main focus is to sell products to the student market. Warning: all parents should hold on to their credit cards when viewing this site.

Student Center

studentcenter.com

Eve Yohalem, StudentCenter LLC
31 West 21st Street, Suite 1102, New York, NY 10010
Ph: 212-929-7980   Fax: 212-255-6357   E-mail: info@studentcenter.com

Jobs: **Yes**	
Cost to post jobs: **Fee**	
Cost to see jobs: **Free**	
Resumes: **No**	
Cost to post resumes: N/A	
Cost to see resumes: N/A	
E-mail Alert (Push): N/A	
Specialty: **College**	
Industry: **All**	
Feature: **Meta-links (Internships)**	
Location: **US**	

StudentCenter.com has a new look and new owners, TMP Worldwide, the owners of OCC, Monster Board, AboutWork and others. Career content, advice and internships are the "hub" of **StudentCenter**, and it continues to grow in this arena. Site provides interesting career articles for those still trying to decide what to be when they grow up. A free newsletter that will be e-mailed to all who register is available. A live chatroom, and now alliances with the sister sites, will make for an interesting future.

St. Louis Area Companies on the Net

www.st-louis.mo.us/st-louis/companies.html

Brian Smith, Washington University
School of Engineering, St.Louis, MO
Ph: 314-935-4850   E-mail: brians@cait.wustl.edu

Jobs: **No** Cost to post jobs: N/A Cost to see jobs: N/A
Resumes: **No** Cost to post resumes: N/A Cost to see resumes: N/A
E-mail Alert (Push): N/A
Specialty: **All**
Industry: **All**
Feature: **Meta-links**
Location: **US/MW/MO/St. Louis**

St. Louis Area Companies on the Net has one of the longest meta-link lists we have seen on the web. If you are looking for a job in St. Louis, this is your one-stop, link shop. One-line description gives you all the information you need to proceed. Hundreds of links.

St. Thomas Human Resource Centre

ein.ccia.st-thomas.hrdc-drhc.gc.ca/english.html

HR Department Canada, Human Resources Development Canada
451 Talbot Street, St. Thomas, Ontario, Canada NSP 3V6
Ph: 519-631-5470   E-mail: (See Notes)

Jobs: **Yes** Cost to post jobs: **Free** Cost to see jobs: **Free**
Resumes: **No** Cost to post resumes: N/A Cost to see resumes: N/A
E-mail Alert (Push): **Job Seeker**
Specialty: **All**
Industry: **All**
Feature: **Meta-links**
Location: **Int'l/Canada**

St. Thomas Human Resource Centre typifies why some countries understand the power of the web, and others are slow to follow. Register your e-mail, and the 'Electronic Labour Exchange" will match your skills with local employers, and send you the information. Site also maintains listings of job bank kiosks. If you cannot get to the web, your telephone will give you 24-hour job vacancy notices. The Centre job bank provides direct contact information. They even differentiate between jobs received within the last 24 hours. This site and its links definitely get it. Their e-mail is: Roshan@ein.ccia.st-thomas.on.ca.

Summer Jobs

www.summerjobs.com

Jeff Allen
1050 Cemetery Lane, Aspen, CO 81611
Ph: 970-544-5461   Fax: 970-920-3071   E-mail: jobs@resortjobs.com

Jobs: **Yes** Cost to post jobs: **Free** (See Notes) Cost to see jobs: **Free**	
Resumes: **No** Cost to post resumes: N/A Cost to see resumes: N/A	
E-mail Alert (Push): N/A	
Specialty: **College/** **Summer Internships**	
Industry: **All**	
Feature: N/A	
Location: **Int'l/US**	

Summer Jobs is the place to be to find that special position for those long hot (wish I was on vacation) months. Positions can be posted for free throughout the world. If recruiters want their position to be at the top of the chart there is a price to pay (prices range from $50 to $150 for the first 20 jobs in each category on a "first come, first served" basis). Hundreds of openings are listed with direct contact information. Search engine gives you a smooth ride to the opening of your choice. Job seekers can view jobs by country, position or any key word. Owners state they will always allow job posting for free.

Supermarket News

www.supermarketnews.com

Fairchild Publishing
7 East 12th Street, New York, NY 10003
Ph: 800-423-3314   Fax: 212-630-4634   E-mail: info@supermarketnews.com

Jobs: **Yes** Cost to post jobs: **Fee** Cost to see jobs: **Free**	
Resumes: **No** Cost to post resumes: N/A Cost to see resumes: N/A	
E-mail Alert (Push): N/A	
Specialty: **Retail/Food/** **Supermarket**	
Industry: **Retail/Supermarket**	
Feature: N/A	
Location: **US**	

Supermarket News is a trade publication for the retail grocery marketplace. Employers pay for the print to have the opportunity to post on the web as well. There were nine jobs posted on our visit with direct contact information. You'll have to bag your own.

Surf-IT.net

www.jobsurfshop.com

David Buback,
305 Warm Springs Dr., Roswell, GA 30075
Ph: 770-998-3902   E-mail: membership@jobsurfshop.com

Jobs: **Yes** Cost to post jobs: **Free** Cost to see jobs: **Free**	
Resumes: **Yes** Cost to post resumes: **Free** Cost to see resumes: **Free**	
E-mail Alert (Push): N/A	
Specialty: **IT**	
Industry: **All**	
Feature: N/A	
Location: **US**	

Surf-It.net (formerly the JobBoard Surf Shop) is for the IT field for technical positions in computers, engineering and telecommunications. Site allows professionals to search and post jobs and search and post resumes for free. All contact information and date of posting are available for job seekers to see. Jobs are posted for 120 days, and are also posted to newsgroups. Site's search engine allows the job seeker to hunt by skills sets or job categories for easy viewing. Banners can be purchased. Price is right, but our question is: "How do they make $$$ other then the banners?" Answer: When you pay $49 per month to become a member, your job postings move closer to the top of the charts. Jobs will then be automatically linked to your company home page, and they receive a "tag" stating "member" so they stick out from the pack. Different.

Talent Alliance

www.talentalliance.com

John McMorrow,
100 Southgate Parkway, Room 3G10, Morristown, NJ 07960
Ph: 888-967-5929   Fax: 404-810-8298   E-mail: tainfo@talentalliance.org

Jobs: **No** Cost to post jobs: N/A Cost to see jobs: N/A
Resumes: **No** Cost to post resumes: N/A Cost to see resumes: N/A
E-mail Alert (Push): N/A
Specialty: **All**
Industry: **All**
Feature: N/A
Location: **US**

Talent Alliance is a group of companies (AT&T, CBSI, Ceridian, Dupont, GTE, Kelly Services, MetLife, TRW, Unisys, UPS) that form the core of a new concept with enormous implications—to provide long-term employability to the consortium's employees, and at the same time, help companies with growth needs to quickly locate skilled workers. The Alliance offers its members the following services:
- job and applicant matching through an online database
- shared training resources and best practices.
- online and onsite career centers
- educational forums, research and communication geared toward improving career management strategies.

Most sections on the site require membership. This is a futuristic approach to employee issues.

Talent Hunter

www.3dsite.com/ism/resumes/cgi-bin/talent-hunter.

Charles Anthony Viviani
E-mail: cav@ax.apc.org

Jobs: **Yes** Cost to post jobs: **Free** Cost to see jobs: **Free**	
Resumes: **Yes** Cost to post resumes: **Free** Cost to see resumes: **Free**	
E-mail Alert (Push): N/A	
Specialty: **Graphic Arts**	
Industry: **All**	
Feature: N/A	
Location: **US**	

Talent Hunter is for people in the graphics industry: 3-D, artists, modeling, special effects and those interested in freelance or full-time employment. Once you register as a job seeker or a recruiter, all searches are free. Price is right so give it a try.

Talent Works: The Online Casting Source

www.talentworks.com

Richard Brodsky, Talentworks
862 Sir Francis Drake Blvd., #255, San Anselmo, CA 94960
Ph: 800-978-9911   Fax: 415-456-0588   E-mail: info@talentworks.com

Jobs: **Yes** Cost to post jobs: **Free** Cost to see jobs: **Free**	
Resumes: **Yes** Cost to post resumes: **Fee** Cost to see resumes: **Free**	
E-mail Alert (Push): N/A	
Specialty: **Entertainment**	
Industry: **Entertainment**	
Feature: N/A	
Location: **US**	

Talent Works: The Online Casting Call asks employers several questions: height, weight, hair and eye color of the applicants they wish to interview. Direct contact information from the candidates is shown, along with their picture. Actors can have a ten-day free trial, and pay $50 for one-year membership. Talent agencies pay $250 to show off their clients. Site has a message board and live chatroom so actors can make new contacts and strut their stuff. The site's search engine allows directors to find their next Romeo or Juliet at the touch of a button.

taps.com

www.taps.com

Affie Panayiotou, Internet Appointments
43-44 Albermarle St., London, England W1X 3SE
Ph: 441-714-31997   Fax: 441-714-931886   E-mail: affiep@taps.com

Jobs: **Yes** Cost to post jobs: **Fee** Cost to see jobs: **Free**
Resumes: **Yes** Cost to post resumes: **Free** Cost to see resumes: **Fee**
E-mail Alert (Push): **Job Seeker**
Specialty: **All**
Industry: **All**
Feature: N/A
Location: **Int'l/Europe/UK**

Postions posted to **taps.com** are primarily for the UK and Europe. Recruiters pay seven pounds for each job, and hundreds of positions were posted on our visits. Site will also "Push" open positions to job seekers once they register their e-mail. Search engine is fast and on target.

TCM's HR Careers

www.tcm.com/hr-careers

Eric Snyder, TCM Internet Services
64 Thare Crescent, Nepean, ON, Canada K2J 2P6
Ph: 613-823-0244   Fax: 613-745-8031   E-mail: jobs@TCM.com

Jobs: **Yes**	
Cost to post jobs: **Fee**	
Cost to see jobs: **Free**	
Resumes: **Yes**	
Cost to post resumes: **Free**	
Cost to see resumes: **Fee**	
E-mail Alert (Push): **Job Seeker**	
Specialty: **Human Resources Training**	
Industry: **All**	
Feature: N/A	
Location: **US/Canada**	

TCM is a nationally-recognized site for training professionals. They have recently added an HR section which focuses on job and contract opportunities for generalists and training and multimedia professionals. Recruiters pay $200 per month to post a position, and another $200 to access the resume database. Job seekers can register their skills, and the site will push positions to them via e-mail. Site will also post the job seeker's resume to 1,400+ recruiters for $50, and if they wish, to newsgroups for $25. A newly-created "chat" session, where job seekers and recruiters can have a virtual jobfair, has been created. The site first drew 35 job seekers, with 80 waiting in the wings. Recruiters pay $500 for this turnkey session. That is a bargain. Great training information is provided for all to view.

Teach Oregon

www.ospa.k12.or.us

Barbra Cooper, Northwest Education Technology &
Oregon School Personnel Assoc., Tualatin, OR 07062
Ph: 503-472-1431   E-mail: (See Notes)

Jobs: **Yes** Cost to post jobs: **Free** Cost to see jobs: **Free**	
Resumes: **Yes** Cost to post resumes: **Fee** Cost to see resumes: **N/A**	
E-mail Alert (Push): **N/A**	
Specialty: **Ed/K-12**	
Industry: **Education**	
Feature: **N/A**	
Location: **US/NW/OR**	

Teach Oregon is the site for the Oregon School Personnel Association. Future teachers can electronically apply through a third-party company in Oregon (NY will be coming—www.otas.com). If you want a job in the Northwest, here's a way to get there. Applicants pay $15 to process their application, and submit it to ten Oregon school districts. Click on Oregon Educational Job Search, and you will link to many of the district's job web pages.

TeacherJobs.com

www.teacherjobs.com/

G.A. McDougall, National Educators Employment Review
P.O. Box 60309, Colorado Springs, CO 80960
Ph: 719-632-5877   Fax: 800-377-1146

Jobs: **Yes** Cost to post jobs: **Free** Cost to see jobs: **Fee**	
Resumes: **Yes** Cost to post resumes: **Free** Cost to see resumes: **Free**	
E-mail Alert (Push): **N/A**	
Specialty: **Ed/K-12**	
Industry: **Ed/K-12**	
Feature: **N/A**	
Location: **US**	

The National Educators Employment Review is a monthly publication, and the intent of this site is to get you to spend $52 to subscribe. Recruiters can post positions and see resumes for free, but job seekers can only see a few samples of job openings. To see the bulk of the free postings, you have to subscribe to the publication. Search engine helps job seekers to find jobs by state.

TechJobBank

205.230.23.123

E-mail: info@techjobbank.com

Jobs: **Yes**   Cost to post jobs: **Fee**   Cost to see jobs: **Free**
Resumes: **Yes**   Cost to post resumes: **Free**   Cost to see resumes: **Fee**
E-mail Alert (Push): **N/A**
Specialty: **All**
Industry: **All**
Feature: **Meta-links**
Location: **US**

TechJobBank has an ominous homepage with graphics that aren't particularly inviting. But, dare to enter, and applicants will find links to hundreds of employers and a search engine for the extensive database. We like the "Note Pad" technology where job seekers can then check the jobs they have an interest in and, if their resume is registered, have it sent out to all the checked employers simultaneously. Needs a job alert system to make our top list.

TechJobs SuperSite

supersite.net/techjobs

Wendy Eng, SuperSite.Net
10228 N. Stelling Road, Cupertino, CA 95014
Ph: 408-343-0300   Fax: 408-252-3081   E-mail: sales@supersite.net

Jobs: **Yes**   Cost to post jobs: **Fee**   Cost to see jobs: **Free**
Resumes: **No**   Cost to post resumes: **N/A**   Cost to see resumes: **N/A**
E-mail Alert (Push): **No**
Specialty: **IT & Nonexempt**   **Technical**
Industry: **All**
Feature: **N/A**
Location: **Int'l/UK/US**

TechJobs SuperSite posts technical positions from dozens of corporations. This is one of the few sites that lists "hourly positions" with its own recruiting section. Recruiters can post five jobs for three months for $1,200. Fifteen job banks are listed on this site (left side of home page are the links) in various high-tech/IT areas. Site appears to be the repository (of multiple points of entry) for Sun World, Java World, MacWorld, NCworld, Netscape etc.

Technical Writers to the Rescue

www.mindspring.com/~panin/writers.htm

Nina Panzica, Society for Technical Communications,
E-mail: panin@mindspring.com

Jobs: **No**	
Cost to post jobs: N/A	
Cost to see jobs: N/A	
Resumes: **No**	
Cost to post resumes: **Free**	
Cost to see resumes: **Free**	
E-mail Alert (Push): N/A	
Specialty: **Communications/ Technical Writing**	
Industry: **All**	
Feature: N/A	
Location: **US/Int'l**	

Technical Writers to the Rescue hosts an important connection for technical writing consultants. The site's volunteer, Nina Panzica, is a senior member of the Atlanta chapter of the Society for Technical Communication. Writers who wish to be listed need to e-mail their profile, and up it goes. Resumes from all over the world can be viewed for free.

Telecommuting Jobs

www.tjobs.com

Sol Levine, Levine Communications
1001 Greenbay Road, Winnetka, IL 60093
Ph: 847-835-2180   Fax: 847-835-2183   E-mail: levine@wwa.com

Jobs: **Yes**	
Cost to post jobs: **Free**	
Cost to see jobs: **Free**	
Resumes: **No**	
Cost to post resumes: **Free**	
Cost to see resumes: **Free**	
E-mail Alert (Push): N/A	
Specialty: **Telecommuting**	
Industry: **All**	
Feature: N/A	
Location: **US**	

Telecommuting Jobs will give job seekers and recruiters a great place to discuss this increasingly important work place component. Job seekers can post brief profiles with links to their site, or an online resume for free. Recruiters can post positions and view job seekers profiles...also free.

Telecommuting, Teleworking, and Alternative Officing

www.gilgordon.com

Gil Gordon, Gil Gordon Associates, 10 Donner Court, Monmouth Junction, NJ 08852
Ph: 732-329-2266 Fax: 732-329-2703   E-mail: gil@gilgordon.com

Jobs: **No**	
Cost to post jobs: N/A	
Cost to see jobs: N/A	
Resumes: **No**	
Cost to post resumes: N/A	
Cost to see resumes: N/A	
E-mail Alert (Push): N/A	
Specialty: **All/Telecommuting**	
Industry: **All**	
Feature: N/A	
Location: **US/Int'l**	

Telecommuting Tools is provided by Gil Gordon, one of the world's leading experts on the subject. Great insight into what it takes to work from home or develop a telecommuting effort can be found here.

Television & Radio News Research

www.missouri.edu/~jourvs/index.html

Vernon Stone, Missouri School of Journalism
U. of Missouri, 3805 W. Rollins Road, Columbia, MO 65203
Ph: 573-882-9939   E-mail: jourvs@showme.missouri.edu

Jobs: **No**	
Cost to post jobs: N/A	
Cost to see jobs: N/A	
Resumes: **No**	
Cost to post resumes: N/A	
Cost to see resumes: N/A	
E-mail Alert (Push): N/A	
Specialty: **Communications Broadcast**	
Industry: **Broadcast Media**	
Feature: **Meta-links**	
Location: **US**	

Television and Radio News Research offers the authors articles regarding careers in TV and radio. Industry-related salary survey information is available.

Top Echelon

www.topechelon.com

Top Echelon Network
PO Box 21390, Canton, OH 44701
Ph: 330-455-1433   Fax: 330-455-8813   E-mail: rex@topechelon.com

Jobs: **Yes**	
Cost to post jobs: **Fee**	
Cost to see jobs: **Free**	
Resumes: **No**	
Cost to post resumes: N/A	
Cost to see resumes: N/A	
E-mail Alert (Push): N/A	
Specialty: **All**	
Industry: **All**	
Feature: N/A	
Location: **US**	

Top Echelon is the owner of the "Recruiter's Exchange," an online system for agency recruiters to share resumes and split fees. This service is only open for third-party recruiting firms. There are different levels of service from the web, which start at $29 and up per month. Site claims to have done over 1,500 split placements in 1997, while having signed up over 2,500 agencies in all disciplines. Search engine is a great tool for job seekers to find agencies in their area or discipline.

Top Jobs on the Net

www.mainquad.com

Kevin Watters, Student Advantage
1770 Union Street, San Francisco, CA 94123
Ph: 415-346-4242   Fax: 415-353-0685   E-mail: kevin@mainquad.com

Jobs: **No**	
Cost to post jobs: N/A	
Cost to see jobs: N/A	
Resumes: **No**	
Cost to post resumes: **Free**	
Cost to see resumes: **Fee**	
E-mail Alert (Push): N/A	
Specialty: **College**	
Industry: **All**	
Feature: N/A	
Location: **US**	

Student Advantage has career information for today's college student. An article about internships, and another about making your resume irresistible made for interesting reading. If you are a high school student, check out the pre-college resource center so you can find the $$$ to enter the big time. Site's main focus is to sell products to the student market. Warning: all parents should hold on to their credit cards when viewing this site.

Top Jobs USA

www.topjobsusa.com

David R. Mayne, Jr, DiSX, Inc
385 E. 800 S., Orem, UT 84097
Ph: 888-562-7872   Fax: 801-226-8393   E-mail: sales@topjobsusa.com

Jobs: **Yes**	
Cost to post jobs: **Fee**	
Cost to see jobs: **Free**	
Resumes: **Yes**	
Cost to post resumes: **Free**	
Cost to see resumes: **Fee**	
E-mail Alert (Push): N/A	
Specialty: **All**	
Industry: **All**	
Feature: N/A	
Location: **US**	

TOPjobs USA claims it is the #1 job warehouse for professional, managerial and technical specialists. Recruiters pay from $16 – $125 to post a position depending on the package selected. Using the site's search engine job seekers can view positions by state, title or company. Resume database can be searched for a fee. Positions are updated twice a week. "Joy Club" is a weekly column on how to conduct a successful job search. Lots of alliances drive traffic, but we found more claims than disclosure.

Town Online

www.townonline.com/working

Glenn Gutmacher, Community Newspaper Company
254 Second Avenue, Needham, MA 02194
Ph: 781-433-8213   Fax: 781-433-7888   E-mail: ggutmach@cnc.com

Jobs: **Yes**	
Cost to post jobs: **Fee**	
Cost to see jobs: **Free**	
Resumes: **No**	
Cost to post resumes: N/A	
Cost to see resumes: N/A	
E-mail Alert (Push): **Job Seeker**	
Specialty: **All**	
Industry: **All**	
Feature: N/A	
Location: **US/NE/MA**	

Town Online is the website for many of New England's (MA) local, weekly papers (100+). The "Working" section provides a job agent that will accept your profile and e-mail position matches to your doorstep. Recruiters pay $50 to post a position ($28 each additional) if a print ad appears in the paper. Site's resume database has recently had some problems, and will be back up later in 1999. A Q&A for career questions, legal issues, and Joyce Lain Kennedy's columns make for easy viewing. Links to numerous salary surveys locally and nationally give added value to this site.

Training Net

www.trainingnet.com

Amar Hhaliwal, TrainingNet Computer Services Limited
103-2609 Westview Drive, Ste 405, North Vancouver, BC V7N4N2
Ph: 604-980-0643   Fax: 604-980-4448   E-mail: info@trainingnet.com

Jobs: **Yes** Cost to post jobs: **Free** Cost to see jobs: **Free**	
Resumes: **Yes** Cost to post resumes: **Free** Cost to see resumes: **Free**	
E-mail Alert (Push): N/A	
Specialty: **Human Resources/ T&D**	
Industry: **All**	
Feature: N/A	
Location: **US/Int'l/Canada**	

Training Net gives employers and job seekers free access to jobs and resumes, with direct contact information. Main focus of this site is to provide services to professionals in the training field. Visitors who register will be sent a weekly newsletter on the latest and greatest products in this field. Site also provides live discussions (TeleForums) with experts in different training fields.

Training SuperSite Job Bank

www.trainingsupersite.com/jobset.htm

Jobs: **Yes** Cost to post jobs: **Fee** Cost to see jobs: **Free**	
Resumes: **Yes** Cost to post resumes: **Free** Cost to see resumes: **Fee**	
E-mail Alert (Push): **Job Seeker**	
Specialty: **Human Resources/ T&D**	
Industry: **All**	
Feature: N/A	
Location: **Int'l/Canada/US**	

The Training SuperSite Job Bank uses push technology, and has a niche HR focus (T&D). Job seekers can view positions by company, position, location or specialty, or register to have the positions sent to their e-mail address. Resumes are $200 a month to view. Positions can be posted for $200/month as well.

trans-ACTION

www.trans-action.com

Tim Reeder, Cahners Business Information
201 King of Prussia Road, Radnor, PA 19089
Ph: 800-866-0206   Fax: 610-964-4663   E-mail: treeder@cahners.com

Jobs: **Yes** Cost to post jobs: **Fee** Cost to see jobs: **Free**	
Resumes: **No** Cost to post resumes: N/A Cost to see resumes: N/A	
E-mail Alert (Push): N/A	
Specialty: **All**	
Industry: **All**	
Feature: N/A	
Location: **US**	

trans-ACTION is a publisher's web site for automotive, trucking, electronics, optics & opthamology, industrial equipment, services, food equipment & services, assembly & machinery, logistics/warehousing, metals & metalworking magazines which all have their job postings displayed on this site (web address appears in Chilton's 40+ magazines). Drilling into the site to find the jobs is cumbersome. Recruiters pay $75 per month per job posting.

Troops to Teachers

jobsearch.miningco.com/msubteach.htm

Andrea Sunderville, NJ State Department of Education
P.O. Box 500, Trenton, NJ 08625
Ph: 609-984-6377   Fax: 609-984-3356

Jobs: **Yes** Cost to post jobs: **Free** Cost to see jobs: **Free**	
Resumes: **Yes** Cost to post resumes: **Free** Cost to see resumes: **Free**	
E-mail Alert (Push): N/A	
Specialty: **Ed/K-12**	
Industry: **Education**	
Feature: N/A	
Location: **US**	

Troops to Teachers is geared to professionals coming out of the military who want a career in education. Over 1,000 teaching positions throughout the U.S. were listed at this site. If you wish to post your resume, you need to be in the military or a veteran. School districts must register with the site to obtain a password to post. Great concept, but the password requirement is a bit awkward.

TV Jobs

www.tvjobs.com

Mark Hollowa, Broadcast Employment Services
P.O. Box 4116, Oceanside, CA 92052
Ph: 760-754-8177   Fax: 760-754-2115   E-mail: info@tvjobs.com

Jobs: **Yes** Cost to post jobs: **Free** Cost to see jobs: **Fee**	
Resumes: **Yes** Cost to post resumes: **Free** Cost to see resumes: **Free**	
E-mail Alert (Push): **Job Seeker**	
Specialty: **Entertainment/ Broadcasting**	
Industry: **Entertainment/ Broadcasting**	
Feature: N/A	
Location: **US/Canada/UK**	

TV Jobs gives job seekers a chance to go to the "really big show." Links to over 1,600 stations are provided through the site's search engine, which can be used 11 different ways. Job seekers pay $15 – $75 to post their resume, and $10 per year to view job openings. Recruiters can post positions and see resumes for free. Resumes are exclusively broadcast related.

Twin Cities Job Page

www.fentonnet.com/jobs/html

Michael Fenton, Fentonnet Inc.
3716 42nd Avenue South, Minneapolis, MN 55406
Ph: 612-724-1845   E-mail: info@fentonnet.com

Jobs: **Yes** Cost to post jobs: **Fee** Cost to see jobs: **Free**	
Resumes: **Yes** Cost to post resumes: **Free** Cost to see resumes: **Free**	
E-mail Alert (Push): N/A	
Specialty: **All**	
Industry: **All**	
Feature: N/A	
Location: **US/MW/MN**	

Twin Cities warehouses resumes, and employers can view for free. Have your scrolling digit ready as the resumes are in no particular order. Recruiters pay $50 to post a position, and unfortunately, there were only two companies advertising on our last visit.

US Air Force Employment Home Page

www.af.mil/careers

Don Pelfrey, US Air Force Recruiting Service
Headquarters, 550 D Street, Suite 1, Randolph Air Force Base, TX 78150
Ph: 210-652-5993   E-mail: pelfreyd@hq.afpc.af.mil

Jobs: **Yes** Cost to post jobs: N/A Cost to see jobs: **Free**	**Air Force Careers** has recently revised their site, and includes job and career listings for civilian, enlisted and officer personnel with pay rates.
Resumes: **Yes** Cost to post resumes: **Free** Cost to see resumes: N/A (See Notes)	
E-mail Alert (Push): N/A	
Specialty: **All**	
Industry: **Military**	
Feature: **Military**	
Location: **US**	

US Job Network High Tech Job & Resume Bank

www.usjob.net

Julie Deese, Jaye Communications
550 Interstate North Pkwy, Suite 150, Atlanta, GA 30339
Ph: 770-752-8128   Fax: 770-612-0780   E-mail: julie.deese@usjob.net

Jobs: **Yes** Cost to post jobs: **Fee** Cost to see jobs: **Free**	**US Job Network** is primarily a southeast site, but is expanding to other areas. Recruiters pay $295 per month for unlimited postings, and have the ability to search the resume database. On our visit, 23 corporations had listings on their job boards. Over 1,700 resumes were posted, of which 1,000 were from Georgia companies. Recruiters automatically receive e-mails of new resumes matching employer job requirements. A company profile includes contact information, a listing of all jobs posted, and a direct link to the company website.
Resumes: **Yes** Cost to post resumes: **Free** Cost to see resumes: **Fee**	
E-mail Alert (Push): **Employer**	
Specialty: IT	
Industry: **All**	
Feature: N/A	
Location: **US/SE/GA**	

USM Resources for G/L/B Students

macweb.acs.usm.maine.edu/csce/career_glb.html

Career Services & Coop. Education, Univ. of Southern Maine
100 Payson Smith Hall, P.O. Box 9300, Maine 04104
E-mail: bliss@usm.maine.edu

Jobs: **No** Cost to post jobs: N/A Cost to see jobs: N/A
Resumes: **No** Cost to post resumes: N/A Cost to see resumes: N/A
E-mail Alert (Push): N/A
Specialty: **College**
Industry: **All**
Feature: **Diversity/Meta-link**s
Location: **US**

The **University of Southern Maine** provides links to career counseling resources for gay, lesbian and bisexual individuals. Main features are links to university programs and articles regarding gay work issues.

Virtual Edge

www.virtual-edge.net

Diane Smith
P.O. Box 3, McCarthy Ridge Road, Forksville, PA 08616
Ph: 717-924-4142   Fax: 717-924-4146   E-mail: dsmith@virtual-edge.net

Jobs: **Yes** Cost to post jobs: **Fee** Cost to see jobs: **Free**
Resumes: **Yes** Cost to post resumes: **Free** Cost to see resumes: **Fee**
E-mail Alert (Push): **Job Seeker**
Specialty: **IT/QA**
Industry: **All**
Feature: N/A
Location: **US/Int'l/China/Japan**

Virtual Edge is a brand-new site that has interesting features for recruiting in the IT/high-tech world. All visitors must register to enter the career center, a matching job service. Job seekers select the areas that are of interest, and the site matches your skills with their client employers. Many large firms have links to openings here. A resume bank will soon be a feature on this site, and will cost recruiters $750 per month to try. Posting a position costs $40 for a 60-day run (other packages are available). Site will push openings to all job seekers who register. Very interesting features.

Virtual Interviewing Assistant

www.ukans.edu/cwis/units/coms2/via/index.html

University of Kansas
Department of Communication Studies
Ph: 785-864-3633   Fax: 785-864-5203   E-mail: coms2@raven.cc.ukans.edu

Jobs: **No**	
Cost to post jobs: N/A	
Cost to see jobs: N/A	
Resumes: **No**	
Cost to post resumes: N/A	
Cost to see resumes: N/A	
E-mail Alert (Push): N/A	
Specialty: **All**	
Industry: **All**	
Feature: **Interviewing**	
Location: **US**	

Virtual Interviewing Assistant provides everything you always wanted to know about the process, but were afraid to ask. The initial ten articles are more than worth the price of admission—free. Some of the links may not work, but this site is worth a visit by both college students and experienced professionals.

Wall Street Journal Interactive Edition

careers.wsj.com

Tony Lee, Dow Jones & Company
P.O. Box 300, Princeton, NJ 08543
Ph: 609-520-4305   E-mail: tlee@wsj.dowjones.com

Jobs: **Yes**
Cost to post jobs: **Fee**
Cost to see jobs: **Free**
Resumes: **No**
Cost to post resumes: N/A
Cost to see resumes: N/A
E-mail Alert (Push): N/A
Specialty: **Executive**
Industry: **All**
Feature: N/A
Location: **US/Int'l**

The Wall Street Journal Interactive Edition is like the energizer bunny...it just keeps growing and growing. Extensive career information and a section with dozens of corporations, where job seekers can search on all the company openings (not just the ones that appear in print) anchor the site. **WSJ** also surprised the staffing industry this year announcing an alliance, FutureStep, with Korn Ferry, an executive search firm. **WSJ** markets FutureStep, which registered 72,000 executives in four months. Career columnists, salaries and profiles, job hunting help, advice on advancing at work, HR issues and more are here. For subscribers to WSJ Online, job seekers have the use of a tool to search the entire database to target opportunities by job function, company, industry, educational requirements, location and other criteria. Each job listing on the site is automatically linked to a complete briefing book on the employer. This includes financial data, a profile of the company's business, and all the recent news articles out of the WSJ. The Interactive Journal costs $49 for a one-year subscription. A comprehensive database of 3,500 executive search firms (Kennedy Directory)can also be viewed on this site for a fee. Top site with the backing and ideas to lead.

Washington Post-Career Post

www.washingtonpost.com/wp-adv/classifieds/career

Jamie Hammond, Washington Post
1150-15th Street N.W., Washington, DC 20071
Ph: 202-334-6000   Fax: 202-334-5561   E-mail: (See Notes)

Jobs: **Yes**
Cost to post jobs: **Fee**
Cost to see jobs: **Free**
Resumes: **No**
Cost to post resumes: N/A
Cost to see resumes: N/A
E-mail Alert (Push): N/A
Specialty: **All**
Industry: **All**
Feature: N/A
Location: **US/E/DC**

Washington Post-CareerPost gives added value to the printed word. Jobs and resumes are also on CareerPath.com. Numerous career articles written by Dick Bolles and others can be found on this site. Local job fair information is posted for all to view. One of the first publishers to offer jobseekers the ability to search ALL the jobs posted to a subscribing employers web site using technology developed by Junglee Corporation.

Water Resources Employment Opportunities

www.uwin.siu.edu/announce/jobs/

UWIN c/o UCOWR Headquarters
4543 Faner Hall, Southern Illinois University, Carbondale, IL 62901
Fax: 618-453-2671   E-mail: submit@uwin.siu.edu

Jobs: **Yes**
Cost to post jobs: **Free**
Cost to see jobs: **Free**
Resumes: **No**
Cost to post resumes: N/A
Cost to see resumes: N/A
E-mail Alert (Push): **Job Seeker**
Specialty: **Engineering/Water**
Industry: **Utility/Water**
Feature: N/A
Location: **US**

Water Resources Employment Opportunities is hosted by Southern Illinois University. It was designed as a clearinghouse for jobs in various water resource fields. Positions are posted by academic, nonacademic and student categories. Positions are posted for free, with full contact information, and are date stamped for freshness. Hundreds of jobs are posted here each month.

Water Works Jobs

www.awwa.org

Torey Lightcap, American Water Works Association
6666 West Quincy Avenue, Denver, CO 80235
Ph: 303-347-6166   Fax: 303-794-7310   E-mail: tlightca@awwa.org

Jobs: **Yes** Cost to post jobs: **Free** Cost to see jobs: **Free**
Resumes: **No** Cost to post resumes: N/A Cost to see resumes: N/A
E-mail Alert (Push): N/A
Specialty: **Science/** **Environmental**
Industry: **Water**
Feature: N/A
Location: **US**

Water Works Jobs had over 60 jobs posted for industry-related opportunities. Many articles for career information are also available. Jobs can be e-mailed to the AWWA site, and are posted in two to three days for free. Site can be viewed in English and Spanish

Web Jobs USA

www.webjobsusa.com

Fran Grossman
395 South End Avenue, Suite 15-D, New York, NY 10280
Ph: 212-912-0175   E-mail: jobs@webjobsusa.com

Jobs: **Yes** Cost to post jobs: **Fee** Cost to see jobs: **Free**
Resumes: **Yes** Cost to post resumes: **Free** Cost to see resumes: **Fee**
E-mail Alert (Push): **Job Seeker**
Specialty: **IT/New Media/WWW**
Industry: **All**
Feature: N/A
Location: **US/Int'l**

Web Jobs touts itself as the resource for finding jobs, projects, salary information, training and more—all related to the Internet. Everyone is looking for webmasters, programmers or sales professionals, and this may be the place to find them. Recruiters pay $499 per year to access the resume database, and job posting costs $75 for a 60-day run. For an additional $50, your job will be e-mailed to over 10,000 candidates. Positions are posted throughout the U.S., and recently an international section has been added. Jobs are in 13 specific areas of the U.S., and there is also an overall location category.

Weed Jobs

www.nrcan.gc.ca/~bcampbel

Robert Campbell, Canadian Forest Service
1219 Queen Street East, P.O. Box 490, Sault Ste. Marie, Canada P6A 5M7
Ph: 705-759-5740   Fax: 705-759-5700   E-mail: bcampbel@nrn1.nrcan.gc.ca

Jobs: **Yes**	
Cost to post jobs: **Free**	
Cost to see jobs: **Free**	
Resumes: **No**	
Cost to post resumes: **N/A**	
Cost to see resumes: **N/A**	
E-mail Alert (Push): **No**	
Specialty: **Sci/Weeds & Soil**	
Industry: **Agriculture**	
Feature: N/A	
Location: **Int'l/Canada/US**	

Weed Jobs keeps sprouting positions for scientists, postdoctoral and graduate students, who are studying different areas of weeds and soil. Talk about a niche site! Positions are date posted, and provide direct contact information. Some very large corporations and universities have posted positions here. This site is the official job placement service for the Weed Science Society of America, and has been endorsed by the Canadian Expert Committee on Weeds.

Westech's Virtual Job Fair

www.vjf.com

Bill Lennan, WesTech
4701 Patrick Henry Drive #1901, Santa Clara, CA 95054
Ph: 408-970-8800   Fax: 408-980-5103   E-mail: webmaster@vjf

Jobs: **Yes**	
Cost to post jobs: **Fee**	
Cost to see jobs: **Free**	
Resumes: **Yes**	
Cost to post resumes: **Free**	
Cost to see resumes: **Fee**	
E-mail Alert (Push): **N/A**	
Specialty: **IT**	
Industry: **All**	
Feature: **Job Fairs**	
Location: **US**	

Westech's site has new features and a new look. You can search for jobs by company or title. Your search will take you to a position description, and to a link to the corporation's information page where you can view all positions of that organization. A note pad concept allows the job seeker to enter an access code and password, and their resume will be automatically sent to the employer. This is one of the largest job fair promoters in the U.S. It also combines a print publication with each of its events. Mainly a west coast operation, Westech was acquired by an Arizona publisher in 1997, and then bought an east coast job fair company (Target Career Fair) several months later. Job seekers can register their resume confidentially if they choose. Jobs are listed from corporations in many different states. A site to watch as job fairs continue to change throughout the US.

Will Work 4 Food

www.2020tech.com/ww4f/index.html

E-mail: rich@2020tech.com

Jobs: **Yes** Cost to post jobs: **Fee** Cost to see jobs: **Free**
Resumes: **Yes** Cost to post resumes: **Free** Cost to see resumes: **Free** (See Notes)
E-mail Alert (Push): N/A
Specialty: **Telecommuting**
Industry: **All**
Feature: N/A
Location: **US**

Will Work 4 Food has been created for the world of telecommuting. Recruiters can post positions for free. Consultants pay $20 for a six-month run to announce their skills to the world. Site keeps the 100 most recent posts for each category. As the numbers rise, your opening may disappear. Those that pay, obviously stay. Dozens of interested telecommuters have listed their profiles. Very new when we first visited, and few openings were posted.

Windows for Jobs

www.delphi.com/windowsforjobs

Marc Le Vine, InfoPro Corporation
1000 Rt. 9 North, Suite 102, Woodbridge, NJ 07095
Ph: 732-283-2589   Fax: 732-283-0853   E-mail: mlevine@infoprocorp.com

Jobs: **Yes** Cost to post jobs: **Free** Cost to see jobs: **Free**
Resumes: **Yes** Cost to post resumes: **Free** Cost to see resumes: **Free**
E-mail Alert (Push): N/A
Specialty: **IT**
Industry: **All**
Feature: N/A
Location: **US/NJ**

Windows for Jobs was created for IT professionals to communicate with fellow job seekers. Site is set up as a listserv where messages are exchanged. Brief profiles and job openings are available to anyone who registers. A live chatroom with recruiting experts and IT professionals is also available. Great focus on an idea that can't lose.

Windows NT Resource Center

www.bhs.com/default.asp

Dave Baker, Beverly Hills Software
8845 W. Olympic Blvd., Suite 200, Beverly Hills,, CA 90211
Ph: 310-358-8311 Fax: 310-358-0326 E-mail: jobcenteradmin@bhs.com

Jobs: **Yes**
Cost to post jobs: **Free**
Cost to see jobs: **Free**
Resumes: **Yes**
Cost to post resumes: **Free**
Cost to see resumes: **Free**
E-mail Alert (Push): N/A
Specialty: **IT/Windows NT**
Industry: **All**
Feature: N/A
Location: **US**

Windows NT Resource Center has recently been updated, and the changes make for a smooth ride for professionals with these skills. Resumes and jobs are dated, and can be posted or viewed for free (and you no longer have to register). Recruiters can search resumes, job title, topic, state or country.

WinJobs

www.winjobs.com/marketing

G.D.Prabhu, TMI Network
B-1, Vikrampuri, Secunderabad, Hyderabad, India
Ph: 009-140-7765026 E-mail: winjobs@hd1.vsnl.net.in

Jobs: **Yes**
Cost to post jobs: **Fee**
Cost to see jobs: **Free**
Resumes: **No**
Cost to post resumes: N/A
Cost to see resumes: N/A
E-mail Alert (Push): **Job Seeker**
Specialty: **IT**
Industry: **IT**
Feature: **Diversity**
Location: **Int'l/India**

WinJobs.com is a monthly online IT magazine which posts job opportunities for professionals who want to work in India and elsewhere. Recruiters pay Rs. 15000 per ad, with other packages available. Job seekers who register can have hot jobs "pushed" to them via e-mail. Site has won several awards for its design and functionality.

womenCONNECT.com

ww.womenconnect.com

Mary McGann, WomenConnect.com
8260 Greensboro Drive, Suite 200A, Mclean, VA 22102
Ph: 703-556-9662   Fax: 703-556-9668   E-mail: jriba@womenconnect.com

Jobs: **Yes** Cost to post jobs: **Fee** Cost to see jobs: **Free**	
Resumes: **No** Cost to post resumes: N/A Cost to see resumes: N/A	
E-mail Alert (Push): **Job Seeker**	
Specialty: **All**	
Industry: **All**	
Feature: **Diversity**	
Location: **US**	

womenCONNECT.com has grown tremendously since our last visit. Seventy-five jobs were posted where none were before, and they are all date stamped. Recruiters pay $120 to post a position for one month. Job seekers can cut and paste their resume or view "map blaster" to get directions to their employer of choice. If you register, the site's agent will match your background and e-mail positions to your doorstep. Articles are from *Working Woman* and *Working Mother* magazines. Interesting articles geared to women's issues A new mentoring section (under construction) round out a great effort worth supporting.

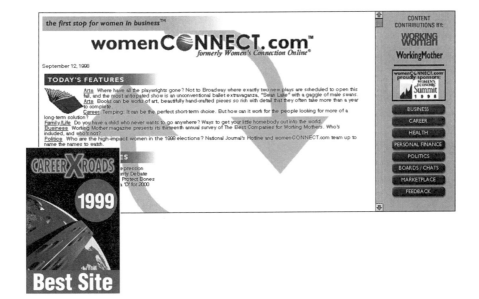

Women in Higher Education

www.wihe.com/index.htm

Mary Conroy-Zenke, WIHE Company
1934 Monroe Street, Madison, WI 53711
Ph: 608-251-3232   Fax: 608-284-0601   E-mail: career@wihe.com

Jobs: **Yes**	
Cost to post jobs: **Fee**	
Cost to see jobs: **Free**	
Resumes: **No**	
Cost to post resumes: **N/A**	
Cost to see resumes: **N/A**	
E-mail Alert (Push): **N/A**	
Specialty: **Teaching**	
Industry: **Higher Education**	
Feature: **C/M**	
Location: **US/Int'l**	

Women in Higher Education provides recruiters access to 12,000 women who work in, or have aspirations for, the field of education. Recruiters pay $360 and up to be in this monthly publication and post jobs on the web. Positions can be viewed by function and region of the U.S. Great opportunities such as president, chancellor, VP, provost, and dean are just a few of the titles listed with direct contact information. Dr. Athena provides career guidance in a Q&A format.

Women in Technology & Industry-WITI

www.witi.com

David Leighton, International Network of Women in Technology
4641 Burnet Ave., Sherman Oaks, CA 91403
Ph: 818-990-6705   Fax: 818-906-3299   E-mail: dave@witi.com

Jobs: **Yes**	
Cost to post jobs: **Fee**	
Cost to see jobs: **Free**	
Resumes: **Yes**	
Cost to post resumes: **N/A**	
Cost to see resumes: **N/A**	
E-mail Alert (Push): **Job Seeker**	
Specialty: **Executive**	
Industry: **All**	
Feature: **Diversity**	
Location: **US/Int'l**	

Women in Int'l. Technology & Industry is a nonprofit organization that partnered with CareerMosaic in 1998. The resume database is now $995/year (you cannot purchase WITI alone). Recruiters pay $160 to post positions for a 30-day run. Job seekers can post their resume, but must return to the site to obtain recruiter responses. Site states it has over 60,000 resumes, but, are those from women in technology or from CareerMosaic's database? This organization is dedicated to increasing the number of women in executive roles, helping women become more financially independent, technology-literate, and to encourage young women to choose careers in science and technology. Managerial level and above positions should be posted. WITI has also built a partnership with *Info World* to publish a special section for the organization during each of their conferences.

WorkAvenue.com

www.workavenue.com

Armand LaCrone, Star Tribune
42 Portland Avenue, Minneapolis, MN 55488
Fax: 612-673-4572

Jobs: **Yes** Cost to post jobs: **Fee** Cost to see jobs: **Free**	
Resumes: **Yes** Cost to post resumes: **Free** Cost to see resumes: **Fee**	
E-mail Alert (Push): N/A	
Specialty: **All**	
Industry: **All**	
Feature: N/A	
Location: **US**	

You might think you're at the classifieds of a major paper. Nah. Although the *Minneapolis Star Tribune* is one of the partners of this regional job and resume site, you won't find thousands of jobs listed here.The cost is right on the money though. Just $35 to post a job, but there is a catch. **WorkAvenue.com** uses its technology to match an employer's posted position with existing resumes, and then makes them available to the recruiter for only $100 each. Fortunately, you only pay for the ones you choose. We understand this model is undergoing reengineering. Maybe somebody noticed that they are competing with their own print product.

Work Zone

www.workzone.net

KAPS Communication
1440 Whalley Avenue, New Haven, CT 06515
Ph: 800-947-4361   E-mail: kjurow@workzone.net

Jobs: **No** Cost to post jobs: N/A Cost to see jobs: N/A	
Resumes: **No** Cost to post resumes: N/A Cost to see resumes: N/A	
E-mail Alert (Push): N/A	
Specialty: **All**	
Industry: **All**	
Feature: N/A	
Location: **US**	

The Work Zone, as described by Lycos' career website, is a "clean-looking and easy-to-navigate site that focuses as much on career transition as it does on the typical job search. It offers interesting overviews and straightforward advice." We agree. The free job search and career transition material available to users is based on the workbook of Nancy Schreter, publisher of *Search Bulletin*.

Workforce Online

www.workforceonline.com

E-mail: markaw@workforceonline.com

Jobs: **Yes**
Cost to post jobs: **Fee**
Cost to see jobs: **Free**
Resumes: **No**
Cost to post resumes: **Free**
Cost to see resumes: **Fee**
E-mail Alert (Push): **Job Seeker**
Specialty: **Human Resources**
Industry: **All**
Feature: N/A
Location: **US**

Workforce Online appears to be in a partnership with E-Span (JobOptions), CareerMosaic and the MonsterBoard. Two of the three allow you to post positions, but we are not sure where they will be posted. MonsterBoard's agent will allow you to register your skills, and place the information into a profile "In" box at the site or you can have leads e-mailed to you. Site is designed for HR Professionals. The "HR Tip of the Day" and "Legal Resources" have interesting articles, and we got a chuckle out of the "HR Humor" section. Recruiters pay $160 to post a job on one side of the house, and $95 on the JobOptions side. More questions than answers here.

The Write Jobs

www.writerswrite.com/jobs

Writers Write, Inc.
5930-E Royal Lane, Suite 106, Dallas, TX 75230
E-mail: advertise@writerswrite.com

Jobs: **Yes**
Cost to post jobs: **Free**
Cost to see jobs: **Free**
Resumes: **No**
Cost to post resumes: N/A
Cost to see resumes: N/A
E-mail Alert (Push): N/A
Specialty: **Commun/Writing**
Industry: **All**
Feature: N/A
Location: **US**

The Write Jobs is a job board that maintains books and listings of current employment opportunities for those with writing skills. Positions listed include positions as editors, staff, freelance and technical writers etc. It's free to see and free to post. Check it out.

Yahoo Classifieds

classifieds.yahoo.com/employment.html

Yahoo
Ph: 408-731-3300

Jobs: **Yes** Cost to post jobs: **Free** Cost to see jobs: **Free**	
Resumes: **Yes** Cost to post resumes: **Free** Cost to see resumes: **Free**	
E-mail Alert (Push): **N/A**	
Specialty: **All**	
Industry: **All**	
Feature: N/A	
Location: **US/Int'l**	

Yahoo is the site that everyone watches to see what they do. Employers post jobs for free. From here, you can see openings in 52 major cities, search by state, or browse national listings. One of the few sites where you know that the statistics on the traffic at the site is not all hype. It does take longer than it should to drill down to the job level, and employers posting an opening will not find it user-friendly—which is why other sites have agreements to post jobs here. Still, **Yahoo** is definitely worth an experiment. Price is right, go for it.

Youth@Work

www.youthatwork.org/

Ph: 408-522-9845   Fax: 408-522-9850   E-mail: admin@youthatwork.org

Jobs: **Yes** Cost to post jobs: **Fee** Cost to see jobs: **Free**	
Resumes: **No** Cost to post resumes: **N/A** Cost to see resumes: **N/A**	
E-mail Alert (Push): **N/A**	
Specialty: **College**	
Industry: **All**	
Feature: N/A	
Location: **US**	

Youth@Work's primary objective is to link job-seeking youths, ages 14-24, with hiring managers throughout Santa Clara and San Mateo Counties in California. With simple buttons that state "Hire Me" or "Work for Me," this site almost has its act together. There are over 900 jobs posted in all categories—from temporary to full-time openings. Search engine works well, but all jobs are coded, and you have to contact a **Youth@Work** office by telephone to obtain additional information.

Cross Reference Index

The sites below are our picks for 1999 as the "best of the best". They include large "career hubs" like CareerMag, MonsterBoard, CareerMosaic and NationJob with well thought through strategies as well as smaller sites like Asia-Net and Career Espresso that fill a marketplace niche. The print media—CareerPath.com, Mercury Center and The Gate— are represented along with companies working together in Talent Alliance, SmartDog and DaVinciTimes and associations like Science Professional Network, SHRM and JobWeb, who are striving to add member benefits and support their respective professions. At the end of the day, your best sites are the ones that work for you. *CAREERXROADS* was designed to give you the information to do just that. Good hunting!

4Work
www.4work.com

American Banker CareerZone
www.americanbanker.com/

America's Employers
www.americasemployers.com

Asia-Net
www.asia-net.com

BenefitsLink
www.benefitslink.com/

BioOnline
www.bio.com

Branch Out
www.branchout.com

CareerBuilder
www.careerbuilder.com

Career City
www.careercity.com

Career Espresso/Emory University
www.sph.emory.edu/studentservice/Career.html

CareerMagazine
www.careermag.com

CareerMosaic
www.careermosaic.com

CareerPath.com
www.careerpath.com

Career Shop
www.careershop.com

CareerWeb
www.cweb.com

College Central Network
www.collegecentral.com

The ComputerJobs Store
www.computerjobs.com

Cool Works
www.coolworks.com

DaVinci Times
www.daVinciTimes.org

DICE High Tech Jobs Online
www.dice.com

Exec-U-Net
www.execunet.com

The (San Francisco Chronicle) Gate
www.sfgate.com/classifieds/

Hard@Work
www.hardatwork.com

HeadHunter.NET
www.headhunter.net

HRSites
www.hrsites

JobDirect.com
www.jobdirect.com

JobNet
www.jobnet.com

JobOptions
www.joboptions.com

JOBTRAK
www.jobtrak.com

JobWeb
www.jobweb.org/

Jobs Careers
www.jobs-careers.com

Jobs for Programmers
www.prgjobs.com

Mercury Center Web
www.sjmercury.com

Minorities' Job Bank
www.minorities-jb.com

The Monster Board
www.monster.com

NationJob Network
www.nationjob.com

NETSHARE
www.netshare.com

Nursing Spectrum
www.nursingspectrum.com

Online Career Center
www.occ.com

Purdue's Job List
www.ups.purdue.edu/student/jobsites.htm

Resumania On-line
www.umn.edu/ohr/ecep/resume

The Riley Guide
www.dbm.com/jobguide

Science Professional Network
www.scienceonline.org

SHRM HR Jobs
www.shrm.org

Smart Dog
www.smartdog.org

**Stern Alumni Outreach
Career Resources Online**
www.stern.nyu.edu/Alumni/career.html

Talent Alliance
www.talentalliance.com

TCM's HR Careers
www.tcm.com/hr-careers

Wall St. Journal Interactive Edition
careers.wsj.com

women CONNECT.com
www.womenconnect.com

CAREER MANAGEMENT

Career Management tools, advice, tips and services. Valuable articles and information can be found on most employment sites but these are chock full.

Acorn Career Counseling
www.acornresume.com

Adguide's Employment Web Site
www.adguide.com

Alumnae Resources
www.ar.org

American Physical Therapy Assoc.
apta.edoc.com

Brave New Work World
www.newwork.com

BRINT (@BRINT)
www.brint.com

Career Action Center
www.careeraction.org/CACpublic/intro.html

Career Babe
www.careerbabe.com

Career Lab
www.careerlab.com

Career Search
www.careersearch.net

Career Talk
www.careertalk.com

Career Tool Box
www.careertoolbox.com

Careers On-Line
disserv3.stu.umn.edu/COL/

CAREERXROADS
www.careerxroads.com

Changing Times
www.lmcia.bc.ca

College Net
www.collegenet.com

Connect to Jobs
www.cabrillo.cc.ca.us/affiliate/

Five O'clock Club
www.fiveoclockclub.com

Forty Plus (Northern Calif.)
web.sirius.com/~40plus/#contact

Getting Past Go: A Survival Guide for College
www.mongen.com/getgo

Global Job Net
riceinfo.rice.edu/projects/careers

Hard@Work
www.hardatwork.com

Health Care Jobs Online
www.hcjobsonline.om

Hire Wire
www.hirewire.com

Jewish Vocational Services
www.jvsjobs.com

Job Smart California Job Search Guide
www.jobsmart.org

Kansas Careers
www-personal.ksu.edu/~dangle/

My Future
www.myfuture.com

National Business Employment Weekly
www.nbew.com

Needle in a Cyberstack
home.revealed.net/albee

NOICC
www.noicc.gov

Quintessential Career & Job Hunting Guide
www.stetson.edu/~rhansen/careers.html

Radio Frame
www.mindspring.com/~coleman/radioframe.html

Resumania On-line
www.umn.edu/ohr/ecep/resume

Student Advantage
www.mainquad.com

Television & Radio News Research
www.missouri.edu/~jourvs/index.html

Virtual Interviewing Assistant
www.ukans.edu/cwis/units/coms2/via/index.html

Women in Technology & Industry-WITI
www.witi.com

Work Zone
www.workzone.net

Seniors looking to get a fast start should consider the sites below but don't forget your own college. Most colleges and universities are now providing extensive links, services and guidance through their website. Recruiter's should analyze their targeted college's sites for additional opportunities to enhance their hiring strategies.

Adguide's Employment Web Site
www.adguide.com

The BLACK COLLEGIAN Online
www.blackcollegian.com

Branch Out
www.branchout.com

BridgePath Employment Services
www.bridgepath.com

Cal State U. Employ. Bd. Job Hunt
csueb.sfsu.edu/jobs.html

Career Central
www.careercentral.com

Career City
www.careercity.com

Career Tech.com
www.careertech.com

Career Tech.com
www.careertech.com

College Central Network
www.collegecentral.com

College Connection
www.careermosaic.com/cm/cc/cc1.html

College Grad Job Hunter
www.collegegrad.com

College News Online
www.collegenews.com/jobs.htm

Entry Level Job Seeker Assistant
members.aol.com/Dylander/jobhome.html

Getting A Job
www.americanexpress.com/student/

Getting Past Go:
A Survival Guide for College
www.mongen.com/getgo

Global Job Net
riceinfo.rice.edu/projects/careers

Great Summer Jobs
www.gsj.petersons.com

Hire Wire
www.hirewire.com

Job Direct.com
www.jobdirect.com

The Job Resource
www.thejobresource.com

JOB TRAK (JOBTRAK)
www.jobtrak.com

Job Web
www.jobweb.org/

My Future
www.myfuture.com

National Alumni Placement Assoc.
www.careers.com

Peterson's Education Center
www.petersons.com

Student Advantage
www.mainquad.com

Student Center
studentcenter.com

Summer Jobs
www.summerjobs.com

Top Jobs on the Net
www.topjobs.net

USM Resources for G/L/B Students
macweb.acs.usm.maine.edu/csce/career_glb.html

Youth@Work
www.youthatwork.org/

DIVERSITY

Everyone is on the net. Here are a few sites devoted to diverse communities. Contact community service centers, libraries, community colleges and other organizations in your locale to find more.

Africa Online Jobs
www.AfricaOnline.com/AfricaOnline/cgi/
showclasscat

Afro-Americ@: The Job Vault
www.afroam.org/information/vault/vault.html

America's Job Bank
www.ajb.dni.us

Arizona Careers Online
www.diversecity.com/jobs.html

Asia-Net
www.asia-net.com

Association for Women in Computing
www.awc-hq.org

Bilingual-Jobs
www.bilingual-jobs.com

The BLACK COLLEGIAN Online
www.blackcollegian.com

**Black Data Processing
Association Online**
www.bdpa.org

Black E.O.E Journal
www.blackeoejournal.com/jobsearch.html

Black Voices
www.blackvoices.com

**Career Center for
Workforce Diversity**
www.eop.com

Career Magazine
www.careermag.com

Career Mosaic
www.careermosaic.com

Career Women
www.careerwomen.com

Careers On-Line
disserv3.stu.umn.edu/COL/

Diversilink
www.diversilink.com

Diversity Careers Online
www.diversitycareers.com

Diversity Link
www.diversitylink.com

Electra a Women's View on Careers
electra.com

**Environmental Careers Org.
(Eco.org)**
www.eco.org

Feminist Career Center
www.feminist.org/911/911jobs.html

Forty Plus (Northern Calif.)
web.sirius.com/~40plus/#contact

Frasernet
www.frasernet.com

Hispanic Online Magazine
www.hisp.com

Inter Career Net
www.rici.com/acw

Interesting Web Sites
www.usbol.com/wjmackey/weblinks.html

Job Web
www.jobweb.org/

Kansas Careers
www-personal.ksu.edu/~dangle/

Latino Web
www.latinoweb.com/jobs/jobs.htm

LATPRO
www.latpro.com

Minorities' Job Bank
www.minorities-jb.com

**National Diversity
Newspaper Job Bank**
www.newsjobs.com

National Society of Black Engineers
www.nsbe.com

Saludos Web
www.saludos.com

SC WIST Work Pathfinder
www.harbour.sfu.ca/scwist/pathfinder/
index.htm.

Sistahspace
www.sistahspace.com

Society of Women Engineers
www.swe.org

USM Resources for G/L/B Students
macweb.acs.usm.maine.edu/csce/
career_glb.html

WinJobs
www.winjobs.com/marketing

women CONNECT.com
ww.womenconnect.com

**Women in Technology & Industry-
WITI**
www.witi.com

They are all here. Some of the biggest and some of the smallest. What is missing are all the companies (and most of the headhunters and placement firms). By next year, jobseekers will be able to search the jobs pages of as many companies as they want directly....and without having to go there one at a time. Already search engines like AltaVista are improving their capability to take you there. Other sites like CareerCast and JobOptions are building exciting new ways to search company databases directly (almost) and, internet services like Junglee Corporation, have enabled sites likatheWall Street Journal, Classifieds 2000, Washington Post and CareerPath.com to offer job seekers another way to search multiple companies for their next job. Much more to come.

SITES RECRUITERS CAN POST FOR A FEE OR FOR FREE

100 Careers in Cyberspace	Fee	Asia-Net	Fee
100 Careers in Wall Street	Fee	Association of Online Professionals	Free
4Work	Fee	Assoc. for Computing Machinery (ACM)	Fee
680 careers.com	Fee	ATI-Net	Free
A1A Computer Jobs	Fee	Au Pair in Europe	Fee
Abag Globe	Free	AutoCAD	Fee
Academe This Week	Fee	Aviation Employee Placement Service	Free
Academic Employment Network	Fee	BA Jobs (SF Bay Area Jobs)	Fee
Academic Physician & Scientist	Fee	Bakery-Net	Free
Accounting .com	Fee	Be the Boss	Fee
AccountingNet	Fee	Benefit News Online	Fee
ActiJob	Fee	Benefits Link	Fee
Adecco	Fee	Best Jobs USA	Fee
Adguide's Employment Web Site	Fee	Bilingual-Jobs	Fee
AdSearch	Fee	Bio Online	Fee
Adweek Online	Fee	BIOCareer Employment Center	Fee
Africa Online Jobs	Free	Bioscience and Medicine	Free
Afro-Americ@: The Job Vault	Fee	BioSpace Career Center	Fee
Airline Employment Ass't. Corps	Free	BIS Careers/Employment	Fee
Airwaves Media Web	Free	The BLACK COLLEGIAN Online	Fee
Allied Health Opportunities Directory	Fee	Black E.O.E Journal	Fee
Alta Vista	Free	Black Voices	Fee
American Assoc. of Fin & Accounting	Fee	Bloomberg Online	Free
American Astronomical Society	Fee	The Blue Line	Free
American Banker CareerZone	Fee	Boldface Jobs	Fee
American Chemical Society Job Bank	Fee	Boston Globe	Fee
American Compensation Association	Fee	Boston Herald Job Find	Fee
American Economic Dev. Council	Fee	Boston Job Bank	Fee
American Institute of Physics	Fee	Boston Search.com	Fee
American Jobs.com	Fee	Branch Out	Fee
American Journalism Review Online	Free	BridgePath Employment Services	Fee
American Medical Association	Fee	Business Week Online Career Center	Fee
American Society for Quality	Fee	California Journalism Job Bank	Fee
American Soc. of Mech. Engineers	Fee	Career America	Fee
American Water Works Jobs	Free	Career Avenue	Fee
America's Employers	Fee	Career Board	Fee
America's Health Care Source	Fee	Career Bridge	Fee
America's Job Bank	Free	Career Builder	Fee
America's Online Help Wanted	Fee	Career Buzz	Fee
America's TV Job Network	Fee	Career Cast	Fee
Antenna's Internet Broadcast Jobs	Free	Career Ctr. for Workforce Diversity	Fee
Arizona Careers Online	Fee	Career Central	Fee
ASAE Career Headquarters	Fee	Career City	Fee
Asia Online	Free	Career Connect	Fee

JOBS

The Career Connection .... **Free**
Career Espresso/Emory University .... **Free**
Career Exchange .... **Fee**
Career Exposure .... **Fee**
Career File .... **Fee**
Career Guide .... **Fee**
Career India .... **Fee**
Career Internetworking .... **Fee**
Career Link .... **Fee**
Career Link USA .... **Fee**
Career Magazine .... **Fee**
Career Mart .... **Fee**
Career Match .... **Free**
Career Mosaic .... **Fee**
Career NET (Career/NET) .... **Fee**
Career Opportunities in Singapore .... **Fee**
Career Path.com .... **Fee**
Career Pro .... **Free**
Career Shop .... **Fee**
Career Site .... **Fee**
Career Spot, The .... **Fee**
Career Tech.com .... **Fee**
Career Tech.com .... **Fee**
Career Web .... **Fee**
Career Women .... **Fee**
Careers On-Line .... **Free**
Carolina Career Center .... **Fee**
Carolinas Career Web .... **Fee**
Casino Careers Online .... **Fee**
Casting Net .... **Free**
CATIA Job Network .... **Fee**
Cell Press .... **Fee**
CFO Magazine .... **Free**
Chemistry & Industry Magazine .... **Free**
Chicago Software News. CareerCat .... **Fee**
Chicago Tribune .... **Fee**
CHIME .... **Fee**
Christian Jobs Online .... **Fee**
Chronicle of Higher Education .... **Fee**
Classified Employment Web Site(CLEWS) **Fee**
Classified Warehouse .... **Fee**
Classifieds 2000 .... **Fee**
CLNET .... **Free**
Coach On-line Service .... **Free**
College Central Network .... **Fee**
College Connection .... **Fee**
College Grad Job Hunter .... **Fee**
College News Online .... **Fee**
Colorado Jobs Online .... **Fee**
Columbia-Williamette Comp. Group .... **Free**
Columbus Dispatch .... **Fee**
Community Career Center .... **Fee**
Computer Jobs Store The .... **Fee**
Computer Work .... **Fee**
Computer World's IT Careers .... **Fee**
Computerwork.com .... **Fee**

Connect to Jobs .... **Fee**
Contract Employment Connection .... **Fee**
Contract Employment Weekly .... **Fee**
Cool Works .... **Fee**
Corporate Gray .... **Fee**
Cowley Job Centre .... **Free**
Creative Freelancers Online .... **Fee**
Crystallography Worldwide .... **Free**
Cyber India Online .... **Fee**
DaVinci Times .... **Fee**
Defense Outplacement Referral Sys. .... **Free**
Design Sphere Online .... **Free**
Developers.net .... **Fee**
DICE High Tech Jobs Online .... **Fee**
Digital Cat (See Note) .... **Fee**
Direct Marketing World Job Center .... **Free**
direct-jobs.com .... **Fee**
Discovery Place Oil & Gas .... **Free**
Diversilink .... **Fee**
Diversity Careers Online .... **Fee**
Diversity Link .... **Fee**
Donohue's RS/6000 Emp. Page .... **Fee**
Drake Beam Morin .... **Free**
Drilling Research Institute .... **Free**
Dr. Dobb's Journal .... **Fee**
Dubuque Iowa .... **Fee**
e Math .... **Fee**
Eagleview .... **Fee**
Eastern & European Job Bank .... **Free**
Ed Physician .... **Free**
Education JobSite .... **Fee**
Educator's Network EDNET .... **Fee**
Electra a Women's View on Careers .... **Fee**
Electric Power NewsLink .... **Fee**
Electronic Engineering Times .... **Fee**
Electronic News OnLine .... **Fee**
Emergency Med. Practice Opp. .... **Fee**
Employment Channel .... **Fee**
Employment Weekly .... **Fee**
Engineering Job Source .... **Fee**
Engineering Jobs.com .... **Free**
Engineering News Record .... **Fee**
Environmental Careers Org. (Eco.org) ..... **Fee**
Environmental Careers World .... **Fee**
Equipment Leasing Association Online .... **Fee**
Escoffier On Line .... **Free**
Exec-U-Net .... **Free**
Federal Jobs Digest (See Note) .... **Free**
Feminist Career Center .... **Free**
Fin Career- Global Financial Careers .... **Free**
Finishing.com .... **Free**
Florida Career Link .... **Fee**
Food and Drug Packaging Online .... **Fee**
Frasernet .... **Fee**
Funeral Net .... **Free**
Future Access Employment Guide .... **Fee**

CAREERXROADS®   The 1999 Directory of Job, Resume & Career Management Sites on the World Wide Web

JOBS

MMWire.com .... **Fee**
The Monster Board .... **Fee**
MTS Group .... **Fee**
Music Pages .... **Free**
NACUBO .... **Fee**
Nation Job Network .... **Fee**
National Alumni Placement Assoc. .... **Fee**
The National Assembly *(See Note)* .... **Free**
National Business Employment Weekly ... **Fee**
National Diversity Newspaper Job Bank .. **Free**
National Educators Employment Review . **Free**
National Society of Black Engineers .... **Fee**
National Soc. of Prof. Engineering HP ...... **Fee**
Nature Biotechnology .... **Fee**
Nat'l. Cncl. of Teachers of Math Jobs ...... **Fee**
Needle in a Cyberstack .... **Free**
Net Cruiting .... **Free**
Net Jobs Information Services .... **Fee**
Net Temps .... **Fee**
NETSHARE .... **Free**
Network World Fusion .... **Fee**
New England Journal of Medicine .... **Fee**
New Jersey Online .... **Fee**
New Media Assoc. of NJ .... **Free**
New York Times .... **Fee**
NJ Job Search .... **Free**
NJ JOBS .... **Fee**
Nursing Spectrum .... **Fee**
NYC Headhunter's Mall *(See Note)* .... **Free**
O Hayo Sensei .... **Fee**
Oil Link .... **Free**
Online Career Center .... **Fee**
Online Sports Career Center .... **Free**
Opportunity Nocs .... **Fee**
OPTICS.ORG Job Search .... **Fee**
ORAsearch .... **Fee**
Orlando Sentinel .... **Fee**
Overseas Jobs Web .... **Fee**
Paralegal .org .... **Fee**
Passport Access .... **Fee**
Perioperative Emp. Opportunities .... **Fee**
Peterson's Education Center .... **Fee**
Philanthropy Journal Online .... **Fee**
Planet Jobs .... **Fee**
Plasma Gate .... **Free**
PolySort .... **Fee**
Position Watch .... **Fee**
Power Magazine .... **Fee**
Private School Employment Network ...... **Fee**
Produce Job Exchange .... **Fee**
Project Connect .... **Free**
Purchasing NAPM .... **Free**
Real Jobs - Real Estate .... **Free**
RealBank .... **Fee**
Recruit Net .... **Fee**
Recruiters Online Network .... **Fee**

Recruitex Technologies *(See Note)* .... **Free**
Rehab Options .... **Fee**
Resort Jobs *(See Note)* .... **Free**
Resumail Network .... **Fee**
Retail JobNet .... **Fee**
Right Management Consultants, Inc. .... **Free**
The RS/6000 Employment Page .... **Fee**
Sales Job.com .... **Fee**
Saludos Web .... **Fee**
Science Professional Network .... **Fee**
ScitechJobs.Com .... **Fee**
Seamless Website, The .... **Free**
SELECT JOBS .... **Fee**
Shawn's Internet Resume Center .... **Fee**
ShowBizJobs.com .... **Fee**
SHRM HR Jobs .... **Fee**
Siam Net .... **Fee**
Sistahspace .... **Free**
Skill Scape .... **Free**
Smart Dog .... **Fee**
Social Service.Com .... **Fee**
Society of Women Engineers .... **Free**
Sorkins Job Bank .... **Fee**
Space Jobs .... **Fee**
Star Chefs .... **Free**
Stern Alumni Outreach .... **Free**
Student Center .... **Fee**
St. Thomas Human Resource Centre .... **Free**
Summer Jobs *(See Note)* .... **Free**
Supermarket News .... **Fee**
Surf IT.net .... **Free**
Talent Hunter .... **Free**
Talent Works .... **Free**
taps.com .... **Fee**
TCM's HR Careers .... **Fee**
Teach Oregon .... **Free**
TeacherJobs.com .... **Free**
TechJobBank .... **Fee**
TechJobs SuperSite .... **Fee**
Telecommuting Jobs .... **Free**
Top Echelon .... **Fee**
Top Jobs on the Net .... **Fee**
Top Jobs USA .... **Fee**
Town Online .... **Fee**
Training Net .... **Free**
Training SuperSite Job Bank .... **Fee**
trans-ACTION .... **Fee**
Troops to Teachers .... **Free**
TV Jobs .... **Free**
Twin Cities Job Page .... **Fee**
US Job Network High Tech Job & Resume
Bank .... **Fee**
Virtual Edge .... **Fee**
Wall Street Journal Interactive Edition ...... **Fee**
Washington Post-Career Post .... **Fee**
Water Resources Emp. Opportunities ...... **Free**
Water Works Jobs .... **Free**

JOBS

LOCATION

There is an enormous growth worldwide of job related sites. US sites are going global as well. Here are a few we've included. The regional sites we've listed below are representative of the thousands of local sites. Large national sites are also developing regional niches to cater to local differences.

INTERNATIONAL: GENERAL

Adecco
Africa Online Jobs
Bioscience and Medicine
BioSpace Career Center
Bloomberg Online
Chemistry & Industry Magazine
Crystallography Worldwide
Engineering Jobs.com
Engineering News Record
Fin Career- Global Financial Careers
Global Careers
Inter Career Net
Job Navigator (South Africa)
Oil Link
Overseas Jobs Web
Plasma Gate
Summer Jobs
Top Jobs on the Net

INTERNATIONAL: (U.S. SITES WITH INTERNATIONAL COMPONENTS)

American Assoc. of Fin & Accounting
American Astronomical Society
American Compensation Association
Career Builder
Career Espresso/Emory University
Career Exposure
Career Link
Career Central
Career Index
Career Mosaic
Career Web
Career Women
Cool Works
Casting Net Chefs
CATIA Job Network (South America)
Cell Press
Coach On-line Service for Football Coaches
Defense Outplacement Referral System
Developers.net Manpower
Diversilink
Dr. Dobb's Journal
Drilling Research Institute
Exec-U-Net
GIS Jobs Clearinghouse
HEALTH BANK USA
Heart
IEEE
Impact Online
Instrument Society of America
INTERNET WORLD
Jobs in Higher Education
LATPRO (Latin America
MBA Free Agents.com
Medzilla
The Monster Board
Nature Biotechnology
Online Career Center
Paralegal .org

Private School Employment Network
RealBank
Recruiters Online Network
Star Resort Jobs
Space Jobs
ScitechJobs.Com
SHRM HR Jobs
Science Professional Network
Wall Street Journal Interactive Edition
Web Jobs USA
Women in Higher Education
Women in Technology & Industry-WITI
Yahoo Classifieds

INTERNATIONAL: CANADA

ActiJob (French Canadian)
Bilingual-Jobs
BIS Careers/Employment
Career Bridge
Career Connect
Career Exchange
Career Internetworking
Classified Warehouse
Discovery Place Oil & Gas
Get Me A Job
Hi Tech Career Centre
IHRIM
Med Hunters
Net Jobs Information Services Position
   Watch
Recruitex Technologies
St. Thomas Human Resource Centre
Training SuperSite Job Bank
Weed Jobs
US and Canadian Connections
DICE
Funeral Net
MBA Careers
Net Temps
SELECT JOBS
TCM's HR Careers
TV Jobs
Training Net

INTERNATIONAL: PACIFIC RIM

Asia-Net
Asia Online
Bilingual-Jobs (Japan)
Career Opportunities in Singapore (Singapore)
Crowley Job Centre (Australia)
Digital Cat (Japan)
Hong Kong Standard (Hong Kong)
IndoScape (Indonesia)
International Pharmajobs
Job Street (Malaysia/Singapore)
Jobs Careers
O Hayo Sensei (Japan & US)
Professionals On-Line (Australia)
Siam Net (Thailand)
Virtual Edge (China/Japan)

INTERNATIONAL: EUROPE

Au Pair in Europe
Career Link (UK/Germany)
Career Central
CATIA Job Network
Donohue's RS/6000 Employment Page
Eastern & European Job Bank
GeoWeb Interactive
Hospitality Net (Netherlands)
Institute of Physics (UK)
International Pharmajobs
Job Lynx
Job Serve: IT Vacancies in the UK (Europe/
   UK)
Job Warehouse (UK/France)
Jobs Careers (Europe/UK)
NETSHARE (US/Europe)
Recruit Net (Int'l/UK)
TechJobs SuperSite (Int'l/UK/US)
ShowBizJobs.com (US/Europe/Canada)
taps.com (UK)
TV Jobs (UK)

INTERNATIONAL: INDIA

WinJobs
Career India
Cyber India Online

U.S.: EAST

100 Careers in Cyberspace
100 Careers in Wall Street (NY/NYC)
Boston Globe (Boston)
Boston Herald Job Find (MA/Boston)
Boston Job Bank (MA/Boston)
Boston Search.com (MA/Boston)
Career Match (NY)
DaVinciTimes (NY/Syracuse)
Employment Weekly (NY/Rochester)
Employment Channel (NJ)
Hartford Courant (CT)
IICS NY Job Listings (NY)
Infoworks, The Computer Job Center (NE)
Jewish Vocational Services (MA)
Job Net (PA/NJ)
Law Employment Center (US/E/NY)Princeton
   Info (NJ)
MTS Group
New Jersey Online (NJ)
New Media Assoc. of NJ (NJ)
New York Times (NY/NYC)
NJ JOBS (NJ)
NJ Job Search (NJ)
Planet Jobs (PA/Phildelphia)
SmartDog (Rochester)
Town Online (MA)
Washington Post-Career Post (DC)
Windows for Jobs (NJ)

U.S.: MIDWEST

Adguide's Employment Web Site (MN)
Career Board (OH)
CareerCat (IL/Chicago)
Career Link USA
Careers On-Line (MN)
Chicago Software Newspaper (IL/Chicago)
Chicago Tribune
College News Online (IL/Chicago)
Columbus Dispatch (OH/Columbus)
Dubuque Iowa (IA)
Engineering Job Source (MI)
Job Keys (MN-OH)
Milwaukee Journal Sentinel (WI)
NationJob Network
Sorkins Job Bank (IL-MO-KS)
The Blue Line (IL-MI-MO-WI)
Twin Cities Job Page (MN)

U.S.: SOUTH/SOUTHEAST/SOUTHWEST

Arizona Careers Online (US/SW/AR)
Black Voices (FL)
Career Guide (GA)
Career Pro (VA)
Career Spot, The (FL/Ft. Lauderdale)
Carolina Career Center (NC)
Carolinas Career Web (NC&SC)
Computer Jobs Store
Florida Career Link (FL)
Houston Chronicle Interactive (TX/Houston)
Job Market, The (FL)
LatPro
Orlando Sentinel (FL/Orlando)
US Job Network High Tech Job & Resume
   Bank (GA)

U.S.: WEST

California
680 careers.com (CA/SF)
Abag Globe (CA/San Francisco)
BA Jobs (Bay Area)
California Journalism Job Bank (CA)
CLNET (CA)
Colorado Jobs Online (CO)
Columbia-Williamette Compensation Group
   (WA-OR)
Forty Plus (Northern Calif.) (CA)
The (San Francisco Chronicle) Gate (CA/San
   Francisco)
Job Keys (OR)
Jobs Jobs Jobs (CA/San Francisco)
Latino Web (CA)
Los Angeles Times (CA/LA)
Job Exchange (CA)
Job Resource (CA)
Mercury Center Web (CA/San Jose)
Mining Co. (CO)
Purchasing NAPM (W)
Saludos Web (CA)
Seamless Website, The (CA)
Silicon Valley Jobs (CA)
Teach Oregon (OR)

META-LINKS

If you are looking to find more sites on your own, here are the biggest and best starting points. Some are industry based and others cover the world. Good hunting.

Acorn Career Counseling
www.acornresume.com

American Association of Finance & Accounting
www.aafa.com/

Aviation Employee Placement Service
www.aeps.com

Bullseye Job Shop
interoz.com/usr/gcbristow

Cal State Univ. Employ. Bd. Job Hunt
csueb.sfsu.edu/jobs.html

Career Espresso/Emory University
www.sph.emory.edu/studentservice/
Career.html

Career Resource Center
www.careers.org

Career Talk
www.careertalk.com

Careers and Jobs
www.starthere.com/jobs

CLNET
latino.sscnet.ucla.edu/

Connect to Jobs
www.cabrillo.cc.ca.us/affiliate/

The Definitive Internet Career Guide
phoenix.placement.oakland.edu/career/
Guide.htm

Employment of People w Disabilities
www.pcepd.gov

Entry Level Job Seeker Assistant
members.aol.com/Dylander/jobhome.html

Escoffier On Line Employment Resources
www.escoffier.com/nonscape/employ.shtml

Hospital Web
neuro-www.mgh.harvard.edu/
hospitalweb.shtml

HR Professionals
hrpro.org/main.html

HRIM Mall
www.hrimmall.com

Interesting Web Sites
www.usbol.com/wjmackey/weblinks.html

Internet Job Surfer
www.rpi.edu/dept/cdc/jobsurfer/jobw.html

Job Hunt: On-Line Job Meta-List
www.job-hunt.org

Job Resources by US Region
www.wm.edu/csrv/career/stualum/
jregion.html

Job Searching - Mining Co.
jobsearchtech.miningco.com

Job Web
www.jobweb.org/

Jobs in Higher Education
volvo.gslis.utexas.edu:80~acadres/jobs/
index.html

Jobs & Career Links
www.owt.com/jobsinfo/jobsinfo.htm

Needle in a Cyberstack
home.revealed.net/albee

Newspaperlinks
www.newspaperlinks.com

Overseas Jobs Web
www.overseasjobs.com

Purdue's Job List
www.ups.purdue.edu/student/jobsites.htm

Quintessential Career & Job Hunting Guide
www.stetson.edu/~rhansen/careers.html

Radio Frame
www.mindspring.com/~coleman/
radioframe.html

Recruiting Links.com
www.recruiting-links.com/

Red Guide to Temp Agencies
www.panix.com/~grvsmth/redguide/
intro.html

The Riley Guide
www.dbm.com/jobguide

SC WIST Work Pathfinder
www.harbour.sfu.ca/scwist/pathfinder/
index.htm.

SenseMedia Surfer Get A Job
sensemedia.net/getajob/

SHRM HR Jobs
www.shrm.org

Silicon Valley Technical Employment Agency
www.sease.com/jobs.html

Space Careers
www.spacelinks.com/SpaceCareers/

Student Center
studentcenter.com

St. Louis Area Companies on the Net
www.st-louis.mo.us/st-louis/companies.html

St. Thomas Human Resource Centre
ein.ccia.st-thomas.hrdc-drhc.gc.ca/
english.html

TechJobBank
205.230.23.123

Television & Radio News Research
www.missouri.edu/~jourvs/index.html

USM Resources for G/L/B Students
macweb.acs.usm.maine.edu/csce/
career_glb.html

How can you beat the convenience of being informed of an opening that matches your (job seekers) interests, or when a resume matches your (recruiter) opening? More and more sites will look to include you in their "community." There are many differences between sites that claim to keep you informed (see Levinstein Article). Some use "push" to entice you back to their site, while others provide all the information you need to go forward. The sophistication and specificity of the technology can only improve with time. Soon companies will add it to the jobs pages on their sites as well.

4Work
www.4work.com

A1A Computer Jobs
www.a1acomputerpros.net/

Adguide's Employment Web Site
www.adguide.com

American Banker CareerZone
www.americanbanker.com/

American Chemical Society Job Bank
www.acs.org

American Economic Dev. Council
www.aedc.org

Asia-Net
www.asia-net.com

Association of Online Professionals
www.aop.org

Aviation Employee Placement Svc.
www.aeps.com

Benefits Link
www.benefitslink.com/

Bilingual-Jobs
www.bilingual-jobs.com

BIS Careers/Employment
bisinc.com/pronet/ccc

Branch Out
www.branchout.com

BridgePath Employment Services
www.bridgepath.com

Business Week Online Career Ctr.
www.businessweek.com/careers/index.html

Career Board
www.careerboard.com

Career Builder
www.careerbuilder.com

Career Buzz
www.careerbuzz.com

Career Connect
www.theglobeandmail.com/careerconnect

Career Exchange
www.careerexchange.com/

Career File
www.careerfile.com

Career India
www.careerindia.com

Career Magazine
www.careermag.com

Career Mart
www.careermart.com

Career Shop
www.tenkey.com

Career Site
www.careersite.com

Career Web
www.cweb.com

CAREERXROADS
www.careerxroads.com

Casino Careers Online
www.casinocareers.com

CATIA Job Network
www.catjn.com

Chemistry & Industry Magazine
pharma.mond.org

CHIME
www.chime-net.org/crc/job/job.htm

Christian Jobs Online
www.christianjobs.com

Classified Warehouse
www.adone.com

College Central Network
www.collegecentral.com

Comprehensive Career Ministries
eab.datastar.net/eab.html

Computer Work
www.computerwork.com

Computer World's IT Careers
www.computerworld.com

Computerwork.com
computerwork.com

Contract Employment Weekly
www.ceweekly.com

Corporate Gray
www.greentogray.com

DaVinci Times
www.daVinciTimes.org

Developers.net
www.developers.net

DICE High Tech Jobs Online
www.dice.com

Diversilink
www.diversilink.com

Dubuque Iowa
www.dubuque-ia.com/jobs.cfm

Eagleview
www.eagleview.com

Electra a Women's View on Careers
electra.com

Engineering Job Source
www.engineerjobs.com

**FedWorld Federal
Job Announcement Search**
www.fedworld.gov

PUSH

Florida Career Link
www.floridacareerlink.com

Funeral Net
www.funeralnet.com/classifieds/index.html

The (San Francisco Chronicle) Gate
www.sfgate.com/classifieds/

GeoWeb Interactive
www.ggrweb.com

Hard@Work
www.hardatwork.com

HeadHunter .NET
www.headhunter.net

Health Career Web
www.HealthCareerWeb.com

Heart
www.career.com

Hi Tech Career Centre
www.hitechcareer.com

Hispanic Online Magazine
www.hisp.com

HRIM Mall
www.hrimmall.com

IndoScape
www.indoscape.com/cfo

InformationWeek Career
www.informationweek.com/career

Institute of Physics
www.iop.org

Inter Career Net
www.rici.com/acw

International Pharmajobs
www.pharmajobs.com

International Seafarers Exchange
www.jobxchange.com/xisetoc.htm

Internet Job Locator
www.joblocator.com

INTERNET WORLD
jobs.internet.com

Irish Jobs
www.exp.ie

Java World
www.javaworld.com

Job Bank USA
www.jobbankusa.com

Job Ctr. Employment Services, Inc.
www.jobcenter.com/

Job Keys
www.jobkeys.com

Job Net
www.jobnet.com

Job Options
www.espan.com

Job Serve: IT Vacancies in the UK
www.jobserve.com

Job Street
www.jobstreet.com

Jobs 4 HR
www.jobs4hr.com

Jobs for Bankers
www.bankjobs.com

Jobs for Programmers
www.prgjobs.com

Jobs in Government
www.jobsingovernment.com

LATPRO
www.latpro.com

Mac Talent.com
www.mactalent.com

Marketing Jobs.com
www.marketingjobs.com

MBA Employment Connection Assoc.
www.mbanetwork.com

MBA Free Agents.com
www.mbafreeagents.com

Medzilla
www.medzilla.com

Mercury Center Web
www.sjmercury.com

Midrange Computing
midrangecomputing.com

The Monster Board
www.monster.com

Nation Job Network
www.nationjob.com

NETSHARE
www.netshare.com

Network World Fusion
www.nwfusion.com

News Page
www.newspage.com

Nursing Spectrum
www.nursingspectrum.com

ORAsearch
www.orasearch.com

Position Watch
www.positionwatch.com

RealBank
www.realbank.com

Recruit Net
recruitnet.guardian.co.uk/

Rehab Options
www.rehaboptions.com

Resucom Resume-Network
www.pbgi.com/resucom/search.htm

Retail JobNet
www.retailjobnet.com

SELECT JOBS
www.selectjobs.com.

ShowBizJobs.com
www.showbizjobs.com

SHRM HR Jobs
www.shrm.org

Siam Net
www.siam.net/jobs/

Skill Scape
www.skillscape.com

Smart Dog
www.smartdog.org

Social Service.Com
www.socialservice.com

Society of Women Engineers
www.swe.org

Space Jobs
www.spacejobs.om

St. Thomas Human Resource Centre
ein.ccia.st-thomas.hrdc-drhc.gc.ca/
english.html

taps.com
www.taps.com

TCM's HR Careers
www.tcm.com/hr-careers

Town Online
www.townonline.com/working

Training SuperSite Job Bank
www.trainingsupersite.com/jobset.htm

TV Jobs
www.tvjobs.com

**US Job Network High Tech Job &
Resume Bank**
www.usjob.net

Virtual Edge
www.virtual-edge.net

Water Resources Employment Opps.
www.uwin.siu.edu/announce/jobs/

Web Jobs USA
www.webjobsusa.com

WinJobs
www.winjobs.com/marketing

women CONNECT.com
ww.womenconnect.com

Women in Tech. & Industry-WITI
www.witi.com

Workforce Online
www.workforceonline.com

RESUMES

Here are all the places we can find that you might consider. One caveat, choose whether you want your resume floating around in newsgroups and other public databases. We recommend that jobseekers restrict their resume posting to sites that protect confidentiality. We also realize that there may be times when that isn't a viable option.

JOBSEEKERS: Post Your Resume for FEE or for FREE

100 Careers in Cyberspace	Fee	Career America	Fee
100 Careers in Wall Street	Fee	Career Avenue	Free
4Work	Free	Career Board	Free
680 careers.com	Free	Career Builder	Free
A1A Computer Jobs	Free	Career Buzz	Free
Abag Globe	Free	Career Cast	Free
Accounting .com	Free	Career Central	Free
AccountingNet	Free	Career City	Free
ActiJob	Free	Career Connect	Free
AdSearch	Free	Career Exchange	Free
Africa Online Jobs	Free	Career Exposure	Free
Airline Employment Ass't. Corps	Fee	Career File	Free
Airwaves Media Web	Free	Career Guide	Free
Alta Vista	Free	Career India	Free
American Banker CareerZone	Free	Career Lab	Fee
American Chemical Society Job Bank	Fee	Career Link USA	Fee
American Compensation Association	Free	Career Magazine	Free
American Economic Dev. Council	Fee	Career Mart	Free
American Jobs.com	Free	Career Match	Free
American Medical Association	Free	Career Mosaic	Free
America's Employers	Free	Career NET Career/NET	Free
America's Health Care Source	Free	Career Opportunities in Singapore	Free
America's Job Bank	Free	Career Path.com	Free
America's Online Help Wanted	Free	Career Pro	Free
America's Talent Bank	Free	Career Shop	Free
America's TV Job Network	Fee	Career Site	Free
Arizona Careers Online	Fee	Career Web	Free
Asia Online	Free	Career Women	Free
Au Pair in Europe	Fee	Careers On-Line	Free
AutoCAD	Free	Carolina Career Center	Free
Aviation Employee Placement Service	Fee	Carolinas Career Web	Free
Bakery-Net	Free	Casino Careers Online	Free
Benefit News Online	Free	CHIME	Free
Benefits Link	Free	Christian Jobs Online	Fee
Best Jobs USA	Free	Classified Employment Web Site	Free
Bilingual-Jobs	Free	Classifieds 2000	Free
Bio Online	Free	Coach On-line Svc.	Fee
Bioscience and Medicine	Free	College Central Network	Free
BIS Careers/Employment	Free	College Connection	Free
The BLACK COLLEGIAN Online	Free	College News Online	Free
Black E.O.E Journal	Free	Colorado Jobs Online	Free
Black Voices	Free	Community Career Center	Fee
Bloomberg Online	Free	Comprehensive Career Ministries	Free
Boldface Jobs	Free	Computer Jobs Store The	Free
Boston Globe	Free	Computer Work	Free
Boston Herald Job Find	Free	Computer World's IT Careers	Free
Boston Job Bank	Free	Computerwork.com	Free
Boston Search.com	Free	Contract Employment Connection	Free
BridgePath Employment Services	Free	Contract Employment Weekly	Free

Corporate Aviation Resume Exchange	**Free**	HR Perc Network Job Opps	**Free**
Corporate Gray	**Free**	HR Recruiting	**Free**
Cowley Job Centre	**Free**	HR World	**Free**
Creative Freelancers Online	**Free**	IACC online	**Free**
Cyber India Online	**Free**	ijob	**Free**
DaVinci Times	**Free**	Imcor Provides Top-Level Executives	**Free**
Design Sphere Online	**Free**	IndoScape	**Free**
Developers.net	**Free**	InformationWeek Career	**Free**
DICE High Tech Jobs Online	**Free**	Infoworks, The Computer Job Center	**Free**
Digital Cat	**Free**	Institute of Physics	**Free**
Direct Marketing World Job Center	**Free**	Instrument Society of America	**Fee**
direct-jobs.com	**Free**	Insurance Career Center	**Free**
Discovery Place Oil & Gas	**Free**	Inter Career Net	**Free**
Diversilink	**Free**	International Pharmajobs	**Free**
Diversity Careers Online	**Free**	International Seafarers Exchange	**Free**
Diversity Link	**Free**	Internet Fashion Exchange	**Free**
Donohue's RS/6000 Employment Page	**Free**	Internet Job Locator	**Free**
Drake Beam Morin	**Fee**	INTERNET WORLD	**Free**
Drilling Research Institute	**Free**	Irish Jobs	**Free**
Dubuque Iowa	**Free**	Jewish Vocational Services	**Free**
e Math *(See Note)*	**Free**	Job Assistant.com	**Free**
Eagleview	**Free**	Job Bank USA	**Free**
Eastern & European Job Bank	**Free**	Job Center Emp. Svcs., Inc. *(See Note)*	**Free**
Electra a Women's View on Careers	**Free**	Job Direct.com	**Free**
Electronic Engineering Times	**Free**	Job Exchange	**Fee**
Employnet	**Fee**	Job Keys	**Free**
Engineering Job Source	**Free**	Job Lynx	**Fee**
Engineering Jobs.com	**Free**	Job Market, The	**Free**
Entry Level Job Seeker Assistant	**Free**	Job Navigator	**Free**
Escoffier On Line	**Free**	Job Net	**Free**
Federal Jobs Digest *(See Note)*	**Free**	Job Options	**Free**
Feminist Career Center	**Free**	The Job Resource	**Free**
Fin Career- Global Financial Careers	**Free**	Job Serve: IT Vacancies in the UK	**Free**
Finishing.com	**Free**	Job Span	**Free**
Florida Career Link	**Free**	Job Street	**Free**
Forty Plus Northern Calif.	**Fee**	JOB TRAK JOBTRAK	**Free**
Frasernet	**Free**	Job Warehouse	**Free**
Funeral Net	**Free**	Jobs 4 HR	**Free**
Future Access Employment Guide	**Free**	Jobs Careers	**Free**
GeoWeb Interactive *(See Note)*	**Free**	Jobs for Bankers	**Free**
Get Me A Job	**Free**	Jobs for Programmers	**Free**
Global Careers	**Free**	Jobs in Government	**Free**
GO Jobs: The Guide to Online Jobs	**Free**	Kelly Services	**Free**
HeadHunter .NET	**Free**	LATPRO	**Fee**
HEALTH BANK USA	**Free**	Layover	**Free**
Health Care Recruitment Online	**Free**	Lee Hecht Harrison *(See Note)*	**Fee**
Health Career Web	**Free**	Lendman Group Job Fairs	**Free**
Health Opps	**Free**	Mac Talent.com	**Fee**
Heart	**Free**	Manpower	**Free**
Help Wanted	**Free**	Manufacturing Job Search	**Free**
Help Wanted USA	**Fee**	Marketing Jobs.com	**Free**
Hi Tech Career Centre	**Free**	MBA Careers	**Free**
Hispanic Online Magazine	**Free**	MBA Employment Connection Assoc.	**Free**
Hollywood Web	**Free**	MBA Free Agents.com *(See Note)*	**Free**
Hong Kong Standard	**Free**	MBA job.com	**Fee**
Hospitality Net	**Free**	Med Hunters	**Free**
Hot Jobs	**Free**	Med Search *(See Note)*	**Free**

RESUMES

Medzilla	Free	Skill Scape	Free
Mercury Center Web	Free	Smart Dog	Free
Midrange Computing	Fee	Software Contractors' Guild	Fee
Ministry Connect	Fee	Sorkins Job Bank	Free
Minorities' Job Bank	Free	Star Chefs	Free
MMWire.com	Free	Stern Alumni Career Res. Online	Fee
The Monster Board	Free	Student Advantage	Free
MTS Group	Free	Surf IT.net	Free
Nation Job Network	Free	Talent Hunter	Free
National Alumni Placement Assoc.	Free	Talent Works	Fee
National Diversity Newspaper Job Bank	Free	taps.com	Free
National Educators Employment Review	Free	TCM's HR Careers	Free
Nat'l. Cncl. of Teachers of Math *(See Note)*	Free	Teach Oregon	Fee
Navy	Free	TeacherJobs.com	Free
Net Jobs Information Services	Fee	TechJobBank	Free
Net Temps	Free	Technical Writers to the Rescue	Free
NETSHARE *(See Note)*	Fee	Telecommuting Jobs	Free
NJ JOBS	Fee	Top Jobs USA	Free
NYC Headhunter's Mall	Free	Training Net	Free
O Hayo Sensei	Free	Training SuperSite Job Bank	Free
OASYS Network	Free	Troops to Teachers	Free
Oil Link	Free	TV Jobs	Free
Omicron Personal Career Center	Free	Twin Cities Job Page	Free
Online Career Center	Free	US Air Force Employment	Free
Online Sports Career Center	Free	US Job Network	Free
Opportunity Nocs	Free	Virtual Edge	Free
OPTICS.ORG Job Search	Free	Web Jobs USA	Free
ORAsearch	Free	Westech's Virtual Job Fair	Free
Overseas Jobs Web	Free	Will Work 4 Food	Free
Paralegal .org	Fee	Windows for Jobs	Free
Passport Access	Free	Windows NT Resource Center	Free
Perioperative Emp. Opps. *(See Note)*	Fee	Work Avenue.com	Free
Position Watch	Free	Workforce Online	Free
Princeton Info	Free	Yahoo Classifieds	Free
Private School Employment Network	Fee		
Produce Job Exchange	Free		
Professionals On-Line	Free		
Purchasing NAPM *(See Note)*	Fee		
Real Jobs–Real Estate	Free		
RealBank	Free		
Recruiters Online Network	Free		
Recruitex Technologies	Free		
Rehab Options	Free		
Resucom Resume-Network	Fee		
Resumail Network	Free		
Resume Link	Free		
Retail JobNet	Fee		
Right Mgmt. Consultants, Inc. *(See Note)*	Fee		
The RS/6000 Employment Page	Free		
Saludos Web	Free		
Science Professional Network *(See Note)*	Free		
Seamless Website, The	Free		
Search Base	Fee		
SELECT JOBS	Free		
Shawn's Internet Resume Center	Free		
ShowBizJobs.com	Fee		
Siam Net	Free		

RECRUITERS: See Resumes for FEE or for FREE

100 Careers in Cyberspace	**Free**	Career Match	**Fee**
100 Careers in Wall Street	**Free**	Career Mosaic	**Fee**
4Work	**Fee**	Career NET Career/NET	**Fee**
A1A Computer Jobs	**Fee**	Career Path.com	**Fee**
Accounting .com	**Fee**	Career Pro	**Free**
AccountingNet	**Free**	Career Shop	**Fee**
Africa Online Jobs	**Free**	Career Site	**Fee**
Airline Employment Ass't. Corps	**Free**	Career Web	**Fee**
Airwaves Media Web	**Free**	Career Women	**Fee**
American Chemical Society Job Bank	**Fee**	Careers On-Line	**Free**
American Compensation Association	**Free**	Carolina Career Center	**Free**
American Medical Association	**Fee**	Carolinas Career Web	**Fee**
America's Employers	**Fee**	Casino Careers Online	**Fee**
America's Health Care Source	**Fee**	CHIME	**Fee**
America's Job Bank	**Free**	Christian Jobs Online	**Fee**
America's Online Help Wanted	**Fee**	Classified Employment Web Site	**Fee**
America's Talent Bank	**Free**	Coach On-line Service	**Free**
America's TV Job Network	**Free**	College Central Network	**Fee**
Arizona Careers Online	**Free**	College Connection	**Free**
Asia Online	**Free**	Colorado Jobs Online	**Free**
AutoCAD	**Fee**	Community Career Center	**Fee**
Aviation Employee Placement Service	**Free**	Comprehensive Career Ministries	**Free**
Bakery-Net	**Free**	Computer Jobs Store The	**Fee**
Benefit News Online	**Free**	Computer Work	**Fee**
Benefits Link	**Free**	Computerwork.com	**Fee**
Best Jobs USA	**Fee**	Contract Employment Connection	**Fee**
Bilingual-Jobs	**Fee**	Contract Employment Weekly	**Fee**
Bio Online	**Fee**	Corporate Aviation Resume Exchange	**Free**
Bioscience and Medicine	**Free**	Corporate Gray	**Fee**
BIS Careers/Employment	**Fee**	Cowley Job Centre	**Free**
The BLACK COLLEGIAN Online	**Fee**	Creative Freelancers Online	**Fee**
Black E.O.E Journal	**Fee**	Cyber India Online	**Free**
Black Voices	**Fee**	DaVinci Times	**Fee**
Bloomberg Online	**Free**	Defense Outplacement Referral Sys.	**Free**
Boldface Jobs	**Free**	Design Sphere Online	**Free**
Boston Globe	**Fee**	DICE High Tech Jobs Online	**Fee**
Boston Herald Job Find	**Fee**	Digital Cat	**Fee**
Boston Job Bank	**Free**	Direct Marketing World Job Center	**Free**
Boston Search.com	**Fee**	direct-jobs.com	**Fee**
BridgePath Employment Services	**Fee**	Discovery Place Oil & Gas	**Free**
Career Avenue	**Fee**	Diversilink	**Fee**
Career Board	**Fee**	Diversity Careers Online	**Fee**
Career Bridge	**Fee**	Diversity Link	**Fee**
Career Cast	**Fee**	Donohue's RS/6000 Employment Page	**Free**
Career Central	**Fee**	Drake Beam Morin	**Free**
Career City	**Fee**	Drilling Research Institute	**Free**
Career Connect	**Fee**	Dubuque Iowa	**Fee**
Career Exchange	**Fee**	e Math *(See Note)*	**Free**
Career Exposure	**Fee**	Eagleview	**Fee**
Career File	**Fee**	Eastern & European Job Bank	**Free**
Career Guide	**Fee**	Electra a Women's View on Careers	**Fee**
Career India	**Fee**	Electronic Engineering Times	**Fee**
Career Link USA	**Free**	Employnet	**Free**
Career Magazine	**Free**	Engineering Job Source	**Fee**
Career Mart	**Fee**	Engineering Jobs.com	**Free**

RESUMES

Entry Level Job Seeker Assistant .... **Free**
Escoffier On Line .... **Free**
Federal Jobs Digest .... **Fee**
Feminist Career Center .... **Free**
Fin Career- Global Financial Careers .... **Fee**
Finishing.com .... **Free**
Florida Career Link .... **Fee**
Forty Plus Northern Calif. .... **Free**
Frasernet .... **Fee**
Funeral Net .... **Free**
Future Access Employment Guide .... **Free**
GeoWeb Interactive .... **Free**
Get Me A Job .... **Free**
Global Careers .... **Free**
GO Jobs: The Guide to Online Jobs .... **Fee**
HeadHunter .NET .... **Free**
HEALTH BANK USA .... **Fee**
Health Career Web .... **Fee**
Health Opps .... **Fee**
Heart .... **Fee**
Help Wanted .... **Free**
Help Wanted USA .... **Free**
Hi Tech Career Centre .... **Fee**
Hispanic Online Magazine .... **Fee**
Hollywood Web .... **Free**
Hospitality Net .... **Free**
Hot Jobs .... **Fee**
HR Perc Network Job Opps .... **Free**
HR Recruiting .... **Fee**
HR World .... **Free**
IACC online .... **Free**
ijob .... **Fee**
Imcor Provides Top-Level Executives ...... **Fee**
IndoScape .... **Fee**
Infoworks, The Computer Job Center ...... **Fee**
Institute of Physics .... **Free**
Instrument Society of America .... **Free**
Insurance Career Center .... **Fee**
Inter Career Net .... **Fee**
International Pharmajobs .... **Fee**
International Seafarers Exchange .... **Fee**
Internet Fashion Exchange .... **Free**
Internet Job Locator .... **Fee**
INTERNET WORLD .... **Fee**
Irish Jobs .... **Fee**
Jewish Vocational Services .... **Free**
Job Assistant.com .... **Free**
Job Bank USA .... **Fee**
Job Center Employment Services, Inc. .... **Free**
Job Direct.com .... **Fee**
Job Exchange .... **Free**
Job Keys .... **Fee**
Job Lynx .... **Free**
Job Market, The .... **Fee**
Job Navigator .... **Fee**
Job Net .... **Fee**
Job Options .... **Fee**

The Job Resource .... **Free**
Job Serve: IT Vacancies in the UK .... **Fee**
Job Span .... **Fee**
Job Street *(See Note)* .... **Fee**
JOB TRAK .... **Fee**
Job Warehouse .... **Fee**
Jobs 4 HR *(See Note)* .... **Fee**
Jobs Careers .... **Fee**
Jobs for Bankers .... **Fee**
Jobs for Programmers .... **Fee**
Jobs in Government .... **Fee**
LATPRO .... **Fee**
Layover .... **Fee**
Lee Hecht Harrison .... **Free**
Lendman Group Job Fairs .... **Fee**
Mac Talent.com .... **Free**
Manufacturing Job Search .... **Fee**
Marketing Jobs.com .... **Fee**
MBA Careers .... **Fee**
MBA Employment Connection Assoc. ...... **Free**
MBA Free Agents.com .... **Fee**
MBA job.com .... **Free**
Med Hunters .... **Fee**
Med Search .... **Fee**
Medzilla .... **Fee**
Midrange Computing .... **Free**
Ministry Connect .... **Free**
Minorities' Job Bank .... **Fee**
MMWire.com .... **Free**
The Monster Board .... **Fee**
MTS Group .... **Fee**
National Educators Emp. Review .... **Free**
Nat'l. Cncl. of Teachers of Math Jobs ...... **Free**
Net Jobs Information Services .... **Free**
Net Temps .... **Fee**
NETSHARE .... **Fee**
NJ JOBS .... **Free**
NYC Headhunter's Mall .... **Fee**
O Hayo Sensei .... **Free**
OASYS Network .... **Fee**
Oil Link .... **Free**
Omicron Personal Career Center .... **Free**
Online Career Center .... **Fee**
OPTICS.ORG Job Search .... **Free**
ORAsearch .... **Fee**
Overseas Jobs Web *(See Note)* .... **Fee**
Paralegal .org .... **Free**
Passport Access .... **Fee**
Perioperative Emp. Opps. .... **Fee**
Princeton Info .... **Free**
Private School Employment Network ...... **Free**
Produce Job Exchange .... **Fee**
Professionals On-Line .... **Free**
Purchasing NAPM .... **Free**
Real Jobs - Real Estate .... **Free**
RealBank .... **Fee**
Recruiters Online Network .... **Fee**

CAREERXROADS® The 1999 Directory of Job, Resume & Career Management Sites on the World Wide Web

RESUMES

SPECIALTY & INDUSTRY

ADVERTISING/GRAPHIC ARTS
Adweek Online
Creative Freelancers Online
Design Sphere Online
OASYS Network
Talent Hunter

AVIATION
Airline Employment Ass't. Corps
Aviation Employee Placement Service
 (Aerospace/Pilot)
Corporate Aviation Resume Exchange
 (Airline Pilots)
NationJob Network

BUSINESS/FINANCE
100 Careers in Wall Street
 (Finance/Business)
Accounting .com (Finance/Accounting)
AccountingNet (Finance/Accounting)
American Assoc. of Fin & Accounting
 (Finance/Accounting)
American Banker CareerZone
 (Finance/Banking)
American Economic Development Council
 (Finance/Economic Development)
Bloomberg Online (Finance/Executive)
Career Central (MBAs/IT)
CFO Magazine (Finance/Accounting)
Equipment Leasing Association Online
Fin Career- Global Financial Careers
 (Finance/Executive)
Jobs for Bankers (Finance/Banking)
Global Careers (Business/Transportation)
Insurance Career Center (Finance/Insurance)
MBA Careers (Business/MBA)
MBA Employment Connection Assoc.
 (Business/MBA)
MBA Free Agents.com (Business/MBA)
MBA job.com (Business/MBA)

COMMUNCATIONS/JOURNALISM
American Journalism Review Online
California Journalism Job Bank
Jobs in Journalism
National Diversity Newspaper Job Bank
The Write Jobs

DOMESTIC
Au Pair in Europe

EDUCATION
Academe This Week (University/Admin.)
Academic Employment Network (University)
Bioscience and Medicine (Science/Bio-
 science)
Chronicle of Higher Education (University)
Coach On-line Service (Coaches (High
 School/Sports Coaching)
Crystallography Worldwide (University/
 Science/Crystallography)
Education JobSite (K-12)
Educator's Network EDNET (K-12)
Institute of Physics (University/Science/
 Physics)
Jobs in Higher Education (University)

NACUBO (Executive)
Nat'l. Council of Teachers of Math Jobs
 Online (Science/Math)
National Educators Employment Review (K-
 12)
O Hayo Sensei (Japan)
Private School Employment Network (K-12)
Project Connect (K-12)
TeacherJobs.com (K-12)
Teach Oregon (K-12)
Troops to Teachers (K-12)
Women in Higher Education (University)

ENGINEERING/MANUFACTURING
ACS Job Bank (Chemical)
American Society of Mechanical Enginers
 (Engineering/Mechanical)
Career Link (Engineering/mfg-hospitality-
 airline-aviation-sales)
DaVinciTimes
Discovery Place Oil & Gas (Chemical)
Diversilink (Engineering/PE)
Diversity Careers Online
Drilling Research Institute (Chemical)
Electric Power NewsLink (Power)
Electronic Engineering Times
Electronic News Online
Engineering Job Source
Engineering Jobs.com
Engineering News Record (Construction/
 Design)
Finishing.com (Finishing)
Food and Drug Packaging Online (Engineer-
 ing/Packaging)
Future Access Employment Guide
IEEE (Engineering/Electrical/Electronic)
Instrument Society of America (Engineering/
 Measurement & Control)
Manufacturing Job Search
National Society of Black Engineers
 (Engineering)
National Society of Professional Engineering
 HP (Engineering/PE)
Oil Link (Chemical)
Power Magazine
Society of Women Engineers
Space Jobs (Aerospace)
Water Resources Employment Opportunities

ENTERTAINMENT/BROADCASTING
Antenna's Internet Broadcast Jobs
Airwaves Media Web (Radio Broadcasting)
Casting Net (Acting)
Hollywood Web
Music Pages (Teaching/Studio Engineers)
ShowBizJobs.com
Talent Works: The Online Casting Source
TV Jobs (Broadcasting)

EXECUTIVE

ASAE Career Headquarters
Career File
Business Week Online Career Center
Exec-U-Net
Imcor Provides Top-Level Executives
NETSHARE
Stern Alumni Outreach Career Resources
  Online
Shawn's Internet Resume Center
Wall Street Journal Interactive Edition
Women in Technology & Industry-WITI

FUNERAL INDUSTRY

Funeral Net

HEALTH CARE

Academic Physician & Scientist (Physician/
  Research)
Allied Health Opportunities Directory (Allied
  Health)
America's Health Care Source (Allied Health)
American Medical Association (MD)
Nursing Spectrum
Career Espresso/Emory University (Public
  Health)
Ed Physician (MD/ER)
Emergency Medicine Practice Opportunity
  (MD)
HEALTH BANK USA
Health Care Jobs Online
Health Care Recruitment Online (Nursing)
Health Career Web (Nursing/MD/Allied
  Health)
Health Opps (Physician/Nursing)
Med Hunters
Med Connect (MD)
New England Journal of Medicine (MD)
Nursing Spectrum
Perioperative Online Employment Opportuni-
  ties (Nursing/OR)
Rehab Options (Rehab/PT/OT/Speech

HOSPITALITY/RETAIL/

Bakery-Net
Casino Careers Online
Cool Works (Sports/Outdoors/Entry)
Escoffier On Line (Food/Chefs)
Hospitality Net
IACC online (Conference Center)
International Seafarers Exchange (Travel)
Internet Fashion Exchange (Retail)
Online Sports Career Center (Recreation)
Produce Job Exchange (Retail/Food)
Resort Jobs (Resort/Summer)
Retail JobNet (Retail)
Star Chefs (Restaurant/Chefs)
Supermarket News
  (Retail/Food/Supermarket)

HUMAN RESOURCES

American Compensation Association
  (Compensation)
Benefits Link (Benefits)
Benefit News Online (Benefits)
Columbia-Williamette Compensation Group
  (Compensation)
HR COMM
HR Network
HR Perc Network Job Opps
HR Recruiting
HR World
HRIM Mall (HRIS)
IFEBP Online (Benefits)
International Personnel Mgmt. Assoc.
International Society for Performance
  Improvement (T&D)
IHRIM (HRIS)
Jobs 4 HR
Net Cruiting (Staffing)
SHRM HR Jobs
TCM's HR Careers (Training)
Training SuperSite Job Bank (T&D)
Training Net (T&D)
Workforce Online

INFORMATION TECHNOLOGY/ HIGH TECH

100 Careers in Cyberspace
A1A Computer Jobs
  (Human Resources/Recruiting)
America's Online Help Wanted
Association for Computing Machinery (ACM)
Association of Online Professionals
  (WWW/Communications)
American Jobs.com (High Tech/Eng)
AutoCAD (CAD)
CareerCat (Software)
Career Exchange
Career India
Career Match
Career NET (Career/NET)
Career Tech.com (Eng/IT)
CATIA Job Network
  (CATIA/CAD/CAM/AutoCAD)
Chicago Software Newspaper
CHIME (CIO)
Computer Jobs Store The
Computer Work
Computerwork.com
Computer World's IT Careers
Contract Employment Connection
Contract Employment Weekly (Engineering)
Cyber India Online
Design Sphere Online (Commuincations)
Developers.net
DICE
Diversity Careers Online
Digital Cat (Java)
Donohue's RS/6000 Employment Page
GeoWeb Interactive (Geographic Systems)
GIS Jobs Clearinghouse (GIS)
HeadHunter.NET
Hot Jobs
IICS NY Job Listings
  (Graphics/Communications)
InformationWeek Career

INFORMATION TECHNOLOGY/
HIGH TECH (Cont'd.)

Infoworks, The Computer Job Center
INTERNET WORLD(Internet)
Java World (JAVA)
Job Keys (Engineering)
Job Navigator
Job Serve: IT Vacancies in the UK
Job Warehouse
   (Programmers/Software Engineers)
Jobs for Programmers
Jobs Jobs Jobs
Mac Talent.com (Macintosh)
Midrange Computing (AS/400 developers)
MMWire.com (Multimedia)
MTS Group
New Media Assoc. of NJ (Multimedia)
Network World Fusion
   (Network/IS Management)
Omicron Personal Career Center
ORAsearch (Oracle)
Position Watch
Professionals On-Line
SELECT JOBS (High Tech)
Software Contractors' Guild
Surf IT.net
TechJobs SuperSite
   (IT & Non-Exempt technical)
The RS/6000 Employment Page
US Job Network High Tech
   Job & Resume Bank
Virtual Edge (QA)
Web Jobs USA (New Media/WWW)
Westech's Virtual Job Fair
Windows for Jobs
Windows NT Resource Center (Windows NT)
WinJobs
Dr. Dobb's Journal

LAW/LAW ENFORCEMENT

The Blue Line (Law Enforcement)
Law Employment Center
Paralegal.org (Law/Paralegal)
Seamless Website, The

NON-PROFIT

ASAE Career Headquarters
Good Works
Impact Online
The National Assembly
Opportunity Nocs
Philanthropy Journal Online
Social Service.Com
   (Social Services/Psychology)
Purchasing
Purchasing NAPM

QUALITY ASSURANCE

American Society for Quality
Real estate
RealBank
Real Jobs
Sales/Marketing
Best Jobs USA
Direct Marketing World Job Center
Marketing Jobs.com (Marketing)
NationJob Network (Sales/Marketing)
Sales Job.com (Sales/Marketing)

SCIENCE

American Chemical Society Job Bank
   (Chemistry/Chem. Eng.)
American Institute of Physics (Physics)
American Astronomical Society (Astronomy)
American Water Works Jobs (Environmental)
ATI-Net (Agriculture)
BIOCareer Employment Center
   (Biotechnology)
Bio Online (Biotechnology)
BioSpace Career Center (Biotechnology)
Cell Press (Biology)
Chemistry & Industry Magazine
   (Pharmaceuticals/Food)
e-Math (Math)
Environmental Careers Org.
Environmental Careers World
International Pharmajobs (Pharmaceuticals)
Job Farm (Agriculture)
Medical Device Link (Medical Device)
Med Search (Biomedical)
Medzilla (Pharmaceutical)
Nature Biotechnology (Biotechnology)
OPTICS.ORG Job Search (Optical Physics)
Plasma Gate (Physics)
PolySort (Chemistry)
Science Professional Network
   (Pharmaceuticals/Biotechnology)
ScitechJobs.Com
Water Works Jobs (Environmental)
Weed Jobs (Weeds & Soil)

TELECOMMUTING/HOME WORK

Telecommuting Jobs
Will Work 4 Food

TRUCKING

Layover